THE ECONO OF WOMEN, MEN, AND WORK

SECOND EDITION

FRANCINE D. BLAU
University of Illinois
at Urbana-Champaign

MARIANNE A. FERBER
University of Illinois
at Urbana-Champaign

PRENTICE-HALL, Englewood Cliffs, New Jersey 07632

Library of Congress Cataloging-in-Publication Data

Blau, Francine D.
    The economics of women, men, and work / Francine D. Blau, Marianne
A. Ferber. -- 2nd ed.
        p.   cm.
    Includes bibliographical references and index.
    ISBN 0-13-233727-4 (pbk.)
    1. Women--United States--Economic conditions. 2. Women--United
States--Social conditions. 3. Women--Employment--United States.
4. Housewives--United States. 5. Sexual division of labor--United
States.   I. Ferber, Marianne A.   II. Title.
HQ1426.B62 1992
305.42'0973--dc20
                                                        92-9296
                                                        CIP

Acquisition Editor: **Stephen Dietrich**
Production Editor: **Carol Burgett**
Production and Interior Design: **Publication Services**
Cover Designer: **Karen Salzbach**
Prepress Buyer: **Trudy Pisciotti**
Manufacturing Buyer: **Robert Anderson**
Editorial Assistant: **Elizabeth Becker**

©1992, 1986 by Prentice-Hall, Inc.
A Simon & Schuster Company
Englewood Cliffs, New Jersey 07632

Printed in the United States of America

10   9   8   7   6   5   4   3   2   1

ISBN 0-13-233727-4

Prentice-Hall International (UK) Limited, *London*
Prentice-Hall of Australia Pty. Limited, *Sydney*
Prentice-Hall Canada Inc., *Toronto*
Prentice-Hall Hispanoamericana, S.A., *Mexico*
Prentice-Hall of India Private Limited, *New Delhi*
Prentice-Hall of Japan, Inc., *Tokyo*
Simon & Schuster Asia Pte. Ltd., *Singapore*
Editora Prentice-Hall do Brasil, Ltda., *Rio de Janeiro*

For

Larry Kahn
Daniel Blau Kahn
Lisa Blau Kahn

and

Bob Ferber
Don Ferber
Ellen Ferber Rogalin

With love

CONTENTS

Chapter 3

THE FAMILY AS AN ECONOMIC UNIT: THE DIVISION OF LABOR BETWEEN HUSBAND AND WIFE

Chapter 4

THE ALLOCATION OF TIME BETWEEN THE HOUSEHOLD AND THE LABOR MARKET

Chapter 5
DIFFERENCES IN OCCUPATIONS AND EARNINGS: OVERVIEW

Chapter 6
DIFFERENCES IN OCCUPATIONS AND EARNINGS: THE HUMAN CAPITAL MODEL

Chapter 7
DIFFERENCES IN OCCUPATIONS AND EARNINGS: THE ROLE OF LABOR MARKET DISCRIMINATION   188

Chapter 10
GENDER DIFFERENCES IN OTHER COUNTRIES: WHAT CAN WE LEARN FROM INTERNATIONAL COMPARISONS?

PREFACE

We wrote *The Economics of Women, Men, and Work* because we saw a need for a text that would acquaint students with the findings of research on women, men, and work in the labor market and the household. We are extremely gratified on the publication of the second edition to reflect that this belief was justified, and hope that this expanded and updated new edition will serve as effectively as the first. The book is written at a level that should both utilize and enhance students' knowledge of economic concepts and analysis but do so in terms intelligible to those not versed in advanced theory. Even though we assume a knowledge of introductory economics on the part of the reader, an interested and determined individual wanting to learn more about the economic status of women as compared to men could benefit considerably from the material offered here.

The text, used in its entirety, is primarily intended for courses specifically concerned with the economic status of women. We think, however, that this book could be used to good advantage in interdisciplinary women's studies courses, as well as introductory-level courses in economic problems. Selected readings would also make a useful supplement to round out a general labor economics course. In addition, it contains enough information about publications in the field to be of use as a reference work for those not familiar with this rapidly growing body of literature.

Since both of us have taught a course on women in the labor market for some time, we believe that the book has benefited from the experience and insights we have gained from our students. We are also greatly indebted to a rather large and diverse group of colleagues, from a number of disciplines, whose comments on the first or second edition were often voluminous and always extremely valuable: Orley C. Ashenfelter, Princeton University; Nancy S. Barrett, Fairleigh Dickinson University; Andrea H. Beller, University of Illinois, Urbana-Champaign; Lourdes Beneria, Cornell University; Barbara R. Bergmann, American University; Charles Brown, University of Michigan; Clair Brown, University of California, Berkeley; Greg J. Duncan, University of Michigan; Margaret C. Dunkle, American Association of University Women Educational Foundation; Paula England, University of Arizona; Belton M. Fleisher, Ohio State University; Claudia D. Goldin, Harvard University;

Daniel S. Hamermesh, Michigan State University; Joan A. Huber, Ohio State University; Joan R. Kahn, University of Maryland; Lawrence M. Kahn, University of Illinois, Urbana-Champaign; Mark R. Killingsworth, Rutgers University; Shelly J. Lundberg, University of Washington, Seattle; Julie A. Matthaei, Wellesley College; Harriet B. Presser, University of Maryland; Barbara B. Reagan, Southern Methodist University; Barbara F. Reskin, Ohio State University; Patricia A. Roos, State University of New York, Stony Brook; Steven H. Sandell, National Commission for Employment Policy; Myra H. Strober, Stanford University; Louise A. Tilly, New School for Social Research; Donald J. Treiman, University of California, Los Angeles; and H. F. (Bill) Williamson, University of Illinois, Urbana-Champaign. Without their help, this book would have had many more deficiencies. For those that remain, as well as for all opinions expressed, we, of course, take complete responsibility.

This list of acknowledgments would be incomplete if we did not also thank Denise Chachere, Barbara Thomas, Michelle Bettler, Jennifer Berdahl, and Amy Courtin, the research assistants who helped us track down sources and references and prepare tables and graphs. We are also grateful to Hope Cook for her competent handling of the numerous drafts of the first edition, and for her assistance, as well as that of Penny Cole, with portions of the second edition.

F. D. B.
M. A. F.

Chapter 1

INTRODUCTION

Courses in economics abound at universities and colleges, and there is an ample supply of texts focusing on the many facets of this discipline. These courses and these books increasingly recognize that women play an important role in the economy as workers and consumers and that in many ways their behavior and their problems differ from those of men. However, male patterns often receive the major emphasis, and gender differences are, at best, just one of many topics covered. For example, workers are often assumed to enter the labor market after completing their education and to remain until their retirement. Similarly, institutions studied are mainly those involved in traditional labor markets, from businesses to labor unions and relevant government agencies. Although women in growing numbers are spending an increasing proportion of their time working for pay, their lives and their world continue to be significantly different from those of men, and much of their time continues to be spent in nonmarket activities.

In recent years, much attention has been focused on the rising labor force participation rates of women, and particularly on the changing economic roles of married women. Much has been made, especially in the popular media, of the often large percentage increases in the number of women in nontraditional occupations, not to mention the publicity received by "the first woman" in a given field, whether it be stockbroker, jockey, or prime minister. All this tends to obscure both the continued responsibility of most women for the bulk of nonmarket work and the large occupational differences between men and women that remain, despite considerable progress in recent years. As long as this situation persists, there is a need to address these issues in depth, as is done in this book.

Although economic behavior is clearly not isolated from the remainder of human existence, the primary focus of this book is on the economic behavior of women and men, on economic institutions, and on economic outcomes. To refresh the memory of students who have some acquaintance with economics, and to provide a minimal background for those who do not, we begin with a brief introduction to the tools of this discipline. Neoclassical or mainstream economic theory provides the major emphasis of this book. But students should be aware that we have endeavored to constantly stretch and challenge the existing theories to shed light on issues related to gender and work. This means that, in addition to presenting conventional analyses, we sometimes develop new applications of the theories or offer critiques of existing approaches. We also tend to emphasize the importance and implications of gender inequities in the labor market and in the household to a greater extent than many of our colleagues might. Finally, we have attempted to take account of institutional factors, alternative perspectives, and the insights of other disciplines where relevant.

Throughout this book, but especially in those segments where we deal with policy (as we do in portions of several chapters), we are confronted by a dilemma common to the social sciences. On the one hand, much of what we present is positive, rather than normative, in the sense that we present facts and research results as we find them. Further, we try to avoid value judgments or prescriptive attitudes, for personal values should not be permitted to intrude upon objective analysis. On the other hand, it is unrealistic to claim that the choice of topics, the emphasis in discussions, and the references provided are, or even can be, entirely value-free. A reasonable solution is to try to present various sides of controversial questions, to make clear that different premises will lead to different conclusions, and that the policies one should adopt depend on the goals one wants to reach. This is the approach we attempt to follow.

Nevertheless, the tenor of this book is undoubtedly colored to some extent by our feminist perspective. This means that we recognize the extent to which persons of the same sex may differ, and persons of the opposite sex may be similar. It means we believe that, as much as possible, individuals should have the opportunity to live up to their potential, rather than be forced to conform to stereotypically male or female roles. Most of all, it means that, while recognizing differences between women and men, some possibly caused by biological factors and others by the way girls and boys are reared in our society, we are less inclined to emphasize the differences between them than the common humanity that unites them.

WHAT ECONOMICS IS ABOUT

Neoclassical economics is concerned with decision making under conditions of **scarcity.** This means that there are not enough resources to satisfy everyone's wants, and choices have to be made about their use. Given this constraint, it is crucial to recognize that using land, labor, and capital to produce one good means that fewer of these inputs will be available for producing other goods. Hence, the real cost of having more of one good is forgoing the opportunity of having more of another.

This concept of **opportunity cost** is fundamental to an understanding of the central **economic problem—how to allocate scarce resources so as to maximize well-being.** In order to make a rational decision whether to spend money to buy a new suit, or whether to spend time going for a hike, it is not sufficient to know how much utility or satisfaction will be derived from each. Because the amount of money and time is limited, and we cannot buy and do everything, it is crucial also to be aware of how much satisfaction is lost by giving up desirable alternatives. **Rationality,** as economists use the term, involves some knowledge of available opportunities and the terms on which they are available. Only on the basis of such information is it possible to weigh the alternatives and choose those that provide more utility than any others.

It is one of the most fundamental assumptions in traditional economics that people may be expected to behave rationally in this sense. This does not mean, as critics have occasionally suggested, that only monetary costs and benefits are considered. It is entirely rational to take into account nonpecuniary factors since *satisfaction,* not, say, money income, is to be maximized. This definition is so broad that almost everyone might be expected to behave this way. Nonetheless, this rationality cannot be taken for granted. It is not satisfactory simply to argue that whatever a person does must provide more satisfaction than any alternative course of action would have because he or she would otherwise have made a different choice. Such an argument amounts to a mere tautology. An individual who does not have the prerequisite knowledge, who blindly follows the traditional course of action without considering costs and benefits, who fails to consider long-run implications or indirect effects, is not necessarily rational. Nor is it uncommon to find persons who, with surprising regularity, make choices that they presently appear to regret. Most of us have probably known someone whose behavior fits one or more of these patterns.

These facts should be kept in mind, lest we accept too readily that whatever people do must be for the best. On the other hand, as a first approximation it is probably more realistic to assume that people tend to try to maximize their well-being, rather than that they are indifferent to it. We shall, for the most part, accept this as a reasonable generalization, while recognizing that it is not necessarily appropriate in every instance. Specifically, it must be kept in mind that the knowledge needed to make optimal decisions is often difficult and costly to obtain. When this cost is likely to exceed the gain derived, it is rational to "satisfice"[1] rather than to insist on maximization. By the same token, however, when additional information can be provided relatively cheaply and easily, it is likely to be useful in improving decision making.

USES OF ECONOMIC THEORY

Assuming that individuals are rational is only one of the many simplifying assumptions economists tend to make in formulating **theories** and building **models.** The justification for making such assumptions is that, much like laboratory experiments in the biological and physical sciences, these abstractions help to focus attention on the particular issue we are attempting to clarify and on the main relationships we want to understand.

In many instances, the approach is explicitly to examine the effects of changes in a single variable, say, price or income, while assuming that all else remains the same. This is not to suggest that economists believe that this ever happens in the real world. An aerospace engineer finds it useful to test a plane in a tunnel where everything except wind speed is artificially stabilized, even though the vehicle will later have to fly in an environment where temperature, atmospheric pressure, and humidity will change. Similarly, the social scientist finds it helpful to begin by abstracting from numerous complications.

A theory is not intended to be a full description of the underlying reality. A description is like a photograph, which shows reality in all its details. A theory may be likened to a modern painting, which at most shows the broad outlines of its subject but may provide deeper insight than a more realistic picture would. Hence, a theory or model should not be judged primarily on its detailed resemblance to reality, but rather in terms of the extent to which it enables us to grasp the salient features of that reality. Thus, economic theory, at its best, can help us to understand the present and to correctly predict the future.

Economists should not, therefore, be faulted for making simplifying assumptions or using abstractions, as long as they are aware of what they are doing and test their conclusions against empirical evidence, which is drawn from the real world with all its complexities. Unfortunately, such testing is not always easy to do. Computers now enable us to process vast amounts of information, and econometricians have made substantial progress in developing better methods for doing so. The availability, timeliness, and quality of the data, however, still leave much to be desired.

---

[1] This concept was first proposed by Herbert Simon in *Models of Man* (New York: Wiley, 1957). He argued that when the knowledge needed to make optimal decisions is difficult and costly to obtain, an individual may be content with selecting a "satisfactory" alternative—one that meets a minimum standard of acceptability.

Collecting data is a slow, expensive, and generally unglamorous undertaking. The U.S. government does more and better work in this respect than governments of many other countries. Even so, collecting, compiling, and publishing the information may take as long as two years. Some data are, in any case, collected only intermittently, other data not at all. For a variety of reasons, including the government's appropriate reluctance to invade certain areas, as well as lack of interest in pursuing topics with no strong political constituency, there are some substantial gaps in official data collection. Private research organizations have endeavored to fill these to a degree, but they are even more likely to be constrained by lack of necessary funds. The data from such special surveys are particularly likely to be collected sporadically or at lengthy intervals. In spite of these difficulties, the possibilities for empirical work have improved beyond the wildest dreams of economists of even one or two generations ago.

When suitable data are available, evidence for some relationships can be obtained using such simple devices as averages and cross-tabulations. In other instances, however, very sophisticated statistical methods are required to analyze the data. Such studies are time-consuming, and rarely are conclusions from any one such study regarded as final. At times there are ambiguities, with different sets of data or various approaches producing inconsistent results. But even these enhance the progress of science, for they help us to identify important areas for future research.

Because of these difficulties of data collection and analysis, timely and definitive answers are simply not available for every question. We have, however, done our best to summarize existing knowledge on each topic considered in this book.

THE SCOPE OF ECONOMICS

Traditionally, and for the most part even today, economics has focused on the market and on the government. In the market, goods and services are sold. Government is itself a major buyer and seller of goods and services and is also an agent that regulates and otherwise influences the economy. Only in recent decades have mainstream economists devoted any significant attention to the allocation of time within the household itself, and even now such material is not always included in general economics courses. Also, the value of nonmarket household production is ignored when aggregate indicators of economic welfare, such as Gross National Product (GNP), are computed. This is a matter for concern because women play the dominant role in the nonmarket sector.

The typical introductory economics course in its microeconomics section puts primary emphasis on the analysis of product market transactions with the firm as seller, concerned with maximizing profits, and the household as buyer, concerned with maximizing satisfaction or utility. Later it introduces markets for factors of production, specifically labor, in which the household is generally the supplier and the firm the purchaser. As a rule, however, this discussion is a brief portion in the section on factors of production, and most students may well come away with a view of the market as chiefly an institution where goods and services are supplied by businesses, and the demand for them comes from the household.

In this book, our interest is specifically in women and men, their work in the labor market and in the household, and the interdependence between individuals within the household and between the household and the market. Therefore, we briefly review supply and demand in this context in the Appendix to this chapter.

In a market economy, the forces of supply and demand for labor determine both the jobs that will be available and how much workers will be paid for doing them. Much of our analysis throughout this book will be concerned with the determinants of the supply of labor. We shall examine how individuals and their families decide to allocate their time between housework and market work and how women's changing roles in this regard are affecting their own well-being and that of their families.

Demand is essentially determined by the behavior of employers, who are in turn influenced by the business climate in which they operate. In the simplest case, their goal is to maximize profits, and their demand for labor is related to its productivity in making the goods or producing the services sold by the firm. Thus, the firm's demand for labor is *derived* from the demand of consumers for its final product. It is, however, possible that employers depart from the dictates of profit maximization and consider aspects of workers that are not directly related to their productivity. Discrimination against women in the labor market and its role in producing economic inequality between women and men is another topic that we shall explore in some depth.

On the supply side, workers may influence their productivity by attending school or getting training on the job. We shall also consider the determinants of such human capital investment decisions and their role in producing pay differences between female and male workers.

INDIVIDUALS, FAMILIES, AND HOUSEHOLDS

Throughout this book, we shall at times focus on the behavior of families and at other times on that of individuals. A **family** is defined as consisting of two or more persons, related by blood, marriage, or adoption, living in the same household.[2] It is, of course, the individual that in the last analysis consumes commodities and supplies labor. Nonetheless, it is often appropriate to treat the family as the

---

[2]This is the official definition used in government statistics. The typical **nuclear family** is composed of parents and children, but single-parent families are becoming increasingly common. An **extended family,** a type of unit more common in some other societies, may include grandparents, uncles, aunts, and other relatives.

relevant economic unit because decisions of various members within a family are interdependent, much of their consumption is joint, and it is common for them to pool income. At the same time, it is important not to lose sight of the fact that the composition of families changes as individuals move in and out and that the interests of members of families may diverge to a greater or lesser extent. We shall return to these issues throughout this book as we discuss the status of women and men within the family and in the labor market.

The broader concept of the **household** is also relevant to economic decision-making and is becoming increasingly more so. A household consists of one or more persons living in one dwelling unit and sharing living expenses. Thus, all families are households, but one-person households, or those composed of unrelated individuals, are not families. The term *household* is more general than *family* and does greater justice to the increasing prevalence of alternative living arrangements; however, since families still constitute a substantial majority of households that include more than one person, and since the term *family* is more familiar and connotes a more uniform set of relationships, we have chosen to use it primarily in this book.

A NOTE ON TERMINOLOGY

Traditionally the terms *sex* and *gender* were used interchangeably to refer to the biological and social differences between women and men. More recently, it has become increasingly common to use the term *sex* to refer to the biological differences between males and females, and *gender* to encompass the distinctions society has erected on this biological base.[3] Thus, *gender* connotes a cultural construct, including distinctions in roles and behaviors as well as mental and emotional characteristics.[4] We see enough merit in this distinction between *sex* and *gender* that we have generally observed it in writing this book.

The question of appropriate language also arises with respect to racial and ethnic groups. Historically, people of African origin in the United States were generally called Negroes. Several decades ago the term *black* came into use, followed more recently by *African American*. For purposes of this book, we decided not to make this latest change, mainly because *black* is the term that continues to be used in the official government statistics on which we frequently rely. For the same reason we decided to use the term *Hispanic* in preference to other alternatives, such as *Spanish origin, Latin American,* or *Latino*.

---

[3]Francine D. Blau, "Gender," in *The New Palgrave: A Dictionary of Economic Theory and Doctrine,* vol. 2, John Eatwell, Murray Milgate, and Peter Newman, eds., (London: The MacMillan Press, 1987), p. 492.

[4]Helen Tierney, ed., *Women's Studies Encyclopedia* (New York: Greenwood Press, 1989), p. 153.

OUTLINE OF THE BOOK

As suggested above, the primary focus of this book is on "economic woman," as she interacts and competes with "economic man." Economic behavior is not, however, treated in isolation from the remainder of human existence. To provide a more comprehensive picture, subsequent chapters will reflect insights from other social sciences, which enhance our understanding of a variety of factors. Such noneconomic factors help to determine economic behavior and how that behavior, in turn, helps to shape other aspects of life.

Chapter 2 deals with the historical evolution of the roles of women and men, focusing particularly on the United States. The following two chapters consider the gender division of labor within the family and analyze the individual's decision about how to allocate his or her time between the household and the labor market.

The next four chapters deal specifically with women's position in the labor market as compared to that of men, beginning with an overview of occupations and earnings and going on to an in-depth examination of the various explanations of the existing situation. Chapter 6 reviews the human capital approach, and Chapter 7 concentrates on discrimination as a cause of women's lower economic status. Chapter 8 rounds out the picture by providing information on individuals in the labor market who are unable to find jobs and exploring the reasons for differentials in the unemployment rates of women and men.

In Chapter 9 we return to the family to examine the impact of women's employment on family structure and on the well-being of family members. Finally, in Chapter 10, we compare the economic status of women relative to men in other countries, with special emphasis on similarities and differences between those countries and the United States. Substantial differences in behaviors suggest that particular outcomes are not inevitable but rather are subject to choice by each society. In instances where a country appears to have impressive achievements in gender equality to its credit, we may be able to learn from the experiences there.

Appendix

A REVIEW OF SUPPLY AND DEMAND
IN THE LABOR MARKET

As we explained in Chapter 1, supply and demand provide economists with a framework for analyzing labor markets. We briefly review these concepts here in the context of a particular type of labor, clerical workers.

Curve *DD* in Figure 1.1 shows the typical downward-sloping **demand curve.** Wage rate (price) is on the vertical axis, and quantity (number of workers) is on the horizontal axis. The demand curve represents the various amounts of labor that would be hired at various prices by firms in this labor market over a given period of time. Everything else remaining the same, including methods of production and prices of other inputs, changes in the wage rate cause movements along this curve. There is a change in the *quantity demanded,* but demand (that is, the demand curve) remains the same. If, on the other hand, other factors do not remain the same, the entire demand curve may be shifted.

Demand curves normally slope downward to the right, which means that the firm will hire more workers at a lower wage rate and fewer at a higher wage rate. There are several reasons for this. The first is that in the short run there is **diminishing marginal productivity** of labor, meaning that additional units of labor provide progressively less additional output when combined with given amounts of capital (plant and equipment). The second is the **substitution effect.** When the

9

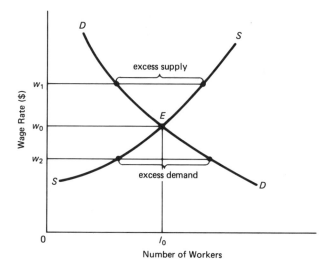

FIGURE 1.1   The Market for Clerical Workers

price of a particular input changes, while that of a potential substitute remains the same, there will be a tendency for profit-maximizing employers to use more of the one that is now relatively cheaper and less of the one that is now relatively more expensive. In the short run, for example, less-skilled labor may be substituted for skilled workers. In the long run, it may be possible to substitute capital for labor. Last, there is the **scale effect,** which may also operate in both the short and long run. As wages increase, the price of the product will go up, less of it will be purchased, and fewer workers will be employed. The scale effect is likely to be especially large when wages constitute a substantial part of the costs of production. These are the factors that cause the quantity of labor hired to decrease as the wage rate increases, but the movements are along the given demand curve and do not involve a shift of demand.

The **supply curve,** shown by *SS* in Figure 1.1, slopes upward and to the right. It shows the number of workers who would be willing to do clerical work at all possible prices. The supply curve is upward sloping because, if rewards for one skill increase while those for all others remain the same, additional workers will be attracted from related occupations. So, for example, an increase in the wages of clerical workers may induce individuals who are currently employed in other jobs to improve their clerical skills and compete for clerical positions. Similarly, if pay for clerical work declines relative to others, the quantity of labor supplied to clerical jobs is expected to decline as workers move to other sectors.

It is important to emphasize that the supply curve depicted in Figure 1.1 represents the number of individuals available for a particular line of work. As we shall see in greater detail in Chapter 4, the number of hours supplied to the market by any particular individual may not increase when wages rise. This may happen because, at a higher wage rate, an individual who participates in the labor market may choose to allocate more of his or her time to nonmarket activities and the satisfactions they bring.

The intersection of the supply and demand curves shown in Figure 1.1 represents a **stable equilibrium.** An equilibrium exists when all persons willing to work at the going rate are able to find employment and all employers willing to hire someone at the going rate are able to find workers. In other words, the quantity demanded and the quantity supplied are equal at E, so there are no forces causing the wage to move from its present level as long as there are no external shocks. In this case, the equilibrium wage is w_0, and the equilibrium quantity of labor employed is l_0. To illustrate why point E represents a *stable* equilibrium, let us assume that, for whatever reason, the wage rate is initially set higher than w_0, say at w_1. At this point, the quantity of labor supplied would exceed the quantity of labor demanded and push wages down toward E. Conversely, if wages were initially set at w_2, the opposite would be true. In short, we have a stable equilibrium where there is no tendency to move away from E. If an external shock were to cause a deviation, there would be a tendency to return toward that point.

External shocks may, of course, also cause shifts in demand, supply, or both, leading to a new equilibrium. Such shocks may come from changes in markets for goods, for nonlabor inputs, or for other types of labor, and they are extremely common. Therefore, a stable equilibrium is not necessarily one that remains fixed for any length of time. It merely means that at any given time there is a tendency toward convergence at the point where the quantity of labor supplied equals the quantity of labor demanded, until conditions cause this point to shift.

It may be instructive to consider a couple of examples in which there are shifts in the supply or demand curves. These sample situations can help to clarify the difference between factors that cause a movement along an existing supply or demand curve and those that cause a shift in the entire curve. We shall also be able to see how the new equilibrium position is established.

Suppose that the government issues a report on the dangers of credit spending and that it is effective enough to cause a reduction in the demand for such services provided by the banking industry. That is, at any given price of these services, consumers demand less of them. Since this industry employs a substantial number of clerical workers, such a change would cause a marked inward shift in the market-wide demand curve for clerical workers, from DD to $D'D'$ in Figure 1.2a. That is, at any given wage rate, firms are willing to hire fewer clerical workers. This illustrates that the demand for labor is a *derived* demand: it is derived from the consumer demand for the goods and services that the workers produce. A new equilibrium will occur at E_1, where the quantity of labor supplied again equals the (new) quantity of labor demanded. At E_1, fewer individuals are employed as clerical workers and a lower wage rate is determined for that occupation.

Shifts in supply curves can also alter the market equilibrium, as shown in Figure 1.2b. For instance, suppose that the government's antidiscrimination policies increase opportunities for women in managerial jobs, raising their wages

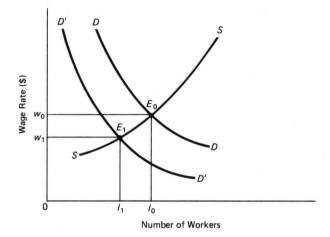

FIGURE 1.2a A Shift in Demand

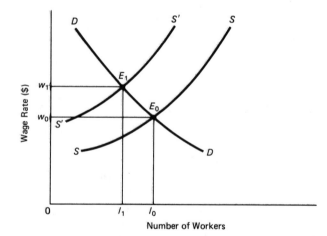

FIGURE 1.2b A Shift in Supply

and making it easier for them to obtain such employment. This will result in a reduction in the supply (inward shift in the supply curve) of clerical workers, an occupation staffed primarily by women. At any given wage, fewer women would be available to work in clerical jobs than previously. At the new equilibrium (E_1), the wages are higher, and the number of workers employed is lower than in the initial situation (E_0). This illustrates that improved opportunities for women in traditionally male jobs can potentially improve the economic welfare even of those women who remain in traditionally female pursuits.

Chapter 2

WOMEN AND MEN: CHANGING ROLES IN A CHANGING ECONOMY

It seems to me that an economic interpretation of history is an indispensable element in the study of society, but it is only one element. In layers below it lie geography, biology and psychology, and in layers above it the investigation of social and political relationships and the history of culture, law and religion.

Joan Robinson, *Freedom and Necessity**

We are constantly told today that we live in an era of rapid change—change in economic conditions, in economic and social institutions, in mores and beliefs. And so we do. Changes in the roles of women and men, their relations to each other, and the nature of the families in which most of them continue to live have been taking place at a speed that is quite possibly unprecedented. This situation has inevitably created stresses and strains. Not surprisingly, people who feel insecure in a world of shifting boundaries and values are prone to look back with nostalgia to the "good old days" when women were women, and men were men, and both knew their proper place.

*Joan Robinson, *Freedom and Necessity: An Introduction to the Study of Society* (London: George Allen and Unwin, 1970), p. 5.

How realistic is this picture some hold of traditional gender roles, unchanging for all time, and pervasive for all places, which is supposed to have existed before the recent era of turmoil and upheaval? The answer to this question has substantial practical implications. If the same roles of women and men have existed always and everywhere, some may conclude that these roles are biologically determined and that they probably cannot, and perhaps should not, be changed. If, on the other hand, there has been a good deal of variation in the roles of men and women over time, it is likely that there is also room for flexibility now and in the future.

For this reason, it is particularly important to gain some insight into the nature of gender roles through the course of human development. There are, of course, other reasons as well. Some awareness of the complexities of history is indispensable for an understanding of the present. It is also crucial if we are to make any progress toward correctly anticipating the future. In our brief historical review, we shall find that, although the rate may have been a great deal slower in the past, there has always been change. Societies, throughout time, have been characterized by an astonishing diversity of economic and social institutions.

We begin by briefly considering the biological and anthropological evidence about the nature of males and females. This takes us somewhat far afield from traditional economics but provides valuable background for the historical analysis that follows. Here we consider the changing roles of men and women in the household and in the economy, and the evolution of the family, in the course of economic development into the period of industrialization in the nineteenth and twentieth centuries. Although other factors are not ignored, economic causation is assigned the predominant role in the shaping of these changes. The focus during the most recent periods is on the United States.

THE NATURE OF MALES AND FEMALES

As recently as the 1970s, a common interpretation of the behavior of, and relation between, men and women emphasized the importance of the biological maternal function of the female in determining the nature and content of her being.[1] In this view, a woman's early life is a preparation for becoming, and her later life is devoted to being, a successful wife and mother. Accordingly, her nature is compliant, not competitive, nurturant, not instrumental. Her activities, though not necessarily confined to the home, at least center around it, for her primary mission is to be a helpmate to her husband and to provide a warm and safe haven for her family. If she does work for pay, she will do best in jobs compatible with her household responsibilities and her "feminine" personality. Men, on the other hand, are not constrained by their paternal function from fully entering the world outside the home. On the contrary, their natural role as provider and protector spurs them on to greater efforts.

[1] See, for example, Lionel Tiger, *Men in Groups* (New York: Random House, 1969).

The popular perception, based to an extent on the work of earlier researchers,[2] has often been that investigations of male and female roles among nonhuman species provided support for the view that biology is destiny. Therefore we, too, begin with a brief look at animals and their behavior. More recent research suggests that no generalization holds for all species and, thus, that extrapolation from animal studies does not support the traditional view. Before summarizing this evidence, we consider the question of why researchers' perceptions of animal behavior have changed over time.

In this area, as in others, scientists confront the problem that their subjective expectations tend to influence how they interpret particular situations and what they notice about them.[3] For example, one male with a group of females is traditionally viewed as the ruler of a dependent harem. From another point of view, it may be a group of dominant females who have no use for more than one male for breeding purposes. Similarly, while attention is frequently focused on individual males who play a dominant role, it goes unnoticed that even the highest-ranking ones may be routed by a group of females who gang up to chase them if they, for instance, disturb the young.

When most researchers were male and, whether male or female, held traditional views of appropriate gender roles among humans, they tended to see confirmation of these views in their observations of animal behavior. As more women have joined the ranks of researchers, and as both men and women have been influenced by changing gender roles in human society, perceptions of animal behavior have accordingly been revised. The new view that has emerged, reflecting as it does a process of reexamination and more careful scrutiny of the evidence, probably can be given more credence than earlier ones. The process of re-evaluation and revision is illustrated in more detail in an insert on pages 17–18, in which a summary of current developments in the study of primates is presented.

As anthropologists have been reconsidering the evidence that studies of animals provide about the nature of females and males, a number of correctives to anthropomorphic models of male dominance and aggressiveness, and of female passivity and nurturance, have been found in new studies of various animal groups.[4] Many of them show evidence of "female dominance, autonomy, and power; of male

---

[2]Foremost among these have been Robert Ardrey, *The Territorial Imperative* (New York: Athenum Press, 1966); Desmond Morris, *The Human Zoo* (New York: McGraw-Hill, 1969); and Lionel Tiger and Robin Fox, *The Imperial Animal* (New York: Holt, Rinehart & Winston, 1971).

[3]This problem is noted in Gordon H. Orians, "On the Evolution of Mating Systems in Birds and Mammals," in *Readings in Behavior,* William van der Kloot, Charles Wolcott, and Benjamin Dane, eds. (New York: Holt, Rinehart & Winston, 1974), pp. 232–47; and Jane B. Lancaster, "In Praise of the Achieving Female Monkey," *Psychology Today*, 7, no. 4 (Sept. 1973): 3236–99.

[4]Some information on various animal species is provided, for instance, in Janet Chafetz, *Masculine, Feminine, or Human?* (Itasca, IL: Peacock Publishers, 1978); Lancaster, "In Praise of the Achieving Female Monkey"; and Clarice S. Stoll, *Female and Male Socialization, Social Roles and Social Structure* (Dubuque, IA: Wm C Brown, 1974).

nurturance and cooperation; and of monogamous behavior as well as promiscuity in both males and females.[5]

Much of the research on sex roles among animals has focused specifically on primates, because they are closer to human beings than are the lower animals. Even there, however, sweeping generalizations are rarely justified. The behavior of these animals is typically dimorphic (that is, certain types of behavior are more typical of one sex than the other). But these differences are generally a matter of degree, not of kind, and there is much overlap. Only among some species such as rhesus monkeys, are males far more aggressive and belligerent than females. Nor do differences in behavior necessarily mean that females are socially inferior. Only among some species, especially baboons and rhesus monkeys, is there a rigidly hierarchical social structure dominated by highly aggressive males. It is particularly interesting that among chimpanzees, the most socially advanced nonhuman primates, females do not appear to occupy a subordinate position. Harem-like groups with dominant males are entirely unknown.[6]

These examples should suffice to make anyone cautious about the argument that any attribute or behavior is always male or female, even if generalizing from animals to humans were otherwise acceptable. But such generalization is itself debatable. An alternative approach suggests that what distinguishes *homo sapiens* from other species is that, for humans, it is primarily the norms and expectations of their societies, not blind animal instincts, that are important in shaping their actions and their relations. In this view, biology constrains, but does not determine, human behavior. Human gender roles are no more limited to those of animals than is human behavior otherwise limited to that of animals.[7]

There are, to be sure, physiological and psychological differences between men and women, but, it is argued, they do not adequately explain all existing variations in behavior or why female traits are so often viewed as socially inferior to male traits. Biological nature, which determines the difference between the sexes, is seen as a broad base upon which a variety of structures, with respect to socially determined gender differences, can be built. This hypothesis is consistent with the diverse male and female roles that sprang up under varying conditions in early societies, in spite of the fact that some differentiation of the work and roles of men and women seems to have been present in all known instances. Recently anthropologists of this school have pointed out that women vary in their social roles and powers, their public status, and their cultural definitions and that the nature, quantity, and social significance of women's activities are far more varied and interesting than has often been assumed.

[5]Cynthia F. Epstein, *Deceptive Distinctions. Sex, Gender, and the Social Order* (New Haven, CT: Yale University Press, 1988), p. 59.

[6]Edward O. Wilson, *Sociobiology: The New Synthesis* (Cambridge, MA: The Belhuan Press of Harvard University Press, 1975).

[7]See anthropologists such as Ernestine Friedl, *Women and Men, An Anthropologists' View* (New York: Holt, Rinehart & Winston, 1975), and Michelle Z. Rosaldo and Louise Lamphere, eds., *Women, Culture and Society* (Stanford: Stanford University Press, 1974).

SEX ROLES AMONG PRIMATES: CHANGING VIEWS

As interest in gender roles among humans has been growing, a large number of scholars, many of them women, have also been studying male and female behavior among animals, particularly primates. Excerpts from an interesting report on recent developments in this field* are presented below.

An explosion of knowledge about monkeys and apes is overturning long-held stereotypes about sex roles and social patterns among the closest kin to humans in the animal world. . . . The new body of research has shown that, although male dominance of groups is common, females of many species are fiercely competitive, resourceful and independent, sexually assertive and promiscuous and, in some cases, more prone than males to wanderlust at puberty.

Soon after the advent of modern primate studies in the early 1960's, many scientists believed they had discovered the key to primate social systems when they described hierarchies of aggressive males competing for the right to mate with seemingly passive females, whose roles appeared limited to the bearing of the young. . . .

"It was as if scientists had projected onto primates a mirror image of the social structure of an American corporation or university," said Sarah Blaffer Hrdy of the University of California at Davis, a leader in the reappraisal of primate behavior. . . .

A common thread through the new findings is that the fundamental evolutionary demand—that parents successfully pass on their genes—imposes different reproductive strategies and behaviors on males and females. But beyond this, Dr. [Jane B.] Lancaster [of the University of Oklahoma] concludes, "It is virtually impossible to generalize about what male primates do or how female primates act." For each species, sex roles have been shaped differently according to its evolutionary history and ecological setting. . . .

Efforts to draw lessons about humans from other primates go to the heart of the age-old debate about nature versus nurture—the respective influences of inborn traits and environment on human behavior. This controversy has heated up over the last 15 years with the advent of sociobiology, which studies how evolutionary pressures cause behavior patterns as well as physical traits to become encoded genetically in animals. Though they deny the charge, some sociobiologists, because of their willingness to speculate about innate human behavioral tendencies on the basis of animal studies, have been accused of promoting a new form of biological determinism.

Most scientists, including many who regard themselves as sociobiologists, reject the notion that the genetic component of human behavior can be isolated. They say human genes determine a biological range of capacity, the expression of which is realized only through environmental influences. In the words of Stephen Jay Gould, a professor at Harvard University, "Biology and culture are inextricable and co-determinant."

*Erik Eckholm, "New View of Female Primates Assails Stereotypes," *The New York Times,* September 18, 1984, pp. 17–18. Copyright ©1984 by The New York Times Company. Reprinted by permission.

The recent field studies have raised questions about the extent to which social behavior is genetically fixed even in wild primates. "We used to talk about 'the monkey' or 'the baboon,'" Dr. Lancaster noted, "but now we've seen that all baboons don't act the same."

A group's ecological setting, its demographic makeup and even its history and traditions—transmitted from one generation to the next by learning rather than genetics—have all been found to influence primate behavior....

Dr. Hrdy holds the view ... that evolution has predisposed human females, like males, not only to intelligence and assertiveness but also to competitiveness. Thus, while attacking old stereotypes that devalue the capacities of women, she also disputes ... "countermyths that emphasize woman's natural innocence from lust for power, her cooperativeness and solidarity with other women."

... The change in perceptions about primates has coincided with ferment in thinking about sex roles in human society and with the entry of women into primate studies in numbers unusually high for the sciences. In addition to the famous field studies of chimpanzees by Jane Goodall and gorillas by Dian Fossey, many women have made important theoretical contributions to primatology. Intriguing questions have been raised about whether social trends and the sex of scientists have affected the course of "objective" science.

Leading primatologists of both sexes agree that men have played key roles in the recent redefining of primate behavior. And the advances in understanding can be explained innocently enough.

Dr. Sherwood L. Washburn of the University of California at Berkeley, who is regarded as the father of modern primate studies, noted that serious field work began only in the early 1960's. "When you get in the field, the obvious creature is the big, dominant male," he said. "The behaviors that were easiest to see were exaggerated in the initial studies. But I don't think this was the result of any bias."

Still, questions about the possible effects on science of a changing social milieu persist. Dr. Hrdy believes that improved methodology, the broad questioning of sexual stereotypes by the women's liberation movement (influencing scientists of both sexes), and the infusion of female scientists have all contributed to the new understanding of primate societies.

FACTORS INFLUENCING WOMEN'S RELATIVE STATUS

In their studies of human societies, anthropologists, particularly the female anthropologists who have given more of their attention to this issue, agree that the relative status of women has varied over time and across societies. There is less agreement on the factors determining their relative position. It is our view that, although it may not be possible to definitively answer this question at present, some important insights can be gained by considering existing theories.

One anthropologist, Ernestine Friedl,[8] has emphasized the importance of environmental constraints in shaping human organization. She argues that the technology employed by a society to produce the necessities of life has tended, in the past, to determine the division of labor on the basis of gender. She also believes that the more important women's role is in production and in controlling distribution outside the family, the higher their status compared to men. Friedl, and others espousing this view, point to the relatively egalitarian situation in primitive societies where men and women shared in providing food, clothing, and shelter for their families, or, in modern days, when both earn an income. In contrast, the status of men and women was very unequal in societies where men provided all the needed resources and women devoted themselves to transforming these resources into usable form and creating a pleasant atmosphere in which they could be used.

Others tend to disagree, at least with the emphasis on the importance of production roles in determining status. In past epochs, slaves did a great deal of productive work without achieving correspondingly high status, and members of the upper class derived their power and prestige from ownership of wealth rather than any work they did. There is little dispute, however, about the fact that property gives owners power over distribution and that this helps to determine status.

We are inclined toward the view that the structure of social relationships and participation in productive work both play a role. Specifically, in the case of women, it appears that sharing in the provision for the family's needs is a necessary, though not a sufficient, ingredient in achieving a greater degree of equality.[9] Clearly, as Michelle Rosaldo[10] points out, the extent to which women's activities are confined to the home, while men monopolize the public sphere, also plays an important role.

In the remainder of this chapter, we explore the effect that changing technology and changing property relations have had on the nature and perception of gender roles, focusing primarily on the United States. First, however, we briefly consider the issue of the relationship between women's roles and economic development in more general terms.

WOMEN'S ROLES AND ECONOMIC DEVELOPMENT

In technologically primitive *hunting and gathering societies*, men and women shared in providing food, clothing, and shelter for their families. At the same time, men hunted large animals and defended the tribe, whereas women gath-

---

[8]Friedl, *Women and Men*. See also Joan Huber and Glenna Spitze, *Sex Stratification: Children, Housework, and Jobs* (New York: Academic Press, 1983).

[9]Joyce M. Nielson, *Sex in Society: Perspectives on Stratification* (Belmont, CA: Wadsworth, 1978).

[10]Michelle Z. Rosaldo, "Women, Culture, and Society: A Theoretical Overview," in *Women, Culture, and Society,* Rosaldo and Lamphere, eds. See also Julie A. Matthaei, *An Economic History of Women in America* (New York: Schocken Books, 1982).

ered a variety of vegetable foods, occasionally hunted small animals,[11] and had the main responsibility for food preparation and care of children. Such a division of labor was undoubtedly expedient when women were pregnant or nursing most of their adult lives, and thus could not participate in activities that would have taken them far from home. The greater strength of men also gave them a considerable advantage for such activities as hunting large animals and fighting.

The extent to which men and women contributed to the necessities of life was determined by the availability of various resources, and women's status appeared to vary accordingly. In general, the fact that men provided for the safety of the tribe and furnished most of the meat, always regarded as the prestige food, gave them the advantage. Nonetheless, the common payment of the bride price suggests that women were also valued for their contributions.

In the somewhat more advanced *horticultural societies,* plants were cultivated in small plots located near the home. Men continued to conduct warfare and also prepared the ground by slashing and burning; women prepared the food and cared for infants. But virtually all other activities were shared. Accordingly, men and women tended to be considerably more equal during this stage.[12]

In *pastoral societies,* on the other hand, men tended to monopolize the herding of large animals; this activity often took them far from home. Herding provided the bulk of what was needed for subsistence. Women's contributions were largely confined to tending the primitive equivalent of hearth and home, and females never reached more than a subservient status.

The situation changed radically when horticultural societies were superceded by *agricultural societies,* which arrived with the introduction of the plow. Although women "helped" in the fields,[13] looked after small animals and gardens, and worked in the now-permanent homes taking care of large families, only men owned and worked the land, and the disparity in power and influence became great indeed. The *dowry,* paid by the father of the bride to the groom, who henceforth undertakes her support, and *purdah,* the practice of hiding women from the sight of men, came into use during that period in some of these societies. Both may be viewed as ways of subordinating women as well as symptoms of their subjugation.

There was one factor that helped to offset this lowly position for at least a small minority of women. As ownership of land and other assets created an upper class of landed gentry, membership in that class entailed great wealth and

---

[11] Some evidence suggests that women may have participated in all hunting more than was acknowledged earlier, especially in tribes where group hunting was common. See, for instance, Agnes Estioko-Griffin and P. Bion Griffin, "Woman the Hunter: The Agta," in *Woman the Gatherer,* Frances Dahlberg, ed. (New Haven, CT: Yale University Press, 1981), pp. 121–52.

[12] This stage perhaps best illustrates the view that, although there was always a division of labor by sex, it was not always hierarchical. See Heidi Hartmann, "Capitalism, Patriarchy, and Job Segregation by Sex," *Signs: Journal of Women in Culture and Society* 1, no. 3, Pt. 2 (Spring 1976): 137–69.

[13] Very poor women also worked as hired laborers and domestic servants.

power. Under these conditions birth in the right family conferred status even on women. Property was generally owned and inherited by men, but in the absence of a male heir in a ruling family, a woman might even become head of state.[14] Hence, there were ruling queens, Elizabeth I of England being the best known. In general, however, while upper-class females enjoyed a rather luxurious lifestyle, they were mainly seen as producers of children, rarely had influence except as behind-the-scenes manipulators, and were typically used as pawns in political and economic alliances. Only in exceptional cases did women achieve important roles in the economy and in the development of culture, aided by achieving high rank in religious orders in some instances, or by the extended absence of fighting men in others.

Women were also more likely to be partners, albeit unequal ones, among the growing class of merchants and artisans in the urban centers that began to grow along with developing agriculture. They participated in what were, in those early days, truly family enterprises, generally took charge when the men traveled on business, and often continued to be in charge after the husband died. Household and work places were not rigidly separated, nor were consumption and production. Father, mother, children, perhaps other relatives, and often apprentices, lived and worked together. Yet their tasks and responsibilities were determined by their age and by their sex. Whenever the father was present, he was the head of the family enterprise.

As we have seen, women tended to have a higher status in horticultural societies than in agricultural ones, in which women's activities came to be increasingly centered within the home. Even so, since much production was concentrated in the household, and since women were active participants, they were perceived as productive members of the family. During the early stages of *industrialization,* on the other hand, much of the production previously concentrated in the household was shifted from the home to the factory and the office. This shift reduced the burden of housekeeping but did little to advance the status of women, who, for the most part, continued to center their activities around the home. Indeed, the perceived importance of their productive role initially tended to decline, as did their relative status. In time, however, continued industrialization began to draw ever-increasing numbers into the paid labor force, paving the way for a "subtle

---

[14]Only recently have any women become heads of state who were not born into the position, and even today they tend to come from the upper classes. The proposition that women were always relegated to a more or less inferior status in all primitive societies, and that at least a few attained power and prestige when class structure developed, is in sharp contrast to the views propounded by Friedrich Engels in *The Origin of Family, Private Property, and the State* (New York: International Publishers, 1884, reprinted 1972, copyright 1942). His contention was that women were powerful matriarchs during the earlier stages of development (primitive communism) and that it was the development of private property that was the root of the subjugation of women. It should be noted, on the other hand, that Engels' emphasis on the mode of production as basic in shaping the roles of women and men underlies our analysis as well.

revolution" in gender roles.[15] In the following sections, we review this process in greater detail, focusing upon the situation in the United States.

The case of the United States is in some respects unique, even in comparison to other advanced industrialized countries. In particular, the frontier experience was shared by only a few of these countries, such as Canada and Australia. Nonetheless, the broad contours of the shifts outlined here are to some extent applicable to many of them. Indeed, the alteration of men's and women's work roles occurring in the United States today may be seen as part of a transformation taking place in much of the industrialized world. (Recent developments in other countries are discussed in greater detail in Chapter 10.)

THE U.S. EXPERIENCE

The Preindustrial Period

In Colonial America, as in other preindustrial economies, the family enterprise was the dominant economic unit, and production was the major function of the family. Most of the necessities for survival were produced in the household, though some goods were generally produced for sale, the proceeds of which were used to purchase some market goods and to accumulate wealth. Cooking; cleaning; care of the young, the old, and the infirm; spinning; weaving; sewing; knitting; soap and candle making; and simple carpentry were carried on in the home. Much of the food and other raw materials were grown on the farm. All members of the family capable of making any contribution participated in production, but there was always some specialization and division of labor.

Among the nonslave population, men were primarily responsible for agriculture and occasionally trade, whereas women did much of the rest of the work, including what would today be characterized as "light manufacturing" activity. But gender-role specialization was by no means complete. Slave women were used to work in the fields. Widows tended to take over the family enterprise when the need arose, and in very early days, single women were on occasion given "maidplots." Even though men and women often had different tasks, and the former were more often involved in production for the market and generally owned all property, everyone participated in productive activity. Even aged grandparents would help with tasks that required responsibility and judgment, and would perhaps also supervise children in carrying out small chores they could adequately perform from a very early age.

All family members, except for infants, had essentially the same economic role. They either contributed goods and services directly or earned money by selling

[15]Ralph E. Smith, "The Movement of Women into the Labor Force," in *The Subtle Revolution: Women at Work,* Ralph E. Smith, ed. (Washington, DC: The Urban Institute, 1979), pp. 1–29.

some of these in the market. The important economic role of children, as well as the plentiful availability of land, encouraged large families. High infant mortality rates provided a further incentive to bear many children. In the eighteenth century, completed fertility may have averaged as many as eight to ten births per woman.[16]

Wealthy women were primarily managers, not workers, within the household. This was, no doubt, a less arduous and possibly a more rewarding level of task but one no less absorbing. For most women, regardless of their affluence, there was little role conflict. The ideal of the frugal, industrious housewife working alongside her family corresponded closely to reality. The only women for whom this was not true were very poor women, who often became indentured servants, and, of course, black women, who were generally slaves. The former were, as a rule, not permitted to marry during their years of servitude; the latter might potentially have their family entirely disrupted by their owners' choice. Both had to work very hard, and slaves did not even have the modest legal protection of rights that indentured servants enjoyed.

The one thing all these diverse groups had in common was that they were productive members of nearly self-sufficient households. Government played a very small role, and although there was some exchange of goods and services, chiefly barter, it was not until well into the nineteenth century that production outside the home, for sale rather than for direct use, came to dominate the economy.

Industrialization

During the early period of industrialization in the late eighteenth and early nineteenth centuries, women in the United States, as elsewhere, worked in the textile mills and other industries that sprang up in the East. Initially, primarily young farm girls were employed in the factories, often contributing part of their pay to supplement family income and using some to accumulate a "dowry" that would make them more desirable marriage partners. The employment of these young women in factories may have appeared quite natural to observers at the time. They were doing much the same type of work they had done in the home, only in a new location and under the supervision of a foreman rather than the head of the household.[17] Once married, women generally left their jobs to look after their own households, which would soon include children.

The earliest available data show that at the end of the nineteenth century, when the labor force participation rate for men was 84 percent, only 18 percent of all women were in the paid labor force, and the percentage of married women

---

[16]For a description of demographic trends, see Karl E. Taeuber and James A. Sweet, in "Family and Work: The Social Life Cycle of Women," *Women and the American Economy: A Look to the 1980's,* Juanita M. Kreps, ed. (Englewood Cliffs, N.J.: Prentice-Hall, 1976), pp. 31–60.

[17]This was pointed out by Edith Abbott, *Women in Industry* (New York: Appleton and Company, 1910).

was 5 percent.[18] The situation was different for black women. Around 25 percent of black wives were employed. Most of these worked either as domestics or in agriculture in the rural South. Although such early industries as textiles, millinery, and cigars did employ women, mainly young single ones, the new, rapidly growing sophisticated industries relied from the beginning almost entirely on male workers.

Among some immigrant groups,[19] however, who in the course of the nineteenth century increasingly replaced American-born workers in factories, it was not uncommon even for married women to be employed. Most of these people came to the "New World" determined to improve their economic condition and particularly to make sure that their children would get a better start than they did. At times, the whole family worked. Often if a choice needed to be made between the children leaving school to supplement family income or the mother seeking employment, the latter choice was made even among groups traditionally reluctant to have women work outside the home. By the same token, maternal employment was associated with dire need and was viewed as a temporary expedient to give the family a better start. Few wives remained in the labor force once the husband earned enough for an adequate living. The immigrants' goal of achieving the desired standard of living included what by then was widely considered the American ideal of the family—the male breadwinner who supported his family and the female homemaker who cared for his domestic needs.

Industrialization and the Evolution of the Family

As an increasingly larger segment of the population began living in urban centers rather than on farms, and family shops were replaced by factories, women found that their household work increasingly came to be confined to the care of children, the nurturing of the husband, and the maintenance of the home. There were no longer a garden or farm animals to take care of, no need for seasonal help with the crops, and no opportunity to participate in a family business. As husbands left the home to earn the income needed to support their families, a more rigid division developed between the female domestic sphere and the male public sphere.

Thus, along with industrialization arose the concept of the **traditional family,** which lingered to a greater or lesser degree well into the twentieth century.[20] The

---

[18] As discussed below, such official figures undoubtedly underestimate the proportion of women who worked for pay. Not only was seasonal work frequently ignored, but work done in the home, such as taking in boarders and bringing home piecework, was often overlooked as well.

[19] Milton Cantor and Bruce Laurie, eds., *Class, Sex and the Woman Worker* (Westport, CT: Greenwood Press, 1977) contains a great deal of interesting information on immigrant women.

[20] Historian Carl N. Degler has termed this the "first transformation." In his view, the second transformation came in the 1940s, when married women began to enter the labor market in large

family shifted from a production unit to a consumption unit, and the responsibility for earning a living came to rest squarely on the shoulders of the husband. Wives (and children) grew to be dependent on his income. Redistribution became an important function of the family, as it provided a mechanism for the transfer of income from the market-productive husband to his market-dependent wife and children. Not only did specific *tasks* differ between men and women, as was always the case, but men and women now had different *economic roles* as well. Many workers and social reformers explicitly advocated that a man should be paid a "family wage," adequate to support not only him but also his wife and children.

As before, among the poor, particularly blacks and immigrants, it was often necessary for wives to enter the labor market. But for the middle-class white wife, and even for the working-class wife whose husband had a steady income, holding a job was frowned upon as inconsistent with her social status. If the wife entered the labor market, it was assumed that she was either compensating for her husband's inadequacy as a breadwinner or that she was selfishly pursuing a career at the expense of her household responsibilities.

The status of children also changed. Only in very poor families would they be expected to help to raise the family's standard of living, though some might work to earn spending money or because their parents thought it would be good for their moral fiber. Furthermore, the age when children came to be considered young adults and were supposed to become productive members of the family increased considerably. By the end of the nineteenth century, child labor laws were passed that prohibit employment of "minors."

As a consequence of industrialization and urbanization, more and more goods and services used by households came to be produced outside the home. Nonetheless, much time and effort was still expended to purchase and maintain these commodities, and to use them to attain the desired standard of living. With soap and bleach purchased at the store, and the washing machine doing the scrubbing, laundry became far less of a chore, but it was done far more frequently, and housewives came to take pride in making it "whiter than white." Groceries bought at the supermarket and a gas or electric range made cooking much easier, but homemakers would now serve elaborate meals rather than a pot of stew. To do otherwise would not be consistent with the role of dedicated mother and wife, whose every thought was for the well-being of her family. The husband might help her, but this was never to interfere with his "work." The children, too, particularly girls, might be expected to assist their mothers, but the basic responsibility for the household rested with the wife.

---

numbers. See his *At Odds: Women and the Family in America from the Revolution to the Present* (New York: Oxford University Press, 1980). It was also during this period that women's work in the household came to be officially classified as unproductive, as pointed out by Nancy Folbre, "The Unproductive Housewife: Her Evolution in Nineteenth-Century Economic Thought," *Signs: Journal of Women in Culture and Society* 16, no. 3 (Spring 1991): 463–84.

The net result of these developments was that the number of hours full-time homemakers devoted to housework, over 50 a week, did not change from the beginning of the century to the 1960s.[21] Two additional trends contributed to this. One was the decline in the number of household servants, whose presence was not uncommon in middle-class households in the nineteenth and early twentieth centuries. Probably more important was the tendency to use the time no longer needed to produce essentials to raise the standard of comfort the family could enjoy, not to increase the wife's leisure time.[22]

Fertility declined with industrialization,[23] in part because of the diminished economic value of children. There was far less opportunity for children to participate in production in urban households, and with growing immigration, hired workers were more readily available as a source of farm labor. Further, the number of years of schooling grew in both towns and rural areas, so that children remained dependent for a longer period of time. Consequently, women born in the early nineteenth century averaged somewhat less than five births, considerably below the rate of their eighteenth-century predecessors, and those born toward the end of the century averaged only about three births. But as the number of children declined, the amount of maternal care per child increased greatly, and the number of years of such care was extended substantially.

Responsibility for spending the family's money and for determining the amount to be saved was not as clear, but there were certain generally accepted norms. The wife made most of the everyday purchases, but was expected to comply with her husband's wishes and to try to please her family.[24] Thus, to some extent, she might be viewed as the purchasing agent rather than an independent decision maker when she did the shopping. The husband determined where the family would live and what major items should be bought, such as larger durables and, particularly, the house.

---

[21] Joann Vanek, "Time Spent in Housework," *Scientific American* 231, no. 5 (Nov. 1974): 116–20, found that even as late as 1966, full-time homemakers were devoting as much time to their work as their grandmothers had in the 1920s. It was not until the late seventies that this situation changed; see Joseph H. Pleck, "Husband's Paid Work and Family Roles: Current Research Issues," in *Research in the Interweave of Social Roles: Families and Jobs,* Helena Lopata and Joseph H. Pleck, eds. (Greenwich, CT: JAI Press, 1983).

[22] Bonnie J. Fox, "Selling the Mechanized Household: 70 Years of Ads in the Ladies Home Journal," *Gender and Society,* 4, no. 1 (March 1990): 25–40, points out that advertisements tended to emphasize improved housekeeping standards and better service to the family rather than liberation from household chores.

[23] Improved methods of birth control are often credited for the declining birth rate. But significant decreases occurred in much of the industrialized world before any major breakthroughs in contraceptive techniques. See Joan Huber, "Toward a Sociotechnological Theory of the Women's Movement," *Social Problems* 23, no. 4 (April 1976): 371–88.

[24] For instance, William H. Chafe, "Looking Backward in Order to Look Forward: Women, Work, and Social Values in America," in *Women and the American Economy,* Kreps, ed., pp. 6–30, suggests that since "woman's divinely ordained task was to support their husbands, care for their children, and provide a haven from the worries of the outside world, the idea that they might wish a career seemed a violation of nature" (pp. 7–8).

The man's authority as "head of the household" was supposed to be absolute in all important matters,[25] for he basically determined the family's lifestyle by providing the money income on which it so crucially depended. Further, the husband's decisions defined the parameters within which the other family members had to operate. Thus, he was dominant within the household as well as in the outside world. It was, however generally assumed that, within the family, he would see to it that benefits were distributed equally, or according to need, as deemed appropriate.

As the economic role of women changed within the family, so too did the image of the ideal wife. Whereas the colonial wife was valued for her industriousness, the growing **cult of true womanhood**[26] that developed with industrialization in the nineteenth century equated piety, purity, domesticity, and submissiveness with the femininity to which all women were expected to aspire. Their role was in the now consumption-oriented home—as daughter, sister, but most of all as wife and mother. This ideal particularly extolled the lifestyle of affluent middle- and upper-class women, who were to a great extent freed even from their domestic chores by the servants their husbands' ample incomes could provide. Understandably, overburdened working-class women might come to look longingly at such a more leisurely existence as something to hope for and strive toward. For men of all social classes, it came to be a mark of success to be the sole wage earner in the family.

This image of the family was fostered not only by the example of the middle and upper middle classes, which was the envy of the poor woman bearing the double burden of paid and unpaid work or toiling at home to make ends meet on a limited budget,[27] but also by male workers and their trade unions. Initially, the availability of women and children for work in industry was welcomed by national leaders, because they provided cheap, competitive labor, while agricultural production could be maintained by men.[28] However, attitudes changed as workers

[25] Arlene S. Skolnick and Jerome H. Skolnick, *Family in Transition,* 2nd ed. (Boston: Little Brown and Company, 1977), p. 68.

[26] This subject is explored in depth by Barbara Easton, "Industrialization and Femininity: A Case Study of Nineteenth Century New England," *Social Problems* 23, no. 4 (April 1976): 389–401; and Barbara Welter, "The Cult of True Womanhood, 1820–1860," in *The American Family in Social-Historical Perspective,* Michael Gordon, ed. (New York: St. Martin's Press, 1978), pp. 313–33. This attitude was by no means confined to the United States. The German equivalent was "Küche, Kirche, Kinder": kitchen, church, and children.

[27] As Louise Tilly and Joan Scott, *Women, Work and Families* (New York: Holt, Rinehart & Winston, 1978) forcefully point out, mothers found it very difficult to combine employment outside the home with housework and child care.

[28] George Washington is quoted as writing to Lafayette, "I conceive much might be done in the way of women, children and others [producing yarn and cloth] without taking one really necessary hand from tilling the earth." Cited in Alice Kessler-Harris, *Women Have Always Worked* (New York: McGraw-Hill, 1981), p. 8.

became more plentiful with the growing influx of immigrants. Working men were particularly eager to get wives out of the labor force and women out of all but the lowest-paid jobs. Their goals were to reserve the better positions for themselves, make sure they would not be underbid, and give greater force to the argument that a "living wage" for a man had to be sufficient to support a dependent wife and children. Thus, women received little, if any, support from organized labor in trying to improve their own working conditions and rewards.[29]

This was the genesis of the traditional family, once accepted as the backbone of American society. As we have seen, it is in fact comparatively recent in origin, dating back only to the mid-nineteenth and early twentieth centuries. Even in its heyday, it was never entirely universal. Many poor, black, and immigrant married women worked outside their homes; in addition, many others earned income at home, taking in boarders or doing piece work. Throughout this period, market work was quite common among single women, and a relatively small number of women chose careers over marriage as a lifelong vocation. Nonetheless, exclusive dedication to the role of mother and wife was widely accepted as the only proper and fulfilling life for a woman. It was not long, however, before this orthodoxy was challenged. Progressive modernization brought about dramatic changes in conditions of production and in the economic roles of men and women, followed by changes in ideas and aspirations that made rigid differentiation, let along ranking of the roles of the sexes, increasingly less appropriate.

As family size continued to shrink, the amount of time and energy needed for childbearing and childrearing declined. At the same time, women were living longer. Although, as previously noted, full-time "housewives" continued to work long hours, thus achieving ever higher standards of homemaking, women had the choice of devoting time to other activities, especially during the years after their children grew up. More and more of the goods and services that were previously provided within the household for its own use were now mass-produced and available for purchase. New appliances facilitated faster and/or easier production of many of the others. Increasingly, the market also provided many new goods and services desired by consumers that could not readily be produced in the home. Under these conditions, it was only a matter of time before large numbers of women and men would decide that a second paycheck would make a greater contribution to the family's standard of living than additional time devoted to upgrading the quality of homemaking. Other factors, to be discussed in a later chapter, such as increased education and changes in the demand for labor, were important in facilitating the influx of women into the labor market. However, the shrinking household and household sphere described earlier were among the basic developments that made it possible.

---

[29] Alice Kessler-Harris, "Organizing the Unorganizable: Three Jewish Women and their Unions," in *Class, Sex and the Woman Worker,* Cantor and Laurie, eds., is very eloquent on this point.

Women in the Labor Market[30]

As suggested previously, there were always women who were economically active beyond taking care of family and home. Among married women, however, such activities frequently took place within the confines of the home and, hence, were not counted as labor force participation. Although the precise definition of the labor force has varied over time, it has never included those who produce goods and services for their own and their family's use in the household. Because women did most of this work, and because in earlier days home production took care of a far larger share of people's needs, much of women's work was not counted.

According to official statistics, 84 percent of men, but only 19 percent of women, and less than 5 percent of married women, were reported to be in the labor force in 1890. It has, however, recently been suggested that, although the census did not severely undercount the paid work of married women outside the home in the early years of collecting separate data for men and women, it did considerably understate paid work in the home (such as taking in boarders or doing piece work) and on the farm.

It has been estimated that women's labor force participation, more broadly defined, was as high as 28 percent in 1890, but decreased thereafter with the decline in the family farm and in paid work done at home, not to reach the previous high again until 1940.[31] Interestingly, this corresponds to the notion, discussed earlier in this chapter (and again in Chapter 10), that women's participation in productive activity is likely first to decline, but to rise once more as the economy moves from one dominated by agriculture through early, and then advanced, industrialization.

Each of the two definitions of labor force participation has merit, depending on whether one is primarily interested in the extent to which women are independent wage earners or in their productive contributions to the household. The issue is mainly relevant for wives because, throughout the period for which data have been available, single women were considerably more likely to be gainfully employed outside the home. As late as 1940, the labor force participation of married women was only 16 percent, while it was 46 percent for single women. One reason for the low rates for married women was the so-called "marriage bar" prohibiting the employment of married women that came into use in the late 1800s and lasted into the mid-1900s. Marriage bars were particularly prevalent in teaching and clerical work, two occupations that were to become among the most common for married women in later years.[32]

Not only were relatively few women employed during the early years of the twentieth century, but they also tended to work in different occupations than

---

[30]Much useful information on the economic status of women in the United States prior to World War II is found in Goldin, *Understanding the Gender Gap,* and Matthaei, *An Economic History of Women in America.*

[31]Claudia Goldin, *Understanding the Gender Gap* (New York: Oxford University Press, 1990).

[32]Goldin, *Understanding the Gender Gap.*

men and were concentrated in a relatively few jobs. According to census data, 42 percent of men were in agriculture and 38 percent in blue-collar jobs, fairly evenly distributed among skilled, semi-skilled, and unskilled. Of the 18 percent who were in white-collar jobs, the largest share was in the category of managers and proprietors, followed by sales occupations, professionals, and clerical occupations.

In contrast, among women almost 39 percent were in domestic service; about one-third of these women were black, one-third foreign-born white, and one-sixth Asian. This occupation may plausibly be seen as an extension of what women do at home. As many as 25 percent were in manufacturing, virtually all in textiles, clothing, and tobacco. Another 18 percent, most of them black, were in agriculture. Finally, 8 percent were in the professions, almost entirely composed of school teachers and nurses. These professions, again, may be regarded as extensions of women's domestic role, though initially almost all school teachers were men.

Ninety percent of all women in the labor force were in this relatively small group of occupations. Like teaching, clerical work was originally a primarily male occupation. As late as the turn of the century, 76 percent of clerical workers were men. It was not until after 1900, when such positions gradually ceased to be viewed as apprenticeships, that women entered this field to any significant extent; in time, as more women entered the labor market, it became predominantly female and absorbed a substantial proportion of employed women.

A wide variety of factors undoubtedly contributed to the rapid growth of clerical jobs. Among these was the growth of large corporations, which greatly increased the volume of paperwork. The large proportion of women with a high school education who needed little or no on-the-job training to perform such work provided an inexpensive labor pool to satisfy the expanding demand. Employers were willing to hire these women, even when they were not expected to stay for a long time; this became all the more common after the separation of purely clerical from apprenticeship functions.

Women, in turn, were likely to find these jobs attractive because relevant skills did not tend to depreciate much during periods out of the labor force and reentry was relatively easy. It is also possible that they preferred clean white-collar jobs to the dirtier, noisier, and at times more physically demanding blue-collar jobs, and they had few other such alternatives.[33]

The growth in the demand for clerical workers undoubtedly facilitated the rapid influx of women into the labor force that began in the 1940s and has continued ever since.[34] The causes of this increase are considered in greater detail in

[33] For analyses of women's occupational choices and of their entry into clerical work see Claudia Goldin, "Historical Evolution of Female Earnings Functions and Occupations," *Explorations in Economic History* 21, no. 1 (Jan. 1984): 1–27; and Margery Davies, "Woman's Place is at the Typewriter: The Feminization of the Clerical Labor Force," in *Labor Market Segmentation,* Richard C. Edwards, Michael Reich, and David M. Gordon, eds. (Lexington, MA: D.C. Heath, 1975), pp. 279–96.

[34] Valerie Oppenheimer, *The Female Labor Force in the United States: Demographic and Economic Factors Governing its Growth and Changing Composition,* (Westport, CT: Greenwood Press, 1976; orig. publ. 1970).

Chapter 4. It is, however, very likely that the steady increase in women's earnings, at least in absolute terms, was a contributing factor. Recent research also provides evidence of gains relative to men during some periods. The pay gap between women and men, which had already narrowed during early industrialization between 1820 and 1850, was reduced considerably further between 1890 and 1930 with increasing education and the rise in clerical work. There was, however, little additional change after that until the late 1970s or early 1980s.[35]

Nonwage benefits, on the other hand, provided little encouragement for women to enter the labor force. Because the foundations of the modern welfare state were laid during the time when the traditional family was still accepted as the norm, the programs generally addressed the needs of traditional families rather than those of two-earner or one-adult households. This was true both for the benefits employers began to provide early in the century, including health insurance, disability coverage, and pensions, and for those introduced by government in the 1930s. Both types of programs were expanded further during World War II, when wage increases were severely restricted by government controls, but it was not until considerably later that attention turned to benefits required particularly by families without full-time homemakers. This subject will be discussed at greater length in later chapters.

How much families and their needs have changed becomes clear when it is recognized that by the 1990s over two-thirds of all employed married men, and over 90 percent of employed married women, had a spouse in the labor force. In addition, over one in ten employed women maintained households by themselves. These changes reflect the rapidly rising labor force participation of women, which had reached 58 percent by 1990, as well as the much higher divorce rates of recent decades. These developments will be discussed in greater detail in following chapters.

CONCLUSIONS

The overview provided here, though very general, permits us to draw some conclusions. The roles of men and women and the social rules that prescribe appropriate behavior for each are not shaped by biology alone. Rather, they are determined by the interaction of technology, the role of women in production, and a variety of social and political factors. There is some reason to believe that women are less likely to be seen as dependents, defined solely in terms of their maternal and family role, when they participate in "productive" work.

It is also likely that the roles of men and women that may have initially developed as a rational response to conditions that existed at one time in the course of economic development continue their hold long after they have

---

[35]Goldin, *Understanding the Gender Gap.*

ceased to be functional.[36] Thus the view that women should devote themselves to homemaking, once a full-time occupation when life was short, families were large, and housekeeping was laborious, lingered long after these conditions had changed substantially. Jobs originally allocated to men, because they required great physical strength, often continued as male preserves when mechanization did away with the need for musclepower. The possibility that such lags in adjustment are not uncommon should be kept in mind when we come to analyze the current situation.

Our review also suggests that neither the role of "housewife" nor that of "working woman" is without significant problems for women. Men's work in the public sphere (that is, outside the family) has usually enjoyed higher status than women's domestic work within the family circle. But even when women have succeeded in entering the world beyond the household to a greater or lesser extent, men have not shown much inclination to share in household work.[37] This, in turn, has made it difficult for women to achieve substantial equality in the public sphere. Many of those who *have* tried have been confronted by the problem of "the double burden" of responsibility for home and market work, or have had to make a choice between a career and marriage.[38] In modern times, machines have largely done away with the need for muscle, and physical strength is no longer required for the most highly valued work. At the same time, childbearing absorbs an increasingly smaller proportion of a woman's adult life and can, for the most part, be timed at will. It is entirely possible that, under these conditions, it is the unequal distribution of labor in the home, rather than women's lesser ability to perform other types of work, that is the main obstacle to equality.

[36]"Although stereotypes are often initially based on fact, they are seldom revised as quickly as the facts change." Ralph E. Smith, "The Movement of Women into the Labor Force," in *The Subtle Revolution: Women at Work,* Ralph E. Smith, ed. (Washington, DC: The Urban Institute, 1979).

[37]It is interesting to note that even Marx, who extolled the virtues of not just specializing in one type of work but rather of participating in a variety of different activities, never included "woman's work" among them. Thus, he suggests that under the ideal conditions of full communism, man will be able to hunt in the morning, fish in the afternoon, raise cattle in the evening, and criticize after dinner. (Karl Marx and Friedrich Engles, *The German Ideology.* Translation by W. Loach and C. P. Magill, London: Lawrence and Wishart, 1938.) Nowhere does he suggest that man might also share in house cleaning, preparing dinner, or putting the children to bed.

[38]Not only does the woman who is employed and retains the primary responsibility as homemaker work long hours, but she is also confronted by a substantially different set of values in the two spheres. In the home, there is emphasis on nurturing, mutual aid, and service to others. In the marketplace, competitive, individualistic behavior is rewarded. Thus, the person whose identity is grounded in the family, who tends to give priority to cooperation and seek approval rather than gain, may well be at a disadvantage. See Clair (Vickery) Brown, "Home Production for Use in a Market Economy," in *Rethinking the Family: Some Feminist Questions,* Barrie Thorne, ed. (New York: Longman, 1981), pp. 151–67.

SUGGESTED READINGS

CHAFETZ, JANET S. *Masculine, Feminine or Human?* Itasca, IL: F. E. Peacock Publishers, 1978.

FRIEDL, ERNESTINE. *Women and Men. An Anthropological View.* New York: Holt, Rinehart & Winston, 1975.

GOLDIN, CLAUDIA. *Understanding the Gender Gap: An Economic History of American Women.* New York: Oxford University Press, 1990.

MATTHAEI, JULIE A. *An Economic History of Women in America.* New York: Schochen Books, 1982.

MORRIS, DESMOND. *The Human Zoo.* New York: McGraw-Hill, 1969.

O'KELLY, CHARLOTTE G. *Women and Men in Society.* New York: D. Van Nostrand Co., 1980.

ROSALDO, MICHELLE Z. and LOUISE LAMPHERE (eds.). *Women, Culture and Society.* Stanford: Stanford University Press, 1974.

STOLL, CLARICE S. *Female and Male. Socialization, Social Roles and Social Structure.* Dubuque, IA: Wm C Brown, 1974.

TIGER, LIONEL and ROBIN FOX. *The Imperial Animal.* New York: Holt, Rinehart & Winston, 1971.

TILLY, LOUISE and JOAN SCOTT. *Women, Work and Family.* New York: Holt, Rinehart & Winston, 1978.

WELTER, BARBARA. "The Cult of True Womanhood, 1820–1860." In *The American Family in Social-Historical Perspective.* Michael Gordon, ed. New York: St. Martin's Press, 1978, pp. 313–33.

Chapter 3

THE FAMILY AS AN ECONOMIC UNIT: THE DIVISION OF LABOR BETWEEN HUSBAND AND WIFE

For a long time, neoclassical economics concerned itself largely with the behavior of "economic man." It was, of course, acknowledged that this man interacted with others, in competition or in cooperation, but it was his individual well-being that he would attempt to maximize. Consumer economics had recognized the existence of the family and its importance as a unit of consumption. However, not until the 1960s, with the path-breaking work of Gary Becker and Jacob Mincer, did mainstream economists begin to concern themselves with the issues confronted by men and women in allocating their time and wealth so as to maximize family well-being.[1] Since then, using sophisticated theory and advanced econometric methods, models have been developed and tested that have produced

---

[1]See Gary S. Becker, "A Theory of the Allocation of Time," *Economic Journal* 75, no. 299 (Sept. 1965): 493–517; and Jacob Mincer, "Labor Force Participation of Married Women," in *Aspects of Labor Economics,* H. Greg Lewis, ed., Universities National Bureau of Economic Research Conference Series, no. 14 (Princeton, NJ: Princeton Univ. Press, 1962), pp. 63–97. An early pioneer was Margaret G. Reid, *Economics of Household Production* (New York: Wiley, 1934), but her interesting ideas had little impact on economists before they were revived in the 1960s, a time when large numbers of women were entering the labor market. Home economists were influenced to a greater extent. A large number of authors have contributed to the growing literature of the "New Home Economics" in recent decades, but much of this work has been conveniently summarized by Gary S. Becker in *A Treatise on the Family* (Cambridge, MA: Harvard University Press, 1981, enlarged edition, 1991).

important insights in this area. Yet these models are not altogether satisfactory, for there is a tendency to treat even this multiperson family as a single-minded, indivisible, utility-maximizing unit.

In this chapter, we draw heavily upon neoclassical economic analysis, with appropriate simplifying assumptions, to better understand the determinants of the division of labor in the family.[2] At the same time, we also present an evaluation and critique of that approach and introduce a more complex reality. In particular, the simple neoclassical model suggests that there are considerable efficiency gains to the traditional division of labor in which the husband specializes in market work and the wife specializes in home work. Though this may be true, it is also the case that such an arrangement is becoming less and less prevalent. We shed light on the reasons for this change by extending the simple model in two ways.[3]

1. We point out that there are other types of economic benefits to forming families besides specialization. Thus, couples may discard specialization and still reap economic gains from living in families.
2. We examine the *disadvantages* of the traditional division of labor, particularly for women, which are not considered in the simple neoclassical model.

We then briefly discuss alternative neoclassical approaches of transaction costs and bargaining models, and we offer an inset based on Heidi Hartmann's work, which illustrates the approach of radical feminists.[4]

Our emphasis upon economic analysis does not mean that we believe families are established or dissolved entirely, or even primarily, for economic reasons. Human need for companionship, sexual attraction, affection, and the urge to perpetuate one's life through children all play a part in family formation. Human need for independence and privacy, preference for a variety of partners, and disappointment when children do not live up to expectations all play a part in family breakups. Nonetheless, it is our belief that economic factors also play an important part and that focusing upon them considerably enhances our understanding of the determinants of the division of labor in the family.

---

[2] We discuss the division of labor between husbands and wives because a substantial majority of people continue to live in families. Much of the analysis is, however, also applicable to unmarried individuals living together in a household. At one time, it would have been suggested that such arrangements tend to be less permanent because they do not involve marriage. But marriages are no longer as enduring as they used to be, so the distinction is not as important as it once was.

[3] Much of this material was first developed in Marianne A. Ferber and Bonnie G. Birnbaum, "The New Home Economics: Retrospect and Prospects," *Journal of Consumer Research* 4, no. 4 (June 1977): 19–28.

[4] See Heidi I. Hartmann, "Capitalism, Patriarchy, and Job Segregation by Sex," *Signs: Journal of Women in Culture and Society,* 1, no. 3 (Spring 1976, p. 2): 137–70, and Heidi I. Hartmann, "The Family as the Locus of Gender, Class and Political Struggle: The Example of Housework," *Signs: Journal of Women in Culture and Society* 6, no. 3 (Spring 1981): 366–94. For another analysis in the Marxist tradition, see Julie A. Matthaei, *An Economic History of Women in America: Women's Work, the Sexual Division of Labor and the Development of Capitalism* (New York: Schocken, 1982). For an institutional approach to the family, see Clair Brown, "Consumption Norms, Work Roles, and Economic Growth," in *Gender in the Workplace,* Clair Brown and Joseph A. Pechman, eds. (Washington, DC: Brookings Institution, 1987).

As we saw in Chapter 2, with industrialization in the nineteenth century, men and women adopted distinct economic roles within the family. Married men, by and large, were viewed as the breadwinners, that is, as having primary responsibility for earning an adequate market income to support the family. Married women, for the most part, were expected to be homemakers, that is, to be responsible for nonmarket work performed in the home. Yet, throughout this century and particularly in recent decades, married women have been entering the labor market and increasingly sharing responsibility for producing an adequate income for the family. In Chapter 4, we examine the trends in female labor force participation in greater detail. Here we need only note that the traditional division of labor, which developed with industrialization, appears to be changing dramatically.

So far, however, changes in the division of nonmarket work have been relatively modest. Only in the late 1970s did the average amount of housework done by husbands begin to increase, and even now the division is far from equal. Married women, including those who are employed outside the home, continue to have primary responsibility for homemaking. They also do a great deal of volunteer work that is widely thought to be very important for the well-being of the community. Later in this chapter, available evidence on the allocation of time to market work, housework, and volunteer work by men and women, as well as changes in this allocation during recent decades, are explored and discussed. This will provide some indication as to what extent we may be moving toward a greater acceptance of the egalitarian marriage, in which both spouses equally share the responsibility for earning a living and for homemaking, and also for making voluntary contributions to their community.

Compared to traditional families, such couples are likely to have fewer children, and these children are increasingly less likely to ever make an economic contribution to their family of origin.[5] This family will not, in the main, be a unit of production or of redistribution of income (except from parents to children) but rather a unit for pooling income and facilitating consumption. As we shall see, much progress has been made in explaining the operation of the family as it has been, though somewhat less in enhancing our understanding of the new type of family that may be emerging.

THE SIMPLE NEOCLASSICAL MODEL: SPECIALIZATION AND EXCHANGE

The basic underlying assumptions of the neoclassical analysis of the family are that it is a unit whose adult members make informed and rational decisions that result in

---

[5]Today's children will be tomorrow's adults, who will then support the older generation through their contributions to the social security system. But for any family, the contribution of their own children is only a tiny and entirely insignificant portion of the whole. Hence, people cannot be expected to have children merely in order to provide their fair share, any more than most of them would voluntarily pay for any public good.

maximizing the utility or well-being of the family. Beginning with these premises, economists have applied the tools of their discipline to the analysis of the division of labor within the family. Models employing these basic economic concepts have also been used to explain women's increasing labor force participation rates, their growing divorce rates and declining fertility, the family's greater emphasis on education of children, and a good many other aspects of human behavior. In this chapter, we first single out the division of labor within the family to illustrate both the strengths and weaknesses of such models. In the following chapter we discuss in considerable depth women's labor force participation decisions.

As noted earlier, the simplest model of the family assumes that the family's goal is to maximize its utility or satisfaction by selecting the combination of **commodities** from which it derives the greatest possible amount of utility. Commodities are produced by combining the home time of family members with goods and services purchased in the market, using labor market earnings.

Virtually all market-purchased goods and services require an infusion of home time to transform them into the commodities from which we may derive utility—from food that needs to be bought and prepared and furniture that needs to be purchased, arranged in the home, and maintained, to day-care centers where children must be dropped off and picked up. Similarly, even time spent in leisure generally requires the input of market goods and services to be enjoyable—from television sets and stereos to concerts and baseball games. Thus, time spent on paid work produces the income necessary to purchase market goods, which in turn are needed together with home time to produce commodities. A crucial question for the family is how time should be allocated between home and market most efficiently in order to maximize satisfaction.

Comparative Advantage

Under certain conditions, commodity production is carried out most efficiently if one member of the family specializes, to some extent, in market production while the other specializes, to some extent, in home production. They may then exchange their output or pool the fruits of their labor to achieve their utility-maximizing combination of market-purchased goods and home-produced goods. In order for this to be true, it is necessary only for the two individuals to have differing **comparative advantages** for home and market production. That is to say, one must have a higher value of time spent at home *relative to* market earning power as compared to the other person.

Is it generally the case that women are relatively more productive in the home and men are relatively more productive in the market? Whether or not one assumes that women are biologically better suited for housework because they are the ones who bear children,[6] it will frequently be the case that women have a comparative

---

[6]Some sociobiologists suggest not only that women's childbearing function is crucial but, also, that women are better suited than men to the far more time-consuming task of childrearing. Their views were discussed in Chapter 2.

advantage in household production and that men have a comparative advantage in market work. This can be true because men and women are traditionally raised with different expectations and receive different education and training. Or it may be the case that women have been discriminated against in the labor market, lowering their market earnings. Or, even if women and men have identical skills initially, the traditional division of labor itself is likely to generate differences in skills, because both homemaking and market skills tend to increase with experience "on the job."

Although each of the above factors tends to produce gender differences in the comparative advantage for homemaking, it is not necessarily the case that the traditional division of labor is the optimal outcome. Treating children according to gender rather than individual talents and discriminating against women workers in the labor market clearly introduce distortions. Even more obvious is the fact that circular reasoning is involved when women supposedly specialize in housework because they do it better, but, in fact, they do it better because they specialize in it. To the extent that women's relative advantage for homemaking is socially determined and reflects unequal access to market opportunities, the traditional division of labor is not always efficient, let alone desirable, particularly when, as we shall see, it entails many disadvantages for women.

In the following discussion, we assume that women have a comparative advantage in housework relative to men because the reality that we seek to explain is one in which women generally have primary responsibility for housework. We do not mean to imply, however, that the traditional division of labor is inevitable or that it will persist indefinitely into the future. Indeed, we are also concerned with better understanding the reasons why traditional patterns are changing.

Specialization and Exchange: Numerical Examples

Two examples will help to clarify the notion of comparative advantage and to illustrate the efficiency of specialization and exchange. The analysis is analogous to the standard proof of gains from international trade and is illustrated in Tables 3.1a and b.

Absolute advantage. The simplest case is when one individual has an absolute advantage in market work and the other individual has an absolute advantage in household production. Suppose John could earn $10 for working one hour in the labor market or could produce a mediocre dinner worth about $5 at home during the same period of time. A second individual, Jane, would earn only $5 an hour in the labor market but is able to prepare an excellent dinner at home worth about

TABLE 3.1a   An Illustration of the Gains from Specialization and Exchange

Case 1: Absolute Advantage

SEPARATE PRODUCTION

	Value of Market Goods		Value of Home Cooking		Total Income
John	(6 hrs. × $10) $ 60	+	(2 hrs. × $5) $ 10	=	$ 70
Jane	(7 hrs. × $5) $ 35	+	(1 hr. × $10) $ 10	=	$ 45
Total (John & Jane)	$ 95		$ 20		$115

SPECIALIZATION AND EXCHANGE

	Value of Market Goods		Value of Home Cooking		Total Income
John	(8 hrs. × $10) $ 80	+	(0 hrs. × $5) $ 0	=	$ 80
Jane	(5 hrs. × $5) $ 25	+	(3 hr. × $10) $ 30	=	$ 55
Total (John & Jane)	$105		$ 30		$135

TABLE 3.1b   An Illustration of the Gains from Specialization and Exchange

Case 2: Comparative Advantage

SEPARATE PRODUCTION

	Value of Market Goods		Value of Home Cooking		Total Income
Dave	(6 hrs. × $10) $ 60	+	(2 hrs. × $5) $10	=	$ 70
Diane	(7 hrs. × $15) $105	+	(1 hr. × $15) $15	=	$120
Total (Dave & Diane)	$165		$25		$190

SPECIALIZATION AND EXCHANGE

	Value of Market Goods		Value of Home Cooking		Total Income
Dave	(8 hrs. × $10) $ 80	+	(0 hrs. × $5) $ 0	=	$ 80
Diane	(6 hrs. × $15) $ 90	+	(2 hr. × $15) $30	=	$120
Total (Dave & Diane)	$170		$30		$200

$10 in one hour. In this case, it is clear that John and Jane's combined level of economic well-being can be increased if they each specialize. John, who has an *absolute advantage* in market work, can spend all his time in the labor market earning money while Jane, who has an *absolute advantage* in cooking, prepares the dinners.

This is illustrated in the top section of Table 3.1a. Initially, John and Jane are each self-sufficient and both allocate some time to market work and the preparation of home-cooked meals. John devotes six hours to earning income and two hours to cooking. His total income (including the value of home-cooked meals) is $70. Jane spends seven hours in the market and one hour on cooking. Her total income is $45. The sum of their two incomes (although they are not necessarily sharing at this point) is $115. If they collaborate, they have the option of each specializing to some extent in one or the other activity and exchanging (or pooling) their output.

The bottom section of Table 3.1a shows that they can produce a higher value of both market goods and home-cooked meals through specialization and exchange and, thus, increase their total income. The concept of *opportunity cost* is useful in understanding this. It may be recalled from Chapter 1 that opportunity cost is the benefit forgone in the next best alternative. John's opportunity cost of obtaining $10 worth of market goods in terms of the value of meals forgone ($5) is lower than Jane's ($20). On the other hand, a home-cooked meal valued at $10 is cheaper for Jane to produce in terms of the value of market goods forgone ($5) than it is for John ($20). Suppose John decides to devote all his time to the market, and Jane transfers two additional hours from market work to cooking. By reallocating their time, the couple is able to raise their total income from $115 to $135.

Comparative advantage. Less obvious is the case where one individual not only earns more in the labor market but is also a better cook. In other words, one individual has an absolute advantage in both types of work. In this situation, the crucial question is for which type of work each has a *comparative advantage*.

This is illustrated in Table 3.1b. Dave earns $10 per hour for time spent in the labor market or can produce a meal worth, say, $5 for an hour spent cooking. Diane is more efficient than Dave in both activities. Her market wage is $15, while she can produce a meal worth $15 in an hour's time. The important point here is that, although Diane is a bit more efficient than Dave in the labor market, she is a far better cook than he is. The opportunity cost (in terms of market goods forgone) of a home-cooked meal worth $10 is lower when Diane produces it than when Dave does. It takes Dave two hours (valued at $20) to produce such a meal, and Diane can do so in 40 minutes (valued at $10). Table 3.1b shows that through specialization and exchange, the couple can increase their total output of both market goods and home-cooked meals and raise their total income from $190 to $200.

Gains to Specialization and Exchange

These examples serve to illustrate the potential gain in output of specialization and exchange. They do not, however, in themselves tell us how much time John and Jane will spend on each type of work. The goal of the family is to maximize utility or satisfaction. Thus, the value attached to various commodities, and the time allocation actually chosen by each couple, will depend on their preferences for market- versus home-produced goods. Many outcomes are possible. For example, it might be that Jane and John would have such a strong preference for market goods that their well-being would be maximized by both of them only working for pay and eating all their meals out. Or Diane and Dave might have such a strong preference for home production that she would entirely specialize in housework, and he would divide his time between market and home. In the Appendix to this chapter, we present a fuller treatment of the decision-making process that explicitly takes into account both the production possibilities available to the couple and their preferences for each type of good.

In any case, however, each couple will seek to produce their desired combination of market and home goods in the most efficient way. Thus, as long as they produce some of each type of good, if the wife has a *comparative* advantage in housework (relative to the husband) and the husband has a *comparative* advantage in market work (relative to the wife), the analysis suggests that they will choose to specialize to some extent in the activities generally associated with women and men.

It would appear, then, that this analysis provides a perfect explanation for the traditional family with a male breadwinner and a female homemaker. One may help the other if there is a high demand for the production he or she is not particularly qualified for, but each has a clearly defined sphere of primary responsibility. For whenever such specialization does not take place, the couple will fail to maximize their output and, potentially, their well-being. Of course, if both spouses happened to have the same comparative advantages, this conclusion no longer follows. It is then not clear, within the framework of this simple analysis what the couple gains from collaborating, for their pooled income will presumably be no greater than the sum of their separate incomes. However, specialization and exchange is not the only economic rationale for joint production and consumption. There are likely to be other economic gains as well, in addition to important noneconomic advantages. Further, the traditional division of labor results in a number of disadvantages, particularly for women, that are not considered in this simple model. We now consider each of these points in turn.

OTHER ADVANTAGES OF JOINT PRODUCTION AND CONSUMPTION

In this section, we review a number of other reasons why individuals may increase their economic well-being by forming families. Where husband and wife do not differ in relative abilities, or do not differ significantly, these provide alternative reasons why they may still find it in their economic self-interest to form families.

Economies of scale. Economies of scale exist when an increase in the scale of operation of a productive unit can result in increased output at decreasing incremental cost. To the extent that a couple is able to benefit from economies of scale, both in the production of some home goods and in purchasing market goods and services, there are economic gains to their living together. For example, ample housing for two may cost less than the combined amount each was paying for their housing separately. Meals for two may take less than twice as much time to prepare as meals for one, and so forth.[7]

Public goods. A public good has the unique characteristic that the consumption or enjoyment of the item by one person does not diminish the consumption or enjoyment of it by others. Within the family, this is likely to be the case with many goods. For example, one partner's enjoyment of a television program is unlikely to be reduced at all by the fact that the other partner is also watching. Similarly, the delight of a parent in his or her child's adorable antics is not apt to be diminished by the other parent's pleasure. Many aspects of housing—the views from the windows, the decoration of the rooms—also have public goods aspects. In fact, the enjoyment of these goods by one partner may even enhance that of the other. To the extent that public goods are important, the gains to joint consumption are increased. This is because two individuals will derive more total satisfaction from sharing a given stock of public goods and services by living together than by living separately.

Externalities. Externalities occur when the consumption of a good or service by one of the partners has an impact on the well-being of the other. For example, a husband's purchase of a new suit may increase his wife's utility as well as his own. Both members of a couple may enjoy their summer vacation more because they are traveling together than they would if each were traveling alone. To the extent that these externalities are positive—one person derives enjoyment from the other's consumption—gains will be greater than indicated by the simple model. When two people care for one another, one partner may derive satisfaction simply from the enjoyment and happiness of the other. This also greatly enhances the gains from joint consumption.

Economic benefits of families. This discussion suggests that the economic gains to individuals joining together to form couples may derive from other factors than simply specialization and exchange. This further implies that, even as men and

---

[7]Economies of scale also explain the advantages of larger groups living together. The fact that such arrangements are not common in affluent societies suggests that most people value additional privacy highly once they can afford it.

women are becoming less differentially specialized in market and home production, marriage may continue to be an important economic institution. However, the decline of this specialization does reduce one of the economic benefits of marriage. From this perspective, it is not surprising that the increased employment of married women has been accompanied by a rising divorce rate.

THE DISADVANTAGES OF SPECIALIZATION

We have just pointed out a variety of economic benefits from family formation. We now return to the issue of specialization and exchange, which the simple model suggests is the economic foundation of marriage. Here we consider the possibility, generally not discussed in the standard models, that such specialization and a gender-based division of labor may not always be desirable, particularly for women.[8]

Sharing of Housework

One correct prediction of the simple model is that, given gender differences in comparative advantage, women's employment outside the home is not necessarily accompanied by an increase in the amount of housework done by her husband. A fuller consideration of the issues, however, suggests a number of reasons why a couple might often find it desirable to share the housework rather than for each spouse to specialize.

First, the sweeping assumption that women have a comparative advantage in all household tasks seems unrealistic. The problem is that the simple model assumes there is only one type of home good. In our numerical example, it was home-cooked meals; more generally it is an aggregate category of "home goods." In fact, tasks typically performed within the household vary from child care, house cleaning, cooking, and shopping to gardening, house repairs, and taking care of the family finances. It is not particularly likely that the wife will have a relative advantage in performing all of these tasks as compared to the husband; rather it is likely that he will have a comparative advantage in at least some of them, even taking his larger market earnings into account. Of course, once the wife is at home because she is better at some, or many, of the household tasks, it may be more efficient for her to undertake other related work as well. But the husband also spends a good bit of time in the home, and not all household tasks are performed in or around the house (for example, shopping or going to the bank). Thus, it seems likely that even a fairly traditional family will find it efficient for the husband to do a bit more housework than suggested by the simple model.

---

[8]These points are stressed in Ferber and Birnbaum, "The New Home Economics." It is also suggested there that more sophisticated models could incorporate many of these complexities.

Second, it is worthwhile to consider the utility or disutility that people derive directly from work. The simple model considers only the utility derived from the consumption of market-produced and home-produced goods. Yet most people spend much of their time working, and their well-being is very much influenced by the satisfaction or dissatisfaction associated directly with their work. If everyone always enjoyed more (or disliked less) the kind of work they do more efficiently, the gains from specialization would be even greater than indicated by the simple model; and this may to a degree be the case. But this line of reasoning ignores the possibility that how we feel about doing particular tasks depends on how much time we have to spend on them. Persons who dislike market or home work to begin with are likely to hate additional time spent on it more as they do increasingly more of it. And even those who like what they are doing are, nonetheless, likely to become less enthusiastic. The stronger this effect, the less likely there are to be the gains in utility from specialization suggested by the simple model.

A similar issue arises with respect to the utility each individual derives from leisure. The model fails to consider adequately that leisure is likely to be more highly valued by the partner who has less of it and that the one who has a great deal of leisure may become bored and also come to feel useless. Thus, the situation in which the wife works in the market and retains full responsibility for housework is not likely to be optimal if, as is often the case, it results in considerably less leisure for her than for her husband; this is especially true during the childrearing years. Alternatively, when the husband has a demanding full-time position, while the responsibilities of the full-time homemaker have become rather modest because the children are growing up, he will be very short of leisure, whereas the wife may well have more of it than she finds desirable.

Finally, some tasks are more efficiently performed by two people together, and many people may enjoy housework more when they do not have to do it alone. Frequently, homemakers spend much of their time isolated, with little possibility for interaction with other adults. For all these reasons, complete specialization by the husband in market work, whether or not the wife specializes completely in housework, may not maximize utility for the family. Nonetheless, the simple model does seem to square with reality to the extent that, on average, husbands devote relatively little time to housework.

Tastes and Bargaining Power

In our development of the simple model, we did not consider how the couple determines the allocation of income and of time to various commodities the family would enjoy. The decision will be relatively easy to make if they both have the same tastes and preferences. Then they will each opt for the same combination of goods and services to be shared. However, if their tastes differ significantly (and this is more likely to be the case as the spouses are more specialized), the question arises as to how they will decide on the combination of commodities to be produced and consumed. Putting the matter somewhat differently, whose preferences (husband's or wife's) will receive greater weight?

Considerable flexibility exists in the case where the couple may pool production but then choose different bundles of commodities for individual consumption, although even here the share of the total going to each partner could be a matter of dispute. But more difficult problems arise in the case of public goods or where commodities have significant externalities. We saw earlier that for people with similar tastes, public goods and positive externalities increase the gains from joint consumption and collaboration. However, where one person's public good is another's public "bad" or where negative externalities exist, consumption of the commodity by one individual may reduce the well-being of the other. For example, one partner may derive enormous satisfaction from the presence of children, whereas the other may dislike having them around. Or the consumption of onions at dinner by one individual may have a negative effect on the enjoyment of the evening for the other.

These difficulties are relevant to the conclusions we derived from the simple model regarding the benefits of specialization. They suggest that conflicts of interest may arise between husband and wife and that relative bargaining power could play a role in resolving these conflicts. In this case, specialization in home work on the part of the wife could have negative consequences for her.

Because the husband earns the money, he may be viewed as having the "power of the purse." He may, thus, be accorded a greater say in spending decisions. There is evidence that a husband is more likely to respect his wife's decision-making ability and to listen to her opinions when she is employed.[9] A number of sociologists also suggest that decision making and allocation of responsibilities are built into the traditional husband-wife roles based on cultural norms and are unrelated to individual skills and interests. Power resides in the position of breadwinner rather than the person. Accordingly, the husband determines what car they will buy, and the wife decides what to serve guests for dinner.[10]

Further, in a money economy, adherence to the traditional division of labor results in the wife being financially dependent on the husband. Since she has more to lose if the marriage breaks up, she may be under greater pressure to subordinate her wishes to her husband's. Indeed, it has been found that the more successful the husband is in fulfilling his economic role, the more the wife tends to give him power to define the norms for decision making.[11] This may reflect not only the greater financial costs to the wife of marital breakup in this case but also that the husband's market success, in a sense, validates his claim to greater competence in familial decision making.

[9]Philip Blumstein and Pepper Schwartz, *American Couples*. New York: William Morrow, 1983.

[10]Harry L. Davis, "Decision Making Within the Household," in *Selected Aspects of Consumer Behavior. A Summary from the Perspective of Different Disciplines,* Robert Ferber, ed. Prepared for National Science Foundation, Directorate for Research Applications, RANN Research Applied to National Needs (Washington, DC: U.S. Government Printing Office, 1976), pp. 73–97.

[11]John H. Scanzoni, *Opportunity and the Family* (New York: Free Press, 1970).

Finally, the lesser outside contacts of the full-time homemaker in comparison to her working husband may make her more dependent on his counsel and judgment than he is on hers. For these and other reasons, a number of studies tend to confirm the dominance of the husband in decision making, given the traditional division of labor.[12] We discuss these points further in the section on Transaction Cost and Bargaining Approaches on page 49.

Life Cycle Changes

A serious shortcoming of the simple model is that it ignores the fact that the comparative advantage of an individual does not necessarily remain the same over the life cycle. As will be explained in greater detail in Chapter 4, the value of home production for women peaks during the childrearing years and then declines as children grow up and become more self-sufficient. At the same time, labor market earnings tend to increase with experience and decline while a person is not employed. If a woman withdraws from the labor force for a considerable period of time for childrearing, she is likely to pay a high price in terms of career advancement and potential earnings. Hence, specializing in home work may not be advantageous to the wife or even to her family in the long run, even if it maximizes family well-being in the short run. Unfortunately, many couples may not be aware of this. Hence, they would fail to realize that it might be worthwhile for the family to make some sacrifices of utility during the early years to keep the wife in the labor market in order to maximize her long-run career prospects and lifetime earnings. As women increasingly value career achievement as an end in itself, the costs of work disruptions are apt to loom even larger. The negative effects of women's shorter, and more discontinuous, labor force participation on their earnings and occupational attainment are considered in greater detail in Chapter 6.

It might be argued that offsetting these disadvantages for the wife's career and the lifetime income of the family is the higher quality of children produced when there is a full-time mother at home. However, recent research concerning the effects that alternative ways of caring for children have on their well-being and achievement levels shows that much depends on the quality as well as the quantity of time mothers spend with children, on the quality of the substitutes provided, on social attitudes toward the family's lifestyle, and on the age and sex of the children who receive out-of-home care.[13] An exhaustive review of this work concluded that "taken by itself, the fact that a mother works outside the home has no universally

---

[12]For instance, Marianne A. Ferber, "Labor Market Participation of Young Married Women: Causes and Effects," *Journal of Marriage and Family* 44, no. 2 (May 1982): 457–68; Dair L. Gillespie, "Who Has the Power? The Marital Struggle," *Journal of Marriage and the Family* 33, no. 3 (August 1971): 445–58; and Hartmann, "The Family as the Locus of Gender, Class, and Political Struggle."

[13]Cheryl D. Hayes, John L. Palmer, and Martha J. Zaslow, eds. *Who Cares for America's Children? Child Care Policy for the 1990's.* Washington, DC: National Academy Press, 1990.

predictable effects on the child."[14] This issue is considered in greater detail in Chapter 9.

Costs of Interdependence

Whatever the probability that the well-being of husband and wife will be maximized under existing circumstances, they will be less well prepared to deal with unforeseen developments. When each spouse is able to manage a household and to earn a living if the need arises, the family will not be devastated if the husband is laid off or does not get a promotion, or if the wife becomes ill and needs care instead of providing it for the rest of the family. Each will also be better equipped to manage alone if the need arises, whether because of divorce, separation, or death.

The difficulties encountered by the wife who has specialized in housework are similar to those discussed above regarding her financial dependency and the negative effect on her potential earnings of time spent out of the labor force. As long as the relationship lasts, both husband and wife may gain from the greater proficiency each acquires in the area in which he or she specializes. However, their skills in the other area are likely to deteriorate, or, at any rate, fail to increase.

This problem will be especially serious for the homemaker. The husband who has concentrated on market work may be seriously inconvenienced by a lack of household skills. But he has market earnings that may be used to purchase household services. The woman who has specialized in household production, on the other hand, is left with no earnings and market skills that may be obsolete. In view of the high divorce rate and the substantially higher life expectancy of women than men, the risk of becoming a "displaced homemaker" is serious.[15] The special problems of female-headed families are discussed more fully in Chapter 9.

There are also potential difficulties for a full-time homemaker even if the partnership lasts until her death or until a time when she is adequately taken care of by a pension or inheritance. As pointed out earlier, the value of the homemaker's contribution to the family is greatest while the children are young. Now that the average number of children is about 2 and female life expectancy is 78, this period is relatively early in a woman's life. After that the value of her contribution at home declines. Because her earning ability (generally lower than her husband's to begin with) also declined during the time she was out of the labor market, her contribution during the latter part of her life is likely to be considerably smaller than her mate's.

[14]Urie Bronfenbrenner and Ann. C. Crouter, "Work and Family Through Time and Space," in *Families That Work: Children in a Changing World* Sheila B. Kamerman and Cheryl D. Hayes, eds. (Washington, DC: National Academy Press, 1982), p. 51.

[15]For example, 40.5 percent of women 65 years old and over lived alone in 1988, as reported in "Studies in Marriage and Family," Bureau of the Census, Current Population Report P-23, No. 162, 1989.

One way of looking at this is that the husband's increasing earnings in the market compensate for her declining productivity, and she can now enjoy her share of the family's total income and a good deal of leisure. Yet, even if her partner is very fond of her, is happy to share his largesse, and/or is grateful to her for the considerable contributions she made earlier, she may come to wonder about her present worth to the family. (Who has not heard of the empty nest syndrome?) But she may not be so lucky. Her spouse may ask what she has done for him lately; he may take advantage of his increasingly greater bargaining power by appropriating a larger share of family income for commodities only he uses or only he wants and, in general, adopting a lifestyle that conforms to his, but not necessarily to her, preferences.

Disadvantages of Specialization: A Summary

Thus we find that the traditional family, in which husband and wife each specialize in a separate sphere, is not as advantageous as the simple economic model presented at the beginning of this chapter suggests. Specializing in home-making is a particularly high-risk undertaking, for the value of home production peaks early in the life cycle. Market skills tend to decline when a person is out of the labor market, and a woman is often socially isolated in the home. Therefore, the homemaker's bargaining power within the family is likely to decline over time, and she will find it difficult to manage on her own if the need arises. But there are risks for the wage earner as well. If the marriage breaks up, he may be confronted with the need to pay alimony or face the problem of avoiding it. Also, he may lack even the minimal skills to keep house for himself. Last, but not least, children of divorced parents may have to live in poverty with a mother unable to earn a decent living or, in rare cases, with a father quite inexperienced in child care.

One may speculate why so many couples continue to opt for a lifestyle that raises so many potential problems. A number of obvious answers come to mind. First, there can be little doubt that most young people in full awareness of the high divorce rate nonetheless expect their own marriage to succeed. This is not so different from the person who starts a small business, fully expecting to make a go of it in spite of the formidable bankruptcy rate. Second, important initial decisions are made at a relatively young age, when concerns for well-being in middle and old age may not loom very large. Third, pressures from relatives and peers toward adoption of traditional family arrangements cannot be entirely discounted. Among some groups it may still take a strong-willed, confident, young person to withstand these pressures. There is, however, no doubt that all this is changing and that surely helps to account for the rising proportion of couples who are rejecting the old breadwinner-homemaker dichotomy.

TRANSACTION COST AND
BARGAINING APPROACHES

One of the shortcomings of the neoclassical model of the family highlighted by the above discussion is that it ignores the internal decision-making structure of the family. It simply assumes that the family operates efficiently and frictionlessly, either because there is consensus on preferences within the family, or because preferences are decided by an altruistic family head and accepted by all other members.[16] Available resources are therefore allocated among family members either on the basis of consensus or according to the dictates of the altruistic head. In this view of the family, power has no relevance.

However, alternative approaches, emphasizing transaction costs and bargaining models, have recently been developed that can be used to highlight the power inequity between men and women that tends to develop as a result of the traditional division of labor. Unlike the new home economics, which essentially ignores the internal organization and structure of families and households, the transaction cost approach focuses on the role of these institutions in structuring complex, long-term relationships so as to minimize transactions costs.[17] In this view, individuals exposed to the risks associated with investing in "marriage-specific" capital seek long-term relationships in order to reduce these hazards.

Marriage-specific human capital is accumulated when individuals put time, effort, and resources into producing commodities that are worth far more within the marriage than they would be if the marriage terminated.[18] An obvious example of such investments is the rearing of children, who are likely to be particularly valued

---

[16]The consensus model was proposed by Paul Samuelson, "Social Indifference Curves," *Quarterly Journal of Economics* 70, no. 1 (Feb. 1956): 1–22. The altruist model is the one introduced by Gary S. Becker, "A Theory of Marriage: Part II," *Journal of Political Economy* 82, no. 2 (Mar./Apr. 1974): S11–26, and Becker, *A Treatise on the Family.* These models, as well some alternatives, are discussed by Robert A. Pollak, "A Transaction Cost Approach to Families and Households," *Journal of Economic Literature* 23, no. 2 (June 1985): 581–602.

[17]"Transaction costs arise from the transfer of ownership or, more generally, of property rights." Jurg Niehans, "Transaction Costs," in *The New Palgrave: A Dictionary of Economics,* John Eatwell, Murray Milgate and Peter Newman, eds. (New York: Stockton Press, 1987, vol. 4, p. 676). Our discussion of the application of transactions cost and bargaining models to the family is based on Pollak, "A Transaction Cost Approach to Families and Households," and Paula England and George Farkas, *Households, Employment and Gender: A Social, Economic, and Demographic View,* (Hawthorne, NY: Aldine, 1986), Chapter 3. Additional references for bargaining models include Marilyn Manser and Murray Brown, "Marriage and Household Decision-Making: A Bargaining Analysis," *International Economic Review* 21, no. 1 (February 1980): 31–44; and Marjorie B. McElroy and Mary J. Horney, "Nash-Bargained Household Decisions: Toward a Generalization of the Theory of Demand," *International Economic Review* 22, no. 2 (June 1981); 333–49. An alternative approach that reaches similar conclusions has been developed by sociologists using social exchange theory; see Anthony F. Heath, *Rational Choice and Social Exchange: A Critique of Exchange Theory* (New York: Cambridge University Press, 1976).

[18]See Gary S. Becker, Elisabeth M. Landes, and Robert T. Michael, "An Economic Analysis of Marital Instability," *Journal of Political Economy* 85, no. 6 (December 1977): 1141–87.

by their parents,[19] but are most often considered to be a liability in the search for a new spouse.

As our earlier discussion of the disadvantages of specialization suggested, much household work, unlike work in the labor market, involves marriage-specific investments and is associated with a decrease in earning power. Consequently, termination of the marriage entails losses for each partner, but especially for the homemaker.

Marriage incorporates both rules about the nature of the ongoing relationship and about the rights of each individual should the union break up. Hence it may be seen as a contractual affiliation that is "flexible enough to allow adaptive sequential decision making in the face of unfolding events,"[20] and also rigid enough to encourage individuals to make marriage-specific investments without undue fear of loss.

Because marriage tends to be a long-term relationship, and since it is not possible to specify in advance how all matters will be settled, bargaining between spouses tends to be important. A major determinant of bargaining power is the next-best alternative available to each spouse outside the marriage. Therefore, women, who generally make greater marriage-specific investments and thus find the value of their next-best alternative reduced, most often have less bargaining power. At the same time, men generally enhance their earnings potential, and hence their alternative opportunities, in case of a break-up. An increased propensity of women to work for pay, coupled with greater opportunities in the labor market, should result in more equal relationships between husbands and wives.

NONMARKET WORK

Economists have traditionally focused their analyses and interests on market work; however, much work is performed outside the market, both in the household and in the voluntary sector. Such unpaid work substantially contributes to the well-being of individuals, their families, and society at large. In this section we consider both types of nonmarket work and how women's and men's involvement in these activities has changed with women's rising labor force participation. This is not only interesting in itself, but also helps to shed considerable light on the relevance of the neoclassical economic model to actual behavior in present-day families.

Work at Home

A number of surveys, mostly dating back to the 1960s and 1970s, provide information on the extent to which husbands and wives shared in paid and unpaid work during those years. Estimates of hours worked, however, show a considerable range. An examination of the individual studies shows why this might be expected. They are based on different samples; some are drawn from different populations.

---

[19]This might well include adoptive as well as natural parents.

[20]Pollak, "A Transaction Cost Approach to Families and Households," p. 595.

A MARXIST-FEMINIST VIEW OF THE FAMILY

Substantially different interpretations of the existing division of labor within the family, and its relation to the position of women and men in the labor market, are offered by a variety of radical economists, Marxists, and Marxist-feminists. Although there are many disagreements among the proponents of these alternative views, there tends to be considerable emphasis on the role of capitalism, patriarchy, or both.

Capitalism describes an economy where the preponderance of capital is privately owned and controlled, even though government may also play a large part, as is the case in the United States. Marxists see such an economy as one in which capitalists wield power over workers who do not own the means of production and are, thus, forced to sell their labor. Patriarchy is the name given to a system in which men are dominant over women.

What follows is a synopsis of the analysis of one prominent exponent of Marxist-Feminist theory, Heidi Hartmann.* It differs from this text's neoclassical approach in its emphasis on power relationships both between men and women in the family and between capitalists and workers in the labor market.

In this model, the family is seen as a primary source of women's oppression and as a locus of struggle. Even though there are often strong emotional ties within the family, it is not primarily shaped by such kinship relations. Rather, it is a unit where production and redistribution of income take place, with emphasis on material aspects of gender relations. The organization of this production within the family, as well as that outside it, has been shaped by both patriarchy and capitalism. Hence, according to this model, production in the family is based on unequal division of labor by class and gender, inevitably bringing about conflict and change.

Individuals within the family are mutually dependent, and to a degree their interests are unified. However, they also act as members of gender categories so that there is room for conflict about many issues. Who does the housework, and how much of it is to be done? Should the woman work outside the home? How should the money be spent? Data indicating that women do the vast majority of the housework, even when they are employed outside the home, and that men are dominant in decision-making power are offered as evidence of patriarchy in the family.

Marxist-feminists argue that capitalism was preceded by a patriarchal system that, in turn, shaped the form modern capitalism took. The primary mechanism for maintaining male superiority in the capitalistic economy is occupational segregation, the restriction of women in the labor market to a small number of predominantly female jobs. Job segregation reinforces the traditional division of domestic labor because it results in lower wages for women and thus makes them economically dependent on men. At the same time, the traditional division of labor in the home reinforces occupational segregation by weakening women's position in the labor market.

The present status of women in the labor market and the current arrangement of sex-segregated jobs are seen as the results of a long process of interaction between patriarchy and capitalism. The actions of male workers and their unions have been an important factor in

*Adapted from Heidi I. Hartmann, "Capitalism, Patriarchy, and Job Segregation by Sex," *Signs: Journal of Women in Culture and Society* 1, no. 3, Pt. 2 (Spring 1976): 137–70; and Heidi I. Hartmann, "The Family as the Locus of Gender, Class and Political Struggle: The Example of Housework," *Signs: Journal of Women in Culture and Society* 6, no. 3 (Spring 1981): 366–94. Adapted by permission.

bringing this about. Marxist-feminists argue that if women's subordination is to end and if men are to begin to escape their own class oppression and exploitation, men will have to be forced to give up their favored positions in the division of labor—in the labor market and at home. Capitalism grew on top of patriarchy; patriarchal capitalism is stratified society par excellence. If non-ruling-class men are to be free, they will have to relinquish their patriarchal benefits as well as struggle against capitalism. If women are to be free, they must fight against both patriarchal power and the capitalist organization of society.

Methods of collecting data and samples vary, as does the definition of what is considered work. Nonetheless, the data presented in Table 3.2 based on four of the most widely cited studies, reveal some interesting patterns, and the fact that they cover years between 1965/66 and 1975/76 enables us to discern some changes over time.

The evidence indicates that nonemployed wives worked the fewest total hours. This was true during both periods but more so during the latter. While they still did far more housework than their husbands, and more than employed wives, they devoted considerably less time to this activity in the 1970s, while still spending (by definition) very little time in the labor market.[21] In the 1960s, the total work time of employed wives was considerably higher than that of any of the other groups, including their husbands. But they also reduced time spent on housework considerably over the decade so that they too worked fewer total hours during the latter period, only very slightly more than their husbands. Meanwhile, the number of hours employed women spent on market work increased somewhat. Husbands of women in the labor market spent somewhat less time on paid work than other husbands but, nonetheless, considerably more than their employed wives. The number of hours spent on housework was small and about the same for husbands of employed and nonemployed wives during both decades.

Although these data suggest that the total workload of husbands and wives in two-earner families became more equal between the 1960s and the 1970s, they also suggest that the division of labor remained quite traditional, with women doing considerably more housework and less market work than men. Regrettably, no recent data are available that provide information separately for families with employed and nonemployed wives. Nonetheless, some more recent evidence, seen in Table 3.3, suggests that differentials between men and women in the use of time have narrowed, although large differences remain.

In 1965, women spent 66.9 percent of total time worked on housework, compared to only 17.2 percent for men. By 1986, the figures were 56.6 and 30.5 percent, respectively. Since these data are for all women, not only those in the labor force, the changes in women's average hours of market work in part reflect their

---

[21]The reason they do report some time in this category is that someone who is employed, but working less than one hour per week, is not included in the labor force, nor are unpaid family workers who put in less than 15 hours.

TABLE 3.2   Range Estimates of Time-Use Data on Housework and Market Work (Hours per Day)

	WIVES			
	NONEMPLOYED		EMPLOYED	
	1960s	*1970s*	*1960s*	*1970s*
Housework	7.6–8.6	4.6–6.8	4.0–5.3	2.3–4.0
Market work	0.0–0.6	0.1–1.9	4.8–5.3	5.0–6.5
Total work	7.6–8.6	6.5–6.8	9.3–10.1	7.9–9.3

	HUSBANDS			
	NONEMPLOYED WIVES		EMPLOYED WIVES	
	1960s	*1970s*	*1960s*	*1970s*
Housework	1.0–1.6	0.6–1.8	1.1–1.6	0.6–1.9
Market Work	7.5–7.8	7.0–7.7	6.3–6.9	6.9–7.1
Total Work	8.4–8.5	8.3–8.9	7.9–8.0	7.7–8.8

Sources:
Martin Meissner, Elizabeth W. Humphreys, Scott W. Meis, and William J. Scheu, "No Exit for Wives: Sexual Division of Labour and the Cumulation of Household Demands," *Canadian Review of Sociology and Anthropology* 12, no.4 (November 1975): 424–39.

Joseph H. Pleck, "Husband's Paid Work and Family Roles: Current Research Issues," *Research in the Interweave of Social Roles: Jobs and Families* 3, (1983): 251–333.

John P. Robinson, *Changes in America's Use of Time* (Cleveland: Communications Research Center, Cleveland State University, 1977).

Kathryn E. Walker and Margaret E. Woods, *Time Use: A Measure of Household Production of Family Goods and Services* (Washington, DC: American Home Economics Association, 1976).

TABLE 3.3   Hours of Time Spent on Housework and Market Work (Hours per Week)

	WOMEN		MEN	
	1965	*1986*	*1965*	*1986*
Housework	37.8	31.9	10.0	18.1
Market work	18.7	24.5	48.3	41.3
Total	56.5	56.4	58.3	59.4
Percent time spent on housework	66.9	56.6	17.2	30.5

Source: United Nations, *The World's Women 1970–1990: Trends and Statistics* (New York: United Nations, 1991).

increased labor force participation. Further, changes for both sexes may in part be due to a decrease in the proportion of the population that is married. However, according to one study, the amount of time married men spent on housework increased by somewhat more than that of all men, and the amount spent by married women declined slightly more than that of all women.[22] It seems reasonable to infer that the trend towards more housework for husbands held for both the husbands of employed women and the husbands of full-time homemakers. If anything, it may be stronger for working couples, where the rationale for husbands to take on a larger share is greater. This speculation is supported by a recent study, which found that husbands of employed women were likely to spend more time on child care.[23] The data in Table 3.3 also indicate that the total amount of time men and women worked was virtually the same in 1965 and has changed very little since then.

As heartening as these trends are to proponents of an egalitarian division of labor, it is important to bear in mind that such data tend to underestimate the problems of employed women. First, nearly 30 percent of women are employed part-time, and their situation is quite different from the remainder who are employed full-time. Women who work part-time are likely to face a smaller and less attractive choice of jobs, lower earnings and fringe benefits, and fewer opportunities for promotion. Those who work full-time face a considerably higher workload.[24] Similarly, the data do not show the very large burdens of employed women with young children. Their difficulties are particularly serious, because many are also likely to be of the age when workers need to prove themselves on the job, and to begin to show that they are upwardly mobile if they are to make much progress. Moreover, these extra responsibilities are apt to make it more difficult for them to compete with their male counterparts, at least to some extent. Thus, whichever route employed wives choose, be it part-time or full-time work, the unequal division of labor in the home is likely to adversely affect their success in the labor market.[25]

On the other hand, it has been argued that the unequal division of labor is in some ways less of a problem than it superficially seems to be. First, many tasks women perform are no longer as physically exacting as those their grandmothers did. Second, such activities as shopping and, to a considerable extent, child care, may be enjoyable enough to be regarded as quasi-leisure.[26] But much of paid work

---

[22]John P. Robinson, "Who's Doing the Housework?" *American Demographics* 10, no. 12 (Dec. 1988): 24–28, 63.

[23]The survey was carried out by Joseph Pleck and James Levine. The results were reported in the Wellesley College Center for Research on Women, *Research Report* 4, no. 1 (Fall 1984): 1, 4.

[24]Joann Vanek, "Household Work, Wage Work, and Sexual Equality," in *Women and Household Labor,* S. F. Berg, ed. (Beverly Hills, CA: Sage, 1980), pp. 75–89.

[25]The issues confronting different women, depending on their marital, parental, and employment status are thoroughly discussed in Barbara R. Bergmann, *The Economic Emergence of Women* (New York: Basic Books, 1986).

[26]These points are discussed by Glen G. Cain, "Women and Work: Trends in Time Spent in Housework," Institute for Research on Poverty, University of Wisconsin, Discussion Paper 747–84 (April 1984).

has also become less onerous, and such time on the job as chatting with fellow workers and entertaining clients is as much quasi-leisure as any family work. In fact, a recent study indicates that, on the whole, people enjoy child care more than any other activities included in a comprehensive list, but enjoy their jobs far more than any other types of housework and considerably more than many leisure activities.[27]

Although the unequal division of tasks between men and women in the home remains a problem, the evidence suggests that as women are spending increasing amounts of time on paid work, men are finally increasing their participation in housework. The proportion of time spent on the two different types of work moved more rapidly toward equality for women and men during the last two decades than during preceding years. It is, however, likely that the ultimate locus of responsibility for homemaking even today continues to rest with women and that they are accordingly the ones who are expected to give family needs priority over market work when unexpected problems and small emergencies come up.[28] Nonetheless, the more egalitarian distribution of unpaid work would be expected to have a positive impact on women's occupational attainment and earnings. These topics are discussed further in Chapters 6 and 7.

Whatever the precise amount of time employed wives and their husbands spend on housework, there is no doubt that it is considerably less than that devoted to work at home by families with nonemployed wives. It is less clear exactly how this reduction is accomplished.

It has often been assumed that families with wives who work outside the home compensate for less household time by purchasing more labor-saving devices and more services available in the market. Research does not fully support this view, however. Child care expenditures are higher for working wife families; however, a number of studies have failed to find any other marked differences in expenditures between employed and nonemployed-wife families at the same income level, except for outlays on directly work-related items such as transportation.[29]

[27] F. Thomas Juster, "Preferences for Work and Leisure," in F. Thomas Juster and Frank P. Stafford, eds. *Time, Goods and Well-Being* (Ann Arbor: Institute for Social Research, The University of Michigan, 1985).

[28] "A Wellesley College study of 160 middle-class families in the Boston suburb of Dedham, Massachusetts, found that fathers with working wives spent more time alone with their children than other fathers, but that nearly all of the women were in charge of remembering, planning, and scheduling children's activities" ("Working Fathers Feel Pressure Deriving from Child-Rearing Duties," *Wall Street Journal* [Sept. 7, 1984]). It also is still the case that men who feel role strain because of their participation tend to blame it on their wives' employment, whereas women tend to blame such strain on their own labor force participation.

[29] See particularly Myra H. Strober and Charles B. Weinberg, "Strategies Used by Working and Nonworking Wives to Reduce Time Pressures," *Journal of Consumer Research* 6, no. 4 (Mar. 1980): 338–48; Myra H. Strober, "Wives' Labor Force Behavior and Family Consumption Patterns," *American Economic Review* 67, no. 1 (Feb. 1977): 410–17.

Part of the story is that employed women have, on the average, fewer and older children. It is, therefore, plausible to assume that, even though there is little evidence that children of employed mothers do more housework, they at least take care of their own needs to a greater extent. This tends to be substantiated by detailed time diaries that show that when the wife enters the labor market, she reduces time spent in the care of other family members more than on other types of housework.

It has also been suggested that homemakers' behavior illustrates Parkinson's law—they tend to stretch out their work to fill the available time.[30] This would make it easier to get more work done in a shorter time when the need arises. Or women may reduce the amount or quality of services they offer their family. No evidence is available to date that would enable us to determine to what extent each of these possible solutions is used.

Two other interesting developments with respect to the allocation of time in the family are that, since 1965, men have reduced the number of hours spent on the job, and, as we have seen, full-time homemakers have reduced the amount of time spent on housework. The former is readily explained. Both rising real-wage rates of men over that period and the earnings of the growing proportion of women who are in the labor market reduce, at least to some extent, the incentive for the husbands to work long hours for pay. The latter might be considered more surprising in view of the failure of hours worked in the household of nonemployed women to decrease over about 50 years prior to the 1960s.[31] It might be conjectured that women who choose or agree to be full-time homemakers will increasingly do so only on favorable terms, that is, that they too are "liberated" from some of the household chores that were formerly expected. This would help to explain why their families spend as much on many purchased services and on labor-saving durables as do two-earner units at the same income level. In any case, although evidence of a major shift in the allocation of household work among the general population is still scanty, the conclusion that a move toward a more egalitarian division of labor has begun is not without foundation.

Volunteer Work

In addition to market work and housework, many people also spend an appreciable amount of time on volunteer work. To distinguish voluntary activities from other work, they are defined as tasks, performed without direct reward in money or in kind, that mainly benefit others rather than the individuals themselves or their immediate family.

[30] Joann Vanek, "Time Spent in Housework," *Scientific American* 231, no. 5 (Nov. 1974): 116–20.

[31] Joann Vanek, "Time Spent in Housework."

Thus volunteer work is neither a way of earning a living, nor is it an integral part of homemaking.[32] Nonetheless, much business is transacted, and many profitable contacts are made, at the meetings of the Rotarians. People participate in unions at least in part to improve their own working conditions, and in the symphony guild so that they will be able to hear concerts. They are also more likely to participate in the PTA or scouting when they have children who are involved. Further, anything that enhances life in the community influences the well-being of the family at least indirectly, and often the connection is a fairly close one. In principle, the distinction is made in terms of which is the dominant purpose, but in practice it is by no means easy to decide where the line should be drawn.

The issue also arises of how to distinguish volunteer work from leisure activities performed for the direct utility the person derives from them. This problem is often solved by including only services rendered as a part of an organized program. Again, however, the distinction remains fuzzy. Therefore it is not surprising that estimates of the amount of volunteer work done vary widely, depending on the definition used, the questions asked, and the respondent who answers the questions.

In any case, there is no doubt that much valuable volunteer work is performed in this country. On the basis of a 1973 survey, which used a very narrow definition, it was calculated that one-quarter or more of all women, and approximately the same proportion of men, participated in volunteer activities for a total of nearly 6 billion hours. Women constituted a substantial majority in recreational, charitable, and religious organizations. Men involved in volunteer organizations were more highly represented in civic and political groups and dominated among volunteer workers in professional organizations and labor unions.[33]

More recently, it was reported on the basis of information collected as part of the May 1989 Current Population Survey that 38 million people, or only about 20 percent of the population over 16 years of age, volunteered for work without pay for an institution or organization during the year ending that month. Slightly more women than men reported doing volunteer work, about 22 percent compared to 19 percent. Not unlike 1973, there were also some differences by gender in the type of volunteer work done. About 13 percent of women contributed time to health organizations and 19 percent to educational institutions, compared to only 7 percent and 10 percent of men, respectively; whereas 17 percent of men did voluntary work for civic and political organizations and 12 percent for sport and

---

[32]For women, it may be thought of as "social homemaking" or women extending the services they generally perform for their own families to the community. See, for instance, Julie A. Matthai, "Capitalism and Sexual Division of Labor: An Essay in U.S. Economic History," *Social Concepts* 1, no. 2 (Sept. 1983): 13–35.

[33]ACTION *American Volunteer 1974* (ACTION Pamphlet 4000-17), (Washington, DC: U.S. Government Printing Office, 1975). Other estimates would suggest a higher figure. Helen Z. Lopata, *Occupation Housewife* (London: Oxford University Press, 1971), found 64 percent of her sample of married women belonged to at least one organization.

recreational organizations, compared to only 10 percent and 5 percent for women, respectively. On the other hand, there were only very small differences in the proportions of women and men involved in social welfare organizations and in religious institutions.[34]

According to the same report, the incidence of volunteering was also found to be higher among persons between 35 and 44 years of age than among those younger or older, among whites than among blacks or Hispanics, and among the college educated than among those with fewer years of schooling.

Another recent survey used a considerably broader definition that includes informal activities such as regularly helping a disabled friend or working for neighborhood improvements.[35] On this basis, as many as 80 million, or 45 percent of adults 18 years and older, were estimated to be involved in some type of volunteer work, on average about 2.2 hours per week. About three-fourths of the total of 19.5 billion hours of volunteer work performed per year were reported to have been done for organizations.

According to this study, men were almost as likely as women to do some volunteer work, and also averaged 2.1 hours per week, compared to 2.2 hours for women. Rather surprisingly, employed persons tended to provide more hours than those not in the labor market, although part-time workers were more likely to do so than full-time workers. It is also interesting to note that, when informal activities are included, blacks were found to provide slightly more hours than whites and substantially more than Hispanics. Participation was greater among members of "other" denominations than Catholics and Protestants, and among persons with some years of college than those less educated.

Many reasons have been given for doing work that, by definition, brings little or no direct material rewards. True altruism, contact with congenial people, dedication to a particular cause, desire for recognition, furthering business, and advancing one's own or a spouse's career all may play a part to a greater or lesser extent. Research also suggests that women who are out of the labor force may believe that volunteer activities will help them to get better jobs when they reenter. Although experience gained in volunteer work is probably not as valuable, in general, as that acquired on the job, women with demanding family responsibilities, such as caring for young children or elderly relatives, will often value the more flexible schedule, and others may enjoy the greater choice of the type of work they prefer to do.[36] Experience in volunteer work is also particularly useful for per-

---

[34]Howard V. Hayghe, "Volunteers in the U.S.: Who Donates the Time?" *Monthly Labor Review* 114, no. 2 (February 1991): 17–23.

[35]"Giving and Volunteering in the United States. Findings from a National Survey," a survey conducted by the Gallup Organization for Independent Sector, 1988.

[36]For a discussion of this subject see Marnie W. Mueller, "Economic Determinants of Volunteer Work by Women," *Signs: Journal of Women in Culture and Society* 1, no. 2 (Winter 1975): 325–38 and Francine D. Blau, "How Voluntary is Volunteer Work? Comment on 'Economic Determinants of Volunteer Work by Women,'" *Signs: Journal of Women in Culture and Society* 21, no. 1 (Autumn 1976): 251–54.

sons interested in running for political office, both because of the skills acquired and the valuable contacts often made. In spite of all these possible advantages, it has been found that most people only join voluntary organizations upon being invited, and even urged, to do so.[37]

From the point of view of society, voluntary organizations also serve a number of useful functions. They offer the opportunity for mediation, integration of subgroups, affirmation of values, and distribution of power. All of these are important, especially in a democratic society. Beyond this, it appears that volunteers provide free services. It is frequently argued that as more and more women enter the labor market and have less time to spend on unpaid work, their contributions to worthy causes will be greatly missed. As we have seen, however, the evidence on this is mixed. On the one hand, the proportion of the population doing volunteer work, narrowly defined, appears to have declined. On the other hand, employed persons are actually likely to do more hours of broadly defined volunteer work. In any case, it must not be overlooked that these women now earn an income. They are therefore able to contribute more money to worthy causes, which incidentally might be considerably more efficient than baking and selling cookies or collecting money door to door. Employed women also pay taxes, thus making additional expenditures on public services possible. Hence workers could be hired to do much of what was earlier done by volunteers.

POLICY ISSUE: SPECIALIZATION AND TAXES

Up to this point, we have been comparing home production and market earnings as though families received the full benefit of each. In fact, the benefits that families actually receive and retain depend upon government transfer and tax policies. Two of the federal government's major programs in this area, income taxes and the social security system, have been particularly criticized as being biased in favor of the traditional, one-earner family. The argument is made that these programs, which evolved when the one-earner family was the norm, need to be modified in the face of the changing structure of American families.

One of the primary rules economists have proposed for fair taxation is **horizontal equity,** which means simply that *equals should be treated equally.*[38] That is, those in similar circumstances should be treated the same. Do current government policies offend against this rule in their treatment of one-earner and

---

[37]David L. Sills, "Voluntary Associations: Sociological Aspects," *International Encyclopedia of Social Sciences* (New York: The Macmillan Company and the Free Press, 1968): 362–76.

[38]"There is a generally accepted standard of equity or fairness with respect to public finance measures: equal treatment of those equally circumstanced." Carl S. Shoup, *Public Finance* (Chicago: Aldine Publishing Company, 1969), p. 23.

two-earner families? We now consider this question for income tax and social security policies.[39]

Income Taxation Policy

It is claimed that government policy in this area is inequitable because the value of goods and services produced in the home is not taxed, whereas money income is subject to taxation. As a result, two couples with the same level of economic well-being are not treated the same way. Suppose, for instance, that Ellen and Ed earn $25,000 each and produce $10,000 worth of goods and services in the household. Suppose too that Jim earns $40,000 and Jane, a full-time homemaker, produces $20,000 worth of goods and services in the home. Although both couples enjoy the same total income of $60,000 when the value of home production is included, Ellen and Ed will be taxed on money income of $50,000, whereas Jim and Jane will be taxed on money income of only $40,000. Given that in 1991 Ellen and Ed would be in the 28 percent tax bracket and Jane and Jim would be in the 15 percent bracket, this adds up to a substantial difference of $2,283 in the amount of taxes they must pay. The difference would obviously be less if both couples were in the 15 percent bracket, and it would be more if Ellen and Ed were in the 31 percent bracket.[40]

One of the concerns with such a policy is that it creates a disincentive for married women to participate in the labor force. Hence, it provides incentives for families to adopt the traditional division of labor. This is the case not only because market earnings are taxed and home production is not; the disincentive to market work is further increased by the **progressivity** of the tax system, meaning that higher levels of family income are taxed at a higher rate than lower levels. In general, progressivity is believed to be a good idea because it is supposed to result in wealthier families bearing a higher share of the tax burden. However, it also means that a married woman can face a relatively high marginal tax rate on her potential income when deciding whether or not to work outside the home.

In addition to this potential inequity, there is also the so-called "marriage penalty," which, even after some 1986 reforms (reducing the highest marginal rate from 50 to 31 percent), creates large taxes on being married for some couples and large subsidies for others. For instance, if Jim earns $40,000 and marries Jane, who has no earnings, his tax liability (based on 1991 rates) declines by $2,494.

---

[39] These topics are discussed in Nancy R. Gordon, "Institutional Responses: The Federal Income Tax System" and "Institutional Responses: The Social Security System," in Ralph E. Smith, ed., *The Subtle Revolution,* (Washington, DC: The Urban Institute, 1979), pp. 201–21, 223–55; and Richard V. Burkhauser and Karen C. Holden, eds., *A Challenge to Social Security: The Changing Roles of Women and Men in American Society* (New York: Academic Press, 1982).

[40] This example assumes that the couples use the standard deduction, have no children, and receive all their income from earnings. Note that the effective marginal tax rate for certain upper-middle-income tax payers is actually a bit higher than 31 percent because this group loses some deductions with higher income.

Conversely, if Ellen and Ed each earn $25,000, their joint tax burden will rise by $945 if they get married. In general, couples receive a subsidy when the spouses' incomes are relatively far apart and are penalized when the incomes are close. Overall, it has been estimated that, in 1988, 40 percent of married couples paid a marriage penalty averaging about $1,000 and 53 percent received a marriage subsidy averaging about $600.[41]

In terms of potential solutions to these perceived inequities, the possibility of taxing household production has received almost no attention. It is doubtful such a proposal would command much popular support. Moreover, it would be extremely difficult to implement, since it would be almost impossible to obtain reliable estimates of the value of household production.

An alternative proposal, which would eliminate both the work disincentive and the marriage penalty, would be to tax each person as an individual. This would equalize tax rates for individuals with equal income, regardless of their marital status. This approach has been adopted in Sweden but has not received much support in this country. Whether it is viewed as more equitable in its treatment of *money* income than the current arrangement (in terms of our definition of horizontal equity) depends on whether the individual or the family is viewed as the appropriate tax unit. Such a change would benefit two-earner couples but would increase the tax liability of one-earner families, even though these families still benefit because in-kind income is not taxed.

Social Security System

The social security system, which covers 9 out of 10 American wage earners, also poses problems of equity between one- and two-earner husband-wife families. As presently constituted, proportional taxes to a specified maximum of earnings are levied, half to be paid by the employer, half by the worker. One controversial aspect of the system centers on the provision of spouse and survivor benefits. The spouse of the covered worker is entitled to receive a spouse benefit equal to 50 percent of the amount received by the covered worker, or a survivor benefit of 100 percent. Since 1977, spouses divorced after at least ten years of marriage are entitled to the same benefit. Alternatively, the spouse may receive a benefit based on his or her own earnings record, whichever amount is greater. Because many married women have substantially lower wages and shorter work lives than their husbands, they are often better off collecting spouse or survivor benefits than

---

[41] The example above again assumes that the couples are childless, receive all their income from earnings, and take the standard deduction. The average estimates of the marriage penalty and subsidy are from Harvey S. Rosen, "The Marriage Penalty Is Down but Not Out," *National Tax Journal* 40, no. 4 (December 1987): 567–75. It is widely believed that this problem was largely remedied by the 1986 tax reforms. Rosen, however, points out that, for low-income couples, the penalties and subsidies tend to be larger now than before 1986, although the opposite tends to be true for couples at high income levels. On average, however, the new law creates a lower marriage penalty than its predecessor.

benefits based on their own earnings. Thus, the additional taxes, which they have paid into the system as workers, have yielded them no increase in benefits. Even those wives who get somewhat higher benefits because of their own participation in the system get a relatively low return on their tax payments. One-earner couples get the highest returns on their payments into the system—only the earner pays social security taxes and the spouse receives a spouse or survivor benefit.

This situation may be considered to violate one rule of horizontal equity— equal contributions into the system do not secure the same return for all individuals (or both types of families). Further, under such circumstances, social security taxes are likely to be a deterrent to labor force participation among wives, for they get little or no return on their social security payments, although they are required to pay the taxes on their market earnings.

One proposed solution to these problems is "earnings sharing" in which an equal share of total household earnings is assigned to each spouse. This proposal recognizes that the division of labor in the home represents a familial decision and that both spouses contribute to family welfare through their market and/or nonmarket work. Earnings sharing is neutral with respect to the work roles of the husband and wife and would, thus, be more encouraging of labor force participation than the current system. The social security system would move in the direction of greater horizontal equity, in that equal contributions yield equal benefits.[42] Two-earner families would no longer be at a disadvantage compared to one-earner families, because spouse benefits would be eliminated. As in the case of individual taxation, support for such a policy is likely to increase with the continued growth of the two-earner family.

CONCLUSION

We have seen in Chapter 2 that the "traditional family" evolved with the man as the breadwinner and the woman as the homemaker, combining her time with the goods and services purchased with the husband's earnings to satisfy the family's needs and wants. The simple neoclassical model explains how such a division of labor may be advantageous under appropriate conditions. But as we have also seen, it cannot be taken for granted that these conditions are satisfied at any given point in time, let alone that they will be for the rest of each person's life.

The traditional specialization may have come about because conditions that existed in earlier times made such an arrangement more nearly optimal than it is today. There are several obvious reasons for this. When cloth was spun, bread was baked, soap was produced at home, the family was large, and there were few opportunities for women to earn a decent market wage, her relative advantage for home work was great. With many children, and a shorter life expectancy, the

---

[42]No social security taxes are paid on the value of what is produced in the household, but neither does the family accumulate benefits.

problem of the decline in the value of housework after the children grew up was far less serious. With severe social and religious sanctions against divorce, women were less likely to find themselves, and their children, dependent on a recalcitrant ex-husband for a living.

However, as these factors have changed, the advantages of the traditional division of labor have decreased and the costs associated with it, particularly for women, have increased. Growing recognition of the drawbacks of the traditional division of responsibilities between husband and wife may be one of the factors that has contributed to the decline in the proportion of families following this pattern. These developments will be analyzed further in the next chapter. Increasing awareness of the potentially high costs of specialization should enable young people to make better-informed decisions and should cause policymakers to reconsider social policies that favor one-earner families and, thus, inhibit more rapid change.

Appendix

SPECIALIZATION AND EXCHANGE: A GRAPHICAL ANALYSIS

As discussed in Chapter 3, a complete analysis of the division of labor between the individuals who make up a couple takes into account both their production
possibilities and their preferences. In this appendix, we do this by providing a fuller
examination of the simple neoclassical model in the context of a graphical analysis.
The same conclusions are reached as to the value of specialization and exchange.

For simplicity, we assume that individuals derive utility from only two types
of goods — home goods, produced with inputs of home time, and market goods,
purchased with market income. In Figure 3.1, H and M measure the dollar value
of household output and market goods, respectively. Two persons, Kathy and Jim,
each allocate their time between market work (M production) and housework (H
production).[43]

If Kathy and Jim are each dependent on their own output, their consumption
opportunities are limited to their individual *production possibility frontiers*. The
production possibility frontier shows the largest feasible combinations of the two

---

[43] We also assume fixed proportions production functions for H and M for each individual. This
means, for example, that an additional hour spent on the production of H by Kathy increases output by
the same amount, regardless of how much H she has already produced. This simplifying assumption
results in the straight line production possibility frontiers shown in Figure 3.1.

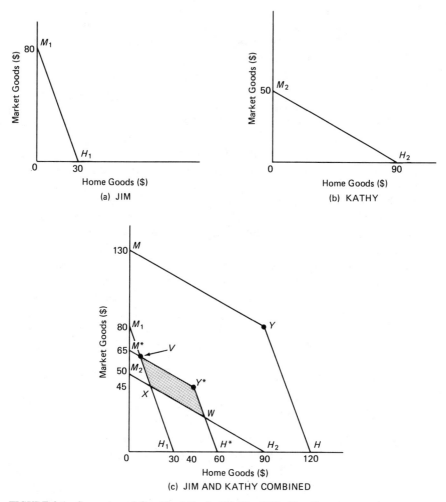

FIGURE 3.1   Separate and Combined Production Possibility Frontiers

outputs that can be produced with given resources (in this case, time inputs) and know-how. M_1H_1 indicates the combinations of household and market outputs available to Jim, while M_2H_2 shows the best options from which Kathy can choose. For example, if Jim devotes full time to market work (M production), he can produce a maximum of $80 worth of market goods. If he spends all his time on household activities, he can produce $30 worth of home goods.

The slope of the line M_1H_1 tells us the money value of the market goods Jim must give up to get an additional dollar of home goods. The fact that M_1H_1 is more steeply sloped than M_2H_2 means that Jim must give up more market goods to get an additional dollar of home goods than Kathy. Specifically, Jim must give up $2.67 of market goods to get an additional dollar of home goods ($80/$30), whereas Kathy needs to give up only $.56 of market goods to get an additional dollar of home goods ($50/$90). Viewing the matter somewhat differently, Kathy must forgo more home goods to get an additional dollar of market goods than Jim. Kathy would have to give up $1.80 worth of home goods to get an additional dollar of market goods ($90/$50), while Jim needs to give up only $.38 worth of home goods to get an additional dollar of market goods ($30/$80). Thus, Jim has a comparative advantage in market work and Kathy has a comparative advantage in home production.

If Jim and Kathy decide to collaborate, their combined production possibility curve will be *MYH*, as show in panel c. At point *M* both Jim and Kathy specialize entirely in market work, producing $130 ($80 + $50) of market goods. If they prefer to have some home goods, it will pay for only Kathy to do housework, up to the point where she does no market work at all (point *Y*), because she adds more to home production ($1.80) for every dollar of market goods given up than Jim would add ($.38). Therefore, the segment *MY* has the same slope as M_2H_2, showing that as long as only Kathy is dividing her time between market and home, it is Kathy's slope that is relevant. Jim will do some housework only if a mix of more household production and fewer market goods are desired than segment *MY* represents. Beyond that point, the slope of M_1H_1 becomes relevant, as it is only Jim who is dividing his time between home and market. At the extreme, at point *H*, both Jim and Kathy work only in the home, producing $120 ($30 + $90) of home goods.

The combined production possibility frontier (*MYH*) makes feasible combinations of *M* and *H* that would not be attainable by Kathy and Jim on their separate production possibility frontiers. These gains from specialization and exchange may be illustrated by putting the output combinations represented by production possibility frontier *MYH* on a per capita or per person basis. Dividing *MYH* by two we obtain *M*Y*H**, which may be compared to the options represented by Jim and Kathy's individual production possibility frontiers, M_1H_1 and M_2H_2 (panel c). The shaded area *WXVY** represents the increased per capita output that is now available. This gain in output may potentially be distributed between Jim and Kathy so as to make them both better off than they would have been separately. To obtain the gains represented by *WXVY**, the couple must produce a nontrivial amount of both market- and home-produced goods, for it is the production of both commodities that gives each of them the opportunity to specialize in the area of their comparative advantage.

This analysis also illustrates that the gains to specialization will be larger, the more the two individuals differ in their comparative advantages. To see this, imagine the extreme case in which Kathy and Jim both have the same production possibility frontier, say M_1H_1. The combined production possibility frontier would then be $2 \times M_1H_1$. On a per capita basis (dividing the combined production possibility frontier in half), we would simply be left with M_1H_1. Kathy and Jim would do no better combining forces than they would each do separately. Based on this simple analysis alone, it is not clear what the economic gains to collaborating are. However, as we saw in Chapter 3, there are likely to be economic gains even in this case, mainly because two people can use many goods and services more efficiently than a single person can. Here, we focus on the couple that can potentially increase its income through joint production.

To provide a link between the potential increase in output due to collaboration and the goal of maximizing satisfaction, we need to introduce an additional tool of economic analysis and pursue our inquiry one step further. So far we have only established the various combinations of the two types of outputs that Kathy and Jim could produce. Which of these they would choose depends on their tastes, that is to say, on their preferences for market goods compared to home goods. To considerably simplify the analysis, we will assume that they have identical tastes. If home goods are valued more highly than market goods, the couple will be willing to give up a considerable amount of market goods in order to get an additional dollar of home goods, and vice versa if market goods are valued more highly. This relationship can be illustrated using **indifference curves,** as seen in Figure 3.2.

Let us assume that Kathy and Jim have been told that they could have the combination of market and home goods represented by point A in panel a. They are then asked to find various other combinations of H and M from which they would derive exactly the same amount of satisfaction or utility. These other points can all be connected into one indifference curve, U_2, called that because the couple is indifferent about being at various points on the curve. The U_2 curve is *negatively sloped*. This means that if the amount of market or home goods is decreased, the amount of the other good must be increased for the couple to remain equally well off.

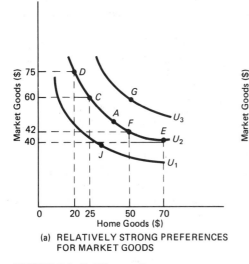

(a) RELATIVELY STRONG PREFERENCES FOR MARKET GOODS

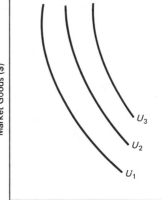

(b) RELATIVELY STRONG PREFERENCES FOR HOME GOODS

FIGURE 3.2   Indifference Curves

Notice too that indifference curve U_2 is convex to the origin. That is, it gets steeper as we move to the left and flatter as we move to the right. What this means is that at a point like C, where M goods are relatively plentiful and H goods are relatively scarce, it takes a fairly large amount of M ($15 worth) to induce the couple to give up a fairly small amount of H ($5 worth) and still remain equally well off. On the other hand, at a point like E, where M goods are relatively scarce and H goods are relatively plentiful, the couple is willing to give up a fairly large amount of H ($20 worth) to get even a small additional amount of scarce M ($2 worth). This is generally realistic to the extent that relatively scarce goods are valued more highly.

However, Kathy and Jim do not have just one indifference curve, but rather a whole family of higher or lower indifference curves. For it is possible to choose a point like G on curve U_3 that offers more of both M and H and is therefore clearly preferable to point A on curve U_2. Hence, all points on curve U_3 will, by extension, be preferable to (give more satisfaction than) all points on curve U_2. Similarly, it is possible to choose a point like J on curve U_1 that offers less of both M and H than at point A. Point J is clearly less desirable than Point A and, by extension, all points on curve U_1 are less desirable (give less satisfaction) than all points on curve U_2.[44]

On the other hand, another couple's preference might look like those depicted in panel b of Figure 3.2. These indifference curves are steeper and show that this couple places a relatively higher value on home goods, compared with market goods, than Kathy and Jim do. In general, it would take a larger amount of market goods to induce them to give up a dollar's worth of home goods while remaining equally well off.

To determine the division of labor (or time allocation) a couple will actually choose, we must consider both their production possibilities and their tastes or preferences. In Figure 3.3, we superimpose the couple's hypothetical indifference map on the production possibility frontier shown in Figure 3.1, panel c. It is then readily possible to determine the combination of home-produced and market-produced goods that a rational couple with those tastes (indifference curves) will choose. It will always be the point where the production possibility curve just touches the highest indifference curve it reaches. The reason is simple—the couple always prefers to be on a higher indifference curve (by definition, as we have seen), but since they are constrained to the possible combinations of output represented by the production possibility frontier, there is no realistic way they can reach an indifference curve that at all points lies above the frontier.

In Figure 3.3, we illustrate the impact of the couple's preferences on their time allocation. The combined production possibility curve for the couple, MYH, shows the various combinations of H and M the couple can produce while taking

___

[44]It should be clear that indifference curves can never intersect. All points on any one curve represent an equal amount of utility, while any point above (below) represents a larger (smaller) amount of utility. At the point where two curves intersect, they clearly represent the same amount of utility, yet at all other points they do not. This is a logical impossibility.

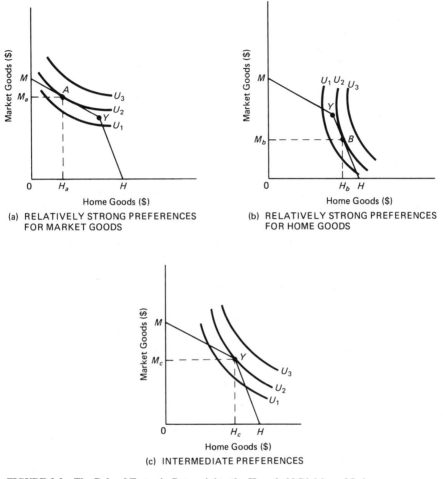

FIGURE 3.3 **The Role of Tastes in Determining the Household Division of Labor**

full advantage of their combined resources and the comparative advantage each has in producing one of the goods. Let us continue to assume that the wife has a comparative advantage in home production and that the husband has a comparative advantage in market work.

As may be seen in panel a, a couple with relatively strong preferences for market goods will maximize satisfaction at point A along segment MY. The husband will specialize entirely in market production and the wife will do all the housework and also supply some time to the market. They will consume M_a dollars of market goods and H_a dollars of home goods.

Panel b shows a couple with stronger preferences for home-produced goods. They will maximize utility at point B. The wife will devote herself entirely to household production, while the husband will do some housework as well as supplying time to the market. Such a couple will consume fewer market goods (M_0) and more home goods (H_0) than a couple with stronger preferences for market goods.

Finally, panel c shows a couple with intermediate tastes. They will maximize utility at point Y. Both wife and husband will each fully specialize in home and market production, respectively, and will consume M_c dollars of market goods and H_c dollars of home woods.

Couples may differ in their allocation of tasks within the family, not solely due to differences in tastes. The relative productivity of each member of the family in the production of market and home goods will also be an important factor. We have already noted that if both husband and wife are equally productive in each endeavor, there will be no gains to specialization or division of labor within the family. However, even if we assume that the wife has a comparative advantage in household production and that the husband has a comparative advantage in market work, the relative productivities of each individual in home and market production are still relevant. This is illustrated in Figure 3.4.

Panel a shows two hypothetical production possibility functions. In *MYH*, the segment corresponding to the wife's frontier (*MY*) is relatively flat, indicating that she is considerably more productive in the home than in the market. For given tastes (represented by indifference curve U), the couple maximizes utility at point Y, where the wife specializes entirely in home production and the husband specializes completely in market work. However, if the couple's production possibility frontier were $M'Y'H'$, even with the same tastes (indifference curve), they would choose point A along segment $M'Y'$. Here the wife will continue to do all the house-

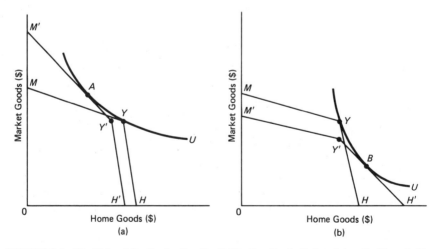

FIGURE 3.4   The Role of the Production Possibility Frontier in Determining the Household Division of Labor

work but will do some market work as well. This is because $M'Y'$ is steeper than MY, indicating a higher ratio of the wife's market productivity relatively to her home productivity. The opportunity cost of home goods in terms of market goods forgone has increased and as a result the family consumes less of them.

Similarly, as shown in panel b, the couple's time allocation may also depend on the husband's relative productivity in the home and the market. For given tastes (represented by indifference curve U), the couple will choose point Y when the husband's productivity in the home is extremely low relative to his market productivity. (This is indicated by the relatively steep slope of segment YH on frontier MYH.) They are more likely to choose a point like B along the flatter segment $Y'H'$ on frontier $M'Y'H'$, where he does some housework as well as market work, when his market productivity is lower relative to his home productivity. At B, the couple consumes more of the now relatively cheaper home-produced goods than at Y.

Figure 3.4 shows how the relative productivity of the husband and the wife in the home and the market influence the division of labor in the family and the combination of home- and market-produced goods that they choose to consume. Nonetheless, as long as the comparative advantages of husband and wife differ in this simple model, specialization will be efficient. As we have seen, the greater the difference between the two in their comparative advantage, the greater the gains to specialization and exchange.

Thus, the fuller analysis presented here supports the conclusions reached on the basis of the numerical example provided in Chapter 3. In this case too, however, the same qualifications hold. First, there are other potential economic benefits to marriage besides specialization and exchange, and, second, there are disadvantages, particularly for women, to the traditional division of labor.

SUGGESTED READINGS

BECKER, GARY S. *A Treatise on the Family.* Harvard University Press, 1991.

FERBER, MARIANNE A. and BONNIE G. BIRNBAUM. "The 'New Home Economics: Retrospects and Prospects," *Journal of Consumer Research* 4, no. 1 (June 1977): 19–28.

GILLESPIE, DAIR L. "Who Has the Power? The Marital Struggle," *Journal of Marriage and the Family* 33, no. 3 (August 1971): 445–58.

HARTMANN, HEIDI I. "The Family as the Locus of Gender, Class and Political Struggle: The Example of Housework," *Signs: Journal of Women in Culture and Society* 6, no. 3 (Spring 1981): 366–94.

JUSTER, F. THOMAS and FRANK P. STAFFORD. "The Allocation of Time: Empirical Findings, Behavioral Models, and Problems of Measurement," *Journal of Economic Literature,* 29, no. 2 (June 1991): 471–522.

POLLAK, ROBERT P. "A Transaction Cost Approach to Families and Households," *Journal of Economic Literature,* 23, no. 2 (June 1985): 581–608.

Chapter 4

THE ALLOCATION OF TIME BETWEEN THE HOUSEHOLD AND THE LABOR MARKET

The continued and increasingly rapid growth in women's labor force participation has been one of the most significant economic and social developments in this country and elsewhere. It is, therefore, important to understand the meaning and nature of this phenomenon before going on to examine its causes and to discuss some of its effects. In this chapter, we first review the definition of the labor force and summarize female and male trends over time in labor force participation. We shall see that, while female participation rates have been increasing, particularly in the post-1940 period, male rates have been declining, albeit not as dramatically. As a consequence of both types of changes, men's and women's labor force participation rates and their patterns of involvement in market work over the life cycle have been becoming increasingly similar. We then turn to the development of some economic concepts for analyzing these trends and use them to provide a better understanding of the reasons for the remarkable influx of women into the labor market. Essentially, the dramatic rise in women's labor force participation is attributed to an increase in the value of their time in the market relative to the value of time spent in the home. In Chapter 9, we examine how the family has changed as a result of women's increasing employment outside the home.

THE LABOR FORCE: SOME DEFINITIONS

Each month, the U.S. Bureau of the Census conducts a survey to gather statistics on the labor force. According to the official definition, the **labor force** includes all those individuals 16 years of age and over who worked for pay or profit during the reference week or actively sought paid employment during the four weeks prior to the reference week. That is, the labor force is comprised of both the employed and the unemployed.

The **employed** group includes all those who worked one hour per week or more as paid employees or were self-employed in their own business or profession or on their own farm. This includes part-time workers who worked less than 35 hours per week, as well as those who worked full-time, 35 hours or more. It also includes all those temporarily absent from paid employment because of bad weather, vacation, labor-management disputes, or personal reasons, whether or not they were paid. An exception to the emphasis on paid employment is that those who worked at least 15 hours as unpaid workers in an enterprise operated by a family member are also included.[1] The **unemployed** include those who do not have a job but who have made specific efforts to find a job within the past four weeks, as well as those not working but waiting to be called back to work or to report for a new job within 30 days.

The **labor force participation rate** of a particular group is equal to the number of its members who are in the labor force divided by the total number in the group who are of working age. Thus, for example, a labor force participation rate of .58 for women means that 58 percent of women 16 years of age and over are labor force participants.

A careful reading of the definition of the labor force makes it clear that being in the labor force is not synonymous with working. Persons who work less than 15 hours a week as unpaid family workers, and those who work only in the household or as volunteer workers, no matter how many hours, are excluded. On the other hand, persons temporarily not working, or unemployed, are included. In large part, this results from the emphasis (in the official definition of the labor force) on being employed in or seeking *market* work. Because women have tended to have primary responsibility for nonmarket work, they constitute a high proportion in the categories that are left out. Thus, their share of the labor force considerably understates their share of work. This was particularly true in earlier days when family enterprises were more common and when most married women

---

[1]The labor force excludes illegal activities such as prostitution and drug trafficking. In the nature of the case, no data are available that would enable us to obtain reliable estimates on the extent of these activities. Further, employment ranging from babysitting to yard work, which is paid for in cash and not reported for tax purposes (the so-called "underground economy"), is likely to be underreported in labor force statistics.

were homemakers.[2] In spite of these reservations, women's labor force participation rate is considered to be an important indicator of their status in a market economy, for work done outside the labor market seldom offers as much prestige, let alone money income, and is sometimes not even viewed as real "work."[3]

TRENDS IN LABOR FORCE PARTICIPATION

The purpose of this section is to briefly review the trends in female and male labor force participation. The reasons for the observed changes are considered later. But here we may obtain an overview of how dramatic these changes have been. Labor force participation rates for selected years since 1890 are shown in Table 4.1.[4] The figures indicate a relatively slow rate of increase in the labor force participation rates of women in the pre-1940 period. Since then, however, more dramatic changes have occurred. In 1940, 28 percent of women were in the labor force; by 1990, the figure had risen to 58 percent, and nearly three-quarters of women between the ages of 25 and 54 were labor force participants. During this time, women workers increased from 25 to 45 percent of the total labor force.

This rapid influx of women into the work force is by no means unique to the United States. On the contrary, as we shall see in Chapter 10, it is typical for most industrialized countries and for many developing countries as well. Further, the labor force participation rate of women is considerably higher than in the United States, not only in Eastern Europe and some developing countries, but also among some nations in Western Europe.

Table 4.1 also indicates the dramatic effect that the mobilization for World War II had on female labor force participation. As males left their civilian jobs to

[2]It has been suggested that such activities as taking in boarders, piecework done at home, and even seasonal work done in factories frequently went unreported, especially when it was the husband who was interviewed. (See, for instance, Milton Cantor and Bruce Laurie, eds., *Class, Sex, and the Woman Worker,* Westport, CT: Greenwood Press, 1977.) How important this undercount may have been is suggested by the fact that when the Census enumerators in 1910 were given instructions to take special care not to overlook women workers, especially unpaid family workers, the participation rate was found to be about 4 percentage points higher than would be expected based on earlier and immediately subsequent decades. It is for this reason that the year 1910 is normally omitted from historical series on women's labor force participation. We follow this practice in Table 4.1.

[3]Most of us have heard a woman say in response to the question whether she works, "No, I am a housewife." Other aspects of the official definition of the labor force have also been the object of criticism at various times. For example, the definition of the unemployed excludes those who would like a job but who have given up searching because they believe no work is available, so-called discouraged workers. Although no definition is likely to be equally satisfactory to all, adherence to a reasonably consistent definition over a long period of time provides useful data for analyzing trends. In some cases, criticism has been accommodated by providing additional data that may be used to construct labor force measures based on different definitions. We take advantage of such data on discouraged workers in our discussion of unemployment in Chapter 8.

[4]Until 1890, published census volumes contain few tabulations of the labor force participation and occupations of women (Claudia Goldin, *Understanding the Gender Gap: An Economic History of American Women,* New York: Oxford University Press, 1990, p. 186).

TABLE 4.1   Labor Force Participation Rates of Men and Women, 1890–1990[a]
(Total Labor Force)

Year	Percent of Men in the Labor Force	Percent of Women in the Labor Force
1890	84.3	18.2
1900	85.7	20.0
1920	84.6	22.7
1930	82.1	23.6
1940	82.5	27.9
1945	87.6	35.8
1947	86.8	31.5
1950	86.8	33.9
1960	84.0	37.8
1970	80.6	43.4
1980	77.9	51.6
1990	76.8	57.5

[a] Prior to 1947 based on population 14 years of age and over; thereafter 16 years and over.

Source: U.S. Department of Commerce, Bureau of the Census, *Historical Statistics of the United States Colonial Times to 1970,* Bicentennial Edition, Part 1, 1975, pp. 131–32; U.S. Department of Labor, *Employment and Training Report of the President,* 1982, table A-1, pp. 147–48; and U.S. Department of Labor, Bureau of Labor Statistics, *Employment and Earnings* 38, no. 1 (January 1991), p.16.

join the armed forces, women entered the labor force in unprecedented numbers. Between 1940 and 1945, the female labor force participation rate increased from 28 to 36 percent. As suggested by the 1947 figures, some decline occurred in the immediate post-World War II period. However, since that time, the female participation rate has continued to increase at a pace considerably in excess of the pre-1940 period.

In contrast to the situation for women, male labor force participation rates began to decline in the 1950s, from 87 percent in 1950 to 77 percent in 1990. As a consequence of these opposing trends, the *difference* between the male and female participation rates has declined sharply from 55 percentage points in 1940 to 19 percentage points in 1990.

We gain a fuller picture of the trends in labor force participation by examining them separately for different subgroups. Table 4.2 shows trends in labor force participation since 1955 by race and Hispanic origin. The participation rate has declined for all groups of men but considerably more so for blacks, who have now fallen considerably behind. Hispanic men, however, are more likely to be in the labor force than other white or black males. The rate has risen for all groups of women but substantially more so for whites and Hispanics. Black women have traditionally had considerably higher labor force participation rates than white women. The gap has now closed, but it should be noted that black women still tend to work longer hours. Hispanic women continue to have a lower labor force participation rate than other white or black women.

TABLE 4.2 **Labor Force Participation Rates of Men and Women by Race and Hispanic Origin, 1955–1990**[a] **(percent)**

	MALES			FEMALES		
	White	*Black*[b]	*Hispanic*[c]	*White*	*Black*[b]	*Hispanic*[c]
1955	85.4	85.0	n.a.	34.5	46.1	n.a.
1965	80.8	79.6	n.a.	38.1	48.6	n.a.
1975	78.7	70.9	80.7	45.9	48.8	43.1
1985	77.0	70.8	80.3	54.1	53.1	49.3
1990	76.9	70.1	81.2	57.5	57.8	53.0

[a]Civilian labor force, includes population aged 16 and over.
[b]Prior to 1975, includes other nonwhites.
[c]Hispanics are also included under the relevant racial category.
n.a. Not available.
Source: U.S. Department of Labor, Bureau of Labor Statistics, *Working Women: A Databook,* 1977, pp. 44–5; U.S. Department of Labor, *Handbook of Labor Statistics* (August 1989), pp. 25–30; and U.S. Department of Labor, *Employment and Earnings* 38, no. 1 (January 1991), pp. 208.

The influx of women into the labor market that has occurred since 1940 has been accompanied by pronounced changes in the patterns of female labor force participation over the life cycle. Before 1940, the typical female worker was young and single, since women tended to leave the labor force permanently upon marriage and childbearing. As Figure 4.1 shows, at that time, the peak age-specific participation rate occurred among women 20 to 24 years of age and declined for each successive age group after that.[5] Over the next 20 years, older married women with school-age or grown children entered or reentered the labor force in increasing numbers, while the labor force participation rates of women between the ages of 20 and 34 remained relatively constant. The proportion of women workers who were married increased from 30 percent in 1940 to 54 percent in 1960. The World War II experience may have played some part in encouraging this shift in the behavior of married women, since it was during the war that, for the first time, large numbers of older married women worked outside the home.[6]

[5]Note that when labor force participation rates are changing, cross-sectional data on participation rates by age as shown in Figure 4.1 may give a misleading impression of the actual experiences of individual women over the life cycle. An interesting analysis of cohort patterns of married women's participation is presented in Goldin, *Understanding the Gender Gap,* pp. 21–23. See also June O'Neill, "Women & Wages," *The American Enterprise* 1, no. 6 (Nov/Dec 1990), pp. 27–28.

[6]William H. Chafe (*The American Woman: Her Changing Social, Economic, and Political Role, 1920–1970,* Oxford: Oxford University Press, 1972), argues that the notion of woman's appropriate sphere being in the home was so deeply embedded that it took a cataclysmic event like World War II to break down this normative barrier. Also, Dorothy Sue Cobble ("Reassessing the 'Doldrum Years': Working Class Feminism in the 1940s," paper presented at the Berkshire Conference on the History of Women, June 1990) emphasizes the dramatic impact the war years had on the attitudes of women workers. She particularly points to the emergence of a new consensus on equal pay and a breakdown of the formerly near-universal consensus in favor of protective legislation for women. On the other hand,

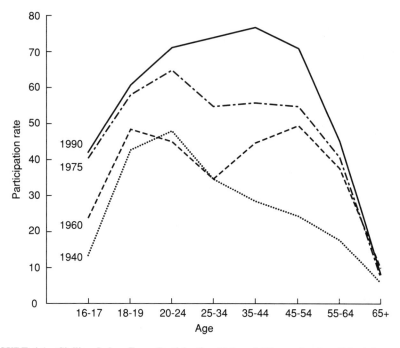

FIGURE 4.1 **Civilian Labor Force Participation Rates of Women by Age, Selected Years, 1940–1990**

Since 1960, there has been a sizable increase in the participation rates of all women under age 55, but particularly among younger women aged 20 to 44. This increase in part reflects declines in the birth rate and increases in the divorce rate over this period. Most notable, however, has been the large increase in the partic- ipation rates of married women with small children. Among those with children less than 6, only 19 percent worked outside the home in 1960, compared to 57 percent in 1988. By 1988, over half (52 percent) of married mothers with infants a year old or less were in the labor force.

As a result of these changes, the pattern of age-specific participation rates among women has come to more closely resemble the male pattern shown in Figure 4.2. Figure 4.2 also shows that the decline in male labor participation rates that occurred during the post-World War II period was concentrated among younger men, particularly those under 20, and among older men, aged 55 and over. Since the 1960s, there has also been a small decrease in the participation rates of men in the so-called prime working ages, not only those 45 to 54 but even those 25 to 44. Participation rates for these age groups remain extremely high, however, with over 90 percent of men in the 25-to-54 age group in the labor force.

Claudia Goldin, "The Role of World War II in the Rise of Women's Work," *American Economic Review* 81, no. 4 (September 1991), tends to give less weight to the influence of World War II on later trends.

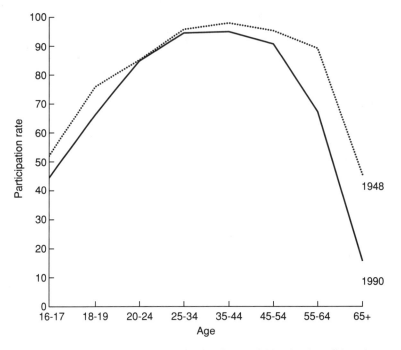

FIGURE 4.2   Civilian Labor Force Participation Rates of Men by Age, Selected
            Years, 1950–1990

TRENDS IN LABOR FORCE ATTACHMENT

The changes in the pattern of women's labor force participation by age that have
occurred since 1940 suggest that rising female participation rates have been associated with an increase in the labor force attachment of women over the life cycle.
That is, women are tending to remain in the labor force more consistently over a
period of time.

Some indication of women's increasing labor force attachment is provided in
Table 4.3. This table shows the **labor force participation rate,** which, it may be
recalled, is the percentage of a particular group (say, women) who are in the labor
force *at a point in time*. It also shows the **labor force experience rate,** which is
the percentage of women who are in the labor force *at some time during the year*.
If the same group of women were in the labor force consistently over the year,
the labor force participation rate would exactly equal the labor force experience
rate, and there would be no *turnover* (change) of the labor force group. Alternatively, if women tended to move into and out of the labor force over the year, the
labor force experience rate would exceed the labor force participation rate. In this
case, the group of labor force participants would include some different individuals
at different points in time (that is, there would be *turnover* in the labor force group).

TABLE 4.3 **Labor Force Turnover of Men and Women Selected Years, 1957–1989**[a] **(percent)**

	MALES			FEMALES		
Year	*Labor Force Participation Rate*[b]	*Labor Force Experience Rate*[c]	*Labor Force Turnover Rate*[d]	*Labor Force Participation Rate*[b]	*Labor Force Experience Rate*[c]	*Labor Force Turnover Rate*[d]
1957	81.9	88.2	7.8	35.8	47.3	32.1
1962	78.4	85.1	8.5	36.6	48.7	32.9
1967	80.4	86.7	7.8	41.1	53.1	29.2
1972	79.0	86.7	8.5	43.9	54.3	23.9
1977	77.7	83.4	7.4	48.4	58.2	20.1
1982	76.6	80.4	5.0	52.6	59.2	12.5
1989	76.4	80.0	4.7	57.4	63.1	9.9

[a]Civilian labor force.

[b]The proportion of individuals in the labor force during the reference week (annual averages).

[c]The proportion of individuals in the labor force at some time during the year.

[d]The difference between the labor force experience rate and the labor force participation rate divided by the labor force participation rate.

Source: 1957–1977 data are from Cynthia B. Lloyd and Beth T. Niemi, *The Economics of Sex Differentials* (NY: Columbia University Press,©1979), Table 2.6, p. 71, reprinted by permission of the publisher; later data are from U.S. Department of Labor, *Employment and Training Report of the President* (1982), Table A-5, p. 155; Ellen Sehgal, "Work Experience in 1983 Reflects the Effects of the Recovery," *Monthly Labor Review* 107, no. 12 (December 1984), Table 1, p. 19; and U.S. Department of Labor, Bureau of Labor Statistics, "Seven Out of Ten Persons in the Working-Age Population had Some Employment During 1989," *News* (August 28, 1990).

The **labor force turnover rate** is equal to the difference between the labor force experience rate and the labor force participation rate divided by the labor force participation rate. It is an indicator of labor force attachment and tells us the extent to which the composition of the labor force group *turns over* during the year.

As may be seen in Table 4.3, the labor force turnover rate of women has been declining since the mid-1960s, indicating that women are becoming more firmly attached to the labor market. Although the rate is still higher than that of men, the gender differential has fallen considerably over the past 30 years. A further indication of women's increasing labor force attachment is that the percentage of women who are full-time, year-round workers has been increasing steadily since the mid-1960s, from 37 percent in 1963 to 51 percent in 1989. Full-time, year-round workers composed 69 percent of the male work force in 1989.

This growing labor force attachment of women has contributed to the increase in their labor force participation rate. The labor force group is increased by entries into the labor force and decreased by exits from the labor force; therefore, when the number of entrants exceeds the number of those who leave the labor force, the size of the labor force is increased. Thus, *both increases* in flows of *entrants* and *decreases* in flows of *exits* may contribute to the growth of the female labor force. And, indeed, the data in Table 4.3 suggest that both these factors have played a role in increasing the female participation rate. That is, labor force experience rates have risen, showing that entries have increased. However, experience rates have declined *relative to* participation rates, indicating that women are remaining in the labor force more continuously (that is, exits have decreased).

As we shall see in greater detail in Chapter 7, work experience is an important determinant of labor market earnings. This is true for women as well as men, though their rewards have not been as great. The lesser amount of work experience of women relative to men has traditionally been cited as an important reason for their lower earnings. For the female population as a whole, rising labor force participation rates have unambiguously worked to increase the average number of years women tend to spend in the labor force over their lifetimes. It is not clear, however, whether recent increases in women's labor force participation have been associated with increases or decreases in the *average* amount of work experience of women who are in the labor force. Two changes, which would tend to have opposite effects, are going on here. On the one hand, the growing number of new entrants, who have worked only a short time, has a negative effect on the average labor market experience of women workers. On the other hand, the growing tendency for women to remain in the labor force for longer periods of time has a positive effect.

Unfortunately, the usual published statistics on labor force participation do not help to answer the question of what the net effect of increased labor force participation on experience has been. From time to time, estimates have, however, been made using longitudinal data that provide information for the same individuals over a period of time, as well as various other types of information. The evidence suggests that before the late 1960s, rising female labor force participation rates were associated with constant or slowly increasing average levels of work experience among women workers. In recent years, notable gains in relative experience have occurred, particularly among younger women.[7] These trends are discussed in greater detail in Chapter 6.

THE LABOR FORCE PARTICIPATION DECISION

In Chapter 3, we examined the division of household and market work between husband and wife. Here we focus upon the closely related question of how an individual decides on the allocation of his or her time between the home and the labor market. We again use a neoclassical model and assume that the goal is to

---

[7]Goldin, *Understanding the Gender Gap,* pp. 37–41; June O'Neill, "The Trend in the Male-Female Wage Gap in the United States," *Journal of Labor Economics* (January 1985, Supp.); James P. Smith and Michael P. Ward, "Time Series Changes in the Female Labor Force," *Journal of Labor Economics* (January 1985, Supp.); M. Anne Hill, "Intercohort Differences in Women's Labor Market Transitions," *American Economic Review* (May 1990): 289–92; and June O'Neil and Solomon Polachek, "Why the Gener Gap in Wages Narrowed in the 1980s," unpublished paper (November 1991).

maximize utility or satisfaction.[8] Individuals decide whether or not to participate in the labor force by comparing the value of their time in the market (w) to the value they place on their time spent at home (w^*). If w is greater than w^*, they participate in the labor force; if w is less than w^*, they remain out of the labor force. In the next section, the long-run increase in women's labor force participation is analyzed in terms of factors that have increased their value of market time and lowered their value of home time.

Now let us examine this model in greater detail. Individuals are viewed as deriving utility from the consumption of *commodities* (goods and services) that are produced using inputs of market goods and nonmarket time.[9] For example, the commodity, a gourmet meal, may be produced using inputs of market goods (like groceries, cooking equipment, etc.) and the individual's own time in preparing the meal. In order to keep this model reasonably simple, we make the following three additional assumptions.

First, we assume that all income earned in the labor market is spent on market goods. This avoids the need to consider the determinants of savings and also means that we may use the terms *market income* and (the money value of) *market goods* interchangeably.

Second, we assume that all nonmarket time is spent in the production of commodities, whether the output is a loaf of bread, a clean house, a healthy child, or a game of golf. This approach not only avoids the need for analyzing a three-way choice among market work, housework, and leisure but also makes the often difficult distinction between nonmarket work (including volunteer work) and leisure unnecessary.[10] We do not wish to suggest, however, that in reality there is no difference between the two. Indeed, one of the concerns about the impact

---

[8]Again, the underpinnings of the analysis are derived from the work of Gary S. Becker ("A Theory of the Allocation of Time," *The Economic Journal* 75, no. 299 (Sept. 1965): 493–517) and Jacob Mincer ("Labor Force Participation of Married Women," ed. H. Gregg Lewis, *Aspects of Labor Economics,* Universities National Bureau of Economic Research Conference Studies, no. 14, Princeton, NJ: Princeton University Press, 1962, pp. 63–97). Major early empirical work on this topic includes Glen G. Cain, *Married Women in the Labor Force* (Chicago: University of Chicago Press, 1966) and William Bowen and T. Aldrich Finegan, *The Economics of Labor Force Participation* (Princeton, NJ: Princeton University Press, 1969). Both Reuben Gronau and James Heckman have contributed greatly to the development of statistical techniques for estimating the theoretical relationships; see, for example, the collection of papers in James P. Smith, ed., *Female Labor Supply: Theory and Estimation* (Princeton, NJ: Princeton University Press, 1980).

[9]Students who have read the Appendix to Chapter 3, where a graphical analysis of specialization and exchange was presented, will recognize that the basic approach employed here is quite similar. However, in this analysis, we do not need to make the rigid distinction between home goods (produced exclusively with inputs of home time) and market goods (produced entirely with market purchased goods) that was used to simplify the analysis in the Appendix to Chapter 3. Indeed, not only can we recognize that market goods and nonmarket time are both inputs into the production of commodities, but also that there may, in many, though not in all, instances, be more than one way to produce the same commodity.

[10]Market work is relatively easy to distinguish as any activity for which there is material, usually monetary, reward. But it is quite problematic to determine whether preparation of a gourmet meal, going to a League of Women Voters meeting, growing flowers, or taking a child for a walk is work or leisure.

of married women's increased labor force participation on their welfare is that it has not been accompanied by a comparable reallocation of household chores. As a result, women are often saddled with the "double burden" of home and market work. This may reduce the leisure time available to them, impede their ability to compete with men in the labor market, or both. These issues were examined more closely in Chapter 3.

Third, and perhaps even more crucially, we focus here on the individual rather than on the family as a whole. Although this is quite realistic when the individual is the only adult in the family, we saw in Chapter 3 that, where more than one adult is present, the division of labor among them, and thus the labor supply decision of each, is reasonably expected to be a family decision. However, we cannot introduce all the complexities of family decision making without causing the exposition to become unduly complex and unwieldy. We do continue to view the individual in a family context by taking into account the impact of the earnings of other family members on each person's labor supply decision, but the labor supply of other members of the household is taken as given and is assumed not to be influenced by the individual's own choice. This assumption is probably not too unreasonable when we consider women's labor supply decisions since, in most American families, husbands are likely to remain in the labor market full-time in any case.[11]

Since both market goods and nonmarket time are used in the production of the commodities from which the individual derives satisfaction, his or her task is to select the utility-maximizing combination of market goods and nonmarket time. Since market goods are purchased with income earned by market work, and all time available is spent either on market work or nonmarket activities, this is the basis of the labor supply decision. In making this choice, the individual must take into account both the options that are open to him or her, given by the *budget constraint* shown in panel a of Figure 4.3, and his or her tastes or preferences expressed in the family of *indifference curves* shown in panel b of Figure 4.3. Let us trace out this decision for the hypothetical case of a married woman named Mary.

The Budget Constraint

The budget constraint shown in panel a gives the various combinations of nonmarket time and market goods Mary has at her disposal, given her potential market wage rate and the nonlabor income available to her. By nonlabor income we mean income other than her own earnings and, hence, unrelated to the amount of time she devotes to the labor market. This may include her husband's earnings, as well as income from interest, dividends, or rental property. Government transfer

---

[11] However, the willingness of husbands to do overtime work and their selection of a job with longer (e.g., 40) vs. shorter (e.g., 37.5) full-time hours are more likely to be affected by their wife's labor force participation and earnings. Further, the labor supply decisions of other family members, such as older children or grandparents, are likely to be more sensitive to the wife's labor supply decision.

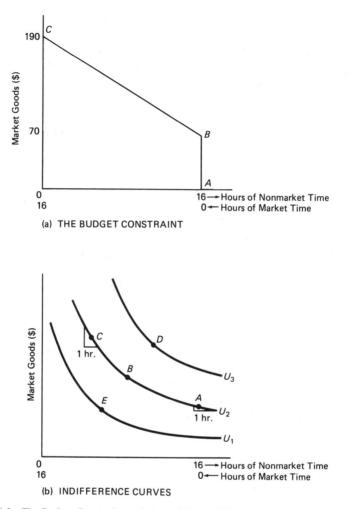

FIGURE 4.3 The Budget Constraint and the Indifference Curves

payments, such as welfare or unemployment insurance, for example, may also be considered nonlabor income, although the amount of income received from such sources is influenced by the amount of time a person supplies to the labor market. Hours of *nonmarket time* are measured from left to right along the horizontal axis. We assume that Mary has a total of 16 hours available to her in a day to allocate between market and nonmarket activities (allowing 8 hours for nondiscretionary activities like sleeping). Since any of this time that Mary does not spend in non-market activities is spent in the market, hours of *market time* are measured from right to left along the horizontal axis.

Mary's nonlabor income is $70 a day. The vertical segment *BA* of the budget constraint shows that Mary has this income available to her even if she supplies no time to the labor market. She may further increase her money income by participating in the labor force. For each additional hour she supplies to the market, she must give up an hour of nonmarket time. In return she receives $7.50, her hourly market wage (w). Thus, segment *CB* is negatively sloped. Its slope is equal to -7.5 or $-w$. If Mary devotes all her time to the market, her total earnings will be $120 ($7.5 \times 16$). Her total income, including her nonlabor income, will be $190 ($120 + $70).

Indifference Curves

Mary's preferences for market goods and nonmarket time are represented by her indifference map, shown in panel b. As discussed above, we can incorporate the family context of decision making into the budget constraint by including the income of other family members as part of the individual's nonlabor income. The matter is thornier when we consider the indifference curves. One possibility would be to view the indifference curves in Figure 4.3 as representing the family's preferences for various combinations of market goods and Mary's nonmarket time. We do not adopt this approach because, as we saw in Chapter 3, preferences among family members may differ, and the process of arriving at family decisions is complex. However, it is important to recognize that our discussion of indifference curves as representing the individual's preferences is only an approximation. In fact, we expect that the individual's decisions are made in the context of the family and that the preferences of other family members have been taken into account in the decision-making process. Bearing this in mind, we now take a closer look at the indifference curves.

Suppose Mary is told that she could have the combination of market goods and nonmarket time represented by point *B*. She is then asked to find various other combinations of market goods and nonmarket time from which she would get exactly the same amount of satisfaction or utility. She then identifies the combinations represented by points *A* and *C*. These and other points, which represent equal satisfaction, can all be connected into one indifference curve, called that because she is indifferent about being at various points on the curve. Thus, each indifference curve indicates the various combinations of market goods and nonmarket time that provide Mary with the same amount of utility or satisfaction.

Mary, however, has not just one indifference curve, but a whole family of higher or lower curves. A point like *D* on indifference curve U_3 is clearly preferable to *B* since it offers more of both market goods and nonmarket time. Thus, by extension, all points on U_3 are preferred to all points on U_2. Similarly, *B* is preferred to *E* and, thus, all the points on U_2 are preferred to all the points on

U_1.[12] As we move out from the origin in a northeasterly direction, consumption possibilities, and thus potential satisfaction, increase.

Indifference curves are generally assumed to be convex to the origin. That is, they become flatter as we move from left to right and steeper as we move from right to left. This is the case because it is believed that individuals generally value relatively scarcer commodities more highly than relatively more plentiful ones. At point A, where nonmarket time is relatively plentiful and market goods are relatively scarce, Mary would be willing to exchange an hour of nonmarket time for a relatively small amount of income (market goods) and still feel equally well-off. However, at a point like C, where market goods are relatively plentiful, it would take a lot of income (market goods) to induce her to give up an additional hour of scarce nonmarket time.

It is interesting to consider more closely the way in which an individual like Mary may substitute market goods for nonmarket time (or vice versa) along an indifference curve while still remaining equally well off. It is important to recognize that we assume she does not derive satisfaction directly from market goods and nonmarket time. Rather, she values them only insofar as they can be used to produce commodities.[13] Thus, broadly speaking, two types of substitution are involved.

Substitution in consumption. Some commodities are relatively *goods intensive* to produce. That is, they are produced using relatively large amounts of market goods and relatively little nonmarket time. Examples of these include buying expensive antiques, furniture, and clothing or recreational activities such as dining out at an elegant restaurant or flying to the Riviera for a short vacation.

Other commodities are relatively *time intensive*. That is, they are produced using relatively large inputs of nonmarket time and relatively fewer inputs of market goods. Examples of these include recreational activities like hiking, bird watching, going to a baseball game, or taking a cycling trip across the country. Also, as anyone who has spent time caring for youngsters can attest, small children are a relatively time-intensive "commodity."

Substitution in production. In many instances, the same commodity can be produced using a relatively time-intensive technique or a relatively goods-intensive technique. For example, a meal may be prepared from scratch at home, made with the use of convenience foods, or purchased at a restaurant. A clean house may be

---

[12]It should be clear that indifference curves can never intersect. All points on any one curve represent an equal amount of utility while any point above (below) represents a larger (smaller) amount of utility. At the point where two curves intersect, they clearly represent the same utility. Yet at all other points they do not. This is a logical impossibility.

[13]Students who read the Appendix to Chapter 3 will recognize that this was not the case in the analysis presented there. In that case, families derived utility directly from market and home goods. The indifference curves used in this chapter are a graphical representation of what has been termed the individual's "indirect utility function." See Becker, "A Theory of the Allocation of Time."

produced by an individual doing the work himself or herself or by hiring cleaning help. A small child may be cared for entirely by a parent, have a babysitter for a few hours a day, or spend all day at a child care center.

As an individual like Mary moves from point A to point B to point C along indifference curve U_2 in Figure 4.3, she will exploit opportunities for substitution in consumption and production. That is, she will substitute goods-intensive commodities for time-intensive commodities, and/or goods-intensive for time-intensive production techniques. As she continues to do so, she will exhaust many of the obvious possibilities. It will take larger increments of market goods to induce her to part with her scarcer nonmarket time. This is why the indifference curves are believed to get steeper as we move from right to left.

Substitution between market goods and nonmarket time. Comparing across individuals, the steepness of the indifference curve is influenced by how difficult or easy it is for them to substitute market goods for nonmarket time while remaining equally well-off. This, in turn, will depend on their opportunities for substituting one for the other in production or consumption, or both. For example, those who enjoy hiking very much will not easily be induced to decrease the time they spend on it. They will have steeper indifference curves, reflecting that they have greater difficulty in substituting market goods for nonmarket time in consumption than those who care less for such time-intensive activities.

Similarly, we would expect those whose services are in greater demand in the home (say, because small children are present) to have steeper indifference curves, reflecting their greater difficulty in substituting market goods for nonmarket time in production. Tastes and preferences will be a factor here, too. People who feel very strongly that children should be cared for full-time by their own parent and that alternative care is an extremely poor substitute will have steeper indifference curves than those who believe that adequate alternative care can be provided.

This analysis assumes that there is some degree of substitutability between market goods and nonmarket time. However, it has been pointed out, quite correctly, that there are some commodities that cannot be purchased in the market. Various personal services and management tasks provided in the home may be of this nature. Similarly, there are some commodities available in the market that cannot be produced at home. Examples of this range from sophisticated medical care and advanced education to means of transportation and communication, insurance, and many consumer durables.[14] Nonetheless, it is highly likely that when all commodities are aggregated together (as in the indifference curves shown in Figure 4.3) some substitution possibilities between market goods and nonmarket time exist. Given that, the ease or difficulty of substitution is represented by the steepness of the indifference curves.

---

[14]Clair (Vickery) Brown, "Home Production for Use in a Market Economy," in *Rethinking the Family: Some Feminist Questions,* Barrie Thorne, ed. (New York: Longman, Inc., 1981).

Tastes. Beyond considerations of this kind, economists generally do not analyze the determinants of individuals' preferences for income (market goods) versus nonmarket time. However, it is important to point out that individuals do not operate in a social vacuum. Their tastes and behavior are undoubtedly influenced by social attitudes and norms.[15] For example, the willingness of a woman to substitute purchased services for her own time in child care is undoubtedly influenced by the social acceptability of doing so. Yet it is probably true that attitudes follow behavior to some extent, as well. Thus, it is likely, for example, that it has become more acceptable for mothers of small children to work outside the home in part because it has become more common for them to do so, as well as vice versa.

A woman's relative preference for income (market goods) versus nonmarket time reflects a variety of other factors not generally emphasized by economists. As we saw in Chapter 3, women may value earning their own income for the economic independence it brings and to enhance their relative power position in the family. An increasing number of women value career success in much the same way their male counterparts do, which also affects the shape of their indifference curves.

Although such considerations do not invalidate the use of this model in analyzing women's labor supply decisions, they do serve to make us aware that the term *tastes* (or preferences), as economists use it, covers a lot of ground. This is particularly important as we attempt to explain women's rising labor force participation over time.

The Participation Decision

Let's suppose that Mary's indifference curves and her budget constraint are shown in panel a of Figure 4.4. Mary will maximize utility or satisfaction at point Y where the budget constraint just touches the highest possible indifference curve, U_2. At Y, the amount of income she is willing to accept to give up an additional hour of nonmarket time, given by the slope of the indifference curve at Y, exactly equals the market wage she is offered for that hour, given by the slope of the budget constraint. Mary, therefore, supplies 8 hours per day to the market and spends 8 hours on nonmarket activities. Her daily earnings of $60 ($7.50 × 8) plus her daily nonlabor income of $70 give her (and her family) a total income of $130 per day.

It is interesting to compare the situation at point Y to that at point A, where Mary would supply no time to the labor market. At A, indifference curve U_1 is *flatter* than the budget constraint. This means that Mary values her nonmarket time *less* than the wage the market is willing to pay her for it. Thus, she will certainly choose to supply some time to the market.

Another woman, Joyce, faces the same budget constraint as Mary but has steeper indifference curves (shown in panel b of Figure 4.4). She may have more

---

[15]The importance of social norms is particularly emphasized by Clair Brown, "Consumption Norms, Work Roles, and Economic Growth," in *Gender in the Workplace,* Clair V. Brown and Joseph Pechman, eds. (Washington, DC: Brookings Institution, 1987), pp. 13–58.

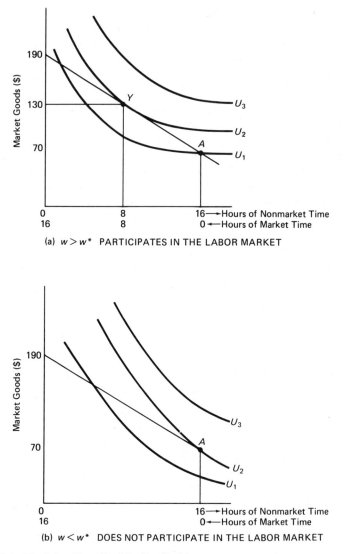

(a) $w > w^*$ PARTICIPATES IN THE LABOR MARKET

(b) $w < w^*$ DOES NOT PARTICIPATE IN THE LABOR MARKET

FIGURE 4.4 The Labor Force Participation Decision

young children to care for than Mary does. In Joyce's case, the budget constraint touches the highest possible indifference curve at point *A*, where the indifference curve is steeper than the budget constraint. This means that Joyce sets a *higher* value on her nonmarket time than does the market. She will maximize her utility by remaining out of the labor force, spending all 16 hours available to her on nonmarket activities. Her consumption of market goods will be limited to her nonlabor income of $70 per day.

The slope of the indifference curve at zero hours of market work (point *A* in panels a and b of Figure 4.4) is termed the **reservation wage** (w^*). It is equal to the value the woman places on her time at home. If the market wage (w) is greater than the reservation wage (w^*), as in panel a, the individual will choose to participate in the labor market. If the market wage (w) is less than the reservation wage (w^*), as in panel b, the individual will choose not to participate in the labor market. Factors that increase w, or the value of market time, while all else remains equal, tend to increase the probability that the individual will choose to participate in the labor force. That is, labor force participation is *positively related* to the wage or the value of market time. On the other hand, factors that increase the value of nonmarket time (w^*) tend to lower the probability of labor force participation, other things being equal. That is, labor force participation is *negatively related* to w^* or the value of nonmarket time.

The Value of Nonmarket Time *(w*)*

As our previous discussion suggests, the value of nonmarket time is influenced by tastes and preferences and also by the demands placed on an individual's nonmarket time. Given the traditional division of labor in most families, the presence of small children, and other circumstances that increase the need for housework, particularly influence women's participation decisions. Over time, the availability of good market substitutes for home time would be a potential factor increasing women's labor force participation.

Another factor that influences the value placed on nonmarket time is the availability of income from sources other than the individual's own work efforts. Figure 4.5 shows the impact of changes in nonlabor income on the labor force participation decision. Let's suppose that the figure represents the budget constraint and indifference curves for Susan, a married woman with two small children. Suppose that her husband is unemployed and that initially her budget constraint is *ABC*. This represents $30 of nonlabor income (from interest on some bonds the family owns) and her market wage of $7.50. She maximizes utility at point *D*, where she supplies five hours a day to the market and earns $37.50. This brings the family's total daily income to $67.50. Now suppose Susan's husband finds a job. When his earnings ($50) are added to the interest received from the bonds ($30), her nonlabor income becomes $80. Her new budget constraint is *AB'C'*. Note that segment *B'C'* is parallel to (has the same slope as) segment *BC*. This is because Susan's (potential) market wage rate remains unchanged at $7.50.

At the higher income level, Susan's consumption possibilities have increased, and she is able to reach a higher indifference curve. She maximizes utility at *B'* where she consumes more of both market goods and nonmarket time, and supplies less time to the market; in fact, she withdraws from the labor force entirely. This represents the impact of the **income effect.** Ordinarily, as a person has more income, he or she will demand more of a variety of good things. To the extent that nonmarket time is used to produce them, higher income will increase the value of nonmarket

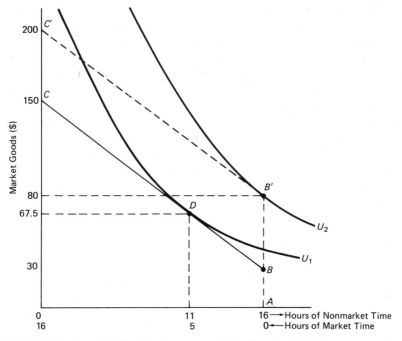

FIGURE 4.5 The Impact of Nonlabor Income on Labor Force Participation

time and result in the person choosing to spend less time in the labor market. The income effect will be relatively large when the demand for time-intensive commodities increases sharply with income. The individual then needs to transfer more time from market to nonmarket activities in order to produce them. This is likely to occur when market goods are not considered to be very good substitutes for home-produced items. So Susan, whose wage rate has not changed while her income increased, may choose to consume more recreation, spend more time caring for her children, or possibly even to bake more cakes and pies.

Table 4.4 illustrates the impact of the value of nonmarket time ($w*$) on women's labor force participation decisions. Marital status reflects in part the availability and level of alternative sources of income. Thus, we see that women who are married and whose spouse is present are generally less likely to work outside the home than those in other marital status categories. (The low overall participation rate of other ever-married women (including widows) is largely due to their being on average an older population, many of retirement age.) Further, studies have found that within the married, spouse-present group, labor force participation is negatively related to husband's income, all else being equal.[16]

___

[16]See, for example, the studies reported in James P. Smith, ed., *Female Labor Supply*. The negative relationship between wife's participation and husband's income is not fully revealed in simple tabulations, because of the impact of other variables. In particular, wife's education is positively associated with both husband's income and wife's labor force participation.

TABLE 4.4 **Labor Force Participation Rates of Women by Marital Status, and Presence and Age of Youngest Child, 1966 and 1988**[a]

Marital Status	Total	No Children Under 18	Children 6-17, None Younger	Children 3-5, None Under 3	Children Under 3
1966					
Never married	40.8	n.a.	n.a.	n.a.	n.a.
Married, husband present	35.4	38.4	43.7	29.1	21.2
Other ever married	39.5	34.7	65.9	57.5	38.6
1988					
Never married	65.2	67.3	67.1	53.9	40.1
Married, husband present	56.5	48.9	72.5	61.2	54.5
Other ever married	46.1	38.1	77.5	67.0	52.4

[a]Data are for March of each year and include women 16 years of age and over in 1988 and 14 years of age and over in 1966.

n.a. = Not available.

Source: U.S. Department of Labor, Bureau of Labor Statistics, *Special Labor Force Report, no. 2163,* Table B-5, p. 16 and U.S. Department of Labor, Bureau of Labor Statistics, Bull. 2340 (August 1989), Tables 55–57, pp. 235–44.

Within each marital status category, we see that the presence of small children deters women's participation, because they greatly increase the value of time spent at home. (The lower participation rates for most groups with no children under 18 reflect the higher average age of women in that category.) Of course, the causation may, to some extent, run in the opposite direction. That is, women who are more committed to the labor market and/or face more attractive labor market opportunities may choose to have fewer children. Evidence suggests both that such reverse causation does exist and that the presence of children also has a negative effect on women's labor force participation.[17]

Table 4.4 also shows that, although marital status and presence of children continued to be important determinants of women's labor force participation, married women (husband present) and those with small children were considerably more likely to work outside the home in 1988 than in the 1960s. For example, in 1988, 55 percent of married women with children under three years old were in the labor market, compared to only 21 percent in 1966. Similarly, 61 percent of married women with children between the ages of three and five were labor force participants in 1988, compared to 29 percent in 1966.

[17]For efforts to disentangle this complex causation, see Glen Cain and Martin Dooley, "Estimation of a Model of Labor Supply, Fertility and Wages of Married Women," *Journal of Political Economy* 84, no. 4, pt. 2 (August 1976): S179–S200; Belton M. Fleisher and George F. Rhodes, Jr., "Fertility, Woman's Wage Rates and Labor Supply," *American Economic Review* 69, no. 1 (March 1979): 14–24; and Linda J. Waite and Rafe M. Stolzenberg, "Intended Childbearing and Labor Force Participation of Young Women: Insights from Nonrecursive Models," *American Sociological Review* 41, no. 2 (April 1976): 232–52.

Policy Issue:
Government Subsidy of Child Care[18]

As we have seen, young children are still a significant deterrent to the entry of their mothers into the labor market. At the same time, the labor force participation rate among these women has been increasing more rapidly than for any other group. Hence, availability of suitable and affordable child care is an important issue because it would encourage more young women to enter and stay in the labor market, and because the children of mothers who are employed in any case will be better cared for.

Public policy encouraging and subsidizing purchased child care could increase its supply and reduce its cost. Official approval might also increase its social acceptability. The crucial questions are whether and how this should be done. The outlays involved are potentially very large, and there is little agreement about who should bear them. The effects on fertility and child development must also be considered. These issues will be discussed in Chapter 9. It may be noted that available evidence, with respect to the effect of various types of care on children's development, provides little reason for concern about unfavorable effects of high quality substitutes for family care. Unfortunately, not all child care is of high quality.

In the meantime, the short-run effect of subsidizing child care on labor force participation is quite clear. Suppose panel b of Figure 4.4 represents the situation of Nancy, a woman with small children, before the government subsidy. As we can see, she chooses not to participate in the labor force. When suitable child care becomes available at a lower cost, Nancy's home time becomes relatively less valuable. This is shown by the flatter indifference curves in panel a. In this particular example, the government subsidy results in Nancy deciding to enter the labor force. In general, we would expect the availability of child care at a lower price to increase the labor force participation rate of women with small children.

The policy is also likely to have long-run effects on the women who are influenced by it. Because they would experience fewer (and/or shorter) work force interruptions, they would accumulate longer and more continuous labor market experience. This is expected to have a favorable effect on the quality of jobs they are able to obtain, and on their earnings, and would in turn further reinforce the tendency toward spending more time in the labor market. Therefore, in the long run, child care subsidies are likely not only to raise women's labor force participation, but also to enhance their occupational attainment and earnings. Thus, child care subsidies could contribute to a reduction in labor market inequality between men

---

[18]For further consideration of these issues, see James J. Heckman, "Effects of Child Care Programs on Women's Work Effort," *Journal of Political Economy* 82, no. 2 (March/April 1974, supp.): S136–S163; Myra H. Strober, "Formal Extra Family Child Care—Some Economic Observations," in *Sex, Discrimination, and the Division of Labor*, Cynthia B. Lloyd, ed. (New York: Columbia University Press, 1975); and David M. Blau and Philip K. Robins, "Child-Care Costs and Family Labor Supply," *Review of Economics and Statistics* 70, no. 3 (August 1988): 374–81.

and women. Whether or not they are desirable on other grounds is considered in Chapter 9.

The Value of Market Time *(w)*

As discussed earlier, in addition to the impact of the value of nonmarket time, the labor force participation decision is influenced by the labor market opportunities an individual faces, particularly the wage rate available in the labor market. To see this in greater detail, let us consider the case of Ellen, who initially faces the budget constraint, *ABC,* shown in Figure 4.6. Her potential market wage is only $4.50 per hour, while her nonlabor income (say, equal to her husband's earnings) is $40 per day. Given her tastes (indifference map), she maximizes utility at point *B* where she devotes all her time to nonmarket activities. Note that at point *B* the indifference curve is steeper than the budget line *(BC)*—Ellen's reservation wage *(w*)* is higher than the wage rate offered to her by the market *(w)*.

Now suppose that Ellen's market opportunities improve and her potential market wage increases to $8.00. Her new budget constraint is *ABC'*. Segment *BA* of her budget constraint remains unchanged, because it is still the case that if she remains out of the labor market entirely, she (and her family) will receive $40 a day of nonlabor income. However, *BC'* is steeper than *BC* because now she will receive $8.00 for each hour she supplies to the market rather than $4.50. Another way to see this is to realize that *C'* must lie above *C,* because if Ellen devotes all her time to market work her total income will be higher at a wage of $8.00 per hour than it would have been at a wage of $4.50 per hour.

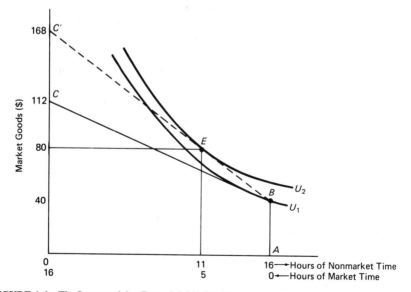

FIGURE 4.6   The Impact of the (Potential) Market Wage on Labor Force Participation

At the higher wage, the budget constraint (BC') is now steeper than the indifference curve at point B—the market wage (w) is greater than the reservation wage (w^*), and Ellen maximizes her utility at point E on indifference curve U_2, where she supplies five hours to the market. Thus, Ellen chooses to participate in the labor force.

This example illustrates the *substitution effect*. An increase in the wage rate, all else being equal, raises the opportunity cost of time spent in nonmarket activities and, hence, the "price" of nonmarket time. Individuals are expected to respond by supplying more time to the market and substituting market goods for nonmarket time in consumption or production. Since the wage increase has clearly enabled Ellen to reach a higher indifference curve, we may conclude that she feels better off with the combination of commodities represented by point E, even though she has less nonmarket time available at E than at B.

Some indication of the impact of the potential market wage on labor force participation may be gained by examining the association between educational attainment and labor force participation (Table 4.5). As we shall see in greater detail in Chapter 7, education appears to increase market productivity and, hence, earnings. This would lead us to expect that education would be positively associated with labor force participation.

For women, in particular, the positive effect of education on labor force participation may be reduced to the extent that additional education also raises the productivity of their nonmarket time. This would be the case if, for example, the time that more-educated women spend with their children contributed more to their children's achievement levels than time spent by less-educated women.

The figures in Table 4.5 suggest, however, that the impact of education on market earnings is greater than on the value of home time. Women with higher levels of education are more likely to be in the labor force. The positive relationship between education and labor force participation may also reflect the fact that younger women who initially plan to spend a relatively high proportion of their mature years in the labor force are more likely to invest in education. Further, given a trend toward rising education attainment, the fact that women at the lowest

TABLE 4.5 Labor Force Participation Rates of Women by Years of Schooling Completed, 1970 and 1988[a]

YEARS OF SCHOOLING COMPLETED	LABOR FORCE PARTICIPATION RATES	
	1970	*1988*
Less than 4 years of high school	43.0	45.4
4 years of high school	51.3	66.9
1–3 years of college	50.9	74.7
4 or more years of college	60.9	80.8

[a]Data are for March of each year and include women aged 25 to 64.

Source: U.S. Department of Labor, Bureau of Labor Statistics, *Handbook of Labor Statistics*, Bull. 2340 (August 1989), Table 66, pp. 282–83.

levels of education have such very low participation rates is in part attributable to the high representation of older individuals among them. Finally, we may note that the jobs held by more educated individuals may have greater nonpecuniary (or nonmonetary) attractions—such as a more pleasant environment, more challenging work, and so on—as well as offering higher wages. This calls attention to the fact that the "value of market work" should ideally take into account not only pecuniary benefits but also other aspects of the job. Table 4.5 also shows that, although education was an important determinant of labor force participation in both 1970 and 1988, participation rates of high school graduates and of college-educated women increased substantially over the period.

Policy Issue:
Taxes and the Decision to Work

As discussed in Chapter 3, not all money earned is actually at the disposal of the worker. Some of it has to be paid out in taxes. Because earnings are taxed and the value of home production is not, labor force participation among married women is discouraged. This effect is increased by the progressive nature of the tax system. Because the family (rather than the individual) is the tax unit, married women, often regarded as secondary earners, face relatively high tax rates on the first dollar of their labor market earnings.

These points may be illustrated by Figure 4.6. Suppose Joan earns $8.00 per hour and faces budget constraint *ABC'*. If we assume she has to pay out 44 percent of her income in taxes, her after-tax wage (or hourly take-home pay) will be only $4.50. This situation is represented by budget constraint *ABC*. Because of this lower wage, Joan chooses to stay out of the labor market.

In general, the higher the tax rate, the lower the after-tax wage and the more likely a woman is to decide not to participate in the labor force. The Tax Reform Act of 1986 reduced the disincentive effects of the federal income tax on married women's labor force participation by making the U.S. tax structure less progressive. For example, the maximum tax rate was lowered from 50 percent prior to 1986 to 31 percent in 1991.[19]

Economic Conditions

Fluctuations in economic conditions also affect labor force participation. These effects are likely to be largest among demographic groups that contain a

---

[19] A more detailed discussion of the tax issue is presented in Chapter 3. Note that the effective marginal tax rate for certain upper-middle-income taxpayers is actually a bit higher than 31 percent because of the loss of some deductions with income increases for this group. Note too that we have simplified the representation of a progressive tax in Figure 4.6 in that we consider only one tax rate. In fact, as long as individuals are below the maximum rate, it is possible that as they work more hours their higher total income will push them into a higher tax bracket. Thus, the after-tax budget constraint may be "kinked," its slope becoming flatter each time the individual enters a higher tax bracket.

relatively high proportion of individuals who are loosely attached to the labor force. This would include teenagers of both sexes, older men, and women. Economists view the response of labor force participation to the changing level of economic activity as being the net result of two opposing effects.

The **added worker effect** predicts that during economic downturns, if the primary earner becomes unemployed, other family members may enter (or postpone their exit from) the labor force in order to maintain family income. Essentially, the decline in their nonlabor income due to the unemployment of the primary earner lowers the value of other family members' nonmarket time (w^*). Such individuals may leave the labor force when economic conditions improve and the primary earner is again employed on a regular basis.

Alternatively, the **discouraged worker effect** holds that during times of high unemployment, when individuals become unemployed, they may become discouraged and drop out of the labor force after a fruitless period of job search. Others who are outside the labor market may postpone labor force entry until economic conditions improve. Discouragement is due to the decline in the perceived reward to market work (w) because of the difficulty of locating an acceptable job. As economic conditions improve, previously discouraged workers may become encouraged and enter the labor force.

Both these effects can operate at the same time for different households. The *net* effect of economic conditions on labor force participation depends on whether the discouraged or added worker effect predominates in the aggregate. This is an empirical question. The data suggest that for the labor force as a whole the discouraged worker effect is probably dominant. One study finds that cyclical sensitivity is particularly pronounced for teenagers, older men, and women under 35. The evidence for older women is less strong. Other researchers report that the cyclical sensitivity of female labor force participation seems to have declined in the 1970s.[20] This finding is consistent with the observation that women are becoming more firmly attached to the labor force, which means they are less likely to move in and out of the labor force with the ups and downs of the business cycle.

THE HOURS DECISION

The impact of a change in the wage rate on the number of hours supplied to the market by those who are already labor force participants is a bit more complex than the impact of a wage change on labor force participation. As may be seen in Figure 4.7, an increase in the wage rate corresponds to a rotation of the budget constraint from CD to CD', since more market goods can now be purchased for every hour

[20] See Kim B. Clark and Lawrence H. Summers, "Demographic Differences in Cyclical Employment Variation," *Journal of Human Resources* 16, no. 1 (Winter 1981): 61–79; and Cynthia B. Lloyd and Beth Niemi, "Sex Differences in Labor Supply Elasticity: The Implications of Sectoral Shifts in Demand," *American Economic Review* 68, no. 2 (May 1978): 78–83.

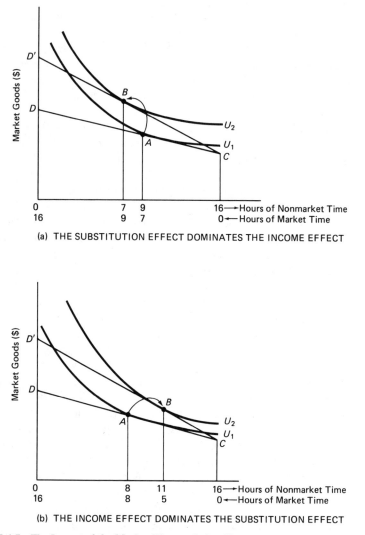

(a) THE SUBSTITUTION EFFECT DOMINATES THE INCOME EFFECT

(b) THE INCOME EFFECT DOMINATES THE SUBSTITUTION EFFECT

FIGURE 4.7   The Impact of the Market Wage on Labor Hours

worked. In both panels a and b, the individual initially maximizes utility at point
A on indifference curve U_1. At a higher wage, he or she is able to reach a higher
indifference curve and selects point B on indifference curve U_2. This may result in
either an increase (panel a) or a decrease (panel b) in hours supplied to the market[21]

___

[21]The diagrammatic representation of the effect of a wage change on work hours is shown in
greater detail in the appendix to this chapter.

because, for those who are labor force participants, an increase in the wage rate has two distinct effects.

On the one hand, the increase in the wage is in one respect like an increase in their income. For any given amount of time supplied to the market *greater than 0 hours,* income is higher along *CD'* than along *CD,* as shown by the fact that higher indifference curves can be reached. This gives rise to an **income effect** that, other things being the same, increases the demand not only for most market goods, but also for nonmarket time, and tends to lower the hours supplied to the market. The increase in the wage, however, also raises the opportunity cost of nonmarket time in terms of market goods that could be purchased. This results in a **substitution effect** that, other things being the same, would cause a reduction in nonmarket time and an increase in the supply of hours to the market.

Thus, when the wage rate rises, the substitution effect will work to increase labor hours supplied, but the income effect will work to reduce labor hours supplied. The net effect is theoretically indeterminate. If the substitution effect dominates the income effect, work hours are increased (panel a). If the income effect dominates the substitution effect, work hours are reduced (panel b). Again, it may be recalled that a wage increase unambiguously raises the probability of labor force participation because, in this case, there is no offsetting income effect, but only a positive substitution effect.

With respect to the hours decision, empirical evidence indicates that, for men, the income effect generally tends to offset or even dominate the substitution effect and that they do not decrease, or may even increase, the amount of nonmarket time as their wage rate goes up. This may be the case because, as a group, men generally have worked full-time in the market and have traditionally devoted most of their nonmarket time to recreation rather than other types of household production. Although it is possible to substitute market goods for nonmarket time in recreational activities, these possibilities are necessarily limited. Thus for men, the substitution effect is likely to be no greater than the income effect.

The situation is quite different for women. For the most part, women spend a great deal of nonmarket time doing housework. This means that they may substitute market work for housework, rather than for recreational activities. To the extent that purchased goods and services are useful substitutes for nonmarket time in producing the commodities the family wants, an increase in the wage rate is very likely to have that result. Hence, the substitution effect is more likely to dominate for women than men. Even so, the situation is complex and empirical findings differ depending on the group studied.[22] Findings also differ depending on whether the

---

[22]Black and white wives were found to respond differently to changes in take-home pay (Jane H. Leuthold, "The Effect of Taxation on the Probability of Labor Force Participation by Married Women," *Public Finance* 33, no. 3 [August 1978]: 280–94) and to varying work incentives provided by AFDC (Frank Levy, "The Labor Supply of Female Household Heads, or AFDC Incentives Don't Work Too Well," *Journal of Human Resources* 14, no. 1 [Winter 1979]: 76–97).

concern is with labor force participation or number of hours worked[23] and whether the focus is on labor supply at a point in time or over the whole life cycle.[24] Nonetheless, empirical studies for the most part find that women's labor supply is strongly positively related to the wage rate,[25] confirming the dominance of the substitution effect.

ANALYZING TRENDS IN WOMEN'S PARTICIPATION: AN OVERVIEW

Having examined how the labor supply decision is made will help us to better understand why women's labor force participation has developed as it has over time. In this section, we give an overview of the factors responsible for the long-term increase in women's labor force participation with industrialization. In the following sections, we take a closer look at a number of subperiods of particular interest.

Why has female labor force participation been rising over the course of the present century? Drawing upon the analysis presented earlier in this chapter, the obvious answer to this question is that a shift toward more market work by women can be explained by a rise in the wage rate (w) or a decrease in the value of time spent in the home (w^*). There is considerable evidence of developments that would be expected to have these effects and also of complex interactions, reinforcing the original results.[26]

[23] As we have seen, an increase in wages always increases the probability that an individual will be in the labor market but, because of the income effect working in the opposite direction, will not necessarily have a positive effect on the number of hours worked.

[24] A thorough discussion of why the two are not the same is found in James J. Heckman, "A Partial Survey of Recent Research on the Labor Supply of Women," *American Economic Review* 68, no. 2 (May 1978): 200–207.

[25] This is the case both for studies that investigate the gross effect of wage changes and even more so for those that estimate the net effect when the change in income is compensated for. Among the former are Orley Ashenfelter and James J. Heckmann, "The Estimation of Income and Substitution Effects in a Model of Family Labor Supply," *Econometrica* 42, no. 1 (January 1974): 73–85; Michael J. Boskin, "The Economics of Labor Supply," in *Income Maintenance and Labor Supply,* G. G. Cain and H. W. Watts, eds. (Chicago: Markham, 1973), pp. 163–81; Robert E. Hall, "Wages, Income and Hours of Work in the U.S. Labor Force," in *Income Maintenance,* Cain and Watts, eds., pp. 102–62. Among the latter are Ashenfelter and Heckman, "The Estimation of Income and Substitution Effects"; Boskin, "The Economics of Labor Supply"; Jane H. Leuthold, "An Empirical Study of Formula Income Transfers and the Work Decision of the Poor," *Journal of Human Resources* 3, no. 3 (Fall 1968): 312–23. For a helpful review of the empirical findings, see Mark R. Killingsworth, *Labor Supply* (Cambridge: Cambridge University Press, 1983).

[26] See Goldin, *Understanding the Gender Gap* for an interesting econometric analysis of these trends in labor force participation.

THE CONTRIBUTION OF NONMARKET PRODUCTION
TO GROSS NATIONAL PRODUCT

Gross National Product (GNP) is the total money value of all the goods and services produced in the economy over a one-year period. No one doubts that unpaid activities like housework and volunteer work are valuable to households and to the community, but at the present time these contributions are not included in GNP. The results of this omission are potentially serious. GNP is considerably underestimated. Comparisons of GNP between countries are distorted to the extent that the relative size of household and market sectors differ. Finally, within a country, the growth in GNP is overstated if women reduce home production as they work more in the labor market.

A major obstacle to including these contributions in GNP is lack of agreement on an acceptable way to estimate the value of time spent in nonmarket production.* There are two fundamentally different methods, each with its own strengths and drawbacks. One is the **opportunity cost approach,** which sets the value of unpaid work equal to the income the person could earn in the labor market. It meshes well with the theory of labor supply in which individuals who participate in the labor force equate the value of nonmarket time to the market wage rate. For individuals who do not participate in the labor market, the value of nonmarket time must be at least as great as the potential market wage.

However, despite its theoretical appeal, there are a number of difficulties with this approach. First, for those who are out of the labor force, we have the nontrivial problem of estimating their potential market earnings. Second, although the market wage is known for those who are employed, the presumption that it accurately represents the value of nonmarket time may not be correct. Many workers do not have the option of working precisely as long as they wish but must work a specified number of hours or forgo an otherwise desirable job. Hence, they may not be able to divide their time so that the value of the last hour spent at home is exactly equal to their wage rate.

In addition to these problems, while correct application of the opportunity cost approach may identify the value of the nonmarket production to individuals and their families, it results in a higher value being placed on the nonmarket production of those whose (potential) *market* productivity is higher. So, for example, an hour spent scrubbing floors by a college graduate is valued more highly than an hour spent by a high school graduate in the same activity. This is the case even if the quantity and quality of their *nonmarket* production is identical. Such estimates are, therefore, not entirely acceptable.

The main alternative to the opportunity cost approach is the so-called **market cost approach,** which sets the value of nonmarket production equal to the cost of hiring someone to do it. This method is not free of difficulties either. The main one is the need to make sure that the purchased item is of equal quality and, for that matter, that it is possible to purchase it. What qualifications must a housecleaner, a cook, a gardener, and a babysitter have to adequately replace the services of a homemaker and parent? Is it possible to delegate such tasks as directing children's upbringing and planning and budgeting for the household?

One approach to estimating market value is to first determine how much time is spent on each individual activity, itself a very difficult task, and then to use the wages of such

---

*For a thorough review of the literature on this subject, see Luisella Goldschmidt-Clermont, *Unpaid Work in the Household: A Review of Economic Evaluation Methods* (Geneva: International Labor Office, 1982). For a fuller consideration of some of the theoretical issues, see Carmel U. Chiswick, "The Value of a Housewife's Time," *Journal of Human Resources* 17, no. 3 (Summer 1982): 413–25.

specialists as cooks, home decorators, chauffeurs, and even child psychologists to estimate the value of nonmarket time. However, this is unrealistic in that it is unlikely that the typical homemaker has all these skills to the same extent that such specialists do. Another alternative is to value unpaid home work at the wage of a domestic worker. But this is not likely to satisfy everyone, especially traditionalists who believe that "a loving wife and mother" will do the job better than any hired help.

Despite these difficulties, both the opportunity cost and the market cost approach have yielded useful estimates of the value of nonmarket production. These estimates suggest that the extent to which we understate GNP by ignoring nonmarket output is 25 percent or more. This also gives some idea of the extent to which real incomes of families are underestimated and their relative size distorted when, as under our current federal income tax laws, the value of nonmarket production (particularly of full-time homemakers) is not included.

Factors Influencing the
Value of Market Time *(w)*

A variety of factors caused the real (inflation-adjusted) wages of women to increase over time. The result was a rotation of the budget constraint as shown in Figure 4.6. Under these circumstances, more women would be expected to find that the wage offered them by the market exceeded their reservation wage and to choose to enter the labor force.

Education. As young women received more education, the wage rate they were able to earn by working in the market also went up and they were more likely to work outside the home. At the same time, once women were more inclined to work for pay, they were likely to want to obtain more market-oriented schooling in order to be able to obtain better-paying jobs.

The magnitude of this phenomenon can be gauged by the enormous increases in the proportion of the population that graduated from high school or obtained college degrees. Between 1940 and 1987, the proportion of women who had completed at least four years of high school increased from 26 to 75 percent. The increase for men was even greater, from 22 to 76 percent, since initially women were more likely to graduate high school than men.[27] During this same period, the proportion of women who completed four or more years of college increased from 3.7 to 16.5 percent, whereas for men the proportion rose from 5.4 to 23.6 percent.

The statistics for higher education reflect the fact that traditionally, more young men than young women completed college and pursued graduate study. However, the gender differential has declined since the late 1960s. Women have

---

[27] The gender difference was even more pronounced earlier in the century. In 1900 only two-thirds as many boys as girls graduated from high school.

been increasing their share of college, graduate, and professional degrees, as well as their representation in traditionally male fields of study. (Data on this are presented in Chapter 6). Hence, although men's educational attainment has also increased over time, gender differences in patterns of educational attainment have narrowed dramatically.

A second development that increased the returns to education was the growing number of years women could expect to live. Life expectancy at birth for women went up from 48 years at the turn of the century to over 78 years in 1987. By that time, a woman aged 20 could expect to live 59 more years. Though most individuals retire by age 65, this increase in life expectancy meant that women were able to reap considerably higher rewards for education and on-the-job training over their lifetime, even if they took some time out for homemaking. As women responded to this increased incentive to invest in education and on-the-job training, their potential lifetime market earnings were increased. The effect was much the same as that of an increase in the wage rate, raising the opportunity cost of nonmarket activities and, thus, increasing labor force participation.

The demand for female labor. It is also frequently suggested that, first with industrialization and then with the movement to the post-industrial economy, the demand for workers in traditionally female clerical and service jobs increased and caused their wages to be higher than they otherwise would have been. The fact that women's occupations, and more recently sex-integrated occupations, have increased more rapidly than male occupations tends to support this view.[28] As discussed in Chapter 2, since married women were barred from clerical employment by many large firms in the 1920s and 1930s, they did not fully benefit from this expansion in demand until the marriage bars were abandoned in the 1950s.[29] It is also quite likely that antidiscrimination legislation has increased the demand for women in traditionally male jobs since its passage in the mid-1960s.

Overall productivity increases. Women, like male workers, have benefited from increases in labor productivity due to growth over time in the capital stock and technological change. This also exerted upward pressure on women's wages, all else being equal.

---

[28] Valerie Oppenheimer, *The Female Labor Force in the United States: Demographic and Economic Factors Governing its Growth and Changing Composition* (Westport, CT: Greenwood Press, 1976; orig. publ. 1970) was the first to emphasize the expansion of female occupations. June O'Neill, "The Trend in the Sex Differential in Wages," was among those to point to the increase in mixed occupations.

[29] Goldin, *Understanding the Gender Gap.* Both Oppenheimer and Goldin attribute the increased willingness of employers to hire older married women in the 1950s to a decrease in the supply of young, single female workers. This was due to the small size of the cohort born during the 1930s coupled with the decline in the marriage age that occurred during the 1950s.

Factors Influencing
the Value of Nonmarket Time (w^*)

It would be a mistake, however, to ascribe the impetus for the persistent influx of women into the labor market entirely to higher wage rates and to overlook those changes that influenced the relative value of nonmarket time. The net result of these factors was to lower the value of nonmarket time relative to market time and, thus, to raise the proportions of women working for pay.

Availability of market substitutes. Among the most obvious of these was the increase in the availability of goods and services that had previously been produced in the home but that became increasingly available for purchase in the market. Not only did fruits and vegetables, in earlier days grown in the family garden, come to be available at the grocery, but in time they were cleaned, canned, frozen, and eventually often included in prepared dishes or even meals. First yarn, earlier spun at home, became commonly available; next it was cloth, and then ready-made clothing, now most often of the easy-care variety. Appliances, from sewing machines, central heating, vacuum cleaners, and electric kitchen ranges to washing machines and dishwashers, became increasingly common in U.S. households. Schools extended the hours and years of care provided. For young children, nursery schools and, recently, day-care centers became more prevalent, while hospitals increasingly care for the sick, and various types of care for the infirm and aged are becoming more common.

These are only a few examples of commodities that in earlier days were produced with large inputs of home time but that today require mainly expenditure of money. Some changes did have the opposite effect, such as the considerably higher cost and greater difficulty of finding domestic help. But by and large, market goods have become more substitutable for nonmarket time. As a result, women would be expected to be more willing to give up time at home in order to be able to do more market work, a change illustrated in Figure 4.4 by the flatter indifference curves shown in panel a as compared to the steeper indifference curves shown in panel b. Thus, we see that the greater availability of goods and services for purchase has resulted in a decrease in the value of women's nonmarket time (w^*) and caused their labor force participation to increase. At the same time, women's rising labor force participation tends to increase the demand for market goods and services that substitute for their time in the home, further encouraging development and production of such products.

Urbanization. Closely related to these changes in households and lifestyles was the growing urbanization of the population. The movement from country to city reduced the opportunity for household production (say, growing and processing vegetables) and increased the convenience of market purchases as well as access to market work. Even leisure activities changed from those that mainly required time—hiking, swimming in the waterhole, and chatting on the front porch—to others that required substantial expenditures—going to the theater, pedaling an exercycle, and watching television.

Demographic trends. Another important change that influenced relative preferences for home vs. market time was the long-run decline in the birth rate alluded to earlier, from 30.1 per 1000 population in 1910 to 15 per 1000 by 1988. Because the rearing of young children, generally considered to be women's responsibility, is very time-intensive, especially in the absence of adequate provision for their care outside the home, their presence used to be one of the strongest barriers to women's entry into the labor market. As we have seen, it is only since the 1960s that mothers of preschoolers are working outside the home to any significant extent, and even now their participation is low relative to that of other groups.

Not only is the period during which there are young children in the home more protracted as their number goes up, but the longer the woman is at home, the less favorable the terms she is likely to encounter in the labor market upon her return, and the more likely she is to remain out permanently. As we have noted, women are, of course, aware of this and to some extent adjust family size to their work plans, as well as vice versa.

Just as women's labor force participation is influenced by, and in turn influences, their fertility, the same is true of marital stability. The divorce rate per 1000 population per year went from 0.9 in 1910 to 4.8 in 1988. At the same time, women's labor force participation rates have been increasing. This is, in part, because divorced women have considerably less nonlabor income and are thus more likely to participate in the labor force. Married women's behavior is affected by rising divorce rates as well. As they have increasingly become aware of the extent to which full-time homemakers are dependent on their spouses for financial support, their preference quite likely has shifted toward market time as a means of safeguarding their standard of living in case of a marital breakup. The other side of the coin is that a two-earner couple can more readily afford to get divorced. The woman can count on her own income, rather than being completely dependent on the often grudging and uncertain support of an ex-husband. The man need not spend resources to fully support, or to avoid support of, an ex-wife.

Rising husband's income. Not all changes have operated in the direction of lowering the value of nonmarket time. In particular, earnings of men have increased more rapidly than the cost of living for most of this century. As the husband's real income goes up, all else being equal, married women's labor force participation is reduced due to the income effect (Figure 4.5). Our previous discussion suggests, however, that, for women, the positive substitution effect of their own rising real wages more than offsets the negative income effect due to the increasing real incomes of their husbands.[30] In addition, since the late 1970s, men's real wages in general have been stagnating, and those of the less-educated and unskilled have been declining in real terms.[31]

Tastes. Over time, the development of many desirable market products that could not be produced efficiently in the home, like automobiles, air conditioning, television and stereos, and most recently personal computers, increased people's preferences for market-produced goods and reduced the relative value placed on nonmarket time.[32]

Last, it is also entirely possible that the trend toward rising female participation rates itself was also responsible for further changes in tastes. To the extent that people tend to be conformist, it was far more difficult for women to enter the labor force when this was the exception than today when it has almost become the rule. Shifting cultural norms, encouraged in part by the example of more women working in the market, have led women to place a higher value on the independence and autonomy that their own earnings bring. Finally, to the extent that people want to keep up with the Joneses in their consumption standards, it takes two paychecks to keep up with the two-earner families of today.

THE WORLD WAR II EXPERIENCE

As noted earlier, during World War II, there was a sharp rise in the female labor force participation rate, particularly among married women. In the immediate post-World War II period, the female participation rate declined sharply, although it remained above pre-War levels (Table 4.1) and began a long-term increase shortly after that. This experience illustrates the importance of economic and social factors in causing changes in female labor force participation.

As men were mobilized for the armed forces and the need for workers rose at the same time, there was a large increase in demand for women to fill the available positions. This increase in labor market opportunities, which included relatively high-paying, traditionally male jobs, increased the potential market wages of women. At the same time, married women were urged to work outside the home to contribute to the war effort. This raised the nonpecuniary benefits of market work for women and lowered their subjective assessment of the value of nonmarket time. In addition, the birth rate, which was already relatively low in the Depression years

---

[30]This was first pointed out by Jacob Mincer in "Labor Force Participation of Married Women." Goldin, *Understanding the Gender Gap,* presents evidence of a declining income elasticity of married women's labor supply over the century.

[31]See Chinhui Juhn, Kevin M. Murphy, and Brooks Pierce, "Wage Inequality and the Rise in Returns to Skill," paper presented at the Conference on Labor Markets in the 1990s, National Bureau of Economic Research, Cambridge, MA, December 1989.

[32]This factor is particularly emphasized by Clair Brown, "Consumption Norms, Work Roles, and Economic Growth."

of the 1930s, remained low during the war because many young men were away in the armed forces.

A further factor that worked to lower the value of home time for married women was that the government and some employers opened day-care centers for children of working mothers.[33] Even though there were not enough places for all such youngsters, this action increased both the supply, and the acceptability, of alternative care of children, at least for the duration of hostilities. Thus, the combination of an increase in the value of market time and a reduction in the value of nonmarket time induced a large increase in the proportion of women working outside the home.

In the immediate post-War period, each of these factors was reversed, helping to bring about the observed decline in participation rates. As men returned to the civilian labor force, many were able to reclaim their former jobs from the women who had held them during the war. This was the case because many union contracts reserved their former jobs for men who had left them for military service. Even in the absence of union agreements, some employers may have voluntarily done this because they felt it was the appropriate recompense for the veteran's wartime contribution. Moreover, whether or not a returning veteran claimed a specific job that had been held by a woman, the influx of returning males into the labor market certainly lowered the demand for women workers.

In addition, social values changed and the employment of married women outside the home was once again frowned upon, now that the wartime emergency was over. Indeed, after enduring the major dislocations of the Great Depression of the 1930s followed by a World War of unprecedented dimensions, there may understandably have been a desire to return to "normalcy," including traditional roles. This swing in attitudes may have also played a role in producing the upsurge in birth rates during the post-War period, discussed in the next section. Finally, when the wartime labor shortage was over, day-care centers were perceived to be no longer needed and were closed. These changes combined to lower the benefits of market work relative to the value of home time and to reduce women's labor force participation rate in the immediate post-World War II period.

The operation of the factors discussed in the preceding section meant that the post-War participation rate, while lower than the wartime peak, exceeded prewar levels. We see the long-term rise in participation rates that followed the war as being primarily due to the fundamental economic and social factors identified above. Yet the wartime experience may well have hastened this process by helping to break

---

[33]Given the public concern, both about stimulating maternal employment in war industries and about possible neglect of children, the federal government provided $52,000,000 during 1941–1943 in matching funds to induce states to provide day-care centers. It has been estimated that 1,600,000 children attended these programs. The best known centers established by large private employers were those by Curtiss-Wright in Buffalo and by Kaiser in Portland. See Bernard Greenblatt, *The Changing Role of Family and State in Child Development.* (San Francisco: Jossey Bass, 1977), pp. 58–60.

down the attitudinal barriers to married women's employment outside the home[34] and giving many women a taste of getting their own income.

THE POST-WORLD WAR II BABY BOOM

As noted above, the long-run downward trend in birth rates was interrupted by the post-World War II baby boom. From 1946 to the mid-1950s, birth rates rose steadily, and they remained at relatively high levels until the early 1960s. Although some of this rise in birth rates was simply a response to the postponement of childbearing that had occurred during the Depression and the war years, much of it did indeed reflect an increase in family size in comparison to earlier periods. At the height of the baby boom, women averaged three births, considerably more than the replacement-level fertility rates of their Depression-era mothers. This means that the decline in the birth rate, which contributed to the rise in female labor force participation over the long run, does not help to explain it during the Baby Boom era.

Why did participation rates increase despite the negative effect of the high birth rate? The first point to be made is that the increase in birth rates would principally affect younger women (under age 35) in the prime childbearing ages, who would be most likely to have small children present. It may be recalled that this was precisely the group for whom labor force participation rates did *not* increase over the 1940 to 1960 period (Figure 4.1). The rising participation rates were primarily due to the entry of older women (over age 35) with school-age or grown children. They were from a generation that benefitted from considerably more education than their elders had received. The rate of high school completion increased from 29 percent in 1930 to 49 percent in 1940. While the baby boom meant that young children would cause mothers to stay home, this was not so as the children grew older and more self-sufficient. Indeed, it might be argued that teenagers, and especially college students, need more money, rather than time.

Second, during this period, economic factors were particularly favorable for rising female participation rates. Real wages were steadily increasing and economic conditions, particularly by current standards, were relatively good.[35] Thus, both the continued rise in participation rates and the pattern of the increase appear explicable in terms of economic and demographic factors.

---

[34]This argument is made by William H. Chafe, in *The American Woman.* For an alternative viewpoint see Goldin, "The Role of World War II in the Rise of Women's Work."

[35]Goldin, *Understanding the Gender Gap,* finds that demand factors, in conjunction with the particularly large wage elasticity of supply that prevailed at that time for married women, largely account for the increase in participation that occurred during this period.

THE 1960s TO THE 1990s:
A PERIOD OF CHANGE

The post-World War II baby boom was followed by a baby bust, during which birth rates fell. By the late 1970s, total fertility rates had fallen below the replacement level and the low rates have continued since that time. In addition, increasing numbers of women began to postpone the birth of their first child into their late 20s, their 30s, or even their early 40s. This pattern of childbearing appears to be associated with stronger attachment to the labor market and a reduction in time spent out of the labor force for childrearing. A further demographic trend that encouraged rising participation rates was the sharp increase in the divorce rate. Currently, it appears to be leveling off but at a very high level. On the basis of past trends, demographers predict that one-half of new marriages will end in divorce. It may be recalled that the younger women (under age 44), who would be most affected by these demographic factors, have posted the largest gains in participation rates since 1960.

During much of the 1960s, rising real wages and relatively low unemployment rates also contributed to the increases in female labor force participation rates. However, during the 1970s and the early 1980s, a stagnating economy resulted in frequent bouts of high unemployment and little progress in real wages. Moreover, while the economy expanded during the mid- to late 1980s, real wages did not increase. This raises the question of why female participation rates continued to rise despite these unfavorable economic conditions.

One obvious explanation is that the positive effect of demographic factors on the participation rate, as well as the continued impact of the other long-run forces we have discussed, outweighed the negative effect of economic conditions. In view of the importance of level of education and presence of young children for women's labor force participation, both the continued increase in years of schooling and the decline in the family size would be expected to have made important contributions. However, one study found that such factors, even together with the effect of the woman's own wage rate, accounted for only about half of the increase in young women's participation rates during the 1970s.[36]

One may speculate that changes in the work expectations of younger women help to explain the portion of their participation increase that was not caused by the above-mentioned factors. It may be recalled that in the pre-World War II period, most women left the labor force permanently upon marriage and childbearing. It is quite likely that the older married women who entered or reentered the labor force during World War II and the early post-War period had not anticipated working during this stage of the life cycle but were drawn into the labor market by prevailing economic and social forces.

---

[36] See David Shapiro and Lois Shaw, "Growth in the Labor Force Attachment of Married Women: Accounting for Changes in the 1970's," *Southern Economic Journal* 50, no. 2 (October 1983): 461–73.

As the reentry pattern of labor force participation became firmly established, most younger women could anticipate spending a substantial portion of their mature years in the labor force. They must also have learned, by observing the experiences of older women, that time spent out of the labor force was costly in terms of career advancement and earnings. To maximize their labor market earnings and to secure intrinsically more interesting and attractive jobs, which were becoming more accessible to women, they would have to keep work force interruptions to a minimum. Thus, the increases in younger women's labor force participation rates, including those of mothers with small children, probably were in part a response to their growing expectation of working for a substantial period of time at a later stage in the life cycle. Further, once it had become socially acceptable for mothers of older children to work outside the home, it was not long before it was socially permissible for women with small children to do so as well.

Two additional factors may have played a role in explaining married women's rising participation rates. First, the entry of the large baby boom cohort into the labor market depressed the wages of younger men. Thus, it has been argued that, in order to attain the consumption standards they aspired to, younger couples needed two wage earners.[37] Second, the unstable economic conditions of the 1970s and early 1980s may have contributed to the growth in participation by giving married women an incentive to enter the labor market as soon as possible rather than waiting to supply labor in a more uncertain future.[38]

ANALYZING TRENDS IN MEN'S PARTICIPATION

The changes in male labor force participation patterns, while less dramatic, are also of interest. The decline in the participation rates of younger men (Figure 4.2) reflects their tendency to remain in school longer. This in turn reflects the ever-increasing skills demanded by our advanced economy. Expenditures on education are more profitable to the individual when they are made relatively early in the life cycle, since this results in a longer period over which to reap the returns to this investment in the form of higher earnings. Finally, with rising real incomes, families no doubt demanded more education for their children. They were better able to afford to pay the bills and also to forgo the contribution their children might otherwise have made to family income.

The declining participation rates of older males are often viewed as evidence of the dominance of the income effect over the substitution effect. As real wages have risen over time, men's demand for nonmarket time appears to have increased. One indicator of this is that the full-time work week declined from 60 hours at the

[37]Valerie Kincade Oppenheimer, "The Easterlin Hypothesis: Another Aspect of the Echo to Consider," *Population and Development Review* 2, nos. 3 and 4 (Sept./Dec. 1976): 433–57.

[38]Francine D. Blau and Adam J. Grossberg, "Wage and Employment Uncertainty and the Labor Force Participation Decisions of Married Women," *Economic Inquiry* 29, no. 4 (October 1991): 678–95.

turn of the century to about 40 hours in the 1940s and remains at about that level today. Further, *annual hours* of full-time workers have declined as paid vacations, holidays, and sick leave have become more prevalent.[39] The increased propensity of men to retire, and to retire at earlier ages, is seen as part of this pattern. In addition, the provision of social security and the growing coverage of private pension schemes, while in part a transfer of income from earlier to later years, also created an income effect that encouraged older males to retire.

The small decline in the participation rate of prime-age males is less well understood. To some extent, it may reflect the greater provision in recent decades of disability income under government programs to older men below conventional retirement age.[40] In the absence of such programs, more disabled men would probably have sought work. It has been argued that black males were particularly affected by programs that provide help for those in need, because they tend to be concentrated at the lower end of the wage distribution, where the opportunity cost to leaving the labor force is relatively low. This, in addition to their high unemployment rates, may help to explain why the participation rates of black males have been declining at a faster pace than those of white males.

The decline in male labor force participation in the prime working years may also, to some extent, reflect the impact of the increased employment of women outside the home. As the two-earner family has become the norm, the additional income may induce some (still relatively few) males to leave the labor force for periods of time, say, to retool for a mid-life career change.

BLACK AND WHITE
PARTICIPATION DIFFERENTIALS:
AN ANALYSIS

In our earlier discussion of labor force participation trends, we noted that, since the 1950s, black male participation rates have been declining faster than those of white males, while black female participation rates have been increasing at a slower pace than those of white females. As a result, black male participation rates have fallen considerably below those of white males, while black female participation rates are now about the same as those of white females.

Table 4.6 compares the participation rates of blacks and whites by marital status in 1988. For both groups, married men are more likely to be in the labor force than men in other marital status categories. Given traditional gender roles, married men living with their wives tend to assume greater financial responsibilities than either single (never married) men or other ever married (separated, divorced,

---

[39] For an analysis of these trends, see Thomas J. Kniesner, "The Full-Time Work Week in the U.S.: 1900–1970," *Industrial and Labor Relations Review* 30, no. 1 (October 1976): 3–15.

[40] Donald Parsons, "The Decline in Male Labor Force Participation," *Journal of Political Economy* 88, no. 1 (February 1980): 117–34.

TABLE 4.6 Labor Force Status by Marital Status, Sex, and Race, 1988

	PARTICIPATION RATES	
Marital Status	*Blacks*	*Whites*
Males		
Total	71.0	76.9
Never married	66.6	76.5
Married, spouse present	78.8	78.5
Other ever married[a]	61.5	68.4
Females		
Total	58.0	56.4
Never married	58.1	70.5
Married, spouse present	65.6	55.9
Other ever married[a]	50.3	45.4

[a] Includes individuals who are separated, divorced, or widowed.

Source: U.S. Department of Labor, Bureau of Labor Statistics, *Handbook of Labor Statistics,* Bulletin 2340, (August 1989) Tables 5 and 6, pp. 28–30 and 34–37.

or widowed) men. They are also more likely to be in the prime working ages than single men who are, on average, considerably younger.

The data indicate that the participation rate of black and white males is quite similar within the married-with-spouse-present category: in 1988, the rate was 79 percent for both blacks and whites. The decrease in the black male participation rate relative to that of white males has been associated with a decline in the relative proportion of black men who are married with spouse present. In 1966, 52 percent of black men were married and living with their wives, in comparison to 67 percent of white men. By 1988, this was true of only 44 percent of blacks, compared to 63 percent of whites.

Marital status is also associated with the declining race differential in participation among women. The participation rate of black married women is higher than that of never-married or other unmarried black women and has traditionally been particularly high relative to married white women. The reasons for the higher participation rate of black married women are not fully understood, but undoubtedly the substantially lower average income of black males plays a role.[41] Although these differences have narrowed in the face of the dramatic increases in white women's labor force participation in the post-World War II period,

[41] Labor force participation of married black women has, however, been found to be higher than that of white women even when husband's income is held constant. For analyses of racial differences in women's participation see Duran Bell, "Why Participation Rates of Black and White Wives Differ," *Journal of Human Resource* 9, no. 4 (Fall 1974): 465–79; Claudia Goldin, "Female Labor Force Participation: The Origin of Black and White Differences, 1870 and 1880," *Journal of Economic History* 37, no. 1 (March 1977): 87–108; and Cain, *Married Women in the Labor Force.*

a substantial gap remains. In 1988, for example, 66 percent of black married women were in the labor force, as compared to 56 percent of whites.

As in the case of males, the decrease in the proportion of black relative to white women who are married with spouse present, has contributed to the decline in their participation rates relative to whites. In 1966, 46 percent of blacks and 61 percent of whites were in this marital status category, in comparison to 32 percent of blacks and 58 percent of whites in 1988. (These proportions are lower for women than for men because there are more women than men in the population, particularly among blacks.)

The reasons for these shifts in racial patterns of labor force participation and marital status in recent years have not been fully identified.[42] However, the disadvantaged economic status of blacks undoubtedly plays a role. The black unemployment rate is considerably higher than the white rate: in 1989, the black rate was 11.4 percent, compared to 4.5 percent for whites. The rate for black teenagers was considerably higher and the race differential even greater. This bleak situation may well impede family formation among young blacks.

High unemployment rates among black youths may also contribute to the considerably lower labor force participation rates of black relative to white single individuals. In 1988, the participation rate of single men was 67 percent among blacks in comparison to 77 percent among whites, and among women, the figures were 58 percent for blacks and 71 percent for whites, respectively. As we saw earlier, the net effect of high unemployment rates, particularly for young people, is to discourage labor force participation. The higher unemployment rates of blacks relative to whites in all age groups, may also contribute to marital breakup as well as to labor force withdrawals associated with the provision of disability benefits.

Finally, the provision of welfare to female-headed families by the Aid to Families with Dependent Children (AFDC) program may reduce the incentive of lower-income women to marry or remarry because husband-wife families are less likely to receive such aid, and may also discourage labor force participation among recipients.[43] This program expanded greatly in the 1960s and the early 1970s and

---

[42] The controversial *Moynihan Report* (Daniel P. Moynihan, "The Negro Family: The Case for National Action," Washington, D.C.: Office of Policy Planning and Research, U.S. Department of Labor, 1965) initially focused public attention of the causes and consequences of the higher incidence of female headship among blacks. See also Heather Ross and Isabel V. Sawhill, *Time of Transition: The Growth of Families Headed by Women* (Washington, D.C.: The Urban Institute, 1975), pp. 67–92; and Irwin Garfinkel and Sara. S. McLanahan, *Single Mothers and Their Children: A New American Dilemma* (Washington, D.C.: The Urban Institute Press, 1986). For studies of the employment issue see Finis Welch, "The Employment of Black Men," *Journal of Labor Economics* 8 (January 1990, pt. 2): S26–S74 and Glen G. Cain and Ross E. Finnie, "The Black-White Difference in Youth Employment: Evidence for Demand-Side Factors," *Journal of Labor Economics* 8 (January 1990, pt. 2): S364–S396.

[43] The evidence suggests that the impact of the AFDC program on family formation is not great; see Garfinkle and McLanahan, *Single Mothers and Their Children*. There is stronger evidence of adverse effects on labor supply of welfare-type programs, see, e.g., Michael C. Keeley, Philip K. Robins, Robert G. Spigelman, and Richard W. West, "The Estimation of Labor Supply Models Using Experimental Data," *American Economic Review* 68, no. 5 (December 1978): 873–87.

the concentration of blacks at the lower end of the wage distribution would make them particularly susceptible to its effects.

CONCLUSION

We began by reviewing the trends in male and female participation rates. We found that while female labor force participation rates have been increasing over the course of the present century—from 20 percent in 1900 to 28 percent in 1940 and 58 percent in 1990—male participation rates have been declining from 87 percent in 1950 to 77 percent in 1990. We then turned to the economic theory of labor supply to gain insight into the determinants of labor force participation in order to better understand these trends, as well as differences in participation across various groups. Last, we applied this theory to an analysis of recent trends.

We conclude this chapter with a fuller consideration of the outlook for the future. Predicting the trend of things to come is always hazardous, and the past record of economists and demographers in this respect is not particularly encouraging. Nonetheless, we shall venture some predictions about changes in labor force participation over the next few decades. In order to do that, however, we must first forecast the variables that are particularly important in influencing labor force participation.

Among the factors particularly relevant to women's entry into the labor market are the rates of marriage, fertility, and divorce. We do not expect any of these to change radically in the foreseeable future. Although there has been a trend toward later marriages, we see no convincing evidence that significantly more people will remain single throughout their lifetime. Though the birthrate has been low, relatively few couples appear to be choosing to remain childless. Thus, we do not expect substantial further declines from current low fertility levels. On the other hand, given the fundamental structural shifts that have increased women's commitment to market work, we also believe a major increase in fertility to be unlikely.[44] Although the divorce rate rose sharply through the 1960s and 1970s, it leveled off and even decreased slightly in the 1980s. A continued constancy of the divorce rate, possibly even a small additional decline, might be expected in the future as the expectations of men and women come more into line with their new, less traditional work roles. The tendency toward later marriages, entered into less because of social pressures and more deliberately than before, should have a similar effect.

Increasing education contributed to the impetus toward greater labor force participation in the past, but there is not much room for further increases in the

---

[44]There was a small increase in the total fertility rate in the late 1980s. (The total fertility rate is the number of births that a cohort of 1000 women would have if they experienced the age-specific birth rates occurring in the current year, throughout their childbearing years.) However, the rate remained relatively low and we do not believe that further large increases are likely. The factors influencing fertility rates are discussed in greater detail in Chapter 9.

extremely high proportion of young women who finish high school. Recent trends in enrollments suggest that the number of college graduates is not likely to go up much further either, at least for the near future, and the rise in the percentage of students who are women must also be expected to level off now that they make up about half of the undergraduates. On the other hand, there is the possibility for further entry of women into nontraditional fields and for further increases in their participation in professional and advanced degree programs.

One factor that may be expected to continue to encourage more women to enter employment is the growing acceptance of career aspirations of women and the declining pressure on them to become full-time homemakers. The concomitant tendency for young women to prepare themselves for more rewarding jobs will in turn result in greater labor force attachment, which will further increase their (potential) market earnings.

Other variables that have been important in the past may continue to exert some influence. New and better household appliances and more goods and services that may be purchased in the market, so that they need not be produced at home, would continue to raise the value of market income compared to home time. Most significant in this category would be greater availability of adequate infant and child care at lower prices, but this may not come about for some time. Nor is there any likelihood that household help will become either more plentiful or less expensive.

Turning from supply-side to demand-side issues, the availability of jobs, and jobs attractive enough to be preferable to full-time homemaking, is of course, crucial. Periods of high unemployment, such as we experienced in the early 1980s and the early 1990s, would be expected to slow down the influx of women into the labor market and may even cause some women to leave it. Of all the variables we are concerned with, this is one of the most unpredictable.

It is not, however, only the general level of unemployment that is important in determining the demand for female labor. There are also the questions of the extent to which specifically female occupations are likely to expand or contract and whether women's entry into mixed occupations and male occupations will continue and, perhaps even accelerate. With the possibility that the telecommunications revolution will reduce the need for clerical workers, where women have been so heavily concentrated, the outlook in this respect may not appear very rosy. On the other hand, with the continued expansion of traditionally female service jobs, declining competition from a shrinking group of teenagers, and young women increasingly preparing for and entering nontraditional occupations, women are likely to avail themselves of growing opportunities wherever these arise, assuming that their ability to enter continues to be safeguarded by the government.

What does all this add up to? We consider it extremely unlikely that women's participation rate will decline in the foreseeable future. At a minimum, we would expect the proportion of women in the labor force to continue at the present level. Even that seems very unlikely, if only because the young women who have a far higher labor force participation even during their childrearing years are much more likely to remain employed up to retirement age than were the older cohorts. Therefore, we would expect a continued upward trend in women's labor force participation, though perhaps at a somewhat slower rate. Only a real labor shortage, as in World War II, or a dramatic shift toward policies encouraging women to enter the labor market (for instance, heavy subsidies for infant and child care) would be likely to result in further acceleration of the rate of increase in labor force participation. Thus, the "moderate growth" projection of the Bureau of Labor Statistics (BLS) that 63 percent of adult women will be in the labor force by the year 2000 appears quite reasonable. Even their "high growth" projection of 64 percent may not be excessive.[45]

As for the labor force participation of men, as long as present attitudes do not change dramatically, many of the factors important for women are not especially relevant here. For instance, marital and parental status and level of education are likely to have considerably less influence on men's participation. One factor is even likely to have the opposite effect on men as opposed to women. As noted earlier in this chapter, rising real income appears to have encouraged men to retire earlier and may do so again as real wages begin to rise consistently once more. But the serious fiscal problems of the social security system, which have resulted in legislation to gradually increase the age when full benefits become available, may offset much or all of this impact.

Unemployment is an important unpredictable variable for men as well as women. We have already discussed its impact on black men and young black men in particular. Other groups may react similarly if confronted by long periods of job shortages. Short of a disastrous depression, however, unemployment rates for whites are not likely to rise to the levels presently experienced in the black community.

Weighing these considerations, we would expect men's labor force participation to continue at the present level or possibly to decline somewhat further, but very little. The BLS projects an additional small decrease of less than one percentage point in the male participation rate under its "moderate growth" scenario. Should there be a dramatic shift toward acceptance of men and women as equally responsible for earning income and homemaking, there could be a larger decline, but we do not anticipate such a change.

Combining the two projections, we fully expect a further reduction in the differential in labor force participation between men and women, though we do not expect it to disappear entirely for a long time to come. Under the BLS's "moderate growth" projection, the gap between the male and female participation rates would decline from 19.3 percentage points in 1990 to 13.3 percentage points in the year 2000. The full magnitude of this change becomes clear when we remember that this differential was 65.7 percentage points at the turn of the century.

[45] See Howard N. Fullerton, "New Labor Force Projections, Spanning 1988 to 2000," *Monthly Labor Review* 112 (November 1989): 3–12.

Appendix

THE INCOME AND SUBSTITUTION EFFECTS: A CLOSER LOOK

As discussed in Chapter 4, for labor force participants, an increase in the wage rate has an uncertain effect on hours supplied, all else being equal. This is illustrated in greater detail in Figure 4.8. The *overall* effect of the wage change is shown (in panels a and b) by the move from point A to point C. It may be broken down into distinct components, attributable to the income and substitution effects.

The income effect is represented by a hypothetical increase in income just large enough to get the individual to the higher indifference curve, U_2, leaving the wage rate unchanged. This would result in a move from point A to point B. For the reasons discussed earlier, the effect of the increase in income, all else being equal, is unambiguously to reduce labor hours supplied to the market. The substitution effect is given by the impact of a hypothetical change in the wage (the slope of the budget constraint) *along a given indifference curve, U_2*. This results in a move from B to C. The substitution effect of an increase in the opportunity cost (or price) of nonmarket time, all else being equal, is unambiguously to increase labor hours supplied.

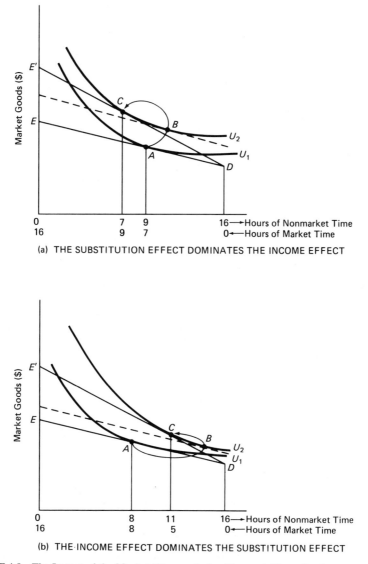

(a) THE SUBSTITUTION EFFECT DOMINATES THE INCOME EFFECT

(b) THE INCOME EFFECT DOMINATES THE SUBSTITUTION EFFECT

FIGURE 4.8 The Impact of the Market Wage on Labor Hours: A Closer Look

The overall effect of the wage change may be either positive or negative depending on whether the substitution effect dominates the income effect (panel a) or the income effect dominates the substitution effect (panel b). Since the prediction of economic theory is ambiguous in this case, empirical evidence is required to resolve this issue in any given case. Such evidence was discussed in Chapter 4.

SUGGESTED READINGS

BECKER, GARY S.   "A Theory of the Allocation of Time." *The Economic Journal* 75, no. 299
    (September 1965): 493–517.

BOWEN, WILLIAM and T. ALDRICH FINEGAN.   *The Economics of Labor Force Participation.*
    Princeton, NJ: Princeton University Press, 1969.

BROWN, CLAIR.   "Consumption Norms, Work Roles, and Economic Growth." In *Gender in the
    Workplace,* Clair Brown and Joseph Pechman, eds. Washington DC: Brookings Institution,
    1987, pp. 13–58.

CAIN, GLEN G.   *Married Women in the Labor Force.* Chicago: University of Chicago Press, 1966.

GOLDIN, CLAUDIA.   *Understanding the Gender Gap.* New York: Oxford University Press, 1990.

KILLINGSWORTH, MARK R.   *Labor Supply.* Cambridge: Cambridge University Press, 1983.

MINCER, JACOB.   "Labor Force Participation of Married Women." In *Aspects of Labor Economics,*
    H. Greg Lewis, ed. Universities National Bureau of Economic Research Conference Studies,
    no. 14. Princeton, NJ: Princeton University Press, 1962, pp. 63–97.

OPPENHEIMER, VALERIE.   *The Female Labor Force in the United States: Demographic and Eco-
    nomic Factors Governing its Growth and Changing Composition.* Westport, CT: Greenwood
    Press, 1976; orig. publ. 1970.

SMITH, JAMES P., ed.   *Female Labor Supply: Theory and Estimation.* Princeton, NJ: University
    Press, 1980.

Chapter 5

DIFFERENCES IN OCCUPATIONS AND EARNINGS: OVERVIEW

The main focus so far has been on the roles of men and women in the family, but Chapter 4 reviewed the dramatic increase in women's labor force participation that has occurred in the post-World War II period. This increase, in conjunction with a decline in male labor force participation rates, has resulted in a steady narrowing of gender differentials in the extent of involvement in market work. Furthermore, the labor force attachment of women has increased as women have become more committed to work outside the home. Although there have been important recent gains, these substantial increases in women's participation in paid work have not been accompanied by comparable improvements in their economic status as compared with men.

In Chapters 6 and 7, we consider alternative theoretical explanations for the observed differences in economic outcomes between men and women. In Chapter 6, we focus on supply-side explanations, particularly the human capital model, which emphasize the role of women's preferences and the choices they make to invest less in job-related education and training, as well as to spend a smaller proportion of their adult years in the labor force. These explanations can also encompass premarket discrimination, or societal discrimination, in which various types of social pressures influence women's choices adversely.

In Chapter 7, we consider demand-side explanations of the gender earnings gap. Emphasis will be on the possible results of gender discrimination in the labor market, which occurs when men and women with equal qualifications find work in different occupations and/or at different wage rates. We also consider that labor market discrimination can indirectly lower women's economic status by reducing their incentives to acquire education and training. In this chapter, we review the extent of gender differences in the two main indicators of economic status—occupational attainment and earnings.

OCCUPATIONAL DIFFERENCES

One way of determining the extent to which men and women do different types of work is to compare the distribution of male and female workers across occupational categories. These distributions are shown in Table 5.1 for 1972 and 1989. In both years, women tended to be concentrated in administrative support (including clerical) and service occupations. In 1989, 46 percent of all women workers were in these two occupations, compared to only 15.3 percent of men. Men were considerably more likely than women to be in operator and laborer jobs and in the precision production, craft, and repair occupations, which are the strongholds of skilled blue-collar workers. Forty percent of male workers were employed in these categories in 1989, as compared to 11 percent of women. Men were also somewhat more highly represented than women in executive, managerial, and administrative positions, whereas women were somewhat more highly represented than men in professional jobs.

Although the situation was fairly similar in both 1972 and 1989, some notable changes occurred between those years. Women were less concentrated in administrative support and service occupations in 1989 than they had been in 1972, when 53 percent held such jobs. Women were also considerably more likely to hold executive and managerial jobs, increasing their share of these positions from 20 percent to 40 percent.[1] Nonetheless, the figures in Table 5.1 amply demonstrate that considerable gender differences in occupational distributions remain.

These differences in the occupational distributions of men and women are associated with gender differences in industrial distributions as well. In 1989, men were more heavily concentrated in construction and manufacturing—33.5 percent of men worked in those industries, as compared to 14.7 percent of women. In contrast, women were considerably more likely to be employed in services and in finance, insurance, and real estate—53.4 percent of women were in these industries, compared to 27.7 percent of men. To some extent, these differences in industrial distributions simply reflect gender differences in occupations. For example, we have

---

[1] It may be that, in the face of government pressure to increase the representation of women in higher-level positions, some women were moved into managerial jobs without being given corresponding responsibility and pay. There can, however, be little doubt that there has also been genuine change.

TABLE 5.1 Distribution of Men and Women by Major Occupational Categories, 1972 and 1989[a]

Occupational Category	1972		1989	
	Men (%)	Women (%)	Men (%)	Women (%)
Executive, administrative, and managerial	11.5	4.6	13.9	11.1
Professional specialty	9.7	12.4	12.0	14.8
Technicians and related support	2.3	2.4	2.9	3.3
Sales occupations	10.0	11.1	11.1	13.1
Administrative support, including clerical	6.4	31.5	5.7	27.8
Service occupations	8.3	21.2	9.6	17.7
Precision production, craft, and repair	19.4	1.6	19.6	2.2
Operators, fabricators, and laborers	25.9	13.4	20.7	8.9
Farming, forestry, and fishing	6.4	1.9	4.4	1.1
Total employed	100.0	100.0	100.0	100.0

[a] Data refer to civilian workers 16 years of age and over.

Source: Department of Labor, Bureau of Labor Statistics, *Employment and Earnings,* January 1984 and 1990.

seen that men are more likely to work as blue-collar workers than women, and a high proportion of such workers are employed in construction and manufacturing. However, there can also be substantial differences in the employment of men and women by firm or industry *within* occupational categories,[2] further contributing to the observed industry differences by gender.

In order to examine occupational differences by race and ethnicity as well as by gender, Table 5.2 provides data separately for black, white, and Hispanic workers. Black and Hispanic men and women were much less likely than whites of the same sex to be employed in the higher-paying managerial and professional positions. At the other end of the scale, they were overrepresented in service occupations, as well as among operators and laborers.

Within each race or ethnic group, however, the patterns of occupational differences by gender showed considerable similarities. Women were heavily overrepresented in administrative support and service occupations and, especially among minority workers, were more likely than men to be in professional and sales jobs. At the same time, women were underrepresented among precision production and craft workers, and among operators and laborers. Minority women were, however, no less likely than minority men to be managerial workers. Overall, gender differences in occupational distributions were larger than racial or ethnic differences.

[2] See for example, Francine D. Blau, *Equal Pay in the Office* (Lexington, MA: Lexington Books, 1977), and Erica L. Groshen, "The Structure of the Female/Male Wage Differential: Is It Who You Are, What You Do, or Where You Work?" *Journal of Human Resources* 26, no. 3 (Summer 1991): 457–72. For historical evidence on this, see Claudia Goldin, *Understanding the Gender Gap: An Economic History of American Women* (New York: Oxford University Press, 1990).

TABLE 5.2   Distribution of Workers by Occupation, Race, Hispanic Origin, and Gender, 1989[a]

Occupational Category	WHITE		BLACK		HISPANIC	
	Men (%)	Women (%)	Men (%)	Women (%)	Men (%)	Women (%)
Executive, administrative, and managerial	14.7	11.6	6.7	7.4	6.9	7.3
Professional specialty	12.4	15.3	6.3	10.8	6.0	8.4
Technicians and related support	2.9	3.2	2.2	3.6	1.9	1.6
Sales occupations	11.7	13.6	5.8	9.4	7.1	12.5
Administrative support, including clerical	5.3	28.2	9.0	25.9	6.4	27.0
Service occupations	8.5	16.4	18.3	27.3	14.8	21.8
Precision production, craft, and repair	20.2	2.2	15.9	2.4	20.5	3.5
Operators, fabricators, and laborers	19.6	8.2	32.7	12.9	28.1	16.6
Farming, forestry, and fishing	4.6	1.2	3.1	0.4	8.2	1.5
Total employed	100.0	100.0	100.0	100.0	100.0	100.0

[a] Data refer to civilian workers 16 years of age and older. Data on Hispanics are for March 1988.

Source: Bureau of the Census, Current Population Reports, Population Characteristics Series P-20, No. 433, *The Hispanic Population in the United States: March 1988* (July 1989); U.S. Department of Labor, *Employment and Earnings,* January 1990.

Occupational Segregation

So far we have discussed gender differences in occupational distributions in a rather general way. Occupational segregation refers to a situation where two groups, in this case men and women, tend to work in a different set of occupations. The **index of segregation** is a widely accepted measure of the degree of such segregation.[3] It gives the percentage of female (or male) workers who would have to change jobs in order for the occupational distribution of the two groups to be the same. The index would equal zero if the distribution of men and women across occupational categories were identical; it would equal 100 if all occupations were either completely male or female. In terms of the data in Table 5.1, the index of occupational segregation by gender was 35.4 in 1989.

The same approach may be used to calculate an index of segregation by race and ethnicity. Using the figures presented in Table 5.2, the index of segregation is 26.6 between black and white men and 19.8 between Hispanic and white men; for women it is 16.1 between blacks and whites, and 15.3 between Hispanics

---

[3] See Otis Dudley Duncan and Beverly Duncan, "A Methodological Analysis of Segregation Indexes," *American Sociological Review* 20, no. 2 (1955): 210–17. The index of occupational segregation by sex is defined as follows:

$$S = \frac{1}{2}\sum_i |M_i - F_i|$$

where M_i = the percentage of males in the labor force employed in occupation i, and F_i = the percentage of females in the labor force employed in occupation i.

and whites. The indexes of gender segregation within each group are considerably higher: 35.9 for whites, 36.1 for blacks, and 35.7 for Hispanics. This confirms our earlier observation that there are greater differences in occupational distribution between men and women than between whites, blacks, and Hispanics of the same sex.

However, data on major occupational categories do not reveal the full extent of occupational segregation by gender. For example, among sales workers, women tend to be employed as retail sales clerks, whereas men are more likely to be manufacturing sales representatives. Information is available on a far larger set of detailed occupations. The precise number has varied over time but is well in excess of 300. The proportion of women in these more narrowly defined occupations within the broader groupings examined earlier does indeed tend to vary considerably. This is illustrated in more detail in Table 5.3, which shows a selection of professional specialty occupations, chosen because we tend to be familiar with the nature and function of the various professions and because both men and women are substantially represented in the category as a whole.

In 1989, 44 percent of all women professionals were in the five predominantly (80 percent or more) female professions shown in the table—dietician, librarian, nurse, prekindergarten and kindergarten teacher, and elementary school teacher. At the same time, this represents a considerable decrease since 1970, when 59 percent were in these jobs. Men also comprised over 80 percent of the incumbents in a number of the professions listed, including the clergy, dentist, engineer, and physician. Together, these four jobs accounted for about one-third of male professional workers. Note, however, that women had made considerable inroads into these traditionally male professions since 1970, and that in 1989, women constituted more than 20 percent in such formerly predominantly male occupations as architect, chemist, computer systems analyst, lawyer, operations researcher, and pharmacist.

A number of studies have calculated the index of occupational segregation for various years using the detailed breakdown of all occupations. For much of the present century, these studies have shown levels of occupational segregation well in excess of 60 percent. Only in the 1980s did the index fall below that figure.[4] (Trends in the extent of occupational segregation will be discussed in greater detail below.) But even these calculations underestimate the full extent of segregation. Job categories used by employers are far more detailed than the census occupations, and

---

[4]See Edward Gross, "Plus Ça Change . . . ? The Sexual Structure of Occupations Over Time," *Social Problems* 16, no. 1 (Fall 1968): 198–208; Francine D. Blau and Wallace E. Hendricks, "Occupational Segregation by Sex: Trends and Prospects," *Journal of Human Resources* 14, no. 2 (Spring 1979): 197–210; Andrea H. Beller, "Trends in Occupational Segregation by Sex and Race: 1960–1981," in *Sex Segregation in the Workplace: Trends, Explanations and Remedies,* Barbara F. Reskin, ed. (Washington, DC: National Academy Press, 1984), pp. 11–26; Suzanne M. Bianchi and Nancy Rytina, "The Decline in Occupational Sex Segregation During the 1970s: Census and CPS Comparisons," *Demography* 23, no. 1 (February 1986): 79–86; Francine D. Blau, "Occupational Segregation by Gender: A Look at the 1980s," paper presented at the American Economic Association Meetings, New York City, December 1988.

TABLE 5.3   Percent Female in Selected Professional Specialty Occupations, 1970, 1989[a]

Occupations	1970	1989
Architects	4.0	20.6
Biological and life scientists	37.8	34.6
Chemists, except biochemists	11.7	27.8
Clergy	2.9	7.8
Computer systems analysts and scientists	13.6	32.4
Dentists	3.5	8.6
Dieticians	92.0	90.8
Economists	15.9	41.3
Editors and reporters	41.6	49.2
Engineers	1.7	7.6
Lawyers	4.9	22.2
Librarians	82.1	87.3
Operations and systems researchers and analysts	11.1	41.1
Pharmacists	12.1	32.3
Physicians	9.7	17.9
Psychologists	38.8	54.0
Public relations specialists	26.6	57.1
Registered nurses	97.3	94.2
Social workers	63.3	68.1
Teachers, except college and university		
Prekindergarten and kindergarten	97.9	97.8
Elementary school	83.9	84.7
Secondary school	49.6	52.6
Teachers, college and university	29.1	38.7

[a] 1970 data are from the 1970 Census and are for the experienced civilian labor force aged 16 and over. 1989 data are annual averages from the Current Population Surveys and are for employed civilians aged 16 and over.

Source: Bureau of the Census, *Detailed Occupation of the Experienced Civilian Labor Force by Sex for the United States and Regions: 1980 and 1970,* Supplementary Report PC80-S1-15, March 1984; and U.S. Department of Labor, *Employment and Earnings* 37 (January 1990).

researchers have found that particular firms often employ only men or women, even in occupations where both sexes are substantially represented.[5] Restaurants, for instance, commonly employ only waiters, or waitresses, but not both. The impact of these factors is revealed in a study of California firms. Using the employers' own job classifications, it was found that 51 percent of firms were completely sex-segregated by job category; no men and women shared the same job title. An additional 8 percent of the firms were single-sex establishments. The mean index of segregation in the remaining firms was 84.1.[6]

[5] See Blau, *Equal Pay in the Office.*

[6] James N. Baron and William T. Bielby, "A Woman's Place Is With Other Women: Sex Segregation in the Work Place," *Sex Segregation in the Workplace,* Reskin, ed. pp. 27–55.

Hierarchies Within Occupations

In addition to differences in their distribution among occupations, men and women also tend to be employed at different levels within occupations. This is often referred to as vertical segregation. No adequate data are available that would enable us to construct economy-wide quantitative measures, but there can be little doubt that such hierarchical differences are substantial.

A good example of this is the hierarchy on university faculties, because they generally use a clear and widely understood set of titles. Table 5.4 provides data on the distribution of men and women by rank in academic years 1974–75 and 1989–90. In both years, women were overrepresented at the lower end of the occupational hierarchy, as Assistant Professors, Instructors, and Lecturers, whereas men were more highly represented at the upper ranks, as Professors and Associate Professors—the categories that tend to have job security in the form of tenure. The data do suggest some improvement over the fifteen-year period, as would be expected if women were initially underrepresented at the higher ranks, at least in part because many of them had been recently hired. By 1989–90, women comprised 26.4 percent of Associate Professors, roughly comparable to their share of Assistant Professors 15 years earlier. Nonetheless, movement into the highest level has proved to be quite slow. The proportion of Professors who were women increased only from 10.1 in 1974–75 to 12.8 percent in 1989–90 and remained considerably below the female share of Associate Professors in 1974–75 (17.3 percent).

This case is not unique. Although women have increased their share of managerial jobs from 19.7 percent in 1972 to 39.8 percent in 1989, their representation in top positions is still extremely sparse. In 1990, of the 4012 directors and highest executives at 799 major companies covered by a *Fortune* study, only 19 were women.[7] Similarly, a recent Korn/Ferry study found that women comprised only 3 percent of top executives at the level of senior vice

TABLE 5.4 Percent Female of Faculty in Institutions of Higher Education by Academic Rank, 1974–75 and 1989–90

Academic Rank	1974–75	1989–90
Professors	10.1	12.8
Associate professors	17.3	26.4
Assistant professors	27.9	39.5
Instructors	48.0	56.5
Lecturers	41.4	52.4
Total	22.5	27.4

Source: *AAUP Bulletin* 61 (August 1975), Table 19 and *Academe* 76 (March-April 1990), Table 16.

[7]Peter Kilborn, "Labor Dept. Wants to Take on Job Bias in the Executive Suite," *New York Times* (July 30, 1990), pp. A1, A12.

president or above. This did, however, represent an increase since 1979, when the figure was 0.5 percent.[8]

Evaluating the Extent of Occupational Segregation

However segregation is measured, and whatever the numerical value of the index arrived at, how can it be determined whether any figure in excess of zero and short of 100 is modest or excessive? The answer depends in part on one's perception of how great the differences are in men's and women's talents, tastes, and motivation and how relevant these are to their occupational distribution and achievements.

Those who argue that occupational segregation is natural and appropriate are at one extreme. In this view, efforts to change the existing situation will merely lead to economic inefficiency and personal frustration. Its proponents emphasize the similarities among individuals within each sex and the differences between the two groups. Those who emphasize the variations among individuals within each sex and similarities between the two groups are at the other extreme. In this view, if men and women were not constrained by gender stereotyping and various barriers to individual choice but were free to follow their own inclinations, they would be far less concentrated in separate occupations. The fact that there are occupations that are predominantly male in some countries but female in others lends some support to the view that socially imposed restrictions play a role in the sex typing of jobs.[9] In this case, removing existing barriers would presumably increase efficiency and decrease frustration, since individuals could seek work suited to their particular aptitudes.

It should be emphasized that even if the present level of occupational segregation is deemed excessive, it would be unreasonable to conclude that the optimal situation would necessarily be a precisely proportional distribution of men and women. Apart from whatever innate differences there may be, past socialization and the prevalent allocation of household responsibilities would make such an outcome unlikely for some time to come.

In addition, the rate of change is limited by the extent to which new people can be hired. Large numbers of people cannot be expected to change jobs on short notice, as the computation of the segregation index perhaps implies. The most that could reasonably be expected is that the underrepresented group would be more highly represented among new hires, to the extent that they are qualified for the available positions, than among those presently employed in the occupation. This may be, at best, a very slow process, especially during periods of recession and retrenchment.

[8]Lori Silver, "Few Women, Minorities at the Top: Survey Finds No Gain in Executive Positions in Past Decade," *The Washington Post,* (August 14, 1990), p. A1.

[9]This subject will be discussed at greater length in Chapter 10.

TRENDS IN OCCUPATIONAL SEGREGATION

The same issues confronted in measuring current occupational segregation also arise in determining the precise extent to which it has changed over time. However, in addition to the concern over how detailed the categories are, or whether hierarchical segregation is taken into account, there is also the question of whether the same occupational definitions are used for the various periods to be compared. The main difficulty is that the definition and number of occupational categories undergo frequent changes. Given constant flux in the economy, this is inevitable. For example, had the Census Bureau rigidly adhered to the occupational categories of an earlier era, jobs such as computer systems analyst and programmer, as well as computer operator and data entry keyer, would not be included. In spite of the best efforts of the people who compile the data and the researchers who use them, data are not entirely comparable over the years and are less so as the years get farther apart.

In spite of these limitations, there is no reason to question the unanimous findings of the studies on this subject, all of which point to little change over a number of decades prior to 1960. The index of segregation was actually reported to have increased by 1.1 percentage points between 1950 and 1960, as predominantly female clerical and professional jobs grew in relative size. Between 1960 and 1970, an inflow of men into female professions and of women into male sales and clerical jobs produced a modest drop in the segregation index of 3.1 percentage points.[10]

During the 1970s, a larger decrease in the segregation index of 8.5 percentage points was found.[11] The decline in segregation continued into the 1980s, although at a somewhat lower pace.[12] The cumulative effect of these changes has been impressive, with the index declining from 67.3 percent in 1970 to 56.7 percent in 1987, a decrease of nearly 11 percentage points.[13] This reduction in segregation was mainly related to the entry of women into formerly male white-collar jobs, particularly professional and managerial occupations. As noted earlier, the data in Table 5.3 indicate that, over the 1970s and the 1980s, women made notable progress in entering a number of professions that were formerly predominantly male, including architecture, engineering, law, pharmacy, and medicine. There were similar large increases in many executive, administrative, and managerial occupations during this period. Examples include a rise in the representation of women between 1970 and 1989 from 7.9 to 31.0 percent of marketing, advertising, and public relations managers, from 8.5 to 25.9 percent of purchasing managers, from 19.4 to 42.7 percent of financial managers, and from 21.1 to 52.6 percent

[10]Blau and Hendricks, "Occupational Segregation."

[11]Bianchi and Rytina, "The Decline in Occupational Sex Segregation During the 1970s." See also Beller, "Trends in Occupational Segregation by Sex."

[12]Blau, "Occupational Segregation by Gender."

[13]Blau, "Occupational Segregation by Gender." This comparison must be interpreted with some caution, because it is based on two different data sets that are not entirely comparable: the Census for 1970 and the Current Population Survey for 1987.

of personnel and labor relations managers. Examples from management-related occupations include increases in female representation from 10.3 to 32.8 percent of management analysts, from 24.6 to 48.6 percent of accountants and auditors, and from 27.8 to 48.8 percent of buyers.

Nonetheless, many highly segregated occupations remain. This can be seen in Table 5.5, which shows some of the most segregated occupations, those that

TABLE 5.5   Selected Occupations Less Than 10 Percent or More Than 90 Percent Female, 1989[a]

Occupations	Less than 10 Percent Female
Airplane pilots and navigators	3.8
Clergy	7.8
Construction laborers	3.0
Construction trades	2.1
Dentists	8.6
Engineers	7.6
Extractive occupations	2.6
Firefighting and fire prevention occupations	3.9
Garbage collectors	4.1
Helpers, construction and extractive occupations	4.4
Material moving equipment operators	3.8
Mechanics and repairers, except supervisors	3.1
Plant and systems operators	5.0
Precision metalworking	6.4
Rail transport occupations	2.8
Supervisors, protective service occupations	8.3
Timber cutting and logging occupations	1.6
Truck drivers, heavy	1.9
Welders and cutters	6.6

	More than 10 Percent Female
Bank tellers	91.0
Bookkeepers, account and auditing clerks	91.7
Child care workers, except private household	96.3
Dental hygienists	99.2
Dieticians	90.8
Health record technologists and technicians	91.3
Licensed practical nurses	96.1
Nursing aides, orderlies and attendants	90.4
Private household occuaptions	95.9
Receptionists	97.2
Registered nurses	94.2
Secretaries, stenographers, and typists	98.3
Teachers' aides	95.1
Teachers, prekindergarten and kindergarten	97.8

[a]Data are for employed civilians aged 16 and over.
Source: U.S. Department of Labor, *Employment and Earnings* (January 1990).

are either less than 10 percent or more than 90 percent female. Many of the predominantly male jobs are blue-collar occupations. Overall, relatively little change occurred in the gender composition of such jobs during the 1970s and the 1980s. The predominantly female categories include, in addition to the traditionally female professions, jobs in the administrative support and service areas.

Thus, the figures indicate that some decline in the amount of segregation has occurred since 1960 and that the pace of change has accelerated since 1970. However, many jobs remain segregated by gender, and the magnitude of the segregation index continues to be substantial. As we have seen, 57 percent of women (or men) would have had to change jobs in 1987 in order for the detailed occupational distribution of the two sex groups to be the same. One reason for this is that the relatively rapid changes in managerial and professional jobs have not been matched in most of the other occupations.

A question that must also be raised is to what extent the observed trends reflect real improvements in opportunities for women.[14] In some cases, firms have responded to government pressures by placing women into nominal management positions that involve little responsibility and little contact with higher levels of management. In other instances, jobs have become increasingly female when skill requirements declined because of technological changes. In such cases, integration may turn out to be a short-run phenomenon, as women increasingly come to dominate such occupations. One example of this trend is the case of insurance adjusters and examiners. Women increased their share of this occupation from 29.6 percent in 1970 to 72.0 percent in 1989. Yet they are employed primarily as "inside adjusters" whose decision making has, to a considerable extent, been computerized and involves little discretion. "Outside adjusters," a better-paid and more prestigious group, remain largely male.[15]

In yet other instances, women may gain access to a sector of an occupation that was always low-paying. For example, the representation of women among bus drivers increased from 28.3 percent in 1970 to 54.8 percent in 1989. But men continue to comprise the majority of full-time workers in metropolitan transportation systems, whereas women are concentrated among part-time school bus drivers.

It is important to point out, however, that women are expected to benefit from the increase in the demand for female labor that results when they are able to enter additional occupations from which they were previously excluded, even when the new jobs are qualitatively similar to those formerly available to them. Moreover, it is likely that much of the observed decline in occupational segregation does represent enhanced labor market opportunities for women and that the

---

[14] These examples are from Barbara F. Reskin and Patricia A. Roos, *Job Queues, Gender Queues: Explaining Women's Inroads into Male Occupations* (Philadelphia: Temple University Press, 1990).

[15] For a study of the insurance industry, see Barbara Baran and Suzanne Teegarden, "Women's Labor in the Office of the Future: A Case Study of the Insurance Industry," in *Women, Households, and the Economy,* Lourdes Beneria and Catharine R. Stimpson, eds. (New Brunswick, NJ: Rutgers University Press, 1987).

COMPANY TRIES HARDER TO FIGHT DISCRIMINATION

The evidence presented in this chapter shows that the situation in the workplace has been changing for women and minorities, albeit slowly. In recent years, these changes have been spurred on by some large, progressive employers who have introduced a variety of innovative programs to attract and retain such workers, and to give them the opportunity to move up to the management level from which they had largely been excluded. Brief excerpts from a newspaper account* provide some information about what one such firm has been doing.

When a black job candidate comes here to Corning Inc. for interviews, managers have a real incentive to hire him. Raises and bonuses for the executives, most of whom are white men, depend largely on recruiting blacks and women and on their success in training and promoting them.

Not only that. One interviewer is a black from the department where the recruit would start work. The interviewer helps put the candidate at ease, and afterward joins in assessing the candidate against intrusions of racism. Once hired, most black recruits and many women are assigned a "coach," someone from another department who shows them the ways of Corning and steers them around the pitfalls that can thwart promotions.

Corning, the giant family-controlled maker of Pyrex, Corning Ware and Steuben crystal, is engaged in one of corporate America's most ambitious experiments in cultural engineering. The company accommodates women and blacks in a score of ways, all ultimately intended to assure them of a good crack at the top jobs in the company. Eventually, the company wants to do the same for other minority members, who are fewer around Corning.

Pressed by advocacy groups and Government, and above all by their own economic self-interest, many big companies nowadays are trying to make affirmative action work better than it did five and 10 years ago. Corning, like many others, managed to hire women and blacks quite easily then, but many promptly fled, blaming entrenched, if often subtle, discrimination. . . .

In their departure interviews, women and blacks said their biggest gripe was evidence that their progress up the ranks was restricted. "We found the reason was not the town but the perceived opportunities," . . .

To prosper and grow in the next decades, Corning says it needs competent managers, scientists and engineers, and irreversible demographic trends oblige the company to turn to women and blacks. . . .

Mr. Houghton [the company Chairman] has set two goals for Corning: one, the better mix of women and blacks in the company's management and professional ranks, and two, making a virtue of the mix. He says he wants a salad, not a purée— blacks who are proud to be black and women who are proud to be mothers and engineers. . . .

White men still far outnumber other groups at Corning, and they still get most promotions. But more are bypassed than ever, too, and there is little the company intends to do about it. . . .

*Peter T. Kilborn, "A Company Recasts Itself to Erase Years of Job Bias," *New York Times* (October 4, 1990), pp. A1, C21. Copyright © 1990 by the New York Times Company. Reprinted by permission.

Some white men assert that management has set lower job standards for women and blacks, but Mr. O'Brien [director of education, training and recruiting] flatly denies it.... "It wouldn't work," he said. "Women and blacks would be the first to complain. And the people would fail...."

Some things the company has done might not seem like much to a white man who can find basic amenities even in a town of 12,000 like Corning. But Corning's blacks could not find programs they liked on radio or television, just as they could not find barbers.

So the company prevailed on the cable television outlet to pipe in a black radio station from Rochester and the Black Entertainment Network from Washington. The company has also helped recruit black teachers for the public schools and an assistant principal who is black.

To recruit women and blacks to Corning, the company offers well-paid internships to [female and black] undergraduates more readily than it offers them to white male students. Blacks and women, much more than white men, tend to drop out of advanced science and engineering courses, and . . . the internships help keep them on course....

More than most companies, Corning also goes to great lengths to find jobs at Corning for recruits' spouses or "significant others," as one official puts it. Several hundred couples work for the company, all subject to only one firm rule— that one spouse not work for the other. In hundreds of other cases, Corning has helped recruits' spouses get jobs around town, including many in businesses that deal primarily with Corning....

"The corporation has been very receptive to just about everything that women and blacks have said they need to be able to do their work better," said Gail Baity, a black woman who started in industrial relations at Corning 14 years ago. She now conducts an intensive two-day course to purge employees of racist attitudes. This course and one on sexism are required for thousands of managers and professional employees....

Blacks and women say the company could do still more. Corning operates a day care center for children 3 to 5 years old, for example, but young parents say they have just as much need for one for infants and toddlers. Some also want paid paternity leave. The company permits unpaid leave for fathers, and so far only one has taken it....

The economics of Corning's accommodations are hard to gauge. The classes, the day care center, the personnel who manage the affirmative action efforts all cost something, but far less than the $4 million a year that Mr. Houghton says the company was spending a few years ago to recruit and train women and blacks to replace those who were quitting. And of course, people who do not anguish over racial and sexual abuse tend to work harder and more happily, helping Corning make money....

For its efforts, the Company has begun to show some real gains. It says 52 percent of the salaried employees it has hired over the past three years are women, and 16 percent are black. Three years ago, the roughly 150 top managers included four white women and one black man. Today the same group has seven women and five blacks, including a black woman who is double counted.

Of 5,365 salaried personnel, the source of the top managers of 20 or 30 years from now, the percentage of women has climbed to 33.6 percent from 17.4 percent. Among blacks the gain has been much smaller, to 5.5 percent from 5.1 percent. But that is well above the levels of most companies, and the percentage of blacks who quit the company has dropped to 10.9 percent last year from 15.1 percent in 1987....

With the change in Corning's personnel mix, a change in the company's gentlemanly ways seems well under way. White men must now contend with women like Wendy E. Luce, 35, who as operations manager of a factory here is the highest-ranking woman in the overwhelmingly male manufacturing side of the company. Ms. Luce says she has no compunctions about yelling when she sees fit. "I'd rather see people get excited," she said.

Roy A. Farr, 60, her deputy at the plant, called her a good boss, but different. "Wendy really feels for people," he said. "She is kinder than men, more considerate, but not to the point where it gets in the way of the business. She knows what she wants to do. She leads. Men demand. She seems to be setting the tone of where Corning wants to go."

---

decrease will continue in the future. The group that can most readily respond to new opportunities, given the difficulty in changing occupations in mid-career, is younger women. And, indeed, the decrease in occupational segregation has been particularly pronounced among this group. This means that change is necessarily something of a slow process but may be expected to gain momentum as more recent cohorts of women who are less occupationally segregated replace older ones.

EARNINGS

For many years, the single best known statistic relevant to the economic status of women in this country probably was that women who worked full-time, year-round, earned about 60 cents to every dollar earned by men working full-time, year-round.[16] One reason for the public awareness of this figure was that the same earnings gap persisted for two decades with only modest fluctuations and no significant trend. As may be seen in Table 5.6 and Figure 5.1, the female-to-male earnings ratios based on annual data hovered close to the 60 percent figure throughout the 1960s and 1970s.[17] In fact, the ratio was actually somewhat higher

[16] Full-time is defined as 35 hours or more per week; year-round is defined as 50 weeks or more per year. The focus on full-time, year-round workers is an effort to adjust annual earnings for gender differences in hours and weeks worked. However, since even women who work full-time work on average 8 to 10 percent fewer hours a week than male full-time workers, a finer adjustment for hours would raise the earnings ratio; see June O'Neill, "Women & Wages," *The American Enterprise* 1, no. 6 (November/December 1990), 25–33.

[17] Median rather than mean earnings are shown because more government data are presented that way. The definition of the median is that half the cases fall above it and half below. In this case, half the individuals have higher earnings and half have lower. The mean, or arithmetic mean, is calculated by adding up the total earnings of all the individuals concerned and dividing by their number. Since there is a relatively small number of persons who have extremely high earnings, the mean tends to be higher than the median.

TABLE 5.6 Female-to-Male Earnings Ratios of Full-Time Workers,
Selected Years 1955–1991

Year	Annual Earnings of Full-Time, Year-Round Workers[a]	Usual Weekly Earnings of Full-time Worker[b]
1955	63.9	
1960	60.8	
1965	60.0	
1970	59.4	62.3
1975	58.8	62.0
1980	60.2	64.4
1985	64.6	68.2
1989	68.7	70.1
1990	71.1	71.8
1991		74.0

[a] Workers aged 16 and over. Prior to 1979, workers aged 14 and over.

[b] Workers aged 16 and over.

Source: U.S. Department of Labor, Women's Bureau, Bulletin 298, *Time of Change: 1984 Handbook on Women Workers;* Bureau of the Census, Population Reports, Consumer Income Series P-60, *Money Income of Households, Families, and Persons in the United States,* and Bureau of the Census, Population Reports, Consumer Income Series P-60, *Money, Income, and Poverty Status in the United States,* various issues; Earl F. Mellor, "Investigating the Differences in Weekly Earnings of Women and Men," *Monthly Labor Review* 107, no. 6 (June 1984); Bureau of Labor Statistics, *Handbook of Labor Statistics,* Bulletin 2340, August 1989; Bureau of Labor Statistics, *Employment and Earnings,* various issues.

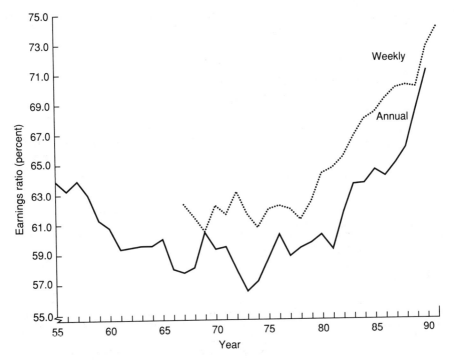

FIGURE 5.1 Female-to-Male Earnings Ratios of Full-Time Workers, 1955–1991

in the 1950s than in the subsequent decades. In the early 1980s, the ratio began to rise. Between 1981 and 1990 it increased from 59.2 percent to 71.1 percent.[18]

Table 5.6 and Figure 5.1 also show the female-to-male earnings ratio calculated using data on the usual weekly earnings of full-time workers. For a variety of reasons, the earnings ratio computed on the basis of weekly earnings is generally higher than the annual figure.[19] Of more interest, however, is that the data for weekly earnings also show a fairly consistent upward trend dating from the late 1970s. Between 1978 and 1991, the earnings ratio, defined in these terms, increased from 61.3 to 74.0 percent.

Changes in the earnings gap between men and women over the life cycle are indicated by the data in Table 5.7. Data are presented for the annual income of full-time, year-round workers by age over the 1960–1990 period.[20] Although women earn less than men in all age groups, the gap tends to widen with age.[21] This fanning out of the male and female earnings profiles in part reflects that women on average accumulate less work experience than men do as they age. This was particularly the case for earlier cohorts.

As was the case for the overall earnings gap, the figures in Table 5.7 suggest that earnings differentials within age groups have also been narrowing. All age groups of women experienced rising relative earnings over the 1980s. For women under 45, earnings ratios began to rise as early as the 1970s, although the 1980s gains were considerably larger. Younger women also experienced the largest increases. Between 1970 and 1990, the earnings ratio among 25- to 34-year-olds increased from 64.9 to 79.1 percent, a rise of 14.2 percentage points. For 35- to 44-year-olds the increase was from 53.9 to 68.9 percent, a rise of 15.0 percentage points.

The fact that the earnings ratio tends to widen with age raises a question as to whether younger women will retain these gains as they age over the life cycle. One way to address this question is to ask what has happened to the relative earnings of prior cohorts as they aged. Using the data in Table 5.7, we can compare the earnings ratio for 25- to 34-year-olds in 1980 to the earnings ratio for 35- to 44-year-olds 10 years later in 1990. This is not by any means a perfect measure of how a given cohort of workers in fact fared over the period, because some of

---

[18] Focusing on all workers, rather than simply those employed full-time, year-round, Francine D. Blau and Andrea H. Beller found evidence of some earnings gains for women during the 1970s, after adjustment for hours and weeks worked; see "Trends in Earnings Differentials by Gender, 1971–1981," *Industrial and Labor Relations Review* 41, no. 4 (July 1988), 513–529.

[19] The reasons for the differences in the weekly and annual series are discussed in Nancy Rytina, "Comparing Annual and Weekly Earnings from the Current Population Survey," *Monthly Labor Review* 106 (April 1983): 32–38.

[20] The focus on income is dictated by data availability. Income includes such items as interest, dividends, and transfer payments, as well as earnings. However, because these items are rather small for the great majority of year-round, full-time workers, income ratios tend to be quite similar to earnings ratios.

[21] An exception to this pattern is that the relative earnings of women increased somewhat in the oldest age group.

TABLE 5.7   Female-to-Male Income Ratios of Full-Time, Year-Round Workers by Age, 1960–1990

Ages	1960	1970	1980	1990
25–34	65.1	64.9	68.6	79.1
35–44	57.6	53.9	56.2	68.9
45–54	58.0	56.3	54.3	61.4
55–64	64.5	60.3	56.7	62.6

Source: 1960–1980: June O'Neill, "Women & Wages," *The American Enterprise* 1 (November/December 1990), p. 29. Reprinted by permission of the American Enterprise Institute for Public Policy Research, Washington D.C. 1989: Bureau of the Census, Consumer Income Series P-60, no. 174, *Money Income of Households, Families, and Persons in the United States: 1990.*

the original group will have exited the labor force by 1990 and some new, less experienced workers will have entered. Such labor force turnover is higher among women than among men, and this will lower their earnings relative to men over the period. Bearing these limitations in mind, the results of such a comparison are nonetheless of interest.

Using this approach, we find a negligible increase in the earnings ratio with age for the group aged 25–34 in 1980—from 68.6 percent to 68.9 percent—while a large decline would be expected on the basis of the 1990 data alone. That is, when we compare 25- to 34-year-olds in 1990 to 35- to 44-year-olds in the same year, the decline in the ratio is much larger, from 79.1 percent to 68.9 percent. Further, the annual income of the 45- to 54-year age group in 1990 was also a larger percentage of men's income than that of 35- to 44-year-olds 10 years earlier, but in this case the increase was 5.2 percentage points. These findings reflect the gains in relative income that women have received in recent years. That is, the comparisons would have been less favorable, particularly for the younger group, had we compared cohorts across 1960 and 1970 or across 1970 and 1980.

These data suggest that younger women may well retain a substantial amount of the improvement in their relative earnings as they age. Moreover, the observation that young women are now entering less traditional occupations and are spending more time in the labor market reinforces our conclusion that they are likely to continue faring better than their predecessors at each point in the life cycle. The overall gender gap in earnings should decline considerably more as earlier cohorts of women with relatively low earnings are replaced increasingly by the more recent cohorts with higher earnings.

These relatively optimistic conclusions must, however, be tempered by the recognition that, although the earnings gap has been closing, men's real wages in many occupations have been declining. Insofar as this is the case, women's progress relative to men does not represent improvement in absolute terms. It is also worthy of note that, as we shall see in Chapter 10, the male-female earnings differential is still considerably larger in the United States than in the Scandinavian countries and Australia. This is the case even though women's qualifications relative to men's

TABLE 5.8   Median Income of Men and Women Working Year-Round, Full-Time, by Years of Schooling 1967 and 1990[a]

	1967			1990		
	INCOME		*Women's Income as Percent of Men's*	INCOME		*Women's Income as Percent of Men's*
Years of Schooling	*Men*	*Women*		*Men*	*Women*	
Elementary:						
Less than 8	$4,831	$2,820	58.4	} $17,394	} $12,251	} 70.4
8	6,133	3,343	54.5			
High school:						
1–3	6,891	3,704	53.8	20,902	14,429	69.0
4	7,732	4,499	58.2	26,653	18,319	68.7
College:						
1–3	8,816	5,253	59.6	31,734	22,227	70.0
4	11,571	6,796	58.7	39,238	28,017	71.4
5 or more	12,510	7,823	62.5	49,304	33,750	68.5

[a]Data refer to workers 25 years of age and older.

Source: Bureau of the Census, Current Population Reports, Consumer Income Series P-60, various issues.

are high in the United States compared to other countries. An important part of the explanation appears to be the higher level of wage inequality in the United States. That is, low-wage workers fare particularly poorly in this country relative to other industrialized nations.[22]

Table 5.8 provides information on incomes of workers by level of education.[23] As was the case for the overall earnings gap and the earnings differentials by age, the gender gap within educational categories has also narrowed over time. Nonetheless, although education has a strong positive effect on the income of both men and women, men continue to earn substantially more than women within each educational category. For instance, female high school graduates earn only slightly more than males with up to eight years of grade school, and female college graduates do not earn much more than male high school graduates.

Table 5.9 reviews the trends in relative income by race and ethnicity as well as by gender. Within each group, women earned less than men in 1990, but the female-to-male income ratio was considerably higher among blacks (86.0 percent) and Hispanics (83.8 percent) than among whites (69.0 percent). The trends in income ratios by gender among whites closely mirror the trends we previously

[22]This is discussed in Francine D. Blau and Lawrence M. Kahn, "The Gender Earnings Gap: Learning from International Comparisons," *American Economic Review* 82, no. 2 (May 1992).

[23]Again, due to data availability, we focus on income rather than earnings of workers. As noted above, earnings and income ratios for full-time, year-round workers tend to be quite similar.

TABLE 5.9   Median Income Ratios of Full-Time, Year-Round Workers by Race, Hispanic Origin, and Gender, Selected Years 1955–1990[a]

Year	White Females -to- White Males	Black Females -to- Black Males	Hispanic Females -to- Hispanic Males	Black Males -to- White Males	Black Females -to- White Females	Hispanic Males -to- White Males	Hispanic Females -to- White Females
1955	65.3	55.1	n.a.	60.9	51.4	n.a.	n.a.
1960	60.6	62.2	n.a.	66.1	67.8	n.a.	n.a.
1965	57.9	62.5	n.a.	62.8	67.9	n.a.	n.a.
1970	58.6	70.5	n.a.	68.1	81.9	n.a.	n.a.
1975	57.5	75.1	68.6	73.2	95.5	71.2	85.0
1980	59.3	78.7	71.7	70.4	93.3	70.0	84.5
1985	64.1	81.2	78.0	70.0	88.5	67.5	82.0
1990	69.0	86.0	83.8	71.4	88.9	64.0	77.7

[a] Prior to 1970, blacks include blacks and other nonwhites. Data for 1980–1989 refer to workers 15 years of age and older; and for 1955–1975 to workers 14 years and older.

Source: Bureau of the Census, Current Population Reports, Consumer Income Series P-60, various issues.

discussed for the population as a whole (of which they comprise the majority), showing little tendency toward a narrowing of the income gap until the 1980s. In contrast, the female-to-male income ratio among blacks has increased considerably from the mid-1950s, when it was 55.1 percent. A sizable increase in the gender income ratio (15.2 percentage points) is also apparent among Hispanics since the mid-1970s, when data became available for this group.

In terms of the racial and ethnic differences shown in the table, we see that minority individuals of both sexes earned less than whites in 1990, but the differential was considerably smaller among women than among men. In 1990, the median income of black males was 71.4 percent of white males' median income, and the figure for Hispanic males was 64.0 percent. These figures were considerably lower than the income ratios of 88.9 percent for black women and 77.7 percent for Hispanic women compared to white women. Among women, black-to-white income ratios increased substantially from the mid-1950s, when the ratio was only 51.4 percent, to the mid-1970s, when it was 95.5 percent. Black men also gained relative to white men, although not as rapidly, from 62.8 percent of white men's income in 1965 to 73.2 percent in 1975. Since the late 1970s, however, income differentials between blacks and whites, and also between Hispanics and whites, have been widening.

CONCLUSION

In this chapter, we presented data on occupations and earnings of women as compared to men in general, as well as for various subgroups, and we briefly

discussed the nature of the differences between them. Although occupational segregation by gender remains substantial, it has been declining slowly but steadily
since the 1960s. The overall gap in the earnings of male and female full-time
workers started to narrow in the late 1970s or early 1980s, although the differential remains large. Perhaps most importantly, occupation and earnings differentials
have declined significantly for younger cohorts, and an analysis of trends suggests
that they are likely to retain much of the relative improvement in their earnings
position as they age. The next two chapters will thoroughly investigate the possible
explanations for the gender differences described here.

Chapter 6

DIFFERENCES IN OCCUPATIONS AND EARNINGS: THE HUMAN CAPITAL MODEL

In this chapter, we present supply-side explanations for the gender differences in earnings and occupations described in Chapter 5. Initially, we simply summarize the arguments of scholars who emphasize this point of view and leave the evaluation of their contributions and the exposition of alternative interpretations for later. In addition, to the extent that supply-side factors are important in causing gender differences in market outcomes, we review government and employer policies that may help to increase women's human capital investments and labor force attachment.

Supply-side explanations focus on the observation that men and women may come to the labor market with different tastes and with different qualifications, such as education, formal training, and experience, or other productivity-related characteristics. Gender differences in tastes might mean, for example, that one group or the other has greater tolerance for an unpleasant, unhealthy, or dangerous environment, for longer work hours or inflexible work schedules, for physical strain, or for boredom, and is more willing to accept these in return for higher wages. Many examples could be offered of gender differences in qualifications related to job performance. A woman may have a college degree in English whereas a man may have a college degree in engineering. Or again, while in the labor market, a woman may make different decisions, even when faced with the same economic incentives as a man. For example, a woman may move in and out of the labor force as her family situation changes, whereas a man's attachment may be more continuous.

Such differences in men's and women's tastes for different types of work, education, and experience could cause women to earn less and to be concentrated in different occupations. Little is known about tastes and their effects on occupational choices and rewards; however, there has been a great deal of research on job-related qualifications. Hence, we too shall concentrate on them.

Before considering the effects of gender differences in qualifications on earnings and occupations, one issue that arises is whether they should be viewed as the result of the voluntary choices men and women make or as the outcome of what has been termed prelabor market or *societal discrimination*. Societal discrimination denotes the multitude of social influences that cause women to make decisions that adversely influence their status in the labor market. Since we are all products of our environments to a greater or lesser extent, it is often difficult to draw the line between voluntary choice and this type of discrimination.

This distinction may in part reflect disciplinary boundaries. The discipline of economics tends to view individual decision making as determined by economic incentives and individual preferences (or tastes). It does not analyze the formation of preferences, and choices are generally viewed as being at least to some extent voluntary. In contrast, sociologists and social psychologists are more apt to examine the role of socialization and social-structural factors in producing what economists classify as individual preferences.[1] Thus, within the context of sociology or social psychology, individual choices are more likely to be seen as stemming from social conditioning or constraints rather than as voluntary.

The tendency to emphasize the role of choice versus societal discrimination may also reflect an implicit value judgment. Those who are reasonably content with the status quo of gender differences in economic outcomes tend to speak mainly of voluntary choices, whereas those who decry sex inequality in pay and occupations are more likely to focus on societal discrimination.

We tend towards the view that at least some of the gender differences in qualifications that currently exist stem from undesirable societal discrimination, although we acknowledge that, particularly in the past and to a lesser extent today, this type of gender differentiation has been regarded as perfectly appropriate. The most important point is that even if societal discrimination is a problem, it is essentially different from *labor market discrimination* (which is discussed in Chapter 7), and a different set of policies is required to deal with it.

A second issue that deserves attention is that distinguishing between supply- and demand-side factors is not as easy as it may at first appear. Labor market discrimination may affect women's economic status *indirectly* by lowering their

---

[1] Sociologists might question the appropriateness of the term "discrimination" in the context of gender socialization. We use it here only to the extent that the socialization process adversely affects the labor market success of young women.

incentives to invest in themselves and to acquire particular job qualifications. Thus, gender differences in productivity-related characteristics may reflect not only the voluntary choices of men and women and the impact of societal discrimination but also the indirect effects of labor market discrimination. This latter point will be developed further in Chapter 7.

HUMAN CAPITAL

Within the economics literature, the major supply-side explanation for gender differentials in economic outcomes has been developed within the context of the human capital model. Most of us are familiar with the notion of investments in **physical capital.** For example, business people expend resources today to build new plants or to purchase new machinery. This augments their firms' productive capabilities and increases their output in future years. They make such decisions based upon a comparison of the expected costs and benefits of these investments. Economists like Theodore Schultz, Gary Becker, and Jacob Mincer have pointed out that individuals and their families make analogous decisions regarding **human capital** investments.[2] In this case, resources are invested in an individual today in order to increase his or her future productivity and earnings. Examples of human capital investments include investments in formal education, on-the-job training, job search, and geographic migration.

Although the analogy between physical and human capital is compelling, there are some important differences between the two. Chiefly, an individual's human capital investment decisions will be influenced to a greater extent by nonpecuniary (nonmonetary) considerations than is typically the case for physical capital investment decisions. Some people enjoy going to school; others do not. Some find indoor, white-collar work attractive; others would prefer to do manual work in the fresh air. This difference between physical and human capital illustrates the general point that although labor markets are similar to other markets, they are not identical to them—in large part because labor services cannot be separated from the individuals who provide them. This does not invalidate the use of economic analysis in the study of labor markets, but it does require us to be more aware of the impact of nonpecuniary factors, which can be very important.

We first focus upon the pecuniary aspects of the human capital investment decision and then consider how nonpecuniary factors might influence the analysis. We emphasize two major kinds of human capital investments—formal schooling and on-the-job training. According to the work of Jacob Mincer and Solomon Polachek, and other human capital theorists, gender differences in these areas—in

[2]See, for example, Theodore W. Schultz, "Investment in Human Capital," *American Economic Review* 51, no. 1 (March 1960): 1–17; Gary S. Becker, *Human Capital: A Theoretical and Empirical Analysis, With Special Reference to Education,* 2nd ed. (Chicago: University of Chicago Press, 1975); Jacob Mincer; "On-the-Job Training: Costs, Returns and Some Implications," *Journal of Political Economy* 70, no. 5, pt. 2 (Oct. 1962): S50–S79.

both the amount and type of investments to make—can produce substantial differences in the pay and occupations of men and women in the labor market.[3]

GENDER DIFFERENCES
IN EDUCATIONAL ATTAINMENT

Gender differences in the educational attainment of men and women in the labor force are shown in Table 6.1 for 1962 and 1989.[4] The table shows that the median years of schooling of women workers were the same as men's in 1989 and actually slightly higher in 1962. However, this overall similarity concealed some significant gender differences in the *pattern* of educational attainment of men and women.

Historically, women have been more likely to complete high school than men, but a higher proportion of men than women have completed college and gone on to post-graduate education. This is reflected in the data for both years shown in the table.

For example, in 1989, 16.4 percent of men, compared to 11.7 percent of women, had completed less than four years of high school. On the other hand, 25.2 percent of men, compared to 22.6 percent of women, had four or more years of college. However, the gender difference in higher education had declined since the 1960s, as younger cohorts with more similar educational attainment entered the labor market. In 1962, a male worker was 23 percent more likely than a female worker to have completed four or more years of college. By 1989, the difference had dropped to 12 percent.

The data in Table 6.1 also show rising educational attainment of both men and women in the labor force over the period, with median years of school completed increasing by almost a year for men and more than half a year for women. A typical worker of either sex was much less likely not to have completed high school in 1989 than in 1962, and considerably more likely to have had some schooling beyond high school.

Educational attainment is shown separately by race and Hispanic origin in Table 6.2. We see that, in 1989, both blacks and Hispanics in the labor force had lower educational attainment than whites. However, the race difference was fairly small and reflected a considerable increase in the relative educational attainment of blacks, particularly since the 1960s. For example, in 1962, the median educational attainment of black males was 3.1 years less than that of white males, but the

---

[3] See, for example, Jacob Mincer and Solomon Polachek, "Family Investments in Human Capital: Earnings of Women," *Journal of Political Economy* 82, no. 2, pt. 2 (March/April 1974): S76–S108; Elizabeth M. Landes, "Sex Differences in Wages and Employment: A Test of the Specific Capital Hypothesis," *Economic Inquiry* 15, no. 4 (Oct. 1977): 523–38; Harriet Zellner, "The Determinants of Occupational Segregation," in *Sex Discrimination and the Division of Labor,* Cynthia B. Lloyd, ed. (New York: Columbia University Press, 1975), pp. 125–45.

[4] The patterns of gender differences are similar for the male and female population as a whole. We present data for the labor force because we are interested in education as a potential explanation for gender differences in labor market outcomes.

TABLE 6.1   Educational Attainment of the Labor Force by Gender, 1962, 1989[a]

Years of School Completed	1962		1989	
	Males (%)	*Females (%)*	*Males (%)*	*Females (%)*
Total	100.0	100.0	100.0	100.0
Less than 4 years of high school	48.0	39.4	16.4	11.7
4 years of high school only	29.6	39.7	38.3	43.2
1 to 3 years of college	10.5	11.2	20.1	22.5
4 or more years of college	11.9	9.7	25.2	22.6
Median school years completed	12.1	12.3	12.9	12.9

[a]Civilian labor force aged 18 to 64 in March of each year.

Source: Data for 1962: U.S. Department of Labor, Bureau of Labor Statistics, Special Labor Force Report Bulletin no. 2191 (April 1984), Table B-1, p. 10; data for 1989 calculated from the microdata file of the March 1989 Current Population Survey.

gap was only 0.3 years in 1989. Among females, the race difference had declined from 1.8 years in 1962 to 0.1 years in 1989. The Hispanic-white differential was larger than the race difference in 1989, particularly for males, but it had declined for that group as well since statistics began to be collected separately for Hispanics in 1974. Nonetheless, minorities, particularly Hispanics, were considerably more likely than whites not to have completed high school and considerably less likely to have completed four or more years of college.

Among minority workers, women had a somewhat higher level of educational attainment than men. This does not, however, represent the situation for the black and Hispanic populations as a whole (including persons not in the labor force).

TABLE 6.2   Educational Attainment of the Labor Force by Gender, Race and Hispanic Origin, 1989[a]

Years of School Completed	WHITES		BLACKS		HISPANICS	
	Males (%)	*Females (%)*	*Males (%)*	*Females (%)*	*Males (%)*	*Females (%)*
Less than 4 years of high school	15.7	10.8	23.4	16.8	46.3	32.9
4 years of high school only	38.2	43.6	43.6	44.2	29.6	36.6
1 to 3 years of college	20.1	22.6	20.1	22.9	14.7	18.5
4 or more years of college	26.0	22.9	12.9	16.1	9.5	12.1
Median school years completed	12.9	12.9	12.6	12.8	12.1	12.5

[a]Civilian labor force aged 18 to 64 in March.

Source: Calculated from the microdata file of the March 1989 Current Population Survey.

Rather, it is due to the greater tendency of more highly educated women to partic-ipate in the labor force.

The trends in higher education by gender, shown in greater detail in Table 6.3, reinforce our impression of declining differences among younger cohorts. In the mid-1960s, women received 42 percent of Bachelor's degrees and 34 percent of Master's degrees. By 1988, slightly over half of these degrees were awarded to women. While women still received a substantially smaller proportion of doctor-ates and first-professional degrees than men in 1988, this represented a substantial increase of the female share since the mid-1960s.

The figures on educational attainment reveal only part of the story of gender differences in formal schooling, however. For at each level of education, men and women differ substantially in the types of courses they take and their fields of specialization. For example, at the secondary level, women tend to take fewer courses in natural sciences and mathematics than men. In terms of vocational courses, they are more likely to take commercial (including secretarial) training and home economics and less likely to take trade or industrial arts.[5] Table 6.4 shows that there were also substantial differences between men and women in fields of specialization at the college level in 1988, but that they had narrowed considerably over the preceding 20 years. Women also posted large gains in the proportion of first professional degrees awarded to them in traditionally male professions (Table 6.5).

In summary, we find that the equality between men and women in median educational attainment conceals some important gender differences that may have

TABLE 6.3 Percentage of Degrees Awarded to Women, by Level of Degree, 1930–1988 (Selected Years)

Year	Bachelor's (%)	Master's (%)	Doctor's (%)	First Professional (%)
1930	39.9[a]	40.4	15.4	n.a.
1966	42.4	33.8	11.6	3.8
1971	43.4	40.1	14.3	6.3
1975	45.3	44.8	21.3	12.4
1981	49.8	50.3	31.1	26.6
1988[b]	52.0	51.5	35.2	35.7

[a]Includes first professional degrees.

[b]Prelimanary data

Source: U.S. Depratment of Education, National Center for Education Statistics, *Digest of Education Statestics 1990*.

[5]Myra and David Sadker, "Sexism in the Schoolroom of the '80s," *Psychology Today* 19 (March 1985): 54–57; Joseph Berger, "All in the Game," *New York Times, Education Life* August 6, 1989, pp. Educ 23–24; and Barbara F. Reskin and Heidi I. Hartmann, *Women's Work, Men's Work: Sex Segregation on the Job* (Washington, DC: National Academy Press, 1986), Ch. 3.

TABLE 6.4   Percentage of Bachelor's Degrees Awarded to Women by Discipline, 1966 and 1988 (Selected Fields)

Discipline	1966 (%)	1988[a] (%)
Agriculture and natural resources	2.7	31.5
Architecture	4.0	26.6
Business	8.5	46.7
Computer and information science	13.0[b]	32.4
Education	75.3	76.9
Engineering	0.4	15.3
English and English literature	66.2	67.9
Foreign languages	70.7	72.8
Health	76.9	85.4
Home economics	97.5	93.0
Life sciences	28.2	50.3
Mathematics	33.3	46.4
Physical sciences	13.6	30.3
Psychology	41.0	70.0
Social sciences	35.0	43.9
Economics	9.8	32.8
History	34.6	37.4
Sociology	59.6	68.8

[a]Preliminary data.

[b]Data are for 1969, the earliest year available.

Source: U.S. Department of Health, Education and Welfare, Office of Education, *Earned Degrees Conferred: 1965–66;* U.S. Department of Education, National Center for Education Statistics, *Digest of Education Statistics, 1990.*

TABLE 6.5   Percentage of First Professional Degrees Awarded to Women by Discipline, 1966 and 1988 (Selected Fields)

Field	1966 (%)	1988[a] (%)
Dentistry	1.1	26.1
Medicine	6.7	33.0
Pharmacy	16.4	59.7
Veterinary Medicine	8.0[b]	50.0
Law	3.8	40.4
Theological professions	4.1	21.4

[a]Preliminary data.

[b]Data are for 1968, the earliest year available.

Source: U.S. Department of Health, Education and Welfare, Office of Education, *Earned Degrees Conferred: 1965–66;* U.S. Department of Education, National Center for Educational Statistics, *Digest of Education Statistics, 1990.*

an impact on women's earnings and occupational attainment in the labor market. Historically, women have been more likely than men to complete high school, but a higher proportion of men than of women have completed four or more years of college. Further, at both the level of secondary and higher education, men and women tend to differ in their fields of specialization. However, all these differences have been narrowing in recent years.

We now turn to a consideration of the human capital theorists' explanation for the historical tendency of men and women to acquire different amounts of education and to specialize in different fields. We then consider the consequences of these decisions for gender differentials in labor market outcomes according to this model.

THE EDUCATIONAL INVESTMENT DECISION

We begin by considering an individual's decision of whether or not to invest in formal education as illustrated in Figure 6.1. Here we consider Daniel's choice between going to college and ending his formal education with high school. Initially, we focus solely upon the pecuniary costs and benefits of investing in education, although later we consider psychic (nonpecuniary) costs and benefits as well. This investment decision entails a comparison between the expected **experience-earnings profiles** (the annual earnings associated with each level of labor market experience) associated with each type of schooling.

In this case, Daniel expects his profile to be *EF* if he enters the labor market after completing high school. Alternatively, if he goes on to college, he will incur out-of-pocket expenses on tuition and books of *OA* dollars per year (negative "earnings") for the four-year period. (He does not anticipate working during school.) Upon graduation, he expects to earn *OC′* dollars. The investment in a college education is believed to increase his productivity and, hence, his earnings above what he could have earned entering the labor force directly after high school (*OE*). Although he initially earns less than he could have if he had worked for four years rather than going to college, over his work life his expected earnings are higher. His experience-earnings profile, if he goes to college, is *ABCG*.

As indicated in Figure 6.1, the earnings of both high school and college graduates are expected to increase with labor market experience over much of the individual's work life. Human capital theory attributes this to the productivity-enhancing effects of on-the-job training, which we discuss later in this chapter. Note that Figure 6.1 shows the college graduate's profile as rising more steeply than that of the high school graduate. This has indeed been found to be the case empirically and suggests that college graduates acquire more training informally on the job as well as formally in school.

Now let us consider how Daniel can use the information in Figure 6.1 to make his investment decision. To do so he considers both the incremental costs and the incremental benefits associated with graduating from college. There are

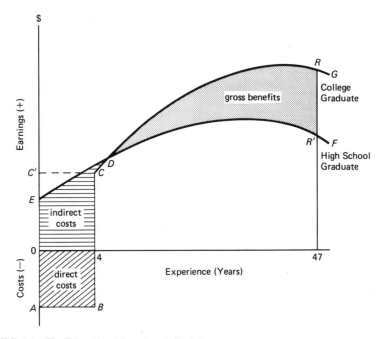

FIGURE 6.1   The Educational Investment Decision

two types of costs of schooling that he must take into account. **Direct costs** are expenditures on such items as tuition, fees, and books. Less obvious, but no less important than direct costs, are the earnings forgone during the time an individual is in school. These **indirect costs** correspond to the opportunity costs of schooling. We have assumed that Daniel does not work while attending college, but even if he did work, his forgone earnings are still likely to be substantial—college students seldom work as many hours or for as high a wage as workers who are not enrolled in school. The full costs of a college education are equal to the sum of the direct and indirect costs, or area *EABCD*.

The gross benefits of a college education are given by the excess of the expected earnings of a college graduate over those of a high school graduate over the work life. The size of these benefits depends on the length of the expected work life. If Daniel expects to work 43 years after college until retirement at age 65, his benefits are equal to the shaded area *DRR'*.

For Daniel to decide in favor of a college education (on an economic basis), the *gross benefits* of this investment must exceed the costs, that is, the *net benefits* must be positive. Further, gross benefits must exceed costs by an amount sufficient to give him an adequate return on his investment. Individuals may differ on the rate of return required to induce them to undertake this investment, but all are likely to require a positive rate of return.

For one thing, instead of investing resources in human capital, Daniel could have put his money into a savings bank or invested it in other assets. Those alternatives provide a positive rate of return and, thus, his human capital investment must also do so in order to be competitive. More fundamentally, Daniel, like most people, prefers income (and the opportunity to spend it) now to income (and the opportunity to spend it) later. To induce him to delay his gratification and receive his income later rather than sooner, the market has to offer him (and others like him) an inducement in the form of a positive rate of return. In Daniel's case, the investment does appear profitable, and he is likely to decide to go on to college. Actual estimates of the average private rate of return to a college education range from 5 to 15 percent.[6] Numerous studies have confirmed that earnings rise with additional education for both men and women, although not necessarily to the same extent (this is illustrated in Figure 6.7).

EDUCATION AND PRODUCTIVITY

Human capital theory postulates that earnings rise with additional education because of the productivity-enhancing effects of education. Intuitively, it seems reasonable that education imparts a variety of skills and knowledge that would potentially be useful on the job, ranging from specific skills like computer programming and accounting to general skills like reasoning ability, writing skills, and proficiency in solving mathematical problems. Educational institutions may also teach certain behaviors that are valued on the job, such as punctuality, following instructions, and habits of predictability and dependability.[7]

Others have suggested an alternative interpretation of the positive relationship between education and earnings in which education functions solely as a **screening device** or a **signal**.[8] In this view, employers have imperfect information on worker productivity and, thus, seek ways to distinguish more productive applicants from less productive applicants before hiring them. At the same time, it is assumed that more able (productive) individuals find the (psychic and monetary) costs of acquiring additional schooling lower than the less able (say, because they find their studies less arduous or because they are awarded scholarships). Having lower costs,

[6]See, for example, Walter W. McMahon and Alan P. Wagner, "The Monetary Returns to Education as Partial Social Efficiency Criteria," *Financing Education, Overcoming Inefficiency and Inequity* (Urbana: University of Illinois Press, 1982), pp. 150–87; George Psacharopoulos, "Returns to Education: An Updated International Comparison," *Comparative Education* 17, no. 3 (1981): 337–28. Calculating the rate of return involves estimating the increase in earnings attributable to additional education as well as all the costs involved in acquiring it, including both forgone earnings and out-of-pocket expenses, then relating the former to the latter. For a critical review of the empirical literature testing the human capital approach, see Mark Blaug, "The Empirical Status of Human Capital Theory: A Slightly Jaundiced Survey," *Journal of Economic Literature* 14, no. 3 (September 1976): 827–55.

[7]See, for example, Richard C. Edwards, "Individual Traits and Organizational Incentives: What Makes a 'Good' Worker?" *The Journal of Human Resources* 11, no. 1 (Winter 1976): 51–68.

[8]See, especially, Michael Spence, *Market Signalling* (Cambridge, MA: Harvard University Press, 1974).

an educational investment may be profitable for the more able when it would not be for the less able. In an extreme version of the signaling model, education is rewarded *solely* because it *signals* higher productivity to the employer and *not* because of any skills it imparts.

Unfortunately, this theoretical disagreement between the human capital and signaling models has proved difficult to resolve empirically. This is the case because the issue is a particularly thorny one—not whether more education is correlated with higher productivity and earnings, but *why*.[9] From the individual's perspective, however, it does not matter whether education raises earnings by increasing productivity or by signaling greater ability. Thus, the decision-making process illustrated in Figure 6.1 would be unaffected.

Nonetheless, there is one potential consequence of the signaling model for gender differences in labor market outcomes that is worth noting. If employers believe that a given level of education signals lower productivity for a woman than for a man, women may have to have higher educational credentials than men to obtain the same job. So, for example, suppose an employer who is hiring for entry-level management positions believes that a college education signals a lower commitment to the labor market for women than for men. He or she may require a woman to have an MBA degree in order to obtain employment, while being perfectly willing to hire a man with only a college degree.[10] This is quite similar to the notion of **statistical discrimination** to be discussed in Chapter 7.

GENDER DIFFERENCES IN
EDUCATIONAL INVESTMENT DECISIONS

Does this analysis suggest that men and women may decide to acquire different amounts and/or types of formal education? According to the analysis we have presented, the major factors to consider are the expected costs and benefits of the investment. Realistically, the definitions of costs and benefits may be extended to include psychic (nonpecuniary), as well as pecuniary, costs and benefits, and we do so below. In addition, because individuals may find it hard to borrow to finance their human capital investments, access to funds is a further consideration of some importance. Thus, we will want to consider why men and women might differ in these respects.

---

[9]For a summary of this literature, see Blaug, "The Empirical Status of Human Capital Theory"; see also John Riley, "Testing the Educational Screening Hypothesis," *Journal of Political Economy* 87, no. 5, pt. 2 (October 1979): S227–S252.

[10]Such "qualifications" discrimination has been emphasized by Dolores A. Conway and Harry V. Roberts, "Reverse Regression, Fairness and Employment Discrimination," *Journal of Business and Economic Statistics* 1, no. 1 (January 1983): 75–85; and Richard F. Kamelich and Solomon W. Polachek, "Discrimination: Fact or Fiction? An Examination Using an Alternative Approach," *Southern Economic Journal* 49, no. 2 (October 1982): 450–61.

Expected Work Life

The major factor emphasized by human capital theorists as producing gender differences in human capital investments is that, given traditional roles in the family, many women anticipate shorter, more disrupted work lives than men. Such women will reach the point sooner when additional investment is no longer worthwhile. Further, it will not pay for them to make the types of human capital investments that require sustained, high-level commitment to the labor force to make them profitable and that depreciate rapidly during periods of work interruptions.

The impact of these factors is illustrated in Figure 6.2, where we have reproduced the earnings profiles shown in Figure 6.1. Note that the horizontal axis now refers to potential experience or the total time elapsed since completing high school. We have done this in order to be able to represent periods of time out of the labor force on this diagram.

A career-oriented woman who anticipates working the same number of years as Daniel will find it equally profitable to invest in a college education, assuming she faces similar costs and has the opportunity to reap the same returns. However, a woman who expects to spend fewer years in the labor market will find her benefits correspondingly reduced.

For example, suppose Adele plans to work for a time—6 years—after college and then to drop out of the labor force for 10 years, say for childrearing. If she, like Daniel, expects to retire at age 65, her expected work life is 33 years in comparison to his 43 years. Her shorter work life reduces the benefits of her human capital investment because she does not earn income during the time she spends out of the labor force. Further, human capital theorists believe that skills depreciate during time spent out of the labor force—that is, when they are not used. They expect that, upon her return to the labor force after an interruption of 10 years, Adele's earnings of e_2 will be less than she was making when she left (e_1) and that she will be faced with profile GH rather than profile CD. We have shown profile GH as approaching CD over time, as Adele retools or becomes less rusty.[11] Nonetheless, the time out of the labor force has cost her a reduction in earnings over the remainder of her working life. In this particular example, the benefits of the investment in a college education, the sum of the two shaded areas, may not be large enough to make it worthwhile.

Thus, the human capital model shows how an adherence to traditional gender roles in the family can explain why women have been less likely than men to pursue college and graduate study. It also suggests one reason why gender differences in

---

[11] For empirical evidence that earnings tend to "rebound" after work force interruptions, see Mary Corcoran, "Work Experience, Labor Force Withdrawals and Women's Earnings: Empirical Results Using the 1976 Panel Survey of Income Dynamics," *Women in the Labor Market,* Cynthia B. Lloyd, Emily Andrews, and Curtis L. Gilroy, eds. (New York: Columbia University Press, 1979), pp. 216–245; Jacob Mincer and Haim Ofek, "Interrupted Work Careers: Depreciation and Restoration of Human Capital," *Journal of Human Resources* 17, no. 1 (Winter 1982): 3–24; and Mary Corcoran, Greg J. Duncan, and Michael Ponza, "A Longitudinal Analysis of White Women's Wages," *Journal of Human Resources* 18, no. 4 (Fall 1983): 497–520.

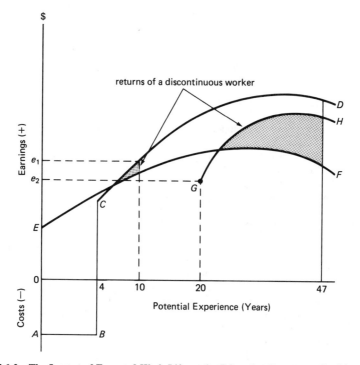

FIGURE 6.2   The Impact of Expected Work Life on the Education Investment Decision

college attendance have been declining. As we saw in Chapter 4, women have increased their labor force participation. As young women anticipate longer and more continuous working lives, it will be more profitable for them to increase their investment in formal education. Further, Figure 6.2 suggests that once women have decided to acquire higher education, for whatever reason, their attachment to the labor force is reinforced because the opportunity cost of time spent out of the labor force is increased.

Although the human capital model suggests a plausible explanation for the historical tendency of men to be more likely to pursue college and graduate study, it does not explain why women have tended in the past to be *more* likely than men to complete high school. The gender disparity was quite sizable at one time. For example, in 1900, only two-thirds as many boys as girls graduated from high school. One possible explanation for this difference is that the opportunity cost of remaining in high school was lower for young women than for young men, since their potential labor market earnings were less. As job opportunities for young men who have not finished high school have declined, so too has the gender differential in high school completion.

The human capital model also suggests that discontinuity of expected labor force participation may help to explain gender differences in fields of specialization. In some fields, as in science and engineering, technological change progresses

SEXISM IN THE SCHOOLROOM

Gender differences in academic achievement and labor market success may be traced in part to differences in the way girls and boys are treated in the classroom. The article* excerpted below describes these important differences and their significance.

If a boy calls out in class, he gets teacher attention, especially intellectual attention. If a girl calls out in class, she is told to raise her hand before speaking. Teachers praise boys more than girls, give boys more academic help and are more likely to accept boys' comments during classroom discussions. These are only a few examples of how teachers favor boys. Through this advantage boys increase their chances for better education and possibly higher pay and quicker promotions. . . .

Education is not a spectator sport. Numerous researchers . . . have shown that when students participate in classroom discussion they hold more positive attitudes toward school, and that positive attitudes enhance learning. It is no coincidence that girls are more passive in the classroom and score lower than boys on SAT's.

Most teachers claim that girls participate and are called on in class as often as boys. But a three-year study we recently completed found that this is not true; vocally, boys clearly dominate the classroom. When we showed teachers and administrators a film of a classroom discussion and asked who was talking more, the teachers overwhelmingly said the girls were. But in reality, the boys in the film were out-talking the girls at a ratio of three to one. Even educators who are active in feminist issues were unable to spot the sex bias until they counted and coded who was talking and who was just watching. Stereotypes of garrulous and gossipy women are so strong that teachers fail to see this communications gender gap even when it is right before their eyes.

Field researchers in our study observed students in more than a hundred fourth-, sixth- and eighth-grade classes in four states and the District of Columbia. The teachers and students were male and female, black and white, from urban, suburban and rural communities. Half of the classrooms covered language arts and English—subjects in which girls traditionally have excelled; the other half covered math and science—traditionally male domains.

We found that at all grade levels, in all communities and in all subject areas, boys dominated classroom communication. They participated in more interactions than girls did and their participation became greater as the year went on.

Our research contradicted the traditional assumption that girls dominate classroom discussion in reading while boys are dominant in math. We found that whether the subject was language arts and English or math and science, boys got more than their fair share of teacher attention.

Some critics claim that if teachers talk more to male students, it is simply because boys are more assertive in grabbing their attention—a classic case of the squeaky wheel getting the educational oil. In fact, our research shows that boys are more assertive in the classroom. While girls sit patiently with their hands

*Myra and David Sadker, "Sexism in the Schoolroom of the '80s," *Psychology Today* 19 (March 1985): pp. 54–57. Reprinted by permission.

raised, boys literally grab teacher attention. They are eight times more likely than girls to call out answers. However, male assertiveness is not the whole answer.

Teachers behave differently, depending on whether boys or girls call out answers during discussions. When boys call out comments without raising their hands, teachers accept their answers. However, when girls call out, teachers reprimand this "inappropriate" behavior with messages such as, "In this class we don't shout out answers, we raise our hands." The message is subtle but powerful: Boys should be academically assertive and grab teacher attention; girls should act like ladies and keep quiet. . . .

Girls are often shortchanged in quality as well as in quantity of teacher attention. In 1975 psychologists Lisa Serbin and K. Daniel O'Leary, then at the State University of New York at Stony Brook, studied classroom interaction at the preschool level and found that teachers gave boys more attention, praised them more often and were at least twice as likely to have extended conversations with them. Serbin and O'Leary also found that teachers were twice as likely to give male students detailed instructions on how to do things for themselves. With female students, teachers were more likely to do it for them instead. The result was that boys learned to become independent, girls learned to become dependent. . . .

Years of experience have shown that the best way to learn something is to do it yourself; classroom chivalry is not only misplaced, it is detrimental. It is also important to give students specific and direct feedback about the quality of their work and answers. During classroom discussion, teachers in our study reacted to boys' answers with dynamic, precise and effective responses, while they often gave girls bland and diffuse reactions. . . .

Too often, girls remain in the dark about the quality of their answers. Teachers rarely tell them if their answers are excellent, need to be improved or are just plain wrong. Unfortunately, acceptance, the imprecise response packing the least educational punch, gets the most equitable sex distribution in classrooms. Active students receiving precise feedback are more likely to achieve academically. And they are more likely to be boys. Consider the following:

- Although girls start school ahead of boys in reading and basic computation, by the time they graduate from high school, boys have higher SAT scores in both areas.
- By high school, some girls become less committed to careers, although their grades and achievement-test scores may be as good as boys'. Many girls' interests turn to marriage or stereotypically female jobs. Part of the reason may be that some women feel that men disapprove of their using their intelligence.
- Girls are less likely to take math and science courses and to participate in special or gifted programs in these subjects, even if they have a talent for them. They are also more likely to believe that they are incapable of pursuing math and science in college and to avoid the subjects.
- Girls are more likely to attribute failure to internal factors, such as ability, rather than to external factors, such as luck. . . .

There is an urgent need to remove sexism from the classroom and give women the same educational encouragement and support that men receive. When women are treated equally in the classroom, they will be more likely to achieve equality in the workplace.

rapidly. A woman returning from a labor force interruption will not only have to contend with her depreciation of skills over the interim but also with the advancement of the field during her absence. On the other hand, in such other fields as teaching history or English, the pace of change is slower. A woman returning from a work force interruption is likely to find that her earnings fall less steeply. Women anticipating traditional roles are, therefore, expected to avoid fields where the rate of technological change is rapid and to concentrate in fields where the cost of work force interruptions is lower.[12] Thus, women's increasing labor force attachment may partially explain their increased representation in traditionally male fields of study.

Societal Discrimination

Although expected working life is a factor that has been particularly emphasized by human capital theorists, societal discrimination may also cause gender differences in educational attainment and field of specialization. To see this, we must consider the psychic as well as the pecuniary costs and benefits of human capital investments. Societal influences may raise the costs of, or lower the returns to, specific types or levels of education for women relative to men. At these higher costs, and/or lower returns, the investment in education may not prove profitable for many women.

This situation is particularly apt to arise in fields that have traditionally been predominantly male. Moreover, it is important to bear in mind that social pressures also help to cause the gender differences in labor force participation emphasized by the human capital theorists. In addition, women's lower labor force participation may to some extent be due to the discrimination they face in the labor market, which reduces their opportunities and lowers their earnings. Such feedback effects of labor market discrimination are considered in greater detail in Chapter 7.

Socialization. Socialization is the name given to the process by which the influence of family, friends, teachers, and the media shape an individual's attitudes and behavior.[13] One of the insets in this chapter illustrates the considerable extent of gender differentiation in the classroom; another points out how even something as innocuous as a children's game can reinforce stereotypical views of appropriate occupations. As another example, it has been found that male characters

---

[12]For evidence in support of lifetime work commitment as a factor causing gender differences in college major, see Solomon W. Polachek, "Sex Differences in College Major," *Industrial and Labor Relations Review* 31, no. 4 (July 1978): 498–508.

[13]For descriptions of the impact of the socialization process on gender roles, see Hilary M. Lips, "Gender-Role Socialization: Lessons in Femininity," in *Women: A Feminist Perspective,* Jo Freeman, ed. (Mountain View, CA: Mayfield, 1989), 4th ed., pp. 197–216; and Margaret M. Marini and Mary C. Brinton, "Sex Stereotyping in Occupational Socialization," in *Sex Segregation in the Work Place: Trends, Explanations, and Remedies,* Barbara Reskin, ed. (Washington, DC: National Academy Press, 1984).

dominate children's television programming; there are very few female characters on children's shows and hardly any in leading roles.[14] Moreover, a study analyzing general viewing fare during the 1989–90 television season concluded that "women are often still depicted on television as half-clad and half-witted, and needing to be rescued by quick-thinking, fully-clothed men."[15]

The socialization process influences the self-esteem of men and women, as well as their perceptions of gender-appropriate competencies and behavior. It also helps to shape the role they expect work to occupy in their lives and the types of jobs to which they aspire. We have already seen how gender differences in the expected importance of market work in their lives may influence men's and women's human capital investment decisions. The consequences of gender differences in occupational orientation are also important. From an early age, boys and girls are taught to aspire to and train for gender-appropriate lines of work. This tends to result in gender differences in fields of specialization. Further, even if, despite these influences, a young woman does form a desire to enter a traditionally male field, the disapproval of her family, teachers, or friends is a psychic cost for her that lowers her subjective evaluation of the net value of this investment.[16] Familial disapproval may also pose practical problems for a young woman, if her family is more reluctant to finance her education than her brother's.

Gender appropriate traits and competencies. Social influences may operate in other ways that are less direct but no less influential. For example, women may be socialized to emphasize appropriate "feminine" personality traits, such as being subordinate, nurturant, and emotional. Traditionally male fields may be stereotyped as requiring "masculine" personality traits such as dominance, competitiveness, and rationality. Having internalized the idea of what is properly female, women may then avoid male fields because they perceive a psychic cost in acting in an "unfeminine" manner or simply because they feel unequipped to do so. In the latter case, they might expect to be less successful in the field, thus lowering their expected returns. Similarly, if women are reared to believe they lack competence in "masculine" subjects like math and science, this would raise their perceived costs and lower their perceived returns to entry into fields emphasizing this knowledge.[17] Men may see traditionally female fields as inappropriate for similar reasons.

---

[14]Bill Carter, "Children's TV, Where Boys are King," *The New York Times,* May 1, 1991, pp. 1, B6.

[15]Andrea Adelson, "Study Attacks Roles of Women in Television," *The New York Times,* November 19, 1990, p. B3.

[16]One study found that women graduate students in the biological and physical sciences received less moral support from their mothers than either the male students in the same field or students of either sex in education. See Helen M. Berg and Marianne A. Ferber, "Men and Women Graduate Students: Who Succeeds and Why?" *Journal of Higher Education* 54, no. 6 (November/December 1983): 629–48.

[17]For analyses of gender differences in mathematics and computer learning, see Sheila Tobias, *Overcoming Math Anxiety* (New York: W. W. Norton, 1978), Ch. 3; and Pamela E. Kramer and Sheila Lehman, "Mismeasuring Women: A Critique of Research on Computer Ability and Avoidance," *Signs: Journal of Women in Culture and Society* 16, no. 1 (Autumn 1990), pp. 158–72.

MISGUIDED GAMESMANSHIP

Societal influences regarding appropriate gender roles are pervasive. Even parents seeking to reinforce nontraditional roles often find themselves bucking more traditional messages from outside the family. In the column reprinted below, the author* criticizes the stereotyped career choices presented in a children's game.

The first call came last week from Pat Reuss, one of the leading women's lobbyists in town. She'd seen an ad in the paper for a new board game from Parker Bros., and she was outraged.

The game is called Careers for Girls. And the careers are—hold on to your MBAs out there—fashion designer, animal doctor, college graduate, schoolteacher, supermom and rock star.

"Have they forgotten Sally Ride?" asked Reuss.

The second call was from one of the most prominent lawyers in town, Marna Tucker. She had gotten a call from another woman lawyer about the game, and that prompted Tucker to go to a toy store and look at it. Among other things, it comes in a hot pink box with all sorts of subliminal messages, including a bracelet that says "baby" in one corner on the back.

Tucker called Parker Bros.' president and got a call back from the company's legal counsel, a woman. The two women lawyers did not see eye to eye on this game.

"I said that I was upset that they had adopted new stereotypes for women's jobs," Tucker said. "This woman, who was very nice, said this was not a game about role models, it was strictly entertainment for preteen girls. I said, 'Oh, is next year's entertainment game going to be Little Black Sambo?' She told me that the jobs were based on marketing surveys, and I said, 'Where were the marketing surveys done? In Saudi Arabia?'

"You can't just use marketing surveys with no sense of responsibility.

"I said, 'I can't believe you can be a woman lawyer in this day and age and not see what is offensive about the game.' "

Deb deSherbinin, senior product manager at Parker Bros., defended the game yesterday and said it was "intended for entertainment purposes only. All the careers in it are good. Parker Brothers had no intention of stereotyping girls at all, and that is really shocking to us. Parker Brothers recognized girls want to have careers just like boys. There's nothing sexist about careers such as a doctor or a rock star. The game was designed by a woman, art was managed by a woman and I'm the marketing woman behind it. It was done by women based on what we saw girls wanted."

Games are among the many tools that societies use to guide boys and girls into growing up the way society wants them to. Black leaders and feminist leaders have long understood the importance of role models and examples both in limiting people's aspirations and in pushing them to strive to new heights. Women of accomplishment who are in their sixties and seventies often say they looked upon the early women pilots, such as Amelia Earhart, as role models.

*Judy Mann, "Misguided Gamesmanship," *Washington Post,* November 21, 1990, p. B3.
© 1990, *The Washington Post.* Reprinted with permission.

What's offensive about Careers for Girls is that the women's movement has spent the last 25 years fighting career tracks and stereotypes about what's appropriate work for women so that women can have the same career choices as men. Women know very well that it is no accident that the professions in which they dominate numerically are the least well paid, and millions of women have gone into so-called nontraditional jobs to have better careers.

In a small sense, Careers for Girls would have represented progress had it come out in the late '60s because it makes the mini-leap from nurse to animal doctor, which was a field then closed to women. But we are now in the '90s, not the '60s, and we have lots of women veterinarians, and we don't need throwbacks that limit the expectations of the next generation of little girls.

What the toymakers ought to be doing is awakening young people of both sexes to the extraordinary range of careers open to them. If there is one unifying message of the modern women's movement, it is that sex-based careers are out. And so are sex-based career games.

Biased evaluations. Even women's possession of "male" traits or competencies and their willingness to display them may not guarantee them an equal amount of success. Studies have found that, among both female and male college students, identical papers were given higher ratings on such dimensions as value, persuasiveness, profundity, writing style, and competence when respondents believed the author to be male rather than female. Similar findings have been obtained in studies requiring both women and men to evaluate the qualifications of applicants for employment.[18] The expectation of inferior performance may eventually cause that inferior performance. Even if it does not, it would lower the expected return to investments in educational credentials.

Discrimination by educational institutions. Discrimination against women in the course of their studies, particularly in male fields, may increase the psychic costs of obtaining the education and/or lower the returns to their investment. It is well to remember that overt discrimination against women in admission to college and professional school was pervasive in the not too distant past. In America, women were not admitted to higher education until 1837 when Oberlin College opened its doors.[19] Women did not gain entrance to medical school until 1847, and it was not until 1915 that the American Medical Association accepted women members. As late as 1869, the U.S. Supreme Court upheld the refusal of the

---

[18] See the studies cited in Virginia E. O'Leary and Ranald D. Hansen, "Trying Hurts Women, Helps Men: The Meaning of Effort," in *Women in the Work Force,* H. John Bernardin, ed. (New York: Praeger, 1982), pp. 102–4.

[19] The information on admissions of women is from Michelle Patterson and Laurie Engleberg, "Women in Male-Dominated Professions," in *Women Working: Theories and Facts in Perspective,* Ann H. Stromberg and Shirley Harkess, eds. (Mountain View, CA: Mayfield, 1978), pp. 266–92.

Illinois State Bar to admit a woman. One of the justices declared that "the natural and proper timidity and delicacy which belongs to the female sex evidently unfit it for many of the occupations of civil life."[20] Nonetheless, a year later, in 1870, the first woman did succeed in graduating from an American law school.

Even after these "firsts," women were not universally admitted to all in-stitutions of higher education in all fields for a very long time. The prestigious Harvard Medical School did not admit women until 1945; the Harvard Law School excluded women until 1950. Similarly, many highly respected undergraduate insti-tutions, like Princeton and Yale, remained male-only until the late 1960s or early 1970s. Others, like Harvard, granted women access to classes and some facilities but officially restricted them to a separate college.

Moreover, the opening of doors to women did not necessarily mean that the doors opened as widely for them as for men. Women continued in many cases to be discriminated against in admissions and financial aid policies long after they gained formal admittance. In some cases, women were held to higher standards than men; in others, overt or informal quotas limited the number of places available to them.[21] Often course requirements for male and female high school students were different, and at all levels, gender-based counseling was prevalent.

Policy issue: The role of government in combatting discrimination. These were the types of policies that Title IX of the Educational Amendments (to the Civil Rights Act of 1964), passed by Congress in 1972, was intended to remedy. It prohibits discrimination on the basis of sex in any educational program or activity receiving federal financial assistance and covers admissions, financial aid, access to programs and activities, as well as employment of teachers and other personnel.

Even though enforcement has not been rigorous, it is likely that this legisla-tion has contributed to the substantial changes in the extent and type of participation of women in the educational system that we have described. The main provisions relevant at the high school level are that all courses and programs, except sex in-struction, chorus, and contact sports, must be available to both males and females. At the university level, the most important provisions probably are for nondis-crimination in admissions[22] and in faculty hiring, and for equal availability of scholarships and fellowships, assistantships, research opportunities, and housing.

Title IX has had a particularly dramatic impact on collegiate athletics. Since its passage, support and facilities for women athletes have greatly increased, as has women's participation in athletics programs.[23] Ironically, as explained in an inset,

[20]Cited in Patterson and Engleberg, "Women in Male-Dominated Professions," p. 277.

[21]See, for example, Ann Sutherland Harris, "The Second Sex in Academe," *AAUP Bulletin* 56, no. 3 (Fall 1970): 283–95; and Mary Frank Fox, "Women and Higher Education: Gender Differences in the Status of Students and Scholars," in *Women: A Feminist Perspective,* Jo Freeman, ed. pp. 217–35.

[22]Private, single-sex undergraduate schools and public undergraduate schools that have been segregated since their inception are exempt, as are religious and military schools.

[23]Fox, "Women and Higher Education."

MORE WOMEN ARE PLAYING, BUT FEWER CALL THE SHOTS

Although implementation of Title IX has given a tremendous boost to women's participation in college athletics, their representation in coaching and administrative positions has fallen. The article* excerpted below explains why.

From basketball to cross-country, more women than ever before are competing in college sports, but fewer are coaching or running athletic programs.

Since 1972, when a Federal law was passed requiring colleges receiving Government money to provide equitable programs for women, opportunities for female athletes have expanded markedly.

But as women's sports gained more money and prestige, an increasing number of men sought and obtained coaching and administrative jobs previously held by women, according to a recent study of intercollegiate athletic programs. . . .

George S. King Jr., the athletic director at Purdue, discussed the resistance to hiring women. "Although there are top-notch women administrators, I'm not sure that coaches making a half-million dollars a year, with specific ideas about their programs, are ready to let a woman on the inside," he said. . . .

Educators, coaches and sports administrators said that some of those jobs had gone to men who were often deemed better qualified because they had coached the big-revenue sport of football or had contacts in the network of sports administrators.

In many cases, they said, women who apply must convince college administrators that they can juggle family responsibilities and a demanding job, a burden male applicants never carry.

"Sports is a flagrant example of discrimination against women," said Donna A. Lopiano, the women's athletic director at the University of Texas-Austin. "It's wild here in the trenches. When a woman goes after a job, she hears: If you're young, you'll have child-bearing problems. If you have a family, you can't handle the time demands. If you're not a parent, you're homosexual."

Lopiano said change would not come until more forceful positions were taken by the Federal Government; the schools and national organizations like the National Collegiate Athletic Association, the National Association of Intercollegiate Athletics and the United States Olympic Committee. . . .

"The small number of women and minorities in coaching and administration is a real concern," said Richard D. Schultz, executive director of the N.C.A.A. Although there are many qualified women, he said: "The pool of women applicants is not what it should be. The question is why. I hope it is not out and out discrimination, but one could certainly believe that's part of it." . . .

In 1972, more than 90 percent of women's teams were coached by women and run by female administrators. By 1978, the year by which schools had to comply with Title IX of the Federal Education Acts Amendment of 1972, only 58 percent of the 4,208 coaching jobs with women's teams were filled by women.

With men's and women's athletic departments merging, male administrators became athletic directors and women became assistants or found their jobs eliminated. Now, women account for only 15.9 percent of the administrators of women's programs and 47.3 percent of the 5,718 coaches for women's teams at the 828 N.C.A.A. schools, according to a recent study.

At the same time, the number of women competing in intercollegiate sports has increased in the last 18 years from approximately 34,000 or 16 percent of the total number of college students in sports, to 158,000, or 30 percent.

The authors of the study of intercollegiate athletic programs, R. Vivian Acosta and Linda J. Carpenter, professors of physical education at Brooklyn College, said the disparity between the increase in female athletes and the drop in women in coaching and administration can be explained by the effects of Title IX. The act required equitable equipment, training and facilities for women's teams and an increase in management salaries. As the pay rose and women's teams gained prestige, they said, men sought and were hired for top management and coaching jobs, beating out the female applicants. . . .

---

this expansion has been accompanied by a decline in the representation of women in coaching and administrative jobs as they have faced more competition from men for these positions.

Subtle barriers. Although most of these overt barriers have been removed, it is important to bear in mind that they did place serious limits on the educational options of older women. Thus, their impact continues to be reflected in the *current* occupational distribution of women. Further, subtle barriers to women's success in the study of traditionally male fields remain a problem.[24]

The male dominance of a given field can itself discourage young women from attempting to enter. In this way, past discrimination continues to have an impact on younger women. Lacking contact with or first-hand knowledge of successful women, they may assume (quite possibly erroneously) that they too would not be able to succeed. Even if they believe that times have changed and that their prospects for success are greater than indicated by the present low representation of women, the scarcity of women may still pose problems for them, limiting their eventual success and lowering the returns to entering predominantly male fields. For example, without older women to serve as **role models,** female entrants face more confusion about acceptable (or successful) modes of behavior and dress than do young men. They also lack access to the knowledge that older women have acquired about successful strategies for combining work roles and family responsibilities.

[24] These types of subtle barriers are well-described in Cynthia Fuchs Epstein, *Women's Place: Options and Limits in Professional Careers* (Berkeley: University of California Press, 1970); Fox, "Women and Higher Education," in *Women: A Feminist Perspective,* Freeman, ed., and Rosabeth Kanter, *Men and Women of the Corporation* (New York: Basic Books, 1977).

Thus, they are forced to be pioneers, and blazing a new trail is undoubtedly more difficult than following along a well-established path.

Women students may also be excluded from the informal relationships desirable for eventual career success. Older individuals who are well established in the field (mentors) often take promising young students (protégés) under their wing—informally socializing them into the norms of the field, giving them access to the latest research in the area, and tying them into their network of professional contacts.

The **mentor-protégé system** is generally the result of the older individual identifying with the younger person. Male mentors may simply not identify with young women. Or they may fear that the development of a close relationship with a young woman would be misunderstood by their colleagues or their wives.[25] Thus, women students are likely to be at a disadvantage in a predominantly male field. Their problems will be aggravated if male students neglect to include them in their **informal network.** Such informal contacts among students include study groups and discussions over lunches, sports, coffee breaks, or a Friday afternoon beer, where important information about the field and career opportunities are exchanged.

Thus, women often lack the support, encouragement, and access to information and job opportunities provided by informal contacts between teachers and students and among students, as well as female role models to emulate. This raises the psychic costs for them in comparison to otherwise similar male students, lowering their incentives to enter traditionally male fields. It also may result in their being less successful than comparable men in the field when they complete their studies. To the extent that they foresee this, their entry into predominantly male fields is further discouraged. Finally, labor market discrimination itself can adversely affect the incentives of women to invest in formal schooling, insofar as it results in a lower return on their investment. We shall consider this possibility in greater detail in the next chapter.

ON-THE-JOB TRAINING

One of the major insights of human capital theory is the observation that individuals can increase their productivity not only through their investment in formal education but also by learning important work skills while they are actually on the job.[26] Sometimes they participate in formal training programs sponsored by their employers. More often, they benefit from the informal instruction of their supervisors or coworkers and grow proficient at their jobs through repetition and

[25]For evidence that lack of mentors is a problem for female graduate students, see Berg and Ferber, "Men and Women Graduate Students."

[26]See, for example, Becker, *Human Capital;* Mincer, "On-the-Job Training: Cost, Returns and Some Implications"; and Walter Oi, "Labor as a Quasi-Fixed Factor," *Journal of Political Economy* 70, no. 6 (December 1962): 538–55.

trial-and-error. Human capital theory suggests that women's weaker attachment to the labor force, and their resulting lesser amount of labor market experience, means that they will acquire less of this valuable on-the-job training. Further, their expectation of spending fewer years in the labor market could result in their making smaller investments in this type of training than men during each year they spend on the job. As will be discussed in Chapter 7, women may also be denied equal access to on-the-job training.

GENDER DIFFERENCES IN
LABOR MARKET EXPERIENCE

Before developing these ideas further, let us look at the actual extent of gender differences in work experience. Unfortunately, this information is not collected by government agencies on a regular basis but must be pieced together from various special surveys.

The available data indicate that, on average, women in the labor market have less work experience than men. In 1984, for example, among employed workers aged 21 to 64, women averaged 5.2 years less labor market experience than men: 2.4 fewer years with their current employer and 2.8 fewer years of prior work experience.[27] On the other hand, the somewhat sketchy information available on recent trends in work experience suggest that gender differences have been narrowing in recent years.

Table 6.6 shows estimated mean years of labor market experience of employed women for the 1950 to 1986 period.[28] All age groups show an increase in labor market experience for the period taken as a whole, with much of the gains occurring in the post-1970 period. The gains since 1970 were largest for women in their thirties whose average experience levels increased by about two years. This reflects the greater continuity of female labor force participation over the life cycle. As may be seen in Table 6.7, gender differences in job tenure (length of time on the current job) also declined. Between 1966 and 1987, the tenure difference fell

---

[27] Calculated from U.S. Bureau of the Census, *Current Population Reports*, Series P-70, No. 10, *Male-Females Differences in Work Experience, Occupation, and Earnings: 1984* (1987).

[28] These estimates are based on information on women's labor force participation and labor force turnover rather than on direct information on actual work experience. However, direct data on experience, where available, suggest these estimates are reasonable. See, for example, June O'Neill, "The Trend in the Male-Female Wage Gap in the United States," *Journal of Labor Economics* 2, no. 4 (Jan. 1985 Supp.); Solomon W. Polachek "Trends in the Male-Female Wage Gap: The 1980s Compared to the 1970s," paper presented at the American Economic Association Meetings, December 1990; June O'Neill and Solomon Polachek, "Why the Gender Gap in Wages Narrowed in the 1980s," unpublished paper, November 1991; and Audrey Light and Manuelita Ureta, "Gender Differences in Wages and Job Turnover Among Continuously Employed Workers," *American Economic Review* 80, no. 2 (May 1990): 293–97. For complementary estimates for an earlier period, see Claudia Goldin, *Understanding the Gender Gap: An Economic History of American Women* (New York: Oxford University Press, 1990), Chapter 2.

TABLE 6.6   Estimated Years of Labor Market Experience of Working Women,
1950–1986

	AGE				
	25	*30*	*35*	*40*	*45*
1950	5.87	7.97	10.57	13.99	16.43
1960	5.76	8.48	11.83	13.68	16.58
1970	5.69	8.68	11.21	14.24	17.21
1980	6.23	9.50	11.70	14.39	16.97
1986	6.52	10.45	13.51	15.47	18.31

Source: Smith, James P., Michael P. Ward, "Women's Wages and Work in the Twentieth Century,"
RAND, R-3119-NICHD, 1984.

by one year among whites (to 1.7 years), and by a half a year among blacks (to
0.1 years).

Although Table 6.6 indicates that average levels of labor market experience within most age groups increased over the 1970s, it appears that the
average level of experience for all women workers actually fell slightly, because
the large increases in labor force participation of younger women (discussed in
Chapter 4) resulted in a decrease in the average age of women workers.[29] This is

TABLE 6.7   Tenure on Current Job of Employed Men and Women by Race
and Age, 1966 and 1987[a]

	MEDIAN YEARS ON THE JOB					
	1966			1987		
	Males	*Females*	*Difference*	*Males*	*Females*	*Difference*
Total, 16 and over	5.2	2.8	2.4	5.0	3.6	1.4
25 to 34 years	3.2	1.9	1.3	3.7	3.1	0.6
35 to 44 years	7.8	3.5	4.3	7.6	4.9	2.7
45 to 54 years	11.5	5.7	5.8	12.3	7.3	5.0
Whites, 16 and over	5.5	2.8	2.7	5.2	3.5	1.7
Blacks, 16 and over[b]	3.4	2.8	0.6	4.4	4.3	0.1

[a] Data are from January of each year; for 1966, totals include all workers 14 years and over.

[b] The data for 1966 include nonwhites.

Sources: 1966: June O'Neill, "The Trend in the Male-Female Wage Gap in the United States," *Journal
of Labor Economics* 2, no. 4 (Jan. 1985 Supp.), Table 6, p. S102; 1987: U.S. Department of Labor,
Bureau of Labor Statistics, "Most Occupational Changes are Voluntary," *News* (October 22, 1987).

[29]Goldin, *Understanding the Gender Gap,* p. 41.

ironic, considering that the growing labor force attachment of women during the child-bearing years would be expected to increase women's experience in the long run. By the 1980s, this process had played itself out and overall female experience levels unambiguously began to rise relative to males.[30]

To summarize, the view that women have, on average, less work experience than men appears to be borne out by the evidence. However, the differences between men and women in the extent of involvement in work outside the home seem to be narrowing over time. We examine below how, according to the human capital model, such differences could result in lower pay and differences in occupational choices between men and women.

THE ON-THE-JOB TRAINING INVESTMENT DECISION

Again we begin with a general analysis of the training investment decision. On-the-job training may be divided into two types:

- General training
- Firm-specific training

General training increases the individual's productivity to the same extent in all (or a large number of) firms. For example, an individual may learn to operate an office machine that is widely used by other firms in the labor market. On the other hand, **firm-specific** training, as its name implies, increases the individual's productivity only at the firm that provides the training. For example, one may learn how to operate and get things done within a particular bureaucracy or to deal with the idiosyncrasies of a particular piece of equipment. Most training probably combines elements of both. However, for simplicity we assume that training may be classified as being entirely general or entirely firm-specific.

General Training

General training is, by definition, completely transferable from the firm providing the training to other firms. The employer would presumably not be willing to foot any part of the bill for such training, because, in a competitive labor market, there is no way for the employer to collect any of the returns. The worker could simply leave the firm after obtaining the training and be paid what he or she is worth elsewhere. Thus, if general training is to occur, the employee must be willing to bear all the costs, since he or she will reap all the returns. As in the case of formal education, an individual decides whether or not to invest in general training by comparing the costs and benefits.

---

[30]Polachek, "Trends in the Male-Female Wage Gap," and O'Neill and Polachek, "Why the Gender Gap in Wages Narrowed in the 1980s."

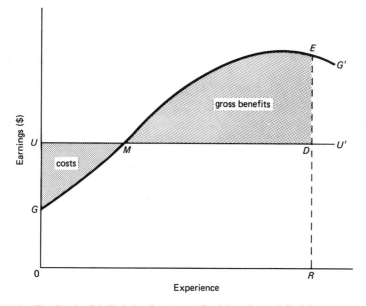

FIGURE 6.3   The On-the-Job Training Investment Decision: General Training

Let us consider Lisa's investment decision, illustrated in Figure 6.3. She will contrast the experience-earnings profile she can expect if she takes a job with no training (UU') to the profile she can expect if she receives general training (GG'). On-the-job training, although often informal, still entails costs just as does formal schooling. Some of these costs may be direct, such as for materials used in the training. Another portion of the costs is indirect, as the worker and his or her coworkers or supervisor transfer their attention from daily production to training activities. The resulting decline in output represents the opportunity cost to the firm of the training activity.

How does Lisa go about "paying" such costs if she decides to invest in general training? She does so by accepting a wage below what she could obtain elsewhere. This lower wage corresponds to her productivity (net of training costs) to the firm during the training period. The costs of the investment in general training are given by the area UGM. As Lisa becomes more skilled, her earnings catch up to and eventually surpass what she could have earned without training. Assuming a total of OR years of labor market experience over her work life, her gross benefits will be equal to the area MED. As in the case of formal schooling, she is likely to undertake the investment if gross benefits exceed costs by a sufficient amount to yield the desired rate of return (as appears to be the case in Figure 6.3).

Firm-Specific Training

Figure 6.4 illustrates Don's decision of whether or not to invest in firm-specific training. His productivity on the job is shown by the profile GG'. This

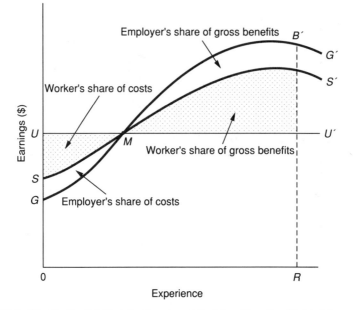

FIGURE 6.4 The On-the-Job Training Investment Decision: Firm-Specific Training

is also what his earnings profile would be if the training were general. However, since firm-specific training is not transferable, Don will not be willing to bear all the costs of the training, because his ability to reap the returns depends upon continued employment at the firm that initially provided the training. Were he to lose his job, his investment would be wiped out (the earnings profile available to him at another firm is UU'). Although Don would have a strong incentive to remain at the firm, the firm would have no particular reason to accord him any special protection from layoffs.

Similarly, the firm is unwilling to shoulder all the costs of firm-specific training because if Don were to quit, the firm would lose its investment. If the firm were to pay all the costs and receive all the returns, Don's profile would be UU'. He would have no special incentive to remain with the firm because he would be earning no more than he could get elsewhere. A temporary shift in demand that resulted in higher wages in another industry or even just more favorable working conditions at another firm might be sufficient to lure him away.

The solution is for the worker and the firm to share the costs of, and returns to, firm-specific training, in which case the specifically trained worker's profile would be SS'. The worker (Don) has an incentive to remain with the firm after completing training because he earns more there than he can get elsewhere (given by profile UU'). The firm also has an incentive to retain a worker who has completed specific training, even in the face of, say, a dip in the demand for the firm's product. This is true because the specifically trained worker (again, Don in this case) is actually being paid less than his productivity—after point M, SS' lies below GG'.

There are two important implications of this analysis of firm-specific training. First, a relatively permanent attachment is likely to develop between the firm and the specifically trained worker. Such workers are less likely either to quit or to be laid off their jobs than untrained or generally trained workers. Second, because employers pay part of the costs of firm-specific training, they will be concerned about the expected employment stability of workers hired into jobs where such training is important. (We further develop this point below.)

As Figures 6.3 and 6.4 suggest, earnings will increase with experience for workers who have invested in training. Considerable empirical evidence does indeed exist of a positive relationship between labor market experience and earnings for workers of both sexes, although the return to experience has been found to be less for women than for men. However, the return to experience for women increased relative to men's over the late 1970s and the 1980s.[31]

EXPERIENCE AND PRODUCTIVITY

Human capital theory suggests that the reason why earnings tend to increase with experience in the labor market is that a worker's productivity is augmented by on-the-job training. However, critics of the human capital explanation have argued that it has not been proven that the productivity-enhancing effects of on-the-job training have actually *caused* the higher earnings.[32]

For example, the rise in earnings with experience may simply reflect the widespread use of seniority arrangements, which appear to govern wage setting to some extent in the nonunion as well as the union sector. Of course, this does not explain why firms would adhere to this practice, if more senior workers were not also generally more able.

One interesting suggestion is that upward sloping earnings profiles, which reward experience with the firm (tenure), raise workers' productivity, because employees are motivated to work hard so as to remain with the firm until retirement and, thus, reap the higher earnings that come with longer tenure.[33] This is in the

---

[31] See, for example, Mincer and Polachek, "Family Investments in Human Capital"; and Mary Corcoran and Greg J. Duncan, "Work History Labor Force Attachment, and Earnings Differences Between Races and Sexes," *Journal of Human Resources* 14, no. 1 (Winter 1979): 3–20. For recent trends, See Polachek and O'Neill, "Why the Gender Gap in Wages Narrowed in the 1980s."

[32] See especially James L. Medoff and Katherine G. Abraham, "Experience, Performance, and Earnings," *Quarterly Journal of Economics* 95, no. 4 (December 1980): 703–36; and James L. Medoff and Katherine G. Abraham, "Are Those Paid More Really More Productive? The Case of Experience," *Journal of Human Resources* 16, no. 2 (Spring 1981): 186–216.

[33] Edward P. Lazear, "Why Is There Mandatory Retirement?" *Journal of Political Economy* 87 (December 1979): 1261–84; and Edward P. Lazear, "Agency, Earnings Profiles, Productivity and Hours Restrictions," *American Economic Review* 71, no. 4 (September 1981): 606–20. See also Joseph E. Stiglitz, "Incentives, Risk and Information: Notes Toward a Theory of Hierarchy," *Bell Journal of Economics* 6, no. 2 (Autumn 1975): 552–79.

interest of both workers and firms because the increased productivity makes possible both higher earnings and higher profits. Note that, although workers are induced to put forth extra effort and be more productive, higher productivity is *not* due to training and productivity does *not* rise with experience. It should also be noted that these alternative explanations focus on the return to tenure (experience with a particular employer) and, thus, do not necessarily challenge the human capital explanation for the return associated with *general* labor market experience.

It is particularly difficult to obtain empirical data to shed light on this controversy, since information on actual productivity of workers is seldom available. Thus far, the empirical evidence on the relationship between tenure and productivity is mixed, with some studies supporting the human capital explanation and others refuting it.[34]

From the perspective of the individual, the factors influencing the investment decision are not affected by the reasons for the upward-sloping experience-earnings profile. It is the magnitude of costs *versus* benefits that is the individual's principal concern. However, when the upward-sloping experience-earnings profile reflects an incentive structure offered to the worker by a particular firm, the situation is similar to **firm-specific training** in that the higher earnings will only be available to the worker at that firm.

GENDER DIFFERENCES IN TRAINING INVESTMENT DECISIONS

Expected Work Life

Does our analysis of the training investment decision suggest that women will be less likely to invest in on-the-job training than men? Putting this somewhat differently, would they be less willing to spend time in poorly-paid entry level positions in order to reap a later return in terms of higher earnings? Again, human capital theory suggests that adherence to traditional gender roles would indeed lower women's incentives to invest.

The impact of women's shorter work lives is illustrated in Figure 6.5. Let us assume TT' represents the earnings profile of a generally trained worker. Here we see that, just as in the case of formal education, the gross return to on-the-job training depends upon the number of years over which the return is earned. Jane, who plans to be in the labor market for a shorter period of time than Lisa, will find the investment in on-the-job training less profitable. For example, suppose

---

[34] Negative studies include Medoff and Abraham, "Experience, Performance, and Earnings," Medoff and Abraham, "Are Those Paid More Really More Productive?" and Katherine G. Abraham and Henry Farber, "Job Duration, Seniority, and Earnings," *American Economic Review* 77, no. 3 (June 1987): 278–97. Those providing more support for the training hypothesis include Robert Topel, "Specific Capital, Mobility and Wages: Wages Rise with Job Seniority," *Journal of Political Economy* 99, no. 1 (February 1991): 145–76; and James Brown, "Why Do Wages Increase with Tenure?" *American Economic Review* 79, no. 5 (December 1989): 971–91.

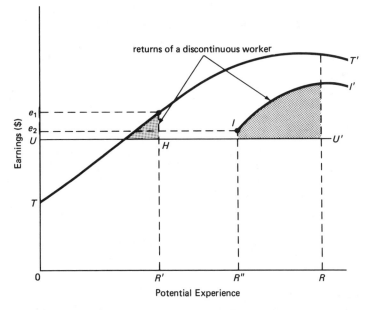

FIGURE 6.5 The Impact of Expected Work Life on the Training Investment Decision

she expects to work R' years, then return after an interruption of $R''-R'$ years. Her benefits are reduced by the time spent out of the labor force when her earnings are zero. Further, human capital theory suggests that the work force interruption after R' years will lower her earnings profile from TT' to II', resulting in a further loss of benefits. Although we have again shown the post-interruption profile (II') as approaching the profile of a continuous worker (TT'),[35] a lifetime loss in earnings still occurs.

Jane's return to her investment in general training is equal to the sum of the two shaded areas, considerably less than Lisa's return shown in Figure 6.3. As we noted in our discussion of field of educational specialization, if occupations differ in the amount of depreciation associated with them, women who anticipate discontinuous work careers are likely to be attracted to fields in which such depreciation is relatively small.[36] Given these reductions in benefits, women following traditional roles are likely to find it profitable to make smaller investments in general training than will career-oriented men. On the other hand, as women's labor force attachment increases, the profitability of such investments for them is also likely to increase. Moreover, we may note that as more women are

---

[35]See footnote 11 for evidence that earnings tend to "rebound" after work force interruptions.

[36]See, especially, Solomon W. Polachek, "Occupational Self-Selection: A Human Capital Approach to Sex Differences in Occupational Structure," *The Review of Economics and Statistics* 63, no. 1 (February 1981): 60–69.

employed in jobs with general training opportunities (profile TT'), the opportunity cost of work force interruptions is increased, and their labor force attachment is reinforced.

The consequences of women's shorter, and more discontinuous, labor force participation for their incentives to invest in firm-specified training may also be illustrated by Figure 6.5. Assume TT' is now the earnings profile of a specifically trained worker. The impact of work interruptions is potentially even more serious in this case, depending crucially on whether or not a woman is able to return to her initial employer.

Suppose Jennifer has been out of the labor force for a substantial period of time and is unable to get her old job back. Because she has acquired specific training, her skills are useless in other firms. Her earnings upon her return to the labor force will be only U dollars (the earnings of an untrained individual), and her new earnings profile will be UU' (the profile of an untrained individual). The returns to Jennifer's investment in firm-specific training have been completely wiped out by her withdrawal from the labor force! That is, the second shaded area shown in Figure 6.5 is eliminated, although she will still receive some return for the brief period before she leaves the labor force. Of course, this conclusion depends on our assumption that she could not return to her original employer. But unless a woman is guaranteed reemployment, she must always face this risk. Thus, human capital theory suggests that women who anticipate work force interruptions of a long or uncertain duration[37] will particularly avoid jobs where firm-specific training is important.

As women increase their labor force attachment, their representation in jobs requiring firm-specific training should increase. The most important factor in this case, however, is attachment to a particular firm. This most probably requires that women keep any work force interruptions within the limits of their employer's leave policy and also raises the question of what such policies should be. We consider this matter later. Figure 6.5 makes clear that, as in the case of the other human capital investments we have discussed, as women take jobs in which they obtain firm-specific training, their incentives to remain in the labor market (and with the firm) are correspondingly increased.

Discrimination

The explanation for gender differences in on-the-job training investment decisions suggested by human capital theory stresses differences between men and women in planned labor force participation over the life cycle. However, it is important to point out that, just as in the case of men's and women's formal education decisions, societal discrimination may be a factor increasing

---

[37] Shorter, fixed-duration interruptions may be covered by an employer's leave policy. Thus, a woman who seeks three months of unpaid leave after the birth of a child is in a very different position from one who quits her job and withdraws from the labor force for an indefinite period.

the (pecuniary and psychic) costs or lowering the (pecuniary and psychic) returns to entry into traditionally male fields. Further, labor market discrimination, which is discussed in greater detail in Chapter 7, may also play a part in reducing women's representation in jobs where training is important. That is, overt or subtle discrimination on the part of employers, coworkers, or customers may prove an obstacle to women seeking access to jobs in such areas.

Consideration of firm-specific training introduces a particular rationale for employer discrimination that may be important in the labor market. As illustrated in Figure 6.4, the employer is expected to share some of the costs of firm-specific training. The returns to the firm's (as well as to the worker's) investment depend on how long the individual remains with the firm. Thus, if an employer believes that women are less likely to remain with the firm, on average, than men, he or she may prefer men for jobs that require specific training. Even to the extent that upward-sloping earnings profiles are offered to workers as an incentive to work hard, employers will prefer men for jobs that offer such incentives if they believe that women tend to be short-term workers who would not be motivated by long-term rewards.

Employers' differential treatment of men and women on the basis of their perceptions of average gender differences in productivity or job stability has been termed **statistical discrimination.** Such behavior on the part of employers can restrict opportunities for career-oriented as well as noncareer-oriented women, if employers cannot easily distinguish between them. Finally, labor market discrimination may indirectly lower women's incentives to invest in themselves by lowering the rewards for doing so.

OCCUPATIONS AND EARNINGS

The consequences predicted by the human capital analysis for gender differences in earnings and employment are fairly straightforward. Human capital theorists argue that most women do indeed anticipate shorter and less continuous work careers than men. Thus, women are expected to select occupations requiring less investment in on-the-job training than those chosen by men. They will particularly avoid jobs in which firm-specific training is important, and employers will be reluctant to hire them for such jobs. Further, they will seek jobs where depreciation of earnings for time spent out of the labor force is minimized.

Hypothetical earnings profiles for predominantly male and predominantly female jobs are shown in Figure 6.6. For simplicity, we assume all workers have the same amount of formal schooling. Earnings profiles in predominantly male jobs are expected to slope steeply upward as does profile MM', since men are expected to undertake substantial investments in on-the-job training. Women, on the other hand, are expected to choose the flatter profile FF', representing smaller amounts of investment in on-the-job training. The existence of the crossover point, H, is crucial to this argument. Before H, profile FF' lies above profile MM'. It is argued

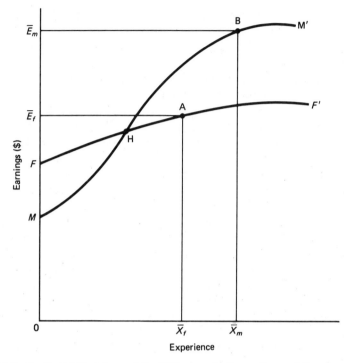

FIGURE 6.6   On-the-Job Training and Sex Differences in Occupations and Earnings

that women choose higher earnings now in preference to greater earnings in the future because they do not expect to be in the labor market long enough for the larger human capital investment to pay off. Thus, we see that the human capital analysis of on-the-job training decisions, in conjunction with our previous discussion of formal education, provides an explanation for the occupational segregation by gender detailed in Chapter 5.

The human capital analysis also provides an explanation for gender differences in earnings. We have already seen why human capital theorists believe women are less likely to make large investments in formal schooling. To the extent that women in the labor force have been less likely than men to obtain a college or graduate education, their earnings would be lowered relative to men's. In terms of median educational attainment, however, this is counterbalanced by their greater likelihood of completing high school. Of potentially more importance in explaining gender differences in earnings would be differences between men and women in fields of specialization, if men are more likely to enter the more lucrative areas.

For given levels of formal education, our consideration of on-the-job training investments also gives us reasons to expect women to earn less, as illustrated in Figure 6.6. Mean female earnings are $\bar{E}_f$ dollars and are less than male mean earnings of $\bar{E}_m$ dollars. Why do women earn less? First, on average they have less labor market experience than men—$\bar{X}_f$ is less than $\bar{X}_m$. Because earnings tend to increase with experience, this lowers their earnings relative to men's. Second, for reasons given earlier, males experience larger increases in earnings for additional years of experience (have steeper profiles). After crossover point H, this produces a widening gap between male and female earnings with increasing labor market experience.

OTHER SUPPLY-SIDE FACTORS

Traditional gender roles may work to produce differences in economic outcomes in a variety of other ways. For example, the longer hours that women tend to spend on housework may lower the effort that they put into their market jobs.[38] In addition, to the extent that families place priority on the husband's, rather than the wife's, career in determining the location of the family, her earnings are likely to be lowered, since the best job for both is not necessarily to be found in the same labor market.[39] Anticipation of lesser ability to determine the geographic location of the family may also lead women to select occupations in which jobs are likely to be readily found in any labor market. Further, if women tend to give greater priority than men to family concerns, they may restrict the amount of daily commuting they are willing to do,[40] their hours or work schedules, as well as their availability for work-related travel. Such constraints may also reduce women's earnings relative to men's and adversely influence their occupational choices. Finally, if women anticipate a shorter work life than men, they may invest less time in searching out the best possible job and, as a consequence, receive lower earnings.[41]

---

[38] See Gary S. Becker, "The Allocation of Effort, Specific Human Capital, and the Differences Between Men and Women in Earnings and Occupations," *Journal of Labor Economics,* 3, no. 1, pt. 2 (January 1985): S33–S58. Empirical evidence consistent with this view is found by Joni Hersch, "Male-Female Differences in Hourly Wages: The Role of Human Capital, Working Conditions, and Housework," *Industrial and Labor Relations Review* 44, no. 4 (July 1991): 746–59, but not by Denise D. Bielby and William T. Bielby "She Works Hard for the Money: Household Responsibilities and the Allocation of Work Effort," *American Journal of Sociology* 93, no. 5 (March 1988): 1031–59.

[39] See Robert H. Frank, "Why Women Earn Less: The Theory and Estimation of Differential Qualification," *American Economic Review* 68, no. 3 (June 1978): 360–73; Steven H. Sandell, "Women and the Economics of Family Migration," *Review of Economics and Statistics,* (November 1977): 406–14; and Jacob Mincer, "Family Migration Decisions," *Journal of Political Economy* 86, no. 5 (October 1978): 749–73.

[40] See Victor Fuchs, "Differences in Hourly Earnings Between Men and Women," *Monthly Labor Review* 94, no. 5 (May 1971); Albert Rees and George P. Shultz, *Workers and Wages in an Urban Labor Market* (Chicago: University of Chicago Press, 1970). Janice Madden has suggested that the lesser willingness of women to commute increases the monopsony power of firms over their wages, thus lowering their wages relative to men's. See her "A Spatial Theory of Sex Discrimination," *Journal of Regional Science* 17, no. 3 (December 1977): 369–80. The monopsony model is discussed further in Chapter 7.

[41] Some evidence consistent with this possibility is found in Steven H. Sandell, "Is the Unemployment Rate of Women Too Low? A Direct Test of the Economic Theory of Job Search," *The Review of Economics and Statistics* 62, no. 4 (November 1980): 634–38.

As with the other supply-side influences we have discussed, it is important to bear in mind that such decisions may reflect social pressures as well as the voluntary choices of women. Further, labor market discrimination, to the extent it exists, reinforces traditional gender roles in the family by lowering the wife's opportunity cost (relative to the husband's) of sacrificing her career objectives to family demands.

THE HUMAN CAPITAL EXPLANATION: AN ASSESSMENT

The human capital model can provide a clear, consistent theoretical explanation for gender differences in earnings and occupations in terms of the voluntary choices women and men make. If it is believed that this model provides the *sole* explanation for gender differences in economic outcomes, economic inequality between men and women in the labor market would perhaps not be considered a serious social problem. Certainly, it would not require policy intervention to combat gender discrimination in employment. We have already pointed out that even to the extent that gender inequality in the labor market is caused by such supply-side factors as emphasized by human capital theorists, societal discrimination against women, as well as their own voluntary choices, may be an important explanatory factor. Further, women's anticipation of and experience with labor market discrimination can also lower their human capital investments. This latter process will be described in greater detail in the following chapter. We now consider two more straightforward issues. Do the factors emphasized by human capital theorists help to explain gender differences in labor market outcomes? If so, do they provide the *full* explanation?

A crude test of explanatory power of the human capital explanation for gender differences in earnings is provided by an examination of the trends in the gender-pay differential. As we saw in Chapter 5, virtually no progress was made in closing the overall male-female pay gap during the 1960s and 1970s. Beginning in the late 1970s or early 1980s, the female-to-male earnings ratio began to increase. How does this correspond to shifts in women's qualifications, particularly their relative educational attainment and experience? In general, women's qualifications have been increasing as the pay gap has been declining. Though their median educational attainment, which used to be somewhat greater than men's, is now only equal, their fields of study and propensity to pursue college and graduate education have been becoming more similar to men's, especially over the 1970s and 1980s. Although women on average continue to have less labor market experience than men, the gender differential appears to have declined here as well. As previously noted, although the average experience levels of women within age groups have tended to increase since the 1970s, the average level of experience of the female labor force did not start to rise relative to men's until the 1980s, due to the increased labor force participation rates of younger women during the 1960s and 1970s.[42]

Thus, both the narrowing of the male-female pay gap and the time pattern of the trend is roughly consistent with the human capital model. So are the trends in earnings ratios by age. Younger women have been most rapidly approaching males in terms of their college-going behavior and fields of study. They have also exhibited the largest increases in labor force attachment in recent years, as growing proportions of them have continued to work during the prime childbearing years. And we did indeed find in Chapter 5 that younger women (those under 45) have experienced a substantial increase in their earnings relative to younger males.

This broad consistency of the human capital explanation with the observed trends in the female-to-male earnings ratio strongly suggests that human capital factors account for at least part of the male-female pay gap. This does not necessarily mean, however, that the human capital model provides the *sole* explanation of pay differences. Other factors may well have contributed to the observed *trends* and may help to account for the existence of a gender pay differential *at any given time*. For example, it appears that demand shifts in the 1980s favored women relative to men in that employment in the manufacturing industries, which disproportionately employ men, declined relative to the service industries, which have a higher concentration of women. This factor may well have contributed to the increase in the relative earnings of women during this period.[43]

We now turn to a more detailed examination of the explanatory power of the human capital model, focusing upon data on gender differences in earnings at a point in time. Figure 6.7 shows the **age-earnings profiles** of individuals by gender for those with four years of high school and four years of college, respectively, in 1990. An age-earnings profile shows how earnings vary with age or potential rather than actual experience. As we saw in Figures 6.2 and 6.5, women's greater likelihood of work force interruptions means that, at any given age, they tend to average less actual labor market experience than men. It is important to bear this in mind in comparing the profiles for males and females shown in Figure 6.7.

The figure suggests that gender differences in earnings are not fully explained by differences in educational attainment of men and women, because within each educational category, women earn less. Indeed, older women college graduates earn less than men who have only completed high school. Of course, gender differences in labor market experience and investments in on-the-job training may also be a factor.

---

[42]Polachek, "Trends in the Male-Female Wage Gap," provides evidence that trends in the male-female experience differential can help to explain the slower narrowing of the gender gap in earnings during the 1970s and the faster closing of the gap during the 1980s.

[43]Lawrence F. Katz and Kevin M. Murphy, "Changes in Relative Wages, 1963–1987: Supply and Demand Factors," National Bureau of Economic Research, Working Paper No. 3927 (December 1991); and Francine D. Blau and Lawrence M. Kahn, "Race and Gender Pay Differentials," in *Research Frontiers in Industrial Relations,* David Lewin, Olivia Mitchell, and Peter Sherer, eds. (Madison, WI: Industrial Relations Research Association, forthcoming).

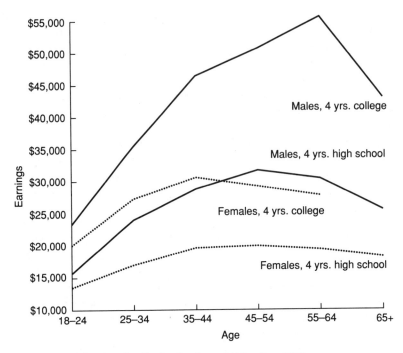

FIGURE 6.7   Age-Earnings Profiles by Gender and Education, 1990

To consider this issue, let us compare Figure 6.7 to Figure 6.6. We see that, as predicted by human capital theorists, women's age-earnings profiles tend to be flatter than men's. This is consistent with less investment in on-the-job training for women than for men. Note, however, that in the hypothetical diagram, Figure 6.6, there is a crossover point *H* between the male and female profiles. This implies that during their early years in the labor market, women should actually earn more than men (with the same education), since the men are investing in on-the-job training and the women are not or are doing so to a lesser extent. However, the actual data shown in Figure 6.7 do not show such a crossover point. On the contrary, within educational categories, men earn more than women at every age, even among the youngest workers who are recent entrants to the labor force. This suggests that gender differences in years of formal education and on-the-job training do not fully explain gender differences in earnings.[44]

[44] Among young women, it has been found that those who expect to work at age 35 have experience-wage profiles that "... begin at a lower point and have a steeper (initial) slope than those of their no-work-plans counterparts" (Steven H. Sandell and David Shapiro, "Work Expectations, Human Capital Accumulation, and the Wages of Young Women," *Journal of Human Resources* 15, no. 3 [Summer 1980]: 343). That is, the women who were more committed to the labor market were moving along an earnings profile like *MM'* in Figure 6.6, whereas the less committed women were moving along a profile like *FF'*. However, the data presented in Figure 6.7 (as well as other evidence of labor market discrimination reviewed in Chapter 7) suggest that *both* groups of women earn less than comparable men. That is, again, that human capital factors do not fully account for the gender pay gap.

Is it possible to determine exactly what proportion of the gender gap in pay is due to differences in qualifications, especially human capital investments? Economists and other social scientists have studied this question extensively. Actual estimates vary depending on the sources of the data used and the types of qualifications examined. Although most studies find that human capital factors, particularly women's lesser labor market experience, do contribute to the gender differential, they also find that a substantial portion of the pay gap cannot be explained by gender differences in qualifications.[45] The portion of the pay gap that is not due to gender differences in qualifications is presumed to be due to labor market discrimination. We discuss this evidence at greater length in Chapter 7.

As suggested by our discussion of Figure 6.6, the human capital model also provides an explanation for occupational segregation by gender in terms of women's optimizing behavior, given the traditional division of labor by gender within the family. Women are believed to choose occupations characterized by flatter experience-earnings profile—illustrated by FF' in Figure 6.6. Men, on the other hand, are willing to undertake the larger human capital investments represented by profile MM'. This implies that women who do enter predominantly male occupations should be those who anticipate more continuous labor force participation and are willing to undertake the larger investments in on-the-job training required in male jobs. In return, they should reap higher returns to each year of their labor market experience. In other words, women in predominantly male jobs should be moving along profile MM', whereas women in predominantly female jobs should be moving along profile FF'. Further, women who anticipate more work interruptions should enter predominantly female jobs where depreciation of earnings due to time spent out of the labor force is less than in predominantly male jobs.

In fact, most of the research in this area does not support the human capital explanation for gender differences in occupations.[46] Women in predominantly male jobs do not earn greater returns to each year of experience than women in predominantly female occupations. Nor is it the case that the earnings of women in predominantly female jobs depreciate less during periods of time spent out of the labor force than do the earnings of women in predominantly male jobs. Finally, women who have discontinuous work histories are not more likely to be

[45]For summaries of this literature, see Francine Blau, "Discrimination Against Women: Theory and Evidence," in *Labor Economics: Modern Views,* William A. Darity, Jr., ed. (Boston: Kluwer-Nijhoff, 1984); Cynthia Lloyd and Beth Niemi, *Economics of Sex Differentials;* Donald J. Treiman and Heidi I. Hartmann, eds., *Women, Work and Wages: Equal Pay for Jobs of Equal Value* (Washington, D.C.: National Academy Press, 1981); and Francine Blau and Marianne Ferber, "Discrimination: Evidence from the United States," *American Economic Review* 77, no. 2 (May 1987): 316–320.

[46]See Paula England, "The Failure of Human Capital Theory to Explain Occupational Sex Segregation," *Journal of Human Resources* 17, no. 3 (Summer 1982): 358–370; Mary Corcoran, Greg J. Duncan, and Michael Ponza, "Work Experience, Job Segregation and Wages," in *Sex Segregation in the Workplace;* and John Abowd and Mark P. Killingsworth, "Sex Discrimination, Atrophy and the Male-Female Wage Differential," *Industrial Relations* 22, no. 3 (Fall 1983): 387–402. On the other hand, results more consistent with the human capital model are obtained by Polachek, "Occupational Self-Selection," and Landes, "A Test of the Specific Capital Hypothesis."

in a predominantly female occupation than are women who have been employed more continuously. Although some other researchers have obtained findings that are more consistent with the human capital explanation for occupational segregation, it appears that this view is not strongly supported by the evidence at this point. However, it is possible that further study will reveal greater support for this view, at least as a partial explanation. Moreover, it should be borne in mind that the available evidence does not rule out the importance of other supply-side factors that may encourage men and women to aspire to and train for "gender appropriate" lines of work.

POLICY ISSUES:
INCREASING WOMEN'S HUMAN CAPITAL
AND LABOR FORCE ATTACHMENT

Although the human capital model does not appear to fully explain gender differences in labor market outcomes, human capital factors undoubtedly contribute to the pay gap. In this section, we consider policies that government or private employers have pursued, or might consider adopting, in order to increase women's human capital and labor force attachment.

Government Training Programs

Particularly since the 1960s, the federal government has been active in providing training and employment programs for disadvantaged or unemployed workers. The most important initial program in this area was the Manpower Development and Training Act (MDTA) of 1962, which emphasized a fairly centralized approach to these problems. It was replaced by the Comprehensive Employment and Training Act (CETA) of 1973, which gave a greater role in decision making and program implementation to local governments. Finally, the Job Training Partnership Act (JTPA), passed in 1982, placed greater reliance on the private sector.

Although the strategies and emphases of these programs have varied, their goal has been the provision of skills to workers to enhance their employability and earnings. The programs provided the government with an excellent opportunity for intervention to reduce occupational segregation by offering women training in traditionally male jobs. Such a strategy would have helped to reduce the male-female pay gap directly, as predominantly male jobs are generally higher paying than predominantly female jobs. Further, training for male-dominated occupations would therefore have increased the opportunity cost of labor withdrawals to a greater extent than training for female-dominated occupations. It could, thus, be expected to increase the labor force attachment of those receiving the training to a greater extent.

Although the evidence available on this topic is sparse, what there is suggests that the training and employment opportunities associated with these training programs have been predominantly sex segregated.[47] It is unfortunate that the opportunity that government training programs offer for reducing occupational segregation and the male-female pay gap have not been realized.[48] Hopefully, a greater priority will be placed on achieving these goals in the future.

The Role of Employers

In Chapter 9, we shall discuss the prospects of employers participating in the provision of child care in order to facilitate the meshing of job and family responsibilities for workers. In this section, we consider a wider variety of policies, such as family leave, flexible work schedules, and others, intended to serve the same purpose. The possibility that employers, as well as workers and their families, might benefit will also be discussed.

The importance of these issues is suggested by the nearly two-thirds of employed male and female workers who had family responsibilities in 1990, either as members of married couples or as single family heads. Of these workers, fully 65 percent of the men and 75.2 percent of women had a spouse who was also in the labor force, and an additional 5.4 percent of the men and 18 percent of the women were living without a spouse.[49] The proportion of families without a full-time homemaker is likely to rise further in the future.

At present, women most often bear the major responsibility for housework as well as care of children and other dependents;[50] they would therefore be the primary beneficiaries of family-oriented policies. Adoption of such policies would not only make it easier for women to meet their "family obligations" and succeed on the job, but also to remain more permanently attached to the labor force. This would increase the incentives of both women themselves and of their employers to invest in the human capital of women workers. At the same time, such policies

---

[47] Barbara F. Reskin and Heidi I. Hartmann, *Women's Work, Men's Work: Sex Segregation on the Job* (Washington, D.C.: National Academy Press, 1986), Ch. 4; Linda J. Waite and Sue E. Berryman, "Occupational Desegregation in CETA Programs," in *Sex Segregation in the Workplace,* Reskin, ed., pp. 292–307; Commission on Skills Development and Vocational Education, *The Job Training Partnership Act: A Report on Services to Women in New York State* (1990), cited in Bureau of National Affairs, *Daily Labor Report,* no. 153, August 8, 1990.

[48] On the other hand, government training programs appear to have been moderately successful in increasing the earnings of program participants over their counterparts of the same sex who did not participate. See, for example, Nicholas M. Kiefer, "The Economic Benefits from Four Government Training Programs," in *Evaluating Manpower Training Programs, Research in Labor Economics,* Farrell E. Bloch, ed., Supp. 1 (1979), pp. 159–86.

[49] Data are from Bureau of Labor Statistics, *Employment and Earnings* (January 1991).

[50] Women not only tend to have primary responsibility for children, but also for other dependents. According to the *Working Caregivers Report* conducted by the Opinion Research Corporation for the American Association of Retired Persons and the Travelers Foundation of Hartford, CN (1989), three out of four employed persons who provide care for the elderly are women.

THE "MOMMY TRACK"

In considering the problems employed women have when juggling job and family, considerable attention has been focused on the relatively small number of women managers. This is probably in part because they tend to be prominent and potentially influential, but also because combining such a position with family responsibilities often does present substantial challenges. It is widely believed that the resulting strains are the cause of high turnover among women executives, and that this in turn creates problems for their employers.

One suggested solution to these difficulties is for women to choose either on the one hand to devote themselves fully to their career, and forgo having children or at least active involvement in rearing them, or on the other hand to settle for a lesser job. In return, employers would be expected to offer adequate flexibility to the latter group, to enable them to do justice to their dual responsibilities to family and paid work. Proponents of such a policy,* the so-called "mommy track," begin from the premise that the basic characteristic that differentiates women from men is their role as mothers. They further hold that bringing this issue into the open is most useful and will permit appropriate adjustments both for the women concerned and their employers.

In this view, maternity involves a continuum that begins with an awareness of the ticking of the biological clock, proceeds to the anticipation of motherhood, includes pregnancy, childbirth, recuperation, and psychological adjustment, and continues to nursing, bonding, and child-rearing. Such a commitment is not considered to make a woman unfit for employment. On the contrary, she may make a valuable and much-needed contribution at a time when a shortage of talented and capable male labor force entrants is anticipated. But only a woman who makes an early decision to devote herself exclusively to her career should expect to join the inner circle of top management.

Among the arguments on the other side** is the lack of hard data showing that businesses at present find it more expensive to employ women managers, or that most of these women are unable to successfully combine career and family. Moreover, making an irreversible decision for a lifetime at a relatively early age is not necessarily desirable. Perhaps most seriously, however, opponents of the "mommy track" are troubled by the stereotyping of women and men, making motherhood categorically different from fatherhood. No one questions that only women bear and nurse children. But for women who currently have a life expectancy of well over 70 years and who have one, two, or even three children, these biological functions absorb only a very small share of their time and energy. It is rather the preparation for parenthood, the psychological adjustment to become a parent, and certainly bonding and child-rearing, that constitute a major commitment. There is no convincing evidence that fathers are not equally capable of such dedication. Hence a more plausible solution is for employers to make adjustments that will enable men and women alike to bear their share of family responsibilities, including needed care not only for children but for other adults in cases of illness, disability, or infirmity.

*See, for example, Felice N. Schwartz. "Management Women and the New Facts of Life," *Harvard Business Review* 67, no. 2 (January–February 1989): 65–76.

**See, for example, letters to the editor in response to Schwartz, *Harvard Business Review* 67, no. 3 (May–June 1989): 182–214.

would make it easier for men to do more homemaking chores, thus promoting a more equal division of labor in the household. Men who already do a substantial share of housework would benefit as well.

To the extent that employers provide family-oriented benefits, they generally do so voluntarily in the United States, although, as we shall see in Chapter 10, such benefits are often mandated by government in other advanced industrialized countries. Profit-maximizing employers are likely to be motivated to institute such programs in lieu of wage increases and other benefits, or when benefits are likely to outweigh their costs. For the individual firm, possible benefits include improved recruitment and retention of workers, and greater productivity as a result of better morale and reductions in tardiness and absenteeism. Popular programs may also improve public relations. Costs, of course, depend on the specific policy under consideration. In addition to other out-of-pocket expenses, they could include scheduling problems, hiring of replacements, and adjustment costs of reformulating existing policies.

Total benefits to the employer increase as the number of workers potentially affected positively by the policies rises. On the other hand, the costs of some policies (for example, family leaves) will also rise as more workers take advantage of them. On balance, however, it is highly likely that employers' incentives to adopt policies of this type will increase as a larger portion of the work force attempts to cope with the difficulties of successfully combining market careers with homemaking responsibilities. As more women take market jobs, and particularly as they move into higher level positions, employers' concern over the retention and job performance of women should become more urgent. Further, as men do a greater share of housework, the pool of potential beneficiaries of these policies will be further increased. Thus, it seems reasonable to expect growing interest on the part of employers in such policies.

Next we examine in greater detail the prevalence of a variety of specific programs, as well as their costs and benefits. Data on the availability of such programs are rather easy to find for large and medium-size firms, but are virtually nonexistent for small firms. (The precise definition of "small" varies from 20 to 50 employees or less.) This is an important omission because more than one-fourth of the labor force is employed in firms with up to 20 employees, and the proportion of women is undoubtedly greater.[51]

Family leaves. Among the most pressing needs of workers with dual responsibilities is that for family leave, to be used, among other reasons, for pregnancy, childbirth, infant care, and tending the ill, whether children, spouses, or other family members. In such circumstances, it is often the case that no alternative can adequately take the place of the employee taking some time off from work. In the absence of provision for family leave at their firm, workers may have to give up

---

[51]This information is provided in Sheila B. Kamerman and Alfred J. Kalin, *The Responsive Workplace* (New York: Columbia University Press, 1987).

their jobs, with loss not only of earnings, but of accrued benefits and seniority. Hence the availability of family leaves, even of relatively short and unpaid ones, with provisions for job security and some other entitlements is often critical for enabling workers, particularly women workers, to retain their tie to the firm in the face of such family demands. This is especially important for increasing women's incentives to invest in firm-specific training, as well as making employers more willing to provide them with such opportunities.

At present, the only legally-mandated provisions are that under the Pregnancy Discrimination Act of 1978 (an amendment to Title VII of the Civil Rights Act of 1964) employers are prohibited from discriminating against workers on the basis of pregnancy. An employer may not, for example, terminate or deny a job to a woman because she is pregnant. Employers who have a medical disability program must also provide paid disability leave for pregnancy and childbirth on the same basis as for other medical disabilities.[52]

In 1988, 89 percent of employees working full-time in medium- and large-size firms in private industry were covered by short-term disability plans that would, by law, cover medical disabilities associated with pregnancy and childbirth.[53] In addition, nearly all such employees received paid vacations, and almost one-quarter were eligible for paid personal leave, which might also be used to care for a new-born. Thus, it is likely that most women working in medium- and large-size firms were able to piece together a short leave of perhaps 2 to 4 months with access to some pay and benefits. But only about a third of full-time workers were employed in firms that provided parental leave beyond this to new mothers, approximately 90 percent of them without pay. The average maximum duration of the leave offered was 19 weeks. Far fewer employees, 17 percent, worked at firms that offered parental leaves to new fathers, even though employers who offer parental leaves not directly tied to pregnancy-disability only to mothers, but not to fathers, lay themselves open to a charges of sex-discrimination against their male employees.[54] It may also be noted that workers employed in small firms are likely to fare substantially worse in terms of benefits than these workers in large and medium-size firms for whom data are available.

In an effort to make unpaid leaves more generally and uniformly available, Congress passed the Family and Medical Leave Act in 1990. It would have required employers to provide up to 12 weeks of unpaid leave to new parents as well as to workers who are seriously ill or who need to care for a sick family member. The Act was, however, vetoed by President Bush.[55] Opponents of the measure

---

[52]Employers who do not have a medical disability program are not required to provide paid disability for pregnancy and childbirth.

[53]These data are from Bureau of Labor Statistics, *Employee Benefits in Medium and Large Firms, 1988* (Washington, DC: U.S. Government Printing Office, 1989).

[54]This is based on a legal interpretation issued by the Equal Employment Opportunity Commission and reported in Bureau of National Affairs, *Daily Labor Report,* no. 224, November 20, 1990.

[55]*New York Times,* July 26, 1990, p. A9.

were particularly concerned about the costs that it would impose on employers. However, a recent study found that providing such unpaid leaves to employees is less expensive for employers than replacing a worker who is forced to resign.[56] Although not all workers would actually resign if denied a leave, this study and others suggest that the costs of providing short, unpaid family leaves may not be unduly onerous to business.[57] This makes the future prospects for the adoption of a national policy better and also suggests that, regardless of federal mandates, employers will increasingly find it in their interests to offer such benefits.[58]

One concern about the provision of family leaves, particularly legally-mandated ones, is that the costs of hiring women is likely to rise, giving employers an increased incentive to discriminate against them. Making parental leave available to fathers as well as mothers might mitigate this problem if men actually took advantage of the opportunity. There is some encouraging evidence from Sweden in this regard. Initially, men tended not to avail themselves of leaves, but by the late 1980s, as many as 85 percent of fathers took a few days of paternity leave at the time of childbirth, and over 20 percent took more extended parental leave for subsequent child care.[59] Similarly, men may be expected to participate in the care of older dependents, which is becoming a growing problem with increasing life expectancy. In any case, it is clearly desirable that, when leaves are provided, they be made available to both men and women so as to encourage men to take on a greater share of family responsibilities.

A constructive employer response to the situation of new parents also involves assistance to employees in adjusting to work upon return from the parental leave. This might take the form of offering part-time work, flextime schedules, or perhaps reallocation to a position requiring less overtime and less travel. One company has a maternity leave coordinator in its personnel department who helps employees both in obtaining leave and in making post-leave arrangements.[60]

[56]The study by William Alpert and Eileen Trzcinski is summarized in Bureau of National Affairs, *Daily Labor Report*, no. 57, March 25, 1991.

[57]For example, a study conducted by the Families and Work Institute found that the majority of employers surveyed in the first four states to adopt parental leave laws (Minnesota, Oregon, Rhode Island, and Wisconsin) said "they were experiencing neither serious increases in costs . . . nor difficulty in administering and implementing the legislation." See *Wall Street Journal*, August 9, 1990, p. B1.

[58]An additional consideration from the perspective of public policy is the impact of alternative care on infants. Some recent research suggests that this effect may be more negative than for older children, perhaps due to the difficulty of locating high quality infant care. This issue is discussed in Chapter 9.

[59]Joseph Pleck, "Family Supportive Employer Policies and Men's Participation." Paper prepared for the Panel on Employer Policies and Working Families, Committee on Women's Employment and Related Social Issues, Commission on Behavioral and Social Sciences, National Research Council, Washington DC: 1989.

[60]Eleanor Byrnes, "Dual Career Couples: How the Company Can Help," in *The Woman in Management: Career and Family Issues*, Jennie Farley, ed. (Ithaca, NY: ILR Press, 1983, pp. 49–53). See also Alan Deutschman, "Pioneers of the New Balance," *Fortune*, May 20, 1991, pp. 60–68.

Work schedules. A decrease in the standard work week of full-time workers would clearly be advantageous to those with time-consuming household responsibilities. As mentioned in Chapter 4, there has been a sizable decline in weekly hours since the turn of the century. However, most of this decrease was accomplished by the 1940s, and little further reduction has occurred since that time. Nor do further reductions in the standard work week appear likely in the near future.

More attention has been focused on alternative work schedules that can permit workers to utilize their off-job time more efficiently or enjoyably, as well as to do some tasks they could not otherwise accomplish, for example, picking a child up from school. *Flextime* permits some degree of variation in work schedules, ranging from modest changes in starting and quitting time to variation in the number of hours worked per day, week, or pay period.[61] An additional advantage of flextime is a reduction in commuting time, if workers are able to avoid rush-hour traffic.

The degree of flexibility that can be offered depends on the nature of the enterprise and the type of work, but in 1987, about 43 percent of firms offered some form of flextime.[62] Since availability of flextime varies considerably by occupation, the proportion of workers on flexible schedules was considerably smaller; only 12.3 percent of full-time workers had flexible schedules in 1985.[63] Interestingly, a somewhat higher proportion of men (13.2 percent) than of women (11.1 percent) had flexible schedules.

An alternative arrangement, *part-time employment,* is already quite common, especially among women. As of 1990, 27 percent of women and 12 percent of men worked less than full-time (defined as at least 35 hours per week) in comparison to 26 percent and 9 percent, respectively, in 1968. The main problems with part-time work as a solution to difficulties in combining job and family responsibilities are the poor compensation and quality of opportunities offered. Part-time workers frequently receive less than proportionate earnings and fringe benefits,[64] and they

---

[61] It is interesting to note that some professionals, for instance university faculty, have always had a great degree of flexibility. They are responsible for teaching classes and attending committee meetings at specified times, but have discretion about when to prepare for classes, grade papers, and do their research.

[62] Howard V. Hayghe, "Employers and Childcare: What Roles Do They Play?" *Monthly Labor Review* 111, no. 9 (September 1988): 38–44.

[63] Earl F. Mellor, "Shift Work and Flextime: How Prevalent are They?" *Monthly Labor Review* 109, no. 11 (November 1986): 14–21. Flextime is considerably more widespread in some Western European countries. Estimates range up to 40 percent of workers covered by such arrangements in Switzerland. See Sheila B. Kamerman and Paul W. Kingston, "Employer Responses to the Family Responsibilities of Employees," in *Families That Work: Children in a Changing World,* Sheila B. Kamerman and Cheryl D. Hayes, eds. (Washington, D.C.: National Academy Press, 1982), pp. 144–208.

[64] All the evidence suggests that part-time workers receive lower fringes. However, with respect to wages, the evidence is more mixed, indicating that some or even all of the observed wage difference between full- and part-time workers may be due to differences in their personal characteristics. See Rebecca M. Blank, "Understanding Part-Time Work," *Research in Labor Economics* 11, 1990: 137–58.

are often excluded from opportunities to be hired for or promoted to high-level jobs. Thus emphasis needs to be placed on improving rewards and long-term career opportunities associated with part-time jobs. One innovative approach to opening more challenging positions to part-time workers is job-sharing, where two individuals share one position. In 1987, 16 percent of firms offered some opportunities for job-sharing.[65]

Flexible Benefit Plans.[66] With recent increases in the labor force participation of women and changes in family composition, the work force is becoming more and more diverse. Some workers have employed spouses and others have spouses who are full-time homemakers. Still others are single family heads or individuals who live alone. Similarly, some workers have responsibilities for small children or for older or disabled relatives and others do not. Flexible plans that provide workers with a choice of benefits to accommodate their particular needs and preferences can increase the value of benefits to the worker. For example, two-earner couples would benefit from the ability to avoid double coverage (which occurs, for example, when both are covered under their own employer's health insurance program and under their spouse's), or parents of young children may prefer to receive child care benefits in exchange for smaller payments into a pension fund. Because standard benefit packages were developed at a time when the typical worker was a married man with a full-time homemaker spouse, nontraditional households, and women workers in particular, will gain as benefit packages are reconsidered and greater flexibility is offered. As employers offer benefits options that more closely match the preferences and needs of women workers, the value of work in the market is enhanced for them and their labor force attachment is likely to increase.

There are two types of flexible benefit plans. "Cafeteria plans" involve the allocation of an amount predetermined by the employer for employee benefits and permit covered employees to select from among a specified assortment. Most often, any monies not used by the end of the year revert to the employer. Reimbursement plans, on the other hand, involve the use of money taken out of paychecks on a pre-tax basis, which may be used by employees for particular job-related expenses, such as care of children and other dependents. It has been estimated that in 1988 about 13 percent of workers in medium and large size firms were covered by one or both of these types of plans.[67]

Managing two careers. As we have noted, frequently in the past when the career demands of the members of a couple have conflicted, women have tended

[65]Hayghe, "Employers and Childcare."

[66]Federal and state tax policy has explicitly encouraged the growth of many employer-paid benefits by excluding them from taxable employee income, while permitting businesses to treat them as a normal business expense. (See Marianne A. Ferber and Brigid O'Farrell, with La Rue Allen, eds., *Work and Family*, Washington, DC: National Academy Press, 1991).

[67]Bureau of Labor Statistics, *Employee Benefits in Medium and Large Firms, 1988.*

to sacrifice their own career advancement for their husband's. Although it is to be hoped that couples will share these adjustment costs more equally in the future, employers can assist two-career couples by reducing the sacrifices that need to be made. For example, 15 of the largest firms in Chicago have formed a spouse employment network. If one of the firms hires a person who is married to a professional, it helps the spouse find work by referring his or her resumé to the network. Participating firms are committed to seriously considering the spouse for employment. Firms can also assist two-career couples by helping the spouse of an employee that is transferred to locate a new job. One firm, for example, hires an outside consultant to do this.[68] Firms can also assist couples by realizing that an employee who declines a transfer or promotion, say because of particularly heavy family responsibilities or difficulties finding employment for a spouse, need not be consigned to the "slow track" forever. When the situation changes, the individual may make an excellent candidate for advancement.

Firms need to scrutinize their internal policies regarding the employment of members of a couple. In the past, anti-nepotism rules often simply forbade the hiring or retaining of a relative of a current employee. If two employees married, usually it turned out to be the wife who would have to go. Today, many firms have gotten rid of such rules. Some, however, retain restrictions on the employment of two family members, for example, prohibiting them from working in the same department. Concern has also been focused on the situation in which two workers form a romantic attachment. In either case, it is feared that if one partner is powerful he or she will exert influence to have the other hired or promoted and that the couple may form a working alliance that will be resented by their coworkers.[69]

Such abuses undoubtedly take place, but there is no evidence that they are any greater than when people simply are or become close friends. In fact, one might expect couples to be somewhat more circumspect, because favoritism would be so obvious. Reducing what risk there is of problems by placing restrictions on the employment of couples must in any case be weighed against the disadvantages of not being able to hire the best qualified people regardless of marital status or other relationships and of not being able to offer a job to a spouse when the firm wants to hire or relocate the other partner. In addition, as long as men are typically the ones in a higher job category, if one member of a couple is asked to leave, the woman will probably be viewed as the most expendable. Thus, any such policy is likely to result in de facto discrimination against women. Further, employment of one member of the couple at another firm may create its own set of problems if that firm turns out to be a competitor.[70] These are probably some of the reasons

[68] Byrnes, "Dual Career Couples."

[69] A particularly negative view on a firm's employment of individuals who are romantically involved is put forth by Eliza G. C. Collins in the September 1983 issue of the *Harvard Business Review* (as reported in *Newsweek,* September 5, 1983, p. 60).

[70] In December 1984, "a California state appeals court affirmed a $300,000 verdict against IBM for wrongfully discharging a female manager because she was dating an employee from a rival office products firm." See Bureau of National Affairs, *Daily Labor Report,* no. 237, December 12, 1984, pp. 2–3.

why a 1984 survey found that 58 percent of firms were relaxing their rules on the hiring and placement of close relatives. Also, in dealing with the growing number of couples who were simply living together, 48 percent of the firms "... said they would rather 'pretend such things don't go on' than be charged with violating rights of privacy."[71]

CONCLUSION

In this chapter, we have examined supply-side explanations for gender differences in occupations and earnings, chiefly focusing upon the human capital model. We have also reviewed government and employer policies that could increase women's human capital investments and promote greater labor force attachment among them. Although the evidence suggests that such factors are undoubtedly important, they explain only part of the story. Discrimination against women in the labor market is also an important factor, to which we turn in the next chapter.

SUGGESTED READINGS

BECKER, GARY S. *Human Capital,* 2nd ed. Chicago: University of Chicago Press, 1975.

CORCORAN, MARY and GREG J. DUNCAN. "Work History, Labor Force Attachment, and Earnings Differences Between the Races and Sexes." *Journal of Human Resources* 14, no. 1 (Winter 1979): 3–20.

ENGLAND, PAULA. "The Failure of Human Capital Theory to Explain Occupational Sex Segregation," *Journal of Human Resources* 17, no. 3 (Summer 1982): 358–70.

FERBER, MARIANNE A. and BRIGID O'FARRELL, with LARUE ALLEN, eds. *Work and Family: Policies for a Changing Workforce.* National Research Council (Washington, D.C.: National Academy Press, 1991).

KANTER, ROSABETH. *Men and Women of the Corporation.* New York: Basic Books, 1977.

LIPS, HILARY M. "Gender-Role Socialization: Lessons in Femininity." In *Women: A Feminist Perspective,* 4th ed., Jo Freeman, ed. Mountain View, CA: Mayfield, 1989.

LLOYD, CYNTHIA B. and BETH T. NIEMI. *The Economics of Sex Differentials.* New York: Columbia University Press, 1979, chs. 3 and 4.

MINCER, JACOB and SOLOMON POLACHEK. "Family Investments in Human Capital: Earnings of Women." *Journal of Political Economy* 82, no. 2, pt. 2 (March/April 1974): S76–S108.

RESKIN, BARBARA F. and HEIDI I. HARTMANN. *Women's Work, Men's Work: Sex Segregation on the Job.* Washington, D.C.: National Academy Press, 1986.

SMITH, JAMES P. and MICHAEL P. WARD. "Women in the Labor Market and in the Family." *Journal of Economic Perspectives* 3, no. 1 (Winter 1989): 9–23.

TOBIAS, SHEILA. *Overcoming Math Anxiety.* New York: W. W. Norton, 1978.

---

[71] *New York Times,* June 17, 1985, p. 20. The survey was conducted by the American Society for Personnel Administration. See also Bureau of National Affairs, *Corporate Affairs: Nepotism, Office Romance, & Sexual Harassment* (1988).

Chapter 7

DIFFERENCES IN OCCUPATIONS AND EARNINGS: THE ROLE OF LABOR MARKET DISCRIMINATION

In the preceding chapter, we examined the role of supply-side factors in producing the gender inequality in earnings and occupational attainment that we observe in the labor market (Chapter 5). We now focus upon the demand side, specifically the role of labor market discrimination. As we explained at the end of Chapter 6, the available evidence suggests that both supply- and demand-side influences are responsible for gender differences in economic outcomes.

In this chapter, we begin by providing a definition of labor market discrimination; then we examine the empirical evidence on the extent of gender discrimination in the labor market with respect to earnings and occupations. We then consider the various explanations that economists have offered for the existence and persistence of such discrimination. Although our focus is on gender discrimination, much of the analysis is equally applicable to discrimination based on race, age, disability, and so on. In fact, most of the models of discrimination that we discuss were initially developed to explain racial discrimination.

Our primary concern here is to determine to what extent discrimination exists and its possible effects on the groups directly involved. However, the issue of misallocation of resources is also potentially serious when workers are not hired, promoted, or rewarded equally when they are equally qualified. This, in addition to consideration of equity or fairness, provides an important rationale for government intervention to combat labor market discrimination. In this chapter, we also review the government's anti-discrimination policies and examine their possible effects.

LABOR MARKET DISCRIMINATION: A DEFINITION

Labor market discrimination exists when *two equally qualified individuals are treated differently solely on the basis of their gender* (race, age, disability, etc.).[1] As we saw in Chapter 1, in the absence of discrimination, profit-maximizing employers in a competitive labor market will pay workers in accordance with their productivity. For similar reasons, they will also find it in their economic self-interest to make other personnel decisions, such as hiring, placement, or promotion decisions, on the same objective basis. An individual's gender (or race, age, disability, etc.) itself would be an irrelevant consideration.

If labor market discrimination nonetheless exists, it is expected to adversely affect the economic status of women *directly* by producing differences in economic outcomes between men and women that are *not* accounted for by differences in productivity-related characteristics or qualifications. That is, men and women who, in the absence of discrimination, would be equally productive and would receive the same pay (or be in the same occupation) do not receive equal rewards. As we shall see, in some economic models of discrimination this inequality occurs because women are paid less than their marginal products due to discrimination. In other views of this process, labor market discrimination *directly* lowers women's productivity as well as their pay, as for instance, when a woman is denied access to an employer-sponsored training program or when customers are reluctant to patronize a female sales person.

If such gender differences in *treatment* of equally qualified men and women are widespread and persistent, the behavior of women themselves may be adversely affected. As we saw in the preceding chapter, productivity differences among workers reflect, in part, the decisions they make whether or not to continue their schooling, participate in a training program, remain continuously in the labor market, and so on. Faced with discrimination in the labor market, women may have less incentive to undertake such human capital investments. If such indirect or **feedback effects** of labor market discrimination exist, they are also expected to lower the economic status of women relative to men.

Much of the theoretical and virtually all of the empirical work on labor market discrimination has focused on its more readily measured *direct* effects; that is, on pay or occupational differences between equally well-qualified (potentially equally productive) men and women. We shall follow that emphasis in this chapter. However, it is important to recognize that the *full* impact of discrimination also

---

[1] This definition is derived from the work of Gary S. Becker, *The Economics of Discrimination,* 2nd ed. (Chicago: University of Chicago Press, 1971).

THE SUBTLE BARRIERS:
DIFFERENT PERCEPTIONS OF MEN AND WOMEN

One of the major difficulties in determining the existence of discrimination is that it may take very subtle forms. One of these is that men and women behaving in similar ways may, nonetheless, be perceived quite differently. Such attitudes are almost impossible to document, let alone measure, but that does not mean they do not exist. Here are some examples of typical reactions.*

The family picture is on HIS desk:
Ah, a solid, responsible family man.

The family picture is on HER desk:
Hmm, her family will come before her career.

HIS desk is cluttered:
He's obviously a hard worker and a busy man.

HER desk is cluttered:
She's obviously a disorganized scatterbrain.

HE's talking with co-workers:
He must be discussing the latest deal.

SHE's talking with co-workers:
She must be gossiping.

HE's not at his desk:
He must be at a meeting.

SHE's not at her desk:
She must be in the ladies' room.

HE's not in the office:
He's meeting customers.

SHE's not in the office:
She must be out shopping.

HE's having lunch with the boss:
He's on his way up.

SHE's having lunch with the boss:
They must be having an affair.

The boss criticized HIM:
He'll improve his performance.

The boss criticized HER:
She'll be very upset.

HE got an unfair deal:
Did he get angry?

SHE got an unfair deal:
Did she cry?

HE's getting married:
He'll get more settled.

SHE's getting married:
She'll get pregnant and leave.

HE'S having a baby:
He'll need a raise.

SHE'S having a baby:
She'll cost the company money in maternity benefits.

HE'S going on a business trip:
It's good for his career.

SHE's going on a business trip:
What does her husband say?

HE'S leaving for a better job:
He recognizes a good opportunity.

SHE's leaving for a better job:
Women are undependable.

*From Natasha Josefowitz, *Paths to Power* © 1990, by Natasha Josefowitz. Reprinted with permission of Addison-Wesley Publishing Company.

includes any feedback effects on women's behavior that result in their being less well-qualified than men.[2] Thus, we also discuss such feedback effects.

EMPIRICAL EVIDENCE

Having defined labor market discrimination, we now consider the empirical evidence as to the existence and extent of such discrimination. We restrict ourselves entirely to the direct effects of such discrimination and, thus, take as given any gender differences in qualifications. We seek to address more fully the two relatively straightforward questions considered in Chapter 6. Are gender differences in labor market outcomes *fully* explained by gender differences in qualifications or (potential) productivity? If not, how large is the unexplained portion of the gender differential? It is this differential that is commonly used as an estimate of the impact of labor market discrimination. Unfortunately, as we shall see, though the questions are fairly simple, the answers are not so easily obtained. We turn first to a consideration of gender differences in earnings and then to an examination of gender differences in occupations.

Earnings Differences

Economists and other social scientists have studied the earnings gap between men and women workers extensively. Actual estimates vary depending on the source of the data used and the types of qualifications examined. However, virtually all studies find that a substantial portion of the pay gap cannot be explained by gender differences in qualifications.[3]

In Tables 7.1 and 7.2 we examine the results of one study of gender discrimination in detail. The data are for a national sample of workers aged 21 to 64 in 1984. Table 7.1 presents the means of some of the various work-related characteristics examined in the study for men and women separately by three levels of education. The three education groups include (1) individuals who did not complete high school (less than 12 years of schooling); (2) individuals who completed high school but not college (12 to 15 years of schooling); and (3) individuals who completed college (16 or more years of schooling).

---

[2]Note that the argument is *not* that *all* differences in qualifications between men and women are due to the indirect effects of discrimination, but, rather, that *some* of these differences may be a response to such discrimination.

[3]For summaries of this literature, see Francine D. Blau and Marianne A. Ferber, "Discrimination: Empirical Evidence from the United States," *American Economic Review* 77, no. 2 (May 1987): 316–20; Glen G. Cain, "The Economics of Discrimination: A Survey," in *Handbook of Labor Economics,* Orley Ashenfelter and Richard Layard, eds. (Amsterdam: North Holland Press, 1986), pp. 693–785; and Janice Madden, "The Persistence of Pay Differentials: The Economics of Sex Discrimination," *Women and Work,* 1 (1985): 76–114.

TABLE 7.1   **Means of Variables for Formal Education, Work Experience, and Gender Composition of Occupation, 1984 (Workers aged 21–64)**

	NOT HIGH SCHOOL GRADUATES		HIGH SCHOOL GRADUATES		COLLEGE GRADUATES	
	Men	*Women*	*Men*	*Women*	*Men*	*Women*
Total years of experience	24.53	18.55	20.58	15.54	19.05	14.34
With current employer	11.02	8.00	9.73	7.19	8.46	6.72
With prior employers	13.51	10.55	10.85	8.35	10.59	7.62
In current occupation	3.53	2.27	2.74	2.21	2.82	2.37
In other occupations	9.98	8.28	8.11	6.14	7.77	5.25
Proportion who usually work full-time	0.97	0.92	0.98	0.93	0.96	0.89
Average proportion of workers in individual's occupation who are female	0.17	0.61	0.21	0.68	0.30	0.61
Proportion in a skilled trade	0.28	0.06	—	—	—	—
Number of math, science, and foreign language courses in high school	—	—	1.94	1.84	3.26	3.18
Proportion:						
Who took academic courses in high school	—	—	0.30	0.30	0.75	0.78
Who obtained master's degree	—	—	—	—	0.19	0.23
Who obtained doctorate	—	—	—	—	0.09	0.03
Whose college field was:						
Law, medicine, or dentistry	—	—	—	—	0.06	0.03
Math or science	—	—	—	—	0.11	0.06
Business or economics	—	—	—	—	0.27	0.17
Engineering	—	—	—	—	0.13	0.02
Education	—	—	—	—	0.09	0.30
Nursing, pharmacy, or health technologies	—	—	—	—	0.01	0.09
Technical or vocational	—	—	—	—	0.03	0.01

Source: U.S. Bureau of the Census, Current Population Reports, Series P–70, No. 10, *Male-Female Differences in Work Experience, Occupation, and Earnings: 1984* (1987).

The gender differences in work-related characteristics shown in Table 7.1 are those we might expect based on our examination of this issue in Chapter 6. At each education level, women have less work experience than men, both with their current employer and with prior employers. Among college graduates, women were less likely than men to have obtained a doctorate (but more likely to have obtained a master's). Women were also less likely to have specialized in engineering, business or economics, math or science, and law, medicine, or dentistry; they were more likely to have studied education, nursing, or pharmacy. Men and women tended

TABLE 7.2   Percentages of the Wage Gap Between Women and Men Explained by Differences in Characteristics

Characteristics	Not High School Graduates	High School Graduates	College Graduates
Formal education[a]	—	0.8	12.7
Experience[b]	13.9	22.2	22.6
Skilled trades[c]	12.9	—	—
Gender composition of occupation[d]	30.3	30.0	17.4
Other characteristics[e]	2.4	7.1	12.8
Unexplained	40.5	39.9	34.5
Total	100.0	100.0	100.0
Wage Differential (%)	29.7	31.0	28.2

[a] Includes type of high school program, number of math, science, and foreign language courses in high school, whether public or private high school (high school and college graduates); highest degree and field of study (college graduates).

[b] Includes number of years with current employer, years in current occupation less years with current employer, years of work experience less years in current occupation, whether usually worked full-time during work years, length of time between current and previous job.

[c] Whether in precision production, craft, or repair occupation.

[d] Includes percent of persons in occupation who are female.

[e] Includes marital status, type of geographic area, whether covered by a union contract, size of firm, class of worker, whether involuntarily left last job, race and Hispanic origin, disability and health status, presence of children.

Source: U.S. Bureau of the Census, Current Population Reports, Series P–70, No. 10, *Male-Female Differences in Work Experience, Occupation, and Earnings: 1984* (1987).

to be concentrated in different occupations, with men working in predominantly male jobs and women working in predominantly female occupations.

The consequences of these differences in work-related characteristics for the male-female wage differential are shown in Table 7.2 Qualifications are found to be important determinants of gender wage differentials. Gender differences in formal education, in this case field of study, are found to explain 13 percent of the wage gap among college graduates. Gender differences in experience explain from 14 to 23 percent. Differences in the gender composition of occupation explain 17 to 30 percent. However, one may question whether gender composition of occupation is appropriately regarded as a work "qualification." Taken together, all these differences (including gender-composition of occupations) explain 60 to 66 percent of the wage difference between men and women with the same level of education.

Although these findings suggest that gender differences in work-related characteristics are important, they are only part of the story. The proportion of the wage differential that is *not* explained by productivity-related characteristics such as these serves as an estimate of the impact of labor market discrimination. It ranges from 35 percent for college graduates to 41 percent among those with less than 12 years of high school. If we were to consider the portion of the pay gap attributed to gender composition of occupation as "unexplained," the unexplained portion of the pay gap would rise to over 50 percent for college graduates and about 70 percent for the other two education groups. These results are particularly striking in light of the many job-related qualifications taken into account in this study.

How conclusive are such estimates? Certainly not entirely so; there are a number of problems with these types of analyses that may result in either upward or downward biases in the estimate of discrimination. One difficulty is that we do not have information on all the qualifications of individuals that are associated with their (potential) productivity. Some of the factors that affect earnings, such as motivation or work effort, cannot easily be quantified. Others (for example, the employees' record of absence or lateness) are frequently unavailable in a particular data set. Hence, in general, it is not possible to include all relevant job qualifications in a study of gender differences in pay. So, for example, although the study reported in Tables 7.1 and 7.2 controls for gender differences in many important work-related variables, it lacks data on these other potentially relevant factors. If men are more highly qualified with respect to the factors that are omitted from the analysis, the extent of labor market discrimination is likely to be *overestimated*. For instance, some portion of the "unexplained" gender differential in Table 7.2 may, in fact, be due to men being more highly motivated or less likely to be absent from work. However, it is also possible that women are more highly qualified in some respects not taken into account, in which case discrimination would be underestimated. In general, more attention has been focused on the possibility that discrimination may be overestimated due to omitted factors.[4]

At the same time, as noted above, some of the lower qualifications of women may be a direct result of labor market discrimination. For example, qualified women may be excluded from particular jobs due to discrimination in hiring or promotion. The study reported in Table 7.2 includes controls for variables like skilled trade and gender composition of the occupation that may be impacted by such discrimination. To the extent that studies of discrimination control for qualifications that themselves reflect the direct effects of discrimination, the impact of discrimination on the pay gap will be *underestimated*.[5]

[4]This problem is a bit less serious than it appears at first glance in that the included factors most likely capture some of the effects of those that cannot be controlled for because of lack of information. For example, it is likely that more-educated individuals are also more intelligent and more able, on the average, than the less-educated. For an interesting explication of the statistical issues raised by imperfect measures of productivity in empirical analyses, see Arthur Goldberger, "Reverse Regression and Salary Discrimination," *Journal of Human Resources* 19, no. 3 (Summer 1984): 293–318.

[5]This point is made by Alan Blinder, "Wage Discrimination: Reduced Form and Structural Estimates," *Journal of Human Resources* 8, no. 4 (Fall 1973): 436–55. For evidence consistent with discrimination against women in access to on-the-job training, see Greg J. Duncan and Saul Hoffman, "On-the-Job Training and Earnings Differences by Race and Sex," *Review of Economics and Statistics* 61, no. 4 (Nov. 1979): 594–603.

Analyses of the type presented in Table 7.2 also neglect the feedback effects of labor market discrimination on the behavior and choices of women themselves. For example, the lesser amount of work experience accumulated by women in comparison to men may be due in part to the lower returns they have traditionally faced. Or, as another example, women may have been less likely to pursue college study in traditionally male fields because of the perception that they would encounter job discrimination in these areas.

Where does this leave us? It suggests that pinpointing the exact portion of the pay gap that is due to labor market discrimination is difficult. Nonetheless, the findings of most studies provide strong evidence of pay differences between men and women that are *not* accounted for by gender differences in qualifications, even when the list of qualifications is quite extensive. Further evidence that labor market discrimination exists is provided by the many employment discrimination cases in which employers have been found guilty of discrimination in pay or have reached out-of-court settlements with the plaintiffs.[6] Finally, it is suggestive that American women believe there is such discrimination. A 1987 Gallup poll found that 56 percent of women thought that women faced discrimination; a figure that, surprisingly, had increased somewhat from 49 percent in 1975. Fifty percent believed that women have a lesser chance of becoming executives than men, even if both have the same abilities; this was a small a reduction from 59 percent in 1975.[7] Similarly, in a 1989 national survey, 55 percent of women with full-time jobs indicated that "at work, most men don't take women seriously."[8] We conclude that discrimination does indeed exist. Although precisely estimating its magnitude is difficult, the evidence suggests that the *direct* effects of labor market discrimination may explain as much as half or more of the pay differential between men and women.

Occupational Differences

As we saw in Chapter 5, not only do women earn less than men, they also tend to be concentrated in different occupations. In this section, we address two questions.

- What are the *consequences* for women of such occupational segregation? In particular, what is its relationship to the pay gap between men and women?
- What are the *causes* of these gender differences in occupational distributions? Specifically, what role does labor market discrimination play?

---

[6]A review of the provisions of the employment discrimination laws and regulations is provided later in this chapter.

[7]"Women See Rise in Job Bias," *The New York Times,* March 20, 1987, p. 11.

[8]Lisa Belkin, "Bars to Equality of Sexes Seen as Eroding, Slowly," *New York Times,* August 20, 1989, cited in John J. Donohue III, "Prohibiting Sex Discrimination in the Workplace: An Economic Perspective," *University of Chicago Law Review* 56, no. 4 (Fall 1989), p. 1339.

From a policy perspective, an understanding of the consequences of segregation is crucial for assessing how important a problem it is, and an analysis of its causes helps us to determine the most effective tools for attacking it.

Consequences of occupational segregation. In Chapter 5, we saw that women are more likely than men to be concentrated in clerical and service jobs, whereas men are more likely than women to work in higher-paying jobs such as managers and skilled craft workers. Similarly, although the representation of men and women in the professional category is about the same, men are more likely to work in lucrative professions such as law, medicine, and engineering, whereas women are more often employed in lower-paying ones such as elementary and secondary school teaching and nursing. Such observations suggest that women are concentrated in relatively low-paying occupations and that this helps to explain the male-female pay gap.

On the other hand, there are factors other than gender composition that may help to account for pay differences between male and female jobs. For example, male jobs may tend to require more education and training than female jobs or call for the exercise of skills, like supervisory responsibility, that are more valuable to the employer. Also, some require more physical strength, inconvenient hours, and so on.

Such characteristics are important, but occupational differences do appear to be a significant factor in explaining the earnings gap, even when productivity-related characteristics of workers are held constant. The findings of the study reported in Table 7.2, for example, suggest that the lower pay in predominantly female jobs accounts for 17 to 30 percent of the male-female pay difference within educational levels.[9] Other research suggests that similar large effects (14 to 23 percent) are obtained even when a variety of occupational and industrial characteristics are also controlled for.[10]

The findings reported above are based on detailed Census occupations. Although the number of occupational categories distinguished by the Census—in excess of 400—is impressive, employers use considerably finer breakdowns. It is very likely that, were such extremely detailed categories available for the economy as a whole, an even higher proportion of the pay gap would be attributed

---

[9]The lower figure is for college graduates where field of study is controlled for and tends to capture some of the effect of sex composition of occupation. To the extent that women have tended to avoid predominantly male fields of study because they expected to encounter labor market discrimination in these areas, it is difficult to disentangle the effects of field of study from gender composition of the occupation.

[10]The 23 percent figure is from Elaine Sorensen, "The Crowding Hypothesis and Comparable Worth Issue," *Journal of Human Resources* 25, no. 1 (Winter 1990): 55–89. The 14 percent figure is from George Johnson and Gary Solon, "Estimates of the Direct Effects of Comparable Worth Policy," *American Economic Review* 76, no. 5 (December 1986): 1117–25. The Sorensen article provides an extremely useful summary of the empirical findings in this area.

to occupational segregation.[11] Moreover, within the same occupational category, women tend to be employed in low-wage firms and industries, whereas men are employed in high-wage enterprises and sectors. For example, in one study, industrial differences were found to account for an additional 12 to 17 percent of the pay gap among equally qualified male and female workers.[12]

In evaluating the negative consequences of occupational segregation on women, it is important to bear in mind that the focus upon earnings does not take into account any adverse nonpecuniary consequences of such segregation for women. For one, it is likely that occupational segregation reinforces cultural notions that there are fundamental differences between men and women in capabilities, preferences, and social and economic roles.

Causes of occupational segregation. As with earnings differences, the causes of occupational segregation may be classified into supply-side versus demand-side factors. It is only the latter—differences in treatment—that represent *direct* labor market discrimination. Of course, the anticipation of or experience with labor market discrimination may indirectly influence women's choices via feedback effects.

In the preceding chapter, we considered a variety of supply-side factors that would influence women's occupational choices, including the socialization process and various barriers to their obtaining training in traditionally male fields. Human capital theory also suggests that, because women generally anticipate shorter and less continuous work lives than men, it will be in their economic self-interest to choose female occupations, which presumably require smaller human capital investments and have lower wage penalties for time spent out of the labor market. On the demand side, employers may contribute to occupational segregation by discriminating against equally qualified women in hiring, placement, access to training programs, and promotion for traditionally male jobs.

Although it is not possible to ascribe a specific portion of gender differences in occupations to supply-side versus demand-side factors, the evidence suggests that both are important. As in the case of pay differences, evidence of discrimination

[11]For example, in one large fiduciary institution it was found that 76 percent of the pay gap between equally qualified men and women was due to gender differences in occupational distribution; see Francine D. Blau, "Occupational Segregation and Labor Market Discrimination," in *Sex Segregation in the Workplace: Trends, Explanations, Remedies,* Barbara Reskin, ed. (Washington, D.C.: National Academy Press, 1984), pp. 117–43.

[12]Sorensen, "The Crowding Hypothesis." For evidence of the importance of gender differences in employment by firm using establishment data, see Francine D. Blau, *Equal Pay in the Office* (Lexington, MA: Lexington Books, 1977); and Erica L. Groshen, "The Structure of the Female/Male Wage Differential: Is It Who You Are, What You Do, or Where You Work?" *Journal of Human Resources,* 26, no.3 (Summer 1991): 457–72.

THE SUBTLE BARRIERS:
GENDER DIFFERENCES IN SPEECH PATTERNS

Women in the workplace are less often confronted with conscious, overt discrimination today than they were in the past. However, subtle barriers continue to hamper their progress. As the excerpt below suggests, even gender differences in speech patterns may create problems for women.*

One of the funniest moments in the movie "Tootsie" is the bar scene in which Dustin Hoffman bats a pair of six-inch eyelashes and, with a perky smile, tells the waiter, "I'll have a Dubonnet on the rocks with a twist, please?"

The actor's questioning intonation at the end of a declarative sentence did more for his characterization of a woman than any number of false eyelashes. This is the way women have been socialized to speak, according to Dr. Lillian Glass, a speech pathologist who coached Mr. Hoffman for his role in "Tootsie," . . . "many casualties in the war between the sexes result from a failure to realize that men and women actually speak different languages" [she said].

The communication gap widens when the scene shifts to the workplace. There, a woman who doesn't understand male shoptalk, with all its sports and military references may find herself at a disadvantage. At a business meeting last week, for example, a male colleague nudged Dr. Jerie McArthur and said, "that looks like a panic pass."

Dr. McArthur, a communications instructor at the University of Minnesota, got the message. She has taken a cram course in football jargon, and she encourages women in her management education seminars to do likewise. Since women tend to be task-oriented, she says, they may not realize what sports metaphors mean to men and even belittle such language. As a result, the men may feel uncomfortable around women.

"In the workplace," Dr. McArthur said, "the male culture is the dominant culture, and women need to understand it if both sexes are going to work together effectively. Coming in and telling men that they have to change is just not very adaptive."

But even women who know the language may not get much chance to use it in mixed company. Recent research on gender differences in male-female conversations suggests that the stereotypical wife who keeps butting in on her husband's jokes was probably never that real. Men interrupt women much more often than they do other men, according to one study, while women are less likely to interrupt either men or women.

At business meetings, Dr. McArthur said, men typically engage in "competitive turn-taking," or grabbing the floor by interrupting another speaker. Women have been conditioned from childhood to believe that to interrupt is impolite. Instead, they will sit for hours waiting for a turn to speak, she said, "while their male colleagues wonder if they'll ever have anything to say."

A woman who does speak up may undermine her credibility in other ways—by using tentative phrases as "I guess," by turning statements into questions

---

*Georgia Dullea, "Relationships, The Sexes: Differences in Speech," *New York Times,* March 19, 1984, p. C10. Copyright © 1984 by The New York Times Company, reprinted by permission.

or by making indirect statements. In a typical scenario, a woman might say at a meeting, "Don't you think it would be better to send them that report first?" A man could then agree, saying, "Yes, it would be better to send that report first." Others at the meeting will come away with the impression that it was the man's idea because, in Dr. McArthur's words, "the woman never really claimed it."

Still another problem for women in the workplace is the use of off-color language by male colleagues. Echoing the view of several female executives interviewed, Ravelle Brickman, vice president at Richard Weiner Inc., a public-relations concern, said that the woman is then faced with a double-edged sword.

"Men in meetings routinely use four-letter words, almost as a way of establishing fraternity," she said. "When a woman is present, the man will often apologize. If the woman wants to be accepted into the fraternity, she cannot accept the apology but must, in fact, respond in kind."

may be found in both academic studies[13] and the many discrimination cases in which employers have been found guilty of such gender discrimination or have settled the cases out of court. As noted above, a 1987 survey found that half of women believed that women have a lesser chance of becoming executives than men, even if both have the same abilities. Similarly, in a national poll conducted in 1984, half of the women surveyed thought that "women are discriminated against in getting skilled labor jobs."[14]

MODELS OF LABOR MARKET DISCRIMINATION

The empirical evidence suggests that there are indeed pay and occupational differences between men and women that are not accounted for by (potential) productivity differences. We now turn to an examination of how discrimination

[13] See for example, Rosabeth Kanter, *Men and Women of the Corporation* (New York: Basic Books, 1977); Greg J. Duncan and Saul Hoffman, "On-the-Job Training and Earnings Differences"; Craig A. Olson and Brian E. Becker, "Sex Discrimination in the Promotion Process," *Industrial and Labor Relations Review* 36, no. 4 (July 1983): 624–41; Robert Cabral, Marianne A. Ferber, and Carole A. Green, "Men and Women in Fiduciary Institutions: A Study of Sex Differences in Career Development," *Review of Economics and Statistics* 63, no. 4 (November 1981): 573–80; and Barbara F. Reskin and Patricia A. Roos, *Job Queues, Gender Queues: Explaining Women's Inroads into Male Occupations* (Philadelphia: Temple University Press, 1990). For reviews of the literature on this topic, see Paula England, "Socioeconomic Explanations of Job Segregation," in *Comparable Worth and Wage Discrimination: Technical Possibilities and Political Realities,* Helen Remick, ed. (Philadelphia: Temple University Press, 1984), pp. 28–46; Patricia A. Roos and Barbara F. Reskin, "Institutional Factors Contributing to Occupational Sex Segregation," in *Sex Segregation in the Workplace,* Reskin, ed. pp. 235–60; and Barbara F. Reskin and Heidi I. Hartmann, eds. *Women's Work, Men's Work: Sex Segregation on the Job* (Washington, D.C.: National Academy Press, 1986).

[14] *Ms. Magazine,* July 1984, p. 56.

produces such gender differences in economic outcomes and why this inequality has persisted over time. Economists have developed a variety of models that may be used to analyze these issues. Unfortunately, empirical research in this area has not yet established which of these approaches most accurately describes the labor market. Indeed, for the most part, these explanations are *not* mutually exclusive and each may shed light on part of the impact of labor market discrimination on women's economic status.

Unless otherwise indicated, the analyses presented here assume that male and female labor are perfect substitutes in production. That is, it is assumed that male and female workers are equally well qualified and, in the absence of discrimination, would be equally productive and receive the same pay. Of course, we know that this assumption is not an accurate description of reality—that is, there are gender differences in qualifications that explain some of the pay gap. However, this assumption is appropriate in that models of discrimination are efforts to explain the portion of the pay gap that is *not* due to differences in qualifications, that is, to explain pay differences between men and women who are (potentially) equally productive.

Tastes for Discrimination

The foundation for the modern neoclassical analysis of labor market discrimination was laid by Gary Becker.[15] Becker conceptualized discrimination as a personal prejudice, or what he termed a *taste,* against associating with a particular group. In his model, employers, coworkers, and/or customers may all potentially have such discriminatory tastes. In contrast to the case of racial discrimination that Becker initially analyzed, it may at first seem odd to hypothesize that men would not like to associate with women when, in fact, they generally live together in families. The issue here may be more one of socially appropriate roles than of the desire to maintain social distance, as Becker postulated was the case with race.[16]

Employers may have no compunctions about hiring women as secretaries but may be reluctant to employ them as pipefitters. Men may be willing to work with women who are in complementary or subordinate positions but dislike interacting with them as equals or superiors. Customers may be delighted to purchase nylons from female clerks but avoid women who sell cars or are attorneys. These discriminatory tastes may be held whether or not it is believed that women

---

[15]Gary S. Becker, *The Economics of Discrimination.* In our presentation of the tastes for discrimination model, we incorporate some of the insights of Kenneth Arrow. See, for example, his "The Theory of Discrimination," in *Discrimination in Labor Markets,* Orley Ashenfelter and Albert Rees, eds. (Princeton, New Jersey: Princeton University Press, 1973), pp. 3–33.

[16]Indeed, the notion of socially appropriate roles may also be a factor in racial discrimination, as when blacks have little difficulty in gaining access to menial jobs but encounter discrimination in obtaining higher-level positions.

are less qualified than men for nontraditional pursuits.[17] This latter possibility is considered under notions of statistical discrimination (see below).

It is important to recognize that discrimination against women by employers, fellow employees, customers or clients is not always or even usually conscious and overt. The subtle barriers of the sort we outlined in Chapter 6 with respect to women's acquisition of formal schooling also operate in the labor market. Women may have fewer opportunities to participate in the beneficial *mentor–protégé* relationships that often develop between senior and junior workers and may be excluded from the *informal networks* that tend to arise among peers at the workplace.

Discrimination may also result from the perception that a woman does not "fit in" with the group as well as a man does. As a female management consultant comments,

> Men I talk to would like to see more women in senior management. . . . But they don't recognize the subtle barriers that stand in the way. . . . At senior management levels, competence is assumed. . . . What you're looking for is someone who fits, someone who gets along, someone you trust. Now that's subtle stuff. How does a group of men feel that a woman is going to fit?

A female vice president of a large bank (who originally worked as a consultant) echoes these sentiments:

> . . . the men just don't feel comfortable. . . . They make all sorts of excuses — that I'm not a banker, that I don't know the culture. There's a smokescreen four miles thick. I attribute it to being a woman.[18]

Evaluations of a female employee's competence may also be tainted by gender stereotypes of appropriate female behavior. For example, in the highly publicized 1990 *Price Waterhouse*[19] case, a woman was denied a partnership in the prestigious Price Waterhouse accounting firm, even though, of the 88 candidates for partnership, she had brought in the most business. She was also the only one of the candidates who was a woman. Her colleagues criticized her for being "overbearing, 'macho' and abrasive and said she would have a better chance of making partner if

---

[17]It should be noted, however, that such preferences on the part of workers or customers for men will cause women to be less productive from the point of view of the employer. For further consideration of the reasons for the origin and persistence of occupational segregation, see Barbara F. Reskin and Patricia A. Roos, *Job Queues, Gender Queues: Explaining Women's Inroads into Male Occupations* (Philadelphia: Temple University Press, 1990) and Myra H. Strober, "Toward a General Theory of Occupational Sex Segregation: The Case of Public School Teaching," in *Sex Segregation in the Workplace: Trends, Explanations, Remedies,* Barbara F. Reskin, ed. (Washington, DC: National Academy Press, 1984), pp. 144-56.

[18]The quotations in the text are from Susan Fraker, "Why Women Aren't Getting to the Top," *Fortune Magazine* 109, no. 8, April 16, 1984, p. 40.

[19]*Hopkins v. Price Waterhouse,* CA DC, No. 84-03040 (1990). For a summary of this case and a text of the opinion, see Bureau of National Affairs, *Daily Labor Report* no. 235, December 6, 1990, pp. A11–A13 and F1–F10.

she would wear makeup and jewelry, and walk, talk and dress 'more femininely.'"
The Court found that Price Waterhouse maintained a partnership evaluation system
that "permitted negative sexually stereotyped comments to influence partnership
selection" and awarded the plaintiff a partnership in the firm.[20]

In general, as Rosabeth Kanter has pointed out, women's position as "tokens"
in male-dominated fields subjects them to special pressures and difficulties that their
male peers do not have to contend with.[21]

In order for such discriminatory tastes to have important consequences for
women's earnings and employment, they must actually influence people's behavior.
According to Becker, individuals with tastes for discrimination against women act as
if there were nonpecuniary costs of associating with women — say, in what is viewed
as a socially inappropriate role.[22] The strength of the individual's discriminatory
taste is measured by his or her **discrimination coefficient** (that is, the size of these
costs in money terms). We now examine the consequences of discrimination based
on employer, employee, and customer preferences, respectively.

Employer discrimination. If an employer has tastes for discrimination
against women, he or she will act as if there were a nonpecuniary cost of employing women equal in dollar terms to d_r (the discrimination coefficient). To this
employer, the costs of employing a man will be his wage, w_m, but the *full* costs of
employing a woman will be her wage *plus* the discrimination coefficient ($w_f + d_r$).
This means that discriminating employers will hire women only at a lower wage
than men ($w_m - d_r = w_f$). Further, if we assume that men are paid in accordance
with their productivity, women will be hired only if they may be paid less than
their productivity.

The consequences of this situation for female workers depend on the prevalence and size of discriminatory tastes among employers, as well as on the number
of women seeking employment. Nondiscriminatory employers are willing to hire
men and women at the same wage rate (that is, their discrimination coefficient
equals 0). If there are a relatively large number of such nondiscriminatory employers or there are relatively few women seeking employment, they may all be
absorbed by the nondiscriminatory firms. In this case, there will be no discriminatory pay differential based on gender, even though some employers have tastes for
discrimination against women.

---

[20] Tamar Lewin, "Partnership Awarded to Woman in Sex Bias Case," *New York Times,* May 16,
1990, pp. A1, A12.

[21] Kanter, *Men and Women of the Corporation.*

[22] Throughout, we assume that employers, coworkers, or customers have tastes for discrimination
against women. It is also possible that they have positive preferences for employing, working with, or
buying from men. This may be termed a kind of *nepotism.* See Matthew Goldberg, "Discrimination,
Nepotism, and Long-Run Wage Differentials," *Quarterly Journal of Economics* 97, no. 2 (May 1982):
307–19 for an interesting analysis of the consequences of nepotism for the persistence of discrimination
in the long run.

However, if discriminatory tastes are widespread, or there are relatively many women seeking employment, some women will have to find jobs at discriminatory firms. As we have seen, the women obtain such employment only if w_f is less than w_m. If we assume that the labor market is competitive, all employers will pay the (same) going rate for labor of a particular sex. This means that, in equilibrium, the market wage differential between men and women must be large enough so that all the women find employment—including those who must find work at the discriminatory firms. Thus, the more prevalent and the stronger employers' discriminatory tastes against women and the larger the number of women seeking employment, the larger will be the aggregate wage gap $(w_m - w_f)$ between men and women.

The model of employer tastes for discrimination is consistent with the inequalities between men and women that we observe in the labor market. There may be a wage differential between equally qualified male and female workers because discriminatory employers will hire women workers only at a wage discount.[23] Further, since less discriminatory employers will hire more women workers than more discriminatory employers, male and female workers may be segregated by firm—as also appears to be the case. Finally, if, as seems likely, employer tastes for discrimination vary across occupations, occupational segregation by gender can also occur.

However, one problem that economists have identified with this model is that discrimination here is not costless to the employer who forgoes the opportunity to hire more of the lower-priced female labor and less of the higher-priced male labor. Therefore, less discriminatory firms should have lower costs of production. Such a competitive advantage would enable them to expand and drive the more discriminatory firms out of business in the long run. As the less discriminatory firms expand, the demand for female labor would be increased and the male-female pay gap would be reduced. If there were enough *entirely* nondiscriminatory firms to absorb all the women workers, the pay gap would be eliminated. Hence, the question is how discrimination, which represents a departure from profit-maximizing behavior, can withstand the impact of competitive pressures.

One answer to this question is that discrimination is likely to be related to lack of competitive pressures in the economy. Becker hypothesized that, on average,

---

[23]Some have proposed testing the employer discrimination model by comparing the gender pay gap among self-employed workers and employees. The claim is that if *employer* discrimination is responsible for the pay differential, female self-employed workers should fare relatively better than female employees, all else being equal. See Victor R. Fuchs, "Differences in Hourly Earnings Between Men and Women," *Monthly Labor Review* 94, no. 5 (May 1971): 9–15; and Robert L. Moore, "Employer Discrimination: Evidence from Self-Employed Workers," *Review of Economics and Statistics* 65, no. 3 (August 1983): 496–501. Although such studies have not supported the employer discrimination model, they do not provide an ideal test. If there are important economies of scale in self-employment, women's lesser endowment of capital, relative to men, could lower their returns. Also, there may be discrimination against women by lenders, suppliers, customers, and so on.

employer discrimination would be less severe in competitive than in monopolistic industries, and some support has been obtained for this prediction.[24] As we shall see, it is also true that women are less highly represented in unionized employment and thus do not benefit from the wage advantage of unionism to the same extent as men.[25]

It has also been suggested that *monopsony* power by employers in the labor market plays a role in producing and perpetuating the gender pay differential.[26] A firm has monopsony power when it is a large buyer of labor relative to the size of the particular market.

To see how this can adversely affect women, consider the not uncommon case of a one-university town. In the past, when the husband's job prospects usually determined the location of the family, the faculty wife with a Ph.D. had little choice but to take whatever the university offered her—most considered themselves fortunate if they were able to obtain employment at all. Even the growing numbers of egalitarian Ph.D. couples cannot entirely avoid this problem. In order to change jobs, they must find *two* acceptable alternatives in a single location.[27] This will obviously be harder to do than to find *one* desirable alternative. Thus, the Ph.D. couple will have fewer options than those with only one Ph.D. in the family. (Similar problems can arise for two-career couples in other fields.)

This situation gives the employer a degree of monopsony power and is likely to lower the pay of both members of the couple relative to Ph.D.s who can relocate more easily. Note that among Ph.D. couples, both the husband's *and* the wife's salary may be adversely affected. However, because women with Ph.D.s are more likely than men Ph.D.s to have a Ph.D. spouse, this factor will probably have a larger adverse effect on academic women as a group than on academic men.[28]

---

[24] See, for example, William A. Luksetich, "Market Power and Sex Discrimination in White-Collar Employment," *Review of Social Economy* 37, no. 2 (October 1979): 211–24; and Orley Ashenfelter and Timothy Hannan, "Sex Discrimination and Product Market Competition: The Case of the Banking Industry," *Quarterly Journal of Economics* 101, no. 1 (February 1986): 149–73.

[25] For analyses of the impact of unions on gender pay differences, see Orley Ashenfelter, "Discrimination and Trade Unions," in *Discrimination in Labor Markets,* Orley Ashenfelter and Albert Rees, eds. (Princeton, NJ: Princeton University Press, 1973); and Richard B. Freeman and Jonathan S. Leonard "Union Maids: Unions and the Female Work Force," in *Gender in the Workplace,* Clair Brown and Joseph A. Pechman, eds. (Washington, D.C.: The Brookings Institution, 1987).

[26] Janice F. Madden, *The Economics of Sex Discrimination* (Lexington, MA: Lexington Books, 1973).

[27] Unless, of course, they adopt the solution of the growing number of two-career couples who work in different locations and see each other, say, on weekends. It is estimated that in 1985 about one million married couples lived apart in order to keep their jobs or advance their careers (*Wall Street Journal,* June 24, 1985), p. 17.

[28] There is evidence, at least for one institution, that both men and women with a spouse who was also a faculty member were paid less. (Marianne A. Ferber and Jane W. Loeb, "Professors, Performance and Rewards," *Industrial Relations* 13, no. 1 [February 1974]: 67–77.) Madden offers the monopsony model as a general explanation for the sex pay gap. She argues that such factors as occupational segregation and the power of male unions may limit women's options and, thus, decrease

Another reason for the persistence of discrimination in the labor market is the possibility (not originally considered by Becker) that the employers' motivation for discriminating against women is not simply personal prejudice but is related to actual or perceived differences between male and female workers in productivity or behavior. We consider such models of "statistical discrimination" later in this chapter. A major contribution of Becker's, however, is the realization that, even if employers themselves have no taste for discrimination against women, their profit-maximizing behavior may result in gender discrimination in the labor market if employees or customers have such tastes. There is no conflict here with profit maximization by employers. Hence, there is no economic reason why this type of discrimination cannot continue. We now consider the possibility of discriminating employees and customers.

Employee discrimination. If a male employee has tastes for discrimination against women, he will act as if there were nonpecuniary costs of working with women equal to his discrimination coefficient, d_e. This is the premium he must be paid to induce him to work with women. This is analogous to the compensating wage differential that economists expect workers to be offered for unpleasant or unsafe working conditions.

What will be the profit-maximizing employer's response to this situation? One solution would be for the employer to hire a sex-segregated work force. This would eliminate the necessity of paying a premium to male workers for associating with female workers. If all employers responded in this way (but had no taste for discrimination themselves), male and female workers would be paid the same wage rate, although they would work in segregated settings.

However, complete segregation may not be profitable where there are substantial costs of adjustment from the previous situation.[29] For example, the hiring of new workers entails recruitment and screening costs for the firm. Further, for jobs in which firm-specific training is important, the firm must incur the costs of these investments as well. Where there are such costs to change, history matters. Given rising female participation rates over time, women, as relatively new entrants, will find men already in place in many sectors. Further, as we saw in

---

their wage elasticity of supply to the firm, all else being equal. Further, women tend to engage in less job search than men and to seek jobs that are closer to home. However, as Francine Blau and Carol Jusenius ("Economists' Approaches to Sex Segregation in the Labor Market: An Appraisal," *Signs: Journal of Women in Culture and Society* 1, no. 3, Pt. 2 [Spring 1976]: 181–99) point out, women's wage elasticity of supply to the firm is increased by the fact that home work provides a viable alternative for those at the margin of labor force participation. Furthermore, if men are more likely than women to acquire firm-specific training that would also lower their mobility relative to women. It seems likely, as suggested by the example we present in the text, that the monopsony explanation is more applicable to specific occupations and specific labor markets than to the aggregate gender pay differential.

[29] Arrow, "The Theory of Discrimination."

Chapter 2, women were heavily concentrated in a few female-dominated activities even when they constituted a small proportion of the labor force. Regardless of the various factors initially causing this segregation, adjustment costs in conjunction with employee tastes for discrimination could help to perpetuate it.

Given employee tastes for discrimination and adjustment costs, marketwide wage differences between male and female workers may result. Again, the size of the wage differential depends on the distribution and intensity of employees' discriminatory tastes, as well as the relative number of women seeking employment. If there is a large proportion of employees with no taste for discrimination against women and/or relatively few women seeking jobs, then it may be possible for all the women to work with nondiscriminatory men. In this case, no pay differential would occur.

However, if discriminatory tastes are widespread, or there is a relatively large number of women seeking jobs, some of the women will have to work with discriminating male workers. Those males will require higher compensation to induce them to work with women. The result will be a wage differential between male and female workers, on the average, since some males will receive this higher pay, and women may be paid less to compensate for this. There also will be more variation in male workers' wage rates than would otherwise be the case. Discriminating male workers who do not work with women do not need to be paid a wage premium, nor do nondiscriminating males, regardless of whether or not they are employed with women.

In an empirical test of this prediction, one study compared the wages of men and women (within the same narrowly defined white-collar occupations) in sex-integrated and sex-segregated firms. It was found that, contrary to what was expected on the basis of the employee discrimination model, men earned *more* in sex-segregated than in integrated firms, and women earned *more* when they worked with men than when they worked only with other women. These findings are more consistent with a situation in which high-wage (for example, monopolistic, unionized) employers are better able to indulge their preferences for hiring men than one in which the pay differential is due to employee discrimination.[30] There may, however, be other areas in which employee discrimination has played an important role.

If, as we speculated earlier, employee tastes for discrimination do exist, and if they vary by occupation, employee discrimination may be a factor causing occupational segregation as well as pay differentials. For example, one reason why women are often not hired for supervisory and managerial positions may be that even male employees who do not mind working with women do not like being supervised by them. Female as well as male employees may not like to have women

[30]Blau, *Equal Pay in the Office.*

supervisors.[31] This could also create a barrier to the employment of women in such jobs.

As Barbara Bergmann and William Darity have pointed out, employee discrimination may also adversely affect the morale and productivity of discriminating male workers who are forced to work with women, a possibility not initially considered by Becker.[32] This would make employers reluctant to hire women, especially when their male employees have considerable firm-specific training and are hard to replace. Further, if employers did hire women under such circumstances, they would pay them less to compensate for the reduction in the productivity of the discriminating male employees. In a sense, a woman's marginal productivity is lower than a man's because adding her to the work force causes a decline in the productivity of previously employed male workers. Adding an additional male worker causes no such decline in output.

Another way in which employee discrimination could affect worker productivity, which was also not initially considered by Becker, is to directly reduce the productivity of women in comparison to men. This is most likely to be a problem in traditionally male fields where the majority of workers are male. For example, on-the-job training frequently occurs informally as supervisors and/or coworkers demonstrate how things are done and give advice and assistance. When male employees have tastes for discrimination against women, they are likely to be unwilling or reluctant to teach them these important skills, and, as a result, women may learn less and be less productive.

The informal barriers we discussed in Chapter 6 with respect to women's acquisition of formal schooling are also relevant here. Women may participate less in the beneficial *mentor-protégé* relationships that often develop between senior and junior workers and may be excluded from the *informal networks* that tend to arise among peers at the workplace. As a result, they will be denied access to important job-related information, skills, and contacts, as well as the informal support systems that male workers generally enjoy. In these cases, although women are *potentially* equally productive, discrimination has the effect of reducing both their productivity and pay.

---

[31]In a 1984 poll of women executives with the title of vice president or higher, 41 percent answered yes to the question, "Have you ever felt that a male subordinate resisted taking orders from you because he felt threatened by a female boss?" (*The Wall Street Journal,* October 29, 1984, p. 31). It is not clear how persistent such attitudes are in the face of actual experience with a female superior. For example, one study found that although both men and women, on the average, expressed a preference for a male boss, both rated women more highly than men among the bosses they ever had. See Marianne A. Ferber, Joan A. Huber, and Glenna Spitze, "Preferences for Men as Bosses and Professionals," *Social Forces* 58, no. 2 (December 1979): 466–76.

[32]Barbara R. Bergmann and William A. Darity, Jr., "Social Relations in the Workplace and Employer Discrimination," *Proceedings of the Thirty-Third Annual Meetings of the Industrial Relations Research Association* (University of Wisconsin, Madison, 1981), pp. 155–62.

Customer discrimination. Customers or clients who have tastes for discrimination against women will act as if there were a nonpecuniary cost associated with purchasing a good or a service from a woman, equal to their discrimination coefficient, d_c. In order to sell as much as a comparable male, a woman would have to charge a lower price. Again, discrimination, this time on the part of possible customers or clients, may result in potentially equally productive women being less productive (in terms of revenue brought in) than comparable males. They are, thus, less desirable employees and receive lower pay. If, as we speculated earlier, such customer discrimination exists in some areas but not in others, occupational segregation may also result.

As in the case of employee discrimination, women as well as men may have these prejudices. A national poll conducted in 1983 found that half of the women surveyed preferred men as doctors and bus drivers, and 36 percent said they would prefer a male accountant. There was also evidence of some intriguing conflicts, suggesting that these views may change as more women (and men) have firsthand experience with women in nontraditional areas. For example, a woman accountant claimed that women made better accountants than men but that men were better doctors and bus drivers than women. On the other hand, a woman bus driver preferred women as bus drivers but said, "men are more shrewd about accounting."[33]

Statistical Discrimination

As noted earlier, models of statistical discrimination developed by Edmund Phelps and others[34] attribute a different motivation to employers for discrimination, one that is consistent with profit maximization and, thus, with the persistence of discrimination in the long run. In this view, employers are constantly faced with the need for decision making under conditions of incomplete information or uncertainty. Even if they carefully study qualifications of applicants, they never know for certain how individuals will perform on the job or how long they will stay with the firm after being hired. Mistakes can be costly, especially where there are substantial hiring and training costs. Promotion decisions entail similar risks, although in this case employers have additional firsthand information on past job performance with the firm.

---

[33] *New York Times* (December 4, 1983): pp. 1, 36. Also Ferber, Huber, and Spitze, "Preferences for Men as Bosses and Professionals," found that both men and women who had ever known any women in a particular profession were less likely to prefer a man in that profession.

[34] See, for example, Edmund S. Phelps, "The Statistical Theory of Racism and Sexism," *American Economic Review* 62, no. 4, September 1972: 659–61; Arrow, "The Theory of Discrimination;" and Dennis J. Aigner and Glen G. Cain, "Statistical Theories of Discrimination in Labor Markets," *Industrial and Labor Relations Review* 30, no. 2, (January 1977): 175–87.

In light of these uncertainties, it is not surprising that employers often use any readily accessible information that may be correlated with productivity or job stability in making difficult personnel decisions. If they believe that, *on average*, women are less productive or less stable employees, *statistical discrimination* against *individual* women may result. That is, employers may judge the individual woman on the basis of their beliefs about group averages. The result is discrimination against women in pay or in hiring and promotion.

For example, suppose an employer is screening applicants for an entry-level managerial position and that the two major qualifications considered are level of education and grades. Assume further that the employer believes that at the same level of qualifications (say, an MBA with an A− average), women as a group will be less likely to remain with the firm than men. Then, for a given level of qualifications, the employer would hire a woman only at a lower wage or, perhaps, simply hire a man rather than a woman for the job. More careful screening of applicants might enable the employer to distinguish more from less career-oriented women (for example, a consideration of the candidate's employment record while a student or of extracurricular activities while in school), but it may not be cost-effective for the employer to invest the additional resources necessary to do this.

Judged on the basis of statements employers themselves make, such beliefs regarding differences in average ability or behavior by sex are quite common. For example, in one study, male managers and administrators compared men and women with respect to a variety of traits that are likely to be related to productivity. Men as a group were rated more highly on understanding the "big picture" of the organization; approaching problems rationally; getting people to work together; understanding financial matters; sizing up situations accurately; administrative capability; leadership potential; setting long-range goals and working toward them; wanting to get ahead; standing up under fire; keeping cool in emergencies; independence and self-sufficiency; and aggressiveness. Women scored more highly on clerical aptitude; being good at detail work; and enjoyment of routine tasks. They were also perceived as crying easily; being sensitive to criticism; timid; jealous; being excessively emotional regarding their jobs; being more likely to be absent and to quit; and putting family matters ahead of their job.[35]

Interviews with male executives generally reveal the recurrent concern that women do not take their careers as seriously as men and the fear that they will quit their jobs when they have children. "For years, women managers say, the feeling was that mothers shouldn't work; now it's that workers shouldn't be mothers." This

---

[35]Benson Rosen and T. H. Jerdee, "Perceived Sex Differences in Managerially Relevant Behavior," *Sex Roles* 4, no. 6 (December 1978): 837–43.

is the case, even though a 1980 study of women managers found that median maternity leave after the birth of the baby was only three months.[36]

If such employer beliefs are simply incorrect or exaggerated or reflect time lags in adjusting to a new reality, actions based on them are clearly unfair and constitute labor market discrimination as we have defined it. That is, they generate wage and occupation differences between men and women that are not accounted for by (potential) productivity differences. If such views are not simply rationalizations for personal prejudice, it might be expected that, over time, they will yield to new information. However, this process may be more sluggish than one would like and, meantime, employers make less than optimal choices.

The situation is different, and a bit more complicated, if the employer views *are* indeed correct *on the average*. Employers make the best choices possible with imperfect knowledge, and, in a sense, labor market discrimination, as we have defined it, does not exist in this case—any resulting wage and employment differences between men and women would be accounted for by *average* productivity differences.

Yet, the consequences for *individual* women are far from satisfactory. A particular woman who would be as productive and as stable an employee as her male counterpart is denied employment or paid a lower wage. It seems fairly clear from a *normative* perspective that basing employment decisions on a characteristic like sex—a characteristic that the individual cannot change—is unfair. Indeed, the practice of judging an *individual* on the basis of *group* characteristics rather than upon his or her own merits seems the very essence of stereotyping and discrimination. Such behavior is certainly not legal under the antidiscrimination laws and regulations that we discuss later in this chapter. Yet it most likely still plays a role in employer thinking. Moreover, statistical discrimination, which is based on employers' *correct* assessment of average gender differences, is not likely to be eroded by the forces of competition.

As Kenneth Arrow has pointed out, the consequences of statistical discrimination are particularly pernicious where there are *feedback effects*.[37] For example, if employers' views of female job instability lead them to give women less firm-specific training and to assign them to jobs where the costs of turnover are minimized, women have little incentive to stay and may respond by exhibiting exactly the unstable behavior that employers expect. Employers' perceptions are confirmed, and they see no reason to change their discriminatory behavior. Yet if employers had believed women to be stable workers and had hired them into positions that rewarded such stability, they might well have been stable workers!

---

[36] Barbara Tolman, "Maternity Costs: Parenthood and Career Overtax Some Women Despite Best Intentions," *Wall Street Journal* (September 7, 1983): pp. 1, 21; see, also, Susan Fraker, "Why Women Aren't Getting to the Top."

[37] Arrow, "The Theory of Discrimination." The example in the text is from Kenneth Arrow, "Economic Dimensions of Occupational Segregation: Comment I," *Signs: Journal of Women in Culture and Society* 1, no. 3, Pt. 2 (Spring 1976): 233–37.

THE SUBTLE BARRIERS:
THE ROLE OF MALE CLUBS*

There are factors influencing women's careers that may at first appear to be only tangentially related to the labor market. For instance, being denied admittance to prestigious all-male private clubs can impede the progress of career women. These "social" clubs are, in fact, places where influential people meet, relationships are developed, and deals are made; they are not simply places where weary businessmen go to relax and socialize. For example, three-quarters of women at the nation's largest law firms responding to a 1989 survey said they did not have the same opportunities as men to cultivate after-hours sports and social activities, which are important to promotions and top assignments. They cited male-only clubs as a particular problem; these clubs were supported by one in five of the law firms at which they worked.**

Studies have shown that most people find their jobs through personal contacts or by word of mouth. Club affiliations give those in executive positions information and contacts that allow them to reap benefits not accessible to those who are excluded. Thus, women's underrepresentation in high-level jobs, and their flatter experience-earnings profiles, may in part be traced to their exclusion from networks that insiders enjoy.

Male executives also belong to other associations and participate in other activities in which women are substantially underrepresented. For example, as students, women generally missed out on the bonding provided by participation in team sports, and female executives are considerably less likely to serve on corporate Boards of Directors. But exclusion from important all-male clubs is an especially serious barrier, because important business and professional meetings often take place there. It is, to say the least, very awkward for a young professional when a prospective employer schedules a luncheon interview at a club where women are only permitted to enter the lobby, or for a female executive to arrive at a club to meet a group of peers, only to be denied entry.

There is no federal law prohibiting gender discrimination by private clubs, and such discrimination is legal in most places. Indeed, in 1990, the Vice President of the United States, Dan Quayle, in response to questioning, stated that he would continue to play golf at a club where women are excluded as members and cannot even play as guests.*** However, a handful of major cities and at least two states, California and Minnesota, have banned gender discrimination by business-oriented private clubs. Such laws have been found constitutional by the Supreme Court.

---

*Portions of this inset are adapted from Robin L. Bartlett, "Clubs that Exclude Women: 'Who You Know' vs. 'What You Know,'" *Committee on the Status of Women in the Economics Profession (CSWEP) Newsletter* (Spring 1984), pp. 11–14. Adapted by permission. See also Robin L. Bartlett and Timothy I. Miller, "Executive Earnings by Gender: A Case Study," *Social Science Quarterly,* 69, no. 4 (December 1988): 892–909.

**Tamar Lewin, "Women Say They Still Face Obstacles as Lawyers," *New York Times,* December 4, 1989, p. 15.

***"Quayle to Keep Golfing at Men-Only Club," *New York Times,* December 31, 1990. The information on the legal status of male-only clubs is from Stuart Taylor, Jr., "Justices Back New York Law Ending Sex Bias by Big Clubs," *New York Times,* June 21, 1988, pp. 1, 12.

Hence, where statistical discrimination is accompanied by feedback effects, even employer behavior that is based on *initially* incorrect assessments of average gender differences may persist in the long run and be fairly impervious to competitive pressures.

Some indication that such feedback effects, essentially self-fulfilling prophecies, are important is provided by studies of male and female "quit" behavior.[38] On average, women are indeed more likely to quit their jobs than men. However, most of this difference is explained by the types of jobs women are in. The evidence suggests that, among both blacks and whites, when a woman worker is confronted with the same incentives to remain on the job in terms of wages, advancement opportunities, and so on, she is no more likely to quit than a comparable male worker. Similarly, it is often thought that blacks are less stable workers than whites. Yet their quit rates appear to be no higher than those of whites on the average. Indeed, given the same job characteristics as whites, blacks are found to be *less* likely to quit than otherwise similar white workers.

The Overcrowding Model

In the models we have previously discussed, gender segregation in employment (by firm or occupation) is a possible consequence of discrimination against women in hiring and job assignments, as are pay differentials. Both wage and employment differences are believed to result either from tastes for discrimination against women (among employers, employees, and/or customers) or from (real or perceived) gender differences in average productivity or job stability. Barbara Bergmann[39] has developed an analysis of the pay gap that gives a more central role to employment segregation.

Although it sheds no new light on the *causes* of segregation, Bergmann's "overcrowding" model demonstrates that, regardless of the reason for segregation (for example, socialization, labor market discrimination), the *consequence* may be a male-female pay differential. This will occur if job opportunities (demand) in the female sector are small relative to the supply of women available for such work. The overcrowding model is consistent with the evidence presented earlier that, all else being equal, earnings tend to be lower in predominantly female than in predominantly male jobs. The fact that men in predominantly female occupations also receive low wages is not necessarily inconsistent with the overcrowding

[38] See Francine D. Blau and Lawrence M. Kahn, "Race and Sex Differences in Quits by Young Workers," *Industrial and Labor Relations Review* 34, no. 4 (July 1981): 563–77; and W. Kip Viscusi, "Sex Differences in Worker Quitting," *Review of Economics and Statistics* 62, no. 3 (August 1980): 388–98. For similar findings with respect to gender differences in absenteeism, see Paul Osterman, "Sex Discrimination in Professional Employment: A Case Study," *Industrial and Labor Relations Review* 32, no. 4 (July 1979): 451–64.

[39] Barbara R. Bergmann, "Occupational Segregation, Wages and Profits When Employers Discriminate by Race or Sex," *Eastern Economic Journal* 1, nos. 1–2 (April–July 1974): 103–10.

hypothesis. Although men as a group are obviously not excluded from the male sector, some of them may, nonetheless, enter female occupations because they have a strong preference or particular skills for this type of work. Or they may be simply unlucky or poorly informed about alternative opportunities. They will accept the lower wages paid in female jobs. However, this lower pay is primarily caused by the many women who enter these jobs for lack of alternative opportunities.

This model is illustrated in Figure 7.1. "F" jobs and "M" jobs are considered. As in the previous models of discrimination, it is assumed that male and female workers are perfect substitutes for each other (that is, they are potentially equally productive). The hypothetical situation in which there is no discrimination is represented by demand curves D_f and D_m and supply curves S_{fo} and S_{mo}. The nondiscriminatory equilibrium points in the two markets (E_{fo} and E_{mo}) are determined so that the wage rate (w_0) is the same for both types of jobs.

To see why this is the case, recall that we have assumed that all workers are equally well-qualified for F and M jobs and that employers are indifferent between hiring male and female workers. Suppose that, by chance, the wage in F jobs is set higher than the wage in M jobs. Then workers attracted by the higher wage rates would transfer from M jobs to F jobs. This process would continue until wages in F jobs were bid down to the level of wages in M jobs. Similarly, if by chance, wages in M jobs were set above those in F jobs, workers would move from F jobs to M jobs until the differential was eliminated. Thus, in the absence of discrimination, worker mobility ensures that the wages paid for both types of work are the same, at least after there has been time to make adjustments.[40]

In the hypothetical example given in Figure 7.1, it is assumed that demand conditions are such that, in equilibrium, L_{fo} workers (25 percent of the labor force) are employed in F jobs and L_{mo} workers (75 percent of the labor force) work in M jobs. F and M jobs have no sex labels associated with them and both women and men are randomly divided between the two sectors.

How does the situation differ when there is discrimination against women in some occupations or when, for a variety of reasons, women choose to concentrate in typically female jobs? The consequences of such segregation may be ascertained by comparing the hypothetical situation in which there is no segregation to one in which M jobs are restricted to men (or women avoid such jobs). In our example, this results in an inward shift of the supply curve to male jobs from S_{mo} to S_{md}, causing wages to be bid up to W_{md}. At this higher wage, only L_{md} workers (60 percent of the labor force) are employed in M jobs. The exclusion of women from M jobs means that all the women must (or choose to) "crowd" into the F jobs. The expanded supply of labor in F jobs, represented by an outward shift of the supply curve from S_{fo} to S_{fd}, depresses wages there to w_{fd}. Now L_{fd} workers (40 percent of the labor force) are employed in F occupations.

---

[40]This also assumes that there are no *nonpecuniary* differences in the relative attractiveness of the two jobs that would result in a compensating wage differential.

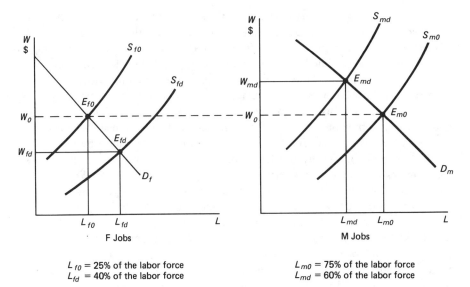

FIGURE 7.1   An Illustration of the Overcrowding Model

The overcrowding model shows how gender segregation in employment may cause a wage differential between otherwise equally productive male and female workers. This occurs if the supply of women seeking employment is large relative to the demand for labor in the F jobs. This may well be what actually occurs in the labor market. Nevertheless, the analysis also shows that gender segregation in employment need not always result in a wage differential between men and women. If it so happens that the wage rate that equates supply and demand in the F sector is the same as the wage that equates supply and demand in the M sector, no wage differential will result (that is, if the female sector is not overcrowded). However, this will happen only by chance. Labor market discrimination (or some other barrier) has eliminated the free mobility of labor between the two sectors that would otherwise ensure wage equality between M and F jobs.

Returning to the more likely situation illustrated in Figure 7.1, in which segregation does lower women's pay, we may examine its impact on the *productivity* of women relative to men. Employers of women in F jobs accommodate a larger number of workers (L_{fd} rather than L_{fo}) by substituting labor for capital. The relatively low wages of the women, w_{fd}, make it profitable to use such labor-intensive production methods. On the other hand, the higher wage in the male sector, w_{md}, encourages employers to substitute capital for labor to economize on relatively high-priced labor. In the overcrowding model, women earn less than men, but both are paid in accordance with their productivity. Discrimination causes both wage and productivity differentials between *potentially* equally productive male and female labor—women are less productive than men because, due to segregation and crowding, they have less capital to work with.

The claim that the supply of labor to a particular occupation (or industry) helps to determine the wage rate is relatively noncontroversial. But the crowding hypothesis, in and of itself, does not explain why so many women are employed in typically female sectors. Controversy has centered on the question of whether this is because men and women have inherently different talents or preferences for different types of work; because, due to differences in socialization or in household responsibilities, women are willing to trade higher wages and steeper lifetime earnings profiles for more favorable job conditions and lower penalties for discontinuous labor force participation; or because employers, coworkers, or customers discriminate against women in some occupations but not in others.

Institutional Models

The theme that the male-female pay gap is closely related to employment segregation is echoed in institutional models of discrimination.[41] Such explanations emphasize that labor markets may not be as flexible as the simple competitive model assumes. Rigidities are introduced both by the institutional arrangements found in many firms and by various barriers to competition introduced by the monopoly power of firms in the product market or of unions in the labor market.

The internal labor market. Institutionalists point out that the job structure of many large firms looks like the illustration in Figure 7.2(a). Firms hire workers from the outside labor market for so-called "entry jobs." The remainder of the jobs are internally allocated by the firm as workers progress along well-defined promotion ladders by acquiring job-related skills, many of which are firm-specific in nature. When firm-specific skills are emphasized and a high proportion of jobs are filled from internal sources, the firm has an *internal labor market.* That is, it determines wages for each job category and the allocation of workers among categories and is insulated to some extent (although not entirely) from the impact of market forces.

To administer their personnel systems, larger firms often take the occupational category as the decision unit, establishing pay rates for each category (with some allowance for seniority and merit considerations), and linking jobs together into promotion ladders. Thus, group treatment of individuals is the norm, and it will be to the employer's advantage to make sure that workers within each job category

---

[41] See, for example, Peter B. Doeringer and Michael J. Piore, *Internal Labor Markets and Manpower Analysis* (Lexington, MA: D. C. Heath and Co., 1971); Michael J. Piore, "The Dual Labor Market: Theory and Implications," in *Problems in Political Economy: An Urban Perspective,* D. M. Gordon, ed. (Lexington, MA: D. C. Heath and Co., 1971), pp. 90–94; Blau and Jusenius, "Economists' Approaches to Sex Segregation in the Labor Market"; Glen G. Cain, "The Challenge of Segmented Labor Market Theories to Orthodox Theory: A Survey," *Journal of Economic Literature* 14, 4 (Dec. 1976): 1215–57; David M. Gordon, Richard Edwards, and Michael Reich, *Segmented Work, Divided Workers: The Historical Transformation of Labor in the United States* (Cambridge: Cambridge University Press, 1982); and Michael Wachter, "Primary and Secondary Labor Markets: A Critique of the Dual Approach," *Brookings Papers on Economic Activity,* no. 3 (1974): 637–94.

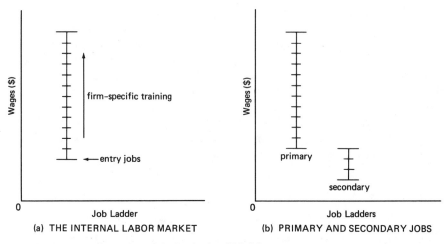

FIGURE 7.2   An Illustration of the Institutional Model

are as similar as possible. If it is believed that men and women (as well as, say, whites and nonwhites) differ in their productivity-related characteristics (like quit and absenteeism rates), statistical discrimination is likely to result in their being channeled into different jobs.

Primary and secondary jobs. The dual labor market model developed by Peter Doeringer and Michael Piore takes this analysis a step further and emphasizes the distinction between primary and secondary jobs.[42] **Primary jobs** emphasize high levels of firm-specific skills and, thus, pay high wages, have good promotion opportunities, and emphasize long-term attachment between workers and firms. In **secondary jobs,** firm-specific skills are not as important. Such jobs will pay less, offer relatively fewer promotion opportunities, and have fairly high rates of labor turnover. This situation is depicted in Figure 7.2(b). Applying the dual labor market model to gender discrimination leads us to expect that men would be more likely to be in primary jobs, women in secondary jobs.

The distinction between primary and secondary jobs may occur within the same firm—say, between the managerial and clerical categories. In addition, it is believed that primary jobs are more likely to be located in monopolistic, unionized industries and that secondary jobs are more likely to be found in competitive industries. This is an additional reason for expecting women to be more concentrated in the competitive sector.

Radical economists further argue that employers as a group benefit from such segmentation of the labor force by gender and race because it prevents workers from seeing their common interests. That is, capitalists (employers) practice "divide and rule" tactics to thwart unionization and other attempts by workers to share power.

---

[42]Doeringer and Piore, *Internal Labor Markets;* and Piore, "The Dual Labor Market."

Radical feminists add another element to this analysis. In their view, one must take into account the effects not only of capitalism, but also of patriarchy, which is defined as a system of male oppression of women. Thus, they point to the role of male workers and of their unions, as well as of employers, in maintaining occupational segregation.[43]

Segmentation of male and female workers into primary and secondary jobs is likely to produce both pay and productivity differences between them due to unequal access to on-the-job training. Institutionalists also argue that feedback effects are likely to magnify any initial productivity differences, as women respond to the lower incentives for worker stability in the secondary factor.

The institutional analysis also reinforces the point made earlier that labor market discrimination against women is not necessarily the outcome of conscious, overt acts by employers. Once men and women are channeled into different types of entry jobs, the normal, everyday operation of the firm—"business as usual"— will virtually ensure gender differences in productivity, promotion opportunities, and pay. This is termed *institutional discrimination.*[44] Even gender differences in initial occupational assignment may be in part due to adherence to traditional policies that tend to work against women. For example:

- Referrals from current male employees or an informal network of male colleagues at other firms
- Sexist recruitment materials picturing women in traditionally female jobs and men in traditionally male jobs
- Lack of encouragement of female applicants to broaden their sights from traditional areas

Feedback Effects

As we have noted several times, labor market discrimination or unequal treatment of women in the labor market may adversely affect women's own decisions and behavior.[45] This is illustrated in Figure 7.3. Human capital theory

---

[43]See Gordon, Edwards, and Reich, *Segmented Work, Divided Workers* for the radical view, and, for the radical feminist analysis, Heidi I. Hartmann, "Capitalism, Patriarchy and Job Segregation by Sex," *Signs: Journal of Women in Culture and Society* 1, no. 3, Pt. 2 (Spring 1976): 137–69.

[44]See Roos and Reskin, "Institutional Factors Contributing to Occupational Sex Segregation," for a description of business practices that tend to adversely affect women.

[45]A number of authors have emphasized the importance of feedback effects in analyzing discrimination in pay and employment. See, for example, Arrow, "The Theory of Discrimination," Barbara R. Bergmann, "Reducing the Pervasiveness of Discrimination," in *Jobs for Americans,* Eli Ginzberg, ed. (Englewood Cliffs, NJ: Prentice-Hall, 1976), pp. 120–41; Blau, *Equal Pay in the Office;* Ferber and Lowry, "The Sex Differential in Earnings"; Shelly J. Lundberg and Richard Startz, "Private Discrimination and Social Intervention in Competitive Labor Markets," *American Economic Review* 73, no. 3 (June 1983): 340–47; Myra H. Strober, "Toward Dimorphics: A Summary Statement to the Conference on Occupational Segregation," *Signs: Journal of Women in Culture and Society* 1, no. 3, Pt. 2 (Spring 1976): 293–302; and Yoram Weiss and Reuben Gronau, "Expected Interruptions in Labour Force Participation and Sex-Related Differences in Earnings Growth," *Review of Economic Studies* 48, no. 4 (October 1981): 607–19.

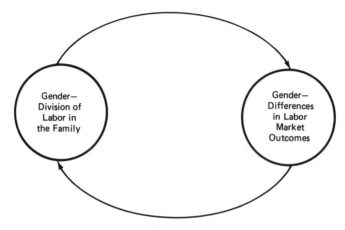

FIGURE 7.3   An Illustration of Feedback Effects

and other supply-side explanations for gender differences in economic outcomes tend to emphasize the role of the gender division of labor in the family in causing differences between men and women in labor market outcomes. This is indicated by the arrow pointing to the right in the figure.

This relationship undoubtedly exists; however, such explanations tend to neglect the impact of labor market discrimination in reinforcing the traditional division of labor (shown by the arrow pointing to the left). Even a relatively small amount of initial labor market discrimination can have greatly magnified effects if it discourages women from making human capital investments, weakens their attachment to the labor force, and provides economic incentives for the family to place priority on the husband's career. Although it is unlikely that labor market discrimination is responsible for initially having caused the traditional division of labor in the family, which clearly predates modern labor markets, it may well help to perpetuate it by inhibiting more rapid movement toward egalitarian sharing of household responsibilities today.

The net result is what might be termed a "vicious circle." Discrimination against women in the labor market reinforces traditional gender roles in the family, while adherence to traditional roles by women provides a rationale for labor market discrimination. However, this also means that effective policies to end labor-market discrimination can have far-reaching effects, particularly when combined with simultaneous changes in social attitudes toward women's roles.

A decrease in labor market discrimination will have feedback effects as the equalization of market incentives between men and women induces further changes in women's supply-side behavior. In addition, as more women enter previously male-dominated fields, the larger number of female role models for younger women is likely to induce still further increases in the availability of women for such jobs. Thus, demand-side policies can be expected to play an important role in sustaining a process of cumulative change in women's economic status.

POLICY ISSUE: THE GOVERNMENT AND EQUAL EMPLOYMENT OPPORTUNITY

Government policies to combat labor market discrimination against women can be justified on two grounds. One is equity or fairness—"a matter of simple justice."[46] Thus, government intervention may be rationalized to assure equal treatment for all participants in the labor market, regardless of gender (or race, ethnic origin, etc.). As well as being unfair, unequal treatment on the basis of gender may result in an inefficient allocation of resources. This provides the second rationale for government intervention. To see this, consider the case where equally productive men and women are hired for different jobs and women's jobs are lower paid (as in the overcrowding model). Under these circumstances, prices do not serve as accurate indicators of social costs. In comparison to the nondiscriminatory situation, society produces "too little" of the outputs that use "overpriced" male labor, given that equally productive female labor is available at a lower price to expand production. Society produces "too much" of the outputs that use "underpriced" female labor, given that the contribution of equally productive labor is valued more highly in the male sector (as measured by its price).

The inefficiency caused by discrimination is even greater when we take into account feedback effects. If women are deterred from investing in their human capital because of discrimination, society loses a valuable resource. Thus, opening doors to women that were previously closed (or only slightly ajar) benefits society as well as individual women by bringing their talents and abilities to bear in new areas. As Nobel laureate Paul A. Samuelson commented about the gains achieved through the mid-1980s, "To the degree that women are getting an opportunity they didn't have in the past, the economy is tapping an important and previously wasted resource."[47]

Weighed against these potential gains are the costs of the increased government intervention in society that may be necessary to produce this result. Some may also fear what they regard as the possible excesses of such policies in the form of "reverse discrimination" or preferential treatment for women and minorities. However, research to date provides no evidence that the increased employment of women and minorities encouraged by legislation has entailed such efficiency costs.[48] We examine the record of government intervention in this area below.[49]

---

[46]This was the title of the Report of the President's Task Force on Women's Rights and Responsibilities (Washington, D.C.: U.S. Government Printing Office, April 1970).

[47]*Business Week,* January 28, 1985, p. 80.

[48]Jonathan S. Leonard, "Antidiscrimination or Reverse Discrimination: The Impact of Changing Demographics, Title VII and Affirmative Action on Productivity," *Journal of Human Resources* 19, no. 2 (Spring 1984): 145–74. Similarly, Marianne A. Ferber and Carole A. Green, "Traditional or Reverse Sex Discrimination? A Case Study of a Large Public University," *Industrial and Labor Relations Review* 35, no. 4 (July 1982): 550–64 found concern with possible reverse discrimination to be misplaced.

[49]For excellent summaries of the legal situation, see Susan Deller Ross and Ann Barcher, *The Rights of Women: The Basic ACLU Guide to a Woman's Rights,* rev. ed. (Toronto: Bantam Books, 1983); and Claire Sherman Thomas, *Sex Discrimination,* Pt. 4 (St. Paul: West Publishing Co., 1982).

Equal Employment Opportunity
Laws and Regulations

Government has long been involved in shaping conditions encountered by women in the labor market. During the period following the Civil War, in response to concern and agitation by workers and their sympathizers, a number of states passed protective labor laws limiting hours and regulating other terms of employment. At first, the Supreme Court struck down these laws as unconstitutional. The justification was that they interfered with the freedom of workers to enter contracts. Subsequently, the Court upheld such laws when they were confined to women alone, arguing that individual rights may be abridged because the state has a legitimate interest in the possible social effects of women's work. In the decision handed down in *Muller v. Oregon* in 1890, Supreme Court Justice Brandeis said the following:

> The two sexes differ in structure of body, in the functions performed by each, in the amount of physical strength, in the capacity for long-continued labor, particularly when done standing, the influence of vigorous health upon the future well-being of the race, the self-reliance which enables one to assert full rights, and in the capacity to maintain the struggle for subsistence. The difference justifies a difference in legislation, and upholds that which is designed to compensate for some of the burdens which rest upon her.

In time, however, the concern shifted from protection to equal opportunity. Indeed, protective laws came eventually to be viewed as undesirable impediments to the advancement of women.[50]

As early as 1961, President Kennedy issued an Executive Order calling for a Presidential Commission on the Status of Women. Two years later, the **Equal Pay Act** of 1963 was passed, which requires employers to pay the same wages to men and women who do substantially equal work, involving equal skill, effort, and responsibility, and performed under similar conditions in the same establishment. By 1964, **Title VII** of the Civil Rights Act, which was originally to prohibit discrimination in employment on the basis of race, religion, and national origin was changed to include the word "sex."[51] Title VII prohibits sex discrimination in virtually all aspects of employment, including hiring and firing, training, promotions, wages, fringe benefits, or other terms and conditions of employment. As amended, it covers all businesses employing 15 or more workers, including federal, state, and local governments and educational institutions. It also prohibits discrimination by employment agencies and labor organizations.

[50] Supreme Court Justice Brennan expressed this view very well in Frontiero v. Richardson: "Traditionally, discrimination was rationalized by an attitude of romantic paternalism which in practical effect put women not on a pedestal but in a cage."

[51] Since it was Howard Smith, a conservative Congressman from Virginia, who proposed this amendment, it is widely believed that the purpose of doing so was to increase opposition to the bill, and reduce the chances of its passage. Although the Act was passed with the word "sex" in it, the application of this law to lesbians and homosexuals has consistently been rejected by the Courts.

The **Equal Employment Opportunity Commission** (EEOC) is the federal agency charged with enforcing the Equal Pay Act and Title VII.

The **Executive Order** 11246 issued in 1965, and amended by Executive Order 11375 in 1967 to include sex, bars discrimination in employment by all employers with federal contracts and subcontracts. It also requires affirmative action for classes of workers disadvantaged by past discrimination. Such contractors are required to analyze their own employment patterns to determine where women and minorities are underrepresented. Whenever such deficiencies are found, they are to set up goals and timetables for the hiring of women and minorities and to make good faith efforts to reach their goals in the specified period. The Executive Order is enforced by the Office of Federal Contract Compliance. Violators face possible loss of their government contracts, although this sanction has been very seldom invoked.

In the years since their passage and implementation, the federal antidiscrimination laws and regulations have been interpreted and clarified by the courts, with the final arbiter being the United States Supreme Court. This process has been especially important for Title VII of the Civil Rights Act, the broadest law and the centerpiece of the Federal government's antidiscrimination enforcement effort. In some cases, the Court's interpretations of the law have changed as the membership on the Court has shifted, and this is likely to continue to be the case in the future. Bearing this is mind, in order to better understand what activities are currently prohibited under Title VII, we turn to a brief summary of some of the more important Court decisions.

Title VII permits exceptions to its ban on gender discrimination when sex is found to be a *bona fide* occupational qualification. The interpretation of this provision was extremely important in that, had it been interpreted broadly, considerable gender discrimination would have been permissible under Title VII. However, both the EEOC and the courts have taken the position that this exception should be interpreted narrowly. That is, men and women are entitled to consideration on the basis of their individual capabilities, rather than on the basis of characteristics generally attributed to the group.[52] Nor can sex in combination with some other factor be used as a legal basis for discrimination under Title VII. The court has held, for example, that an employer cannot refuse to hire women with preschool-age children while men with preschool-age children are hired.[53] Further,

[52]Major cases include *Weeks v. Southern Bell Telephone and Telegraph,* 408 F.2d 228 (5th Cir. 1969); *Rosenfeld v. Southern Pacific Company,* 444 F.2d 1219 (9th Cir. 1971); and *Diaz v. Pan American World Airways, Inc.,* 444 F.2d 385 (5th Cir.). In the only major case to date in which gender was found to be a bona fide occupational qualification (BFOQ), *Dothard v. Rawlinson,* 433 U.S. 321 (1977), the Supreme Court allowed the hiring of males only for the position of guard in Alabama's maximum security male prisons. The court reasoned that due to the nature of the prison population, as well as the atmosphere of the prison, women would be particularly subject to sexual assault, which would interfere with their job performance. Regardless of whether or not one agrees with this reasoning, this case is not likely to result in substantially greater acceptance by the courts of the BFOQ exception, given the unusual circumstances of the case. See Ross and Barcher, *The Rights of Women,* p. 222.

[53]Philips v. Martin Marietta Corp., 400 U.S. 542 (1971).

WOMEN'S JOB RIGHTS VERSUS "FETAL PROTECTION"

One controversial issue raised by the antidiscrimination statutes relates to the employment of women in jobs where they would work with substances like lead that might be hazardous to unborn children. During the 1970s and the 1980s, a number of employers adopted policies excluding fertile women from such employment. These employers' claimed to fear liability in future lawsuits on behalf of children who were born with birth defects caused by their mothers' work environment. They generally barred all women of childbearing age who had not been sterilized, arguing that temporary birth-control measures might fail, and that fetal damage could occur during the early months of pregnancy when many women are unaware that they are pregnant and thus would not request a transfer to a safer job.

Opponents of fetal protection policies, including many women's groups and labor unions, argued that such policies constituted sex discrimination and were illegal under Title VII. Like protective labor laws, fetal protection policies resulted in women being denied access to high-paying jobs. Critics also noted that toxic substances had been found to harm the male as well as the female reproductive system and held that women, like men, should be able to choose whether or not to incur the higher risks in exchange for the higher pay in these jobs. They advocated addressing the safety issue by further efforts to reduce the level of exposure of all workers to toxic substances, rather than by excluding particular groups claimed to be at special risk. Finally, they feared that if fetal protection policies were found to be legal, they would be adopted by many additional employers, eventually affecting millions of women in various industries.

In 1991, the Supreme Court addressed these issues in the *Johnson Controls** case. Johnson Controls is an automobile battery manufacturer that "banned women who could not prove they were infertile from working in areas of the plant where they were exposed to lead, the principal material used in making batteries."** The plaintiffs consisted of all employees who were potentially affected by the policy. Among the individual plaintiffs in the case were a woman who was sterilized to avoid losing her job, a 50-year-old divorced woman who suffered a substantial loss in earnings when she was transferred out of a job where she was exposed to lead, and a man who was denied a leave of absence that he had requested in order to lower his lead level because he intended to become a father. The Court found for the plaintiffs. It held the fetal protection policy to be discriminatory because "fertile men, but not fertile women, are given a choice as to whether they wish to risk their reproductive health for a particular job." It also clarified that the *bona fide* occupational qualification exemption of Title VII "must relate to ability to perform the duties of the job" rather than to any danger or risk to the woman herself. This is in line with the narrow interpretation of this exemption in prior court decisions. Finally, the Court concluded that the risk of employer liability was slight given that " . . . Title VII bans sex-specific fetal-protection policies, the employer fully informs the woman of the risk, and the employer has not acted negligently. . . . "

United Auto Workers v. Johnson Controls, Inc., U.S. Sup. Ct., No. 89-1215 (1991). In this discussion, we draw on the summary of the *Johnson Controls* case and the printed text of the decision in Bureau of National Affairs, *Daily Labor Report:* March 21, 1991 (No. 55), pp. A1–A3 and D1–D11. For the response to the case on the part of business, see also the following issues of the *Daily Labor Report:* March 22, 1991 (No. 55), pp. A11–A13; and April 1, 1991 (No. 62), pp. A2–A4.

**Bureau of National Affairs, *Daily Labor Report:* March 21, 1991, p. A1. The quotations from the Court's decision presented below are from Bureau of National Affairs, *Daily Labor Report,* March 21, 1991.

it is illegal to pay women lower monthly pension benefits than men.[54] In the past, this practice had been justified on the basis that, on average, women live longer and, thus, it would be more costly to provide them with the same monthly benefit. Nonetheless, the courts have ruled that each woman is entitled to be treated as an individual, rather than as a group member.

Another issue addressed by the courts in interpreting Title VII concerns so-called "unintentional" discrimination. This arises when a firm's apparently neutral hiring or promotion practices have a *disparate impact* on women or minorities. Disparate impact means that the practice or practices have a disproportionately adverse effect on women or minorities. An example of this might be a minimum height and weight requirement for the position of police officer that screens out a higher proportion of women than men. On the basis of the Supreme Court's 1971 *Griggs*[55] decision, such practices may be illegal even if the discrimination is not intentional. Under *Griggs,* once the plaintiffs had shown that the practice had a disparate impact, the burden of proof shifted to the employer to show that the practice was a matter of "business necessity" or that the requirement was job related; otherwise there would be a finding of discrimination.

More recently, a 1989 Supreme Court decision in *Wards Cove*[56] held that even after a disparate impact has been demonstrated, the burden of proof remained with the plaintiffs to show that the employer had no business necessity justification for the practice. This decision was widely criticized by civil rights advocates as making it more difficult to win employment discrimination cases. In addition, the decision was questioned on logical grounds in that it is the employer who would be in the best position to know why a practice was necessary to the operation of the business. The original interpretation of the law was reestablished in November 1991, when, after almost two years of debate and a presidential veto, a new civil rights law was passed. In addition, the new law permits women to obtain compensatory and punitive damages for intentional discrimination, although the amounts are limited. (Racial minorities had such rights under existing law.)

Finally, an issue that has been the focus of considerable attention in recent years is sexual harassment.[57] In its 1986 decision in *Meritor,*[58] the Supreme Court

---

[54] *City of Los Angeles, Dept. of Water v. Manhart,* 435 U.S. 702 (1978).

[55] *Griggs v. Duke Power Co.,* 401 U.S. 424 (1971).

[56] *Wards Cove Packing Co. v. Atonio,* 109 S.Ct. 2115 (1989). For a discussion of this case and its implications, see the articles in "Special Report: Setback for Civil Rights? The Supreme Court's 1989 Discrimination Rulings," *ILR Report* 27, no. 2 (Spring 1990).

[57] This issue attracted particular attention during the confirmation hearings of Supreme Court Justice Clarence Thomas, when charges of sexual harassment were made against the nominee by Anita Hill, a law professor who had formerly worked as an assistant to Justice Thomas. Although Justice Thomas was confirmed, the airing of this issue in a national forum greatly heightened public awareness of this problem.

[58] *Meritor Savings Bank v. Vinson,* 106 SCt 2399 (1986). For a useful discussion of the legal status of sexual harassment, see William L. Woerner and Sharon L. Oswald, "Sexual Harassment in the Workplace: A View Through the Eyes of the Courts," *Labor Law Journal* 41, no. 11 (November 1990): 786–93.

held that sexual harassment is illegal under Title VII if it is unwelcome and "sufficiently severe or pervasive to alter the conditions of the victim's employment and create an abusive working environment."[59] Employers may be held liable if they knew or should have known of the alleged harassment.[60] It is widely thought that a strong, well-publicized employer policy against harassment coupled with an effective internal grievance procedure are the best tools currently available to employers to combat sexual harassment at the workplace and to safeguard themselves from liability.

Effectiveness of the Government's Antidiscrimination Effort

Much remains to be learned about the functioning of these laws and regulations. Questions have been raised both about their effectiveness in improving opportunities for the protected categories and about the possibility noted above that they might result in "reverse discrimination" against groups that are not covered.

It is highly likely that the Equal Pay Act has had relatively little impact. The major reason is that men and women rarely do exactly the same kind of work in the same firm. However, the protection offered by this law may become more important as occupational segregation declines.

Considerably less agreement exists on the effects of Title VII and the Executive Order. Although some empirical work has been done examining their effectiveness, the results have not been entirely conclusive, in large part because it is difficult to isolate the effect of legislation from other changes that have been occurring.

A review of the trends in the male-female pay gap was presented in Chapter 5. It gave no indication of a notable increase in women's economic status in the post-1964 period that might be attributable to the effects of the government's antidiscrimination effort, at least through the late 1970s or early 1980s. At the same time, blacks experienced considerable increases in their earnings relative to whites; many people have ascribed these increases in part to the impact of the antidiscrimination laws.[61]

On the other hand, some more detailed studies do find positive effects of the government's policies on women's earnings and occupations.[62] Moreover, the

[59] Cited in "Ending Sexual Harassment: Business is Getting the Message," *Business Week,* March 18, 1991, p. 99.

[60] Woerner and Oswald, "Sexual Harassment in the Workplace."

[61] See Charles Brown, "The Federal Attack on Labor Market Discrimination: The Mouse that Roared?" in *Research in Labor Economics,* Ronald Ehrenberg, ed. (Greenwich, CT: JAI Press, 1982): 33–68.

[62] For example, one study suggests that the trend toward larger male-female earnings differentials was reversed in the middle 1960s, about the time the effect of the government legislation would be expected to become apparent. See Ronald Oaxaca, "The Persistence of Male-Female Earnings Differentials" in *The Distribution of Economic Well-Being,* Thomas F. Juster, ed. (Cambridge, MA:

improvement in women's economic position that began around 1980 could be due in part to the opportunities created by the government's antidiscrimination laws and regulations. This would potentially include both the direct effect of improving the treatment of women in the labor market and, in response to that, the indirect effect of increasing the incentives for women to train for nontraditional jobs.

Affirmative Action

Just as there is disagreement on the effectiveness of the government's antidiscrimination effort, so there is controversy about the form it should take. Debate has particularly centered on the desirability of affirmative action to remedy past underrepresentation of women (or minorities). Affirmative action plans are legally mandated only by the Executive Order or, in some instances, by court orders or out-of-court settlements of discrimination suits. But some employers have adopted such programs voluntarily.

A variety of different views are held about affirmative action. First, there are those who argue that there is no conclusive evidence that there has been serious discrimination in the past and that, even if there had been, removing it would be sufficient and affirmative action is not needed. Second, there are others who accept the need for some form of affirmative action but oppose the use of goals and timetables for fear that they will be too rigidly enforced and become de facto quotas. There is a difference of opinion, even among strong proponents of affirmative action, whether it should take the form of sincere efforts to find and encourage fully qualified candidates from the protected groups or go so far as to hire them preferentially. Some believe that preferential treatment may at times be needed to overcome the effects of past discrimination.

Although employment preferences are controversial, the Supreme Court has found that they are legal under certain circumstances. Specifically, employers can voluntarily give employment preferences to women and minorities as a temporary measure to remedy manifest imbalances in traditionally segregated job categories.[63]

Ballinger Publishing Company, 1977), pp. 303–44. Two other studies that also obtained positive findings attempted to measure the impact of Title VII through regional differences in its enforcement. They report that, between 1967 and 1974, enforcement of Title VII narrowed the sex differential in earnings by about 7 percentage points and sex differences in the probability of being employed in a male occupation by about 6 percentage points, all else equal. See Andrea H. Beller, "The Impact of Equal Employment Opportunity Laws on the Male/Female Earnings Differential," in *Women in the Labor Market*, Cynthia B. Lloyd, Emily Andrews, and Curtis L. Gilroy, eds. (New York: Columbia University Press, 1979), pp. 304–30; and Andrea H. Beller, "Occupational Segregation by Sex: Determinants and Changes," *Journal of Human Resources* 17, no. 3 (Summer 1982): 317–92. On the other hand, a recent study found that affirmative action under the Executive Order has contributed negligibly to women's progress in the workplace; see Jonathan S. Leonard, "Women and Affirmative Action," *Journal of Economic Perspectives* 3, no. 1 (Winter 1989): 61–75.

[63] *Steelworkers v. Weber,* 443 U.S. 193 (1979) and *Johnson v. Santa Clara County Transportation Agency,* 480 U.S. 616 (1987).

At the same time, the Court has stressed the need for affirmative action plans to be flexible, gradual, and limited in their adverse effect on men and whites; it has also tended to disapprove of strict numerical quotas except where necessary to remedy demonstrated cases of severe past discrimination.[64] Further, although the Court has ruled that employers may give preferences to women and minorities in hiring and promotion under certain circumstances, it has rejected the use of such preferences to protect women and minorities from layoffs.[65] This apparent inconsistency may be due to the concern over the rights of third parties, members of nonprotected groups who are adversely affected by the affirmative action program. Being denied a potential benefit like getting hired for a particular job, gaining admittance to a training program, or securing a promotion is viewed as a less serious cost than being laid off from a job, especially after accumulating considerable seniority.

It is important to recognize, however, that most affirmative action programs do not require such preferences. For example, virtually all the employers included in a sample of government contractors stated that no lowering of employment standards was necessary to achieve the company's affirmative action objectives.[66] Interestingly enough, it was found that, in most companies, affirmative action programs had brought about an improvement in personnel management systems. This may be because, in the face of affirmative action pressures, many companies implemented wider and more systematic search procedures and developed more objective criteria and procedures for hiring and promotion. Further evidence that such policies are widely regarded as advantageous comes from a 1984 survey of the chief executive officers of large corporations. More than 90 percent claimed they had established numerical objectives for affirmative action at least in part to satisfy corporate objectives unrelated to government regulations. Even more impressive is that 95 percent stated that they planned to continue to use numerical objectives regardless of government requirements.[67]

Empirical research supports the impression that rigid employment quotas and reverse discrimination are far from being the norm in the labor market. One study found that the employment goals of government contractors covered under the Executive Order were not filled with the rigidity one would expect if they were really quotas. That is, firms tended to fall short of their employment goals

[64] Stuart Taylor, "Court's Change of Course," *New York Times*, March 27, 1987, p. 1.

[65] Steven A. Holmes, "Quotas: Despised by Many, but Just What are They?" *New York Times*, June 2, 1991, p. 20.

[66] The survey was conducted for the Center for National Policy Review and reported in the *BNA's Employee Relations Weekly* 1, no. 2 (September 12, 1983), p. 45.

[67] The survey was conducted by Organization Resources Counselors and reported in Anne B. Fisher, "Businessmen Like to Hire by the Numbers," *Fortune* 112, no. 6 (September 1985): 26–30. The article also reports that in May 1985, the directors of the National Association of Manufacturers adopted a policy statement supporting affirmative action as "good business policy," also stating, however, that "goals, not quotas, are the standards to be followed in the implementation of such programs."

for women and minorities. Nonetheless, the setting of goals did appear to have a positive effect on the employment of these groups in that establishments that promised to employ more women and minorities in the future tended to do so in subsequent years.[68]

As in the case of affirmative action, it has been found, with respect to the broader issue of antidiscrimination policy as a whole, that the increased employment of women has been achieved without substantial reverse discrimination. Specifically, there is no evidence at the industry level that the productivity of women fell relative to men as their employment increased — as would have been the case if there had been substantial reverse discrimination. Direct tests at the company level of the effect of affirmative action pressure, Title VII litigation, and changing demographics on profits also failed to show any adverse effect.[69]

Comparable Worth

In the latter half of the 1970s, impatience with the slow progress in closing the male-female earnings gap, as well as some reluctance to accept the movement of women into different occupations as a necessary component of the solution, led to great interest in a possible alternative approach to increasing women's wages. The new idea, in simple terms, amounts to extending the notion of equal pay for equal work to the broader concept of equal pay for work of comparable worth within the firm.[70] Proponents argue this is a reasonable interpretation of Title VII and a feasible way of achieving a more rapid reduction of the male-female pay gap. Opponents point to the difficulties involved in determining exactly what comparable

[68]Jonathan S. Leonard, "What Promises are Worth: The Impact of Affirmative Action Goals," *Journal of Human Resources* 20, no. 1 (Winter 1985): 3–20.

[69]Jonathan S. Leonard, "Antidiscrimination or Reverse Discrimination: The Impact of Changing Demographics, Title VII, and Affirmative Action on Productivity," *Journal of Human Resources* 19, no. 2 (Spring 1984): 145–74.

[70]For an early article articulating the legal basis for this approach, see Ruth G. Blumrosen, "Wage Discrimination, Job Segregation, and Title VII of the Civil Rights Act of 1964," *University of Michigan Journal of Law Reform* 12, no. 3 (Spring 1979). The issues involved are thoroughly discussed in Treiman and Hartmann, *Women, Work and Wages;* Helen Remick, ed., *Comparable Worth and Wage Discrimination* (Philadelphia: Temple University Press, 1984); Barbara R. Bergmann, *The Economic Emergence of Women* (New York: Basic Books, 1986), Ch. 8; and Mark R. Killingsworth, *The Economics of Comparable Worth* (Kalamazoo, MI: W. E. Upjohn Institute for Employment Research, 1990). For empirical analyses of the impact of comparable worth, see Killingsworth, *The Economics of Comparable Worth;* Ronald G. Ehrenberg and Robert S. Smith, "Comparable-Worth Wage Adjustments and Female Employment in the State and Local Sector," *Journal of Labor Economics* 5 no.1 (January 1987): 43–62; Robert T. Michael, Heidi I. Hartmann, and Brigid O'Farrell, eds., *Pay Equity: Empirical Inquiries* (Washington D.C.: National Academy Press, 1989); Sorensen, "The Crowding Hypothesis and Comparable Worth Issue"; and Roberta E. Robb, "Equal Pay for Work of Equal Value: Issues and Policies," *Canadian Public Policy* 13, no. 4 (1987): 445–61.

worth means in functional terms. They are also concerned about interfering with the working of the free market and the possibility of bringing about a substantial imbalance in the supply of and demand for female workers. Both of these problems deserve serious attention.

Comparing the value to the firm of workers employed in different jobs is a difficult task involving the establishment of equivalences for various fields of education, different types of skill, and varying work environments. Nonetheless, job evaluation is widely used to determine pay scales, not only by governments, but also by many businesses. This certainly shows that the approach is feasible. However, it should be noted that such a procedure is generally used in conjunction with information about market wage rates, rather than as a completely separate alternative to the market. Further, existing job evaluation schemes have been criticized for undervaluing the skills and abilities that are emphasized in female jobs.

Turning to the issue of setting wages at a level other than that determined by the market, the strongest opposition to such a policy comes primarily from those who believe that the existing labor market substantially resembles the neoclassical competitive model. In such a market, only the person's qualifications and tastes limit access to jobs, and all workers are rewarded according to their productivity. In this view, raising women's wages is not only unnecessary but would lead to excess supply, hence unemployment and misallocation of resources.

On the other hand, many of those in favor of the comparable worth approach begin with a view of a segmented labor market, where workers' access to highly paid positions is often limited by discriminating employers, restrictive labor organizations, entrenched internal labor markets, and differences in the prelabor market socialization of men and women. Under such circumstances, the crowding of women into traditional occupations is believed to represent a misallocation of resources, which is permitted to continue by societal and labor market discrimination against women. Mandating higher wages would bring the earnings of those who remain in women's jobs closer to the level of comparably qualified men.

However, raising women's wages without changing the underlying conditions that produced them could still result in job loss. This is illustrated in Figure 7.1. Suppose we begin with the discriminatory situation. The relevant supply curves are S_{fd} and S_{md}, and wages are W_{fd} and W_{md}, in the female and male sectors, respectively. Suppose further that a comparable worth system set wages in female jobs at W_0, the rate that would prevail in the absence of discrimination. At that wage, only L_{f0}, rather than L_{fd} workers, would be demanded by employers. The remainder, $L_{fd} - L_{f0}$, would be displaced from their jobs.

If such shifts were major and abrupt (which, of course, need not be the case), the transition period might be quite protracted. To the extent that not only new entrants but experienced workers were involved, it would be disruptive and painful. Female unemployment rates might well be increased. The costs associated with this policy depend crucially on how many workers are displaced, how quickly, and what happens to them. At present, we simply do not know how severe these problems would be.[71] Some additional light can be shed on these issues by examining what happened in Australia when wages in female occupations were abruptly raised by introducing a comparable worth policy. The experiences of that country will be described in Chapter 10.

It is worth noting that the traditional approach to raising women's pay through the principles of equal pay for equal work and equal employment opportunity also has the potential of increasing the wages even of women who remain in female jobs. This may also be illustrated in Figure 7.1. Suppose that we again begin with the discriminatory situation. If the barriers to entry into the male jobs are reduced, women will transfer from F jobs to M jobs. The supply curve in F jobs will shift inward towards S_{f0} while the supply curve in M jobs shifts outward towards S_{m0}. Wages in the female sector are increased by the reduction of overcrowding there. A completely successful antidiscrimination policy would result in a wage of w_0 being established for both types of jobs. Proponents of comparable worth contend, however, that existing policies have not achieved notable success as yet and that a new strategy is called for.

We have emphasized the economic issues relevant to the subject of comparable worth—issues that are paramount in concluding whether, and for whom, such a policy would be beneficial. However, the courts are making decisions concerning the issue on purely legal grounds. Currently, the status of comparable worth as a legal doctrine under Title VII is unclear, because the matter has not been definitively addressed by the Supreme Court.[72] Nor is there much evidence of the adoption of comparable worth in the private sector, but many state and local governments have implemented or begun to implement some version of comparable

---

[71]One study found that implementation of comparable worth did not appear to cause workers to *lose* their jobs. Rather it tended to reduce employment *growth* below what it otherwise would have been. See Killingsworth, *The Economics of Comparable Worth.*

[72]In the widely publicized case of *County of Washington v. Gunther,* 452 U.S. 161 (1981), the Supreme Court removed a major legal stumbling block to the comparable worth doctrine by ruling that it is not required that a man and woman do "equal work" in order to establish pay discrimination under Title VII. However, many other issues remain unresolved, and the Court stopped short of endorsing the comparable worth approach. See Ross and Barcher, *The Rights of Women,* pp. 23–24. A major legal victory for proponents of comparable worth was attained in September 1983 when a federal court ruled in favor of the American Federation of State, County, and Municipal Employees (AFSCME) and found that the State of Washington had violated Title VII by paying employees in traditionally female job classifications less than employees in traditionally male occupations. A 1974 comparable worth study, commissioned by the state, found that women received 20 percent lower pay than men for jobs requiring equal skill and responsibility. When Washington failed to eliminate the disparity, AFSCME filed suit (Bureau of National Affairs, *Daily Labor Report,* no. 181 [September 16, 1983]). The ruling in favor of the plaintiffs was later overturned on appeal; see *American Federation of State, County and Municipal Employees v. State of Washington* 770 F.2d 1401 (1985). In January 1986, the parties settled out of court ("Washington State Settles Dispute Over Pay Equity," *New York Times,* January 2, 1986, p. A15). Thus the Supreme Court has not issued a definitive ruling on the comparable worth issue.

*JOB EVALUATION**

The implementation of comparable worth requires an evaluation of the contribution of the many different jobs within an enterprise. At present, formal job evaluation procedures are already used by the federal government, a number of state governments, and many large private firms as an aid in determining pay rates. Among the reasons for this policy are, first, that many positions are filled entirely from within the units themselves through promotion and upgrading of the existing work force; and second, that, because some jobs are unique to a particular firm, "going rates" for all jobs are not always available in local labor markets. This puts employers in a position of having to establish wages, rather than simply to accept those determined by the market. This does not mean that market forces are ignored. In setting wages, most firms and governmental units try to take into account whatever information is available on prevailing wages for different types of labor. At the same time, the existence of job evaluation and other procedures for setting wages tend to make wages less responsive to short-term shifts in market conditions than they would otherwise be.

The actual methods used differ in detail but share the same basic rationale and approach. The first step is always a description of all the jobs within the given organization. The next step is to rate each according to all the various features which it is believed determine pay differentials. Last, these ratings are combined to create a score for each job, which may then be used to help determine wages.

Among the factors used to construct job scores are such characteristics as level of education, skills, and responsibility, as well as the environment in which the work is performed. Commonly, multiple regression is used to link these to the existing pay structure. At other times, weights are assigned according to the judgment of the experts constructing the scale. In theory, various jobs can be assigned values objectively, presumably not influenced by irrelevant factors, such as, say, the gender and race of the incumbent, and quite different jobs may be assigned equal values, if warranted.

It would be a mistake, however, to take the objectivity of such procedures for granted. Both prevailing wage structures and the judgments of individuals may be tainted by existing inequalities in the economy and in society, although efforts are under way to develop unbiased compensation schemes.** All one can conclude at this point is that the use of job evaluation to determine pay rates is neither an impractical pipedream, nor a sure-fire cure for discrimination.

---

*Job evaluation is discussed in Donald J. Treiman and Heidi I. Hartmann, eds. *Women, Work and Wages: Equal Pay for Jobs of Equal Value* (Washington, D.C.: National Academy Press, 1981), pp. 71–74. Institutional models, discussed earlier, emphasize the importance of job evaluation and other administrative procedures for determining wages. See Peter B. Doeringer and Michael J. Piore, *Internal Labor Markets and Manpower Analysis* (Lexington, MA: D. C. Heath and Co., 1971).

**See Ronnie Steinberg and Lois Haignere, "Equitable Compensation: Methodological Criteria for Comparable Worth," in *Ingredients for Women's Employment Policy,* Christine Bose and Glenna Spitze, eds. (Albany, NY: State University of New York Press, 1987), pp. 157–82.

worth.[73] In addition, some unions, particularly those in the public sector, have pressed for pay equity as a collective bargaining demand.

POLICY ISSUE: WOMEN AND UNIONS

As discussed above, one of the reasons for the lower wages of women is their relatively low representation in unions. Therefore, in this section we take a closer look at this issue.

Representation of Women in Labor Organizations

As may be seen in Table 7.3, women are underrepresented in labor unions in comparison to their share of the labor force as a whole. Between 1956 and 1990, labor organizations accounted for a shrinking proportion of both male and female workers. In relative terms, however, the underrepresentation of women in unions decreased, as women's share of labor union membership increased more rapidly than their share of total employment. The increase in female unionization occurred primarily in the public sector and among white-collar workers.[74] Table 7.3 also shows that blacks are more likely to be members of labor organizations than whites or Hispanics.

Benefits of Union Membership

The underrepresentation of women in unions is a cause for concern to some, because unions confer benefits on their members that women, thus, enjoy to a lesser extent than men. Unions have been found to increase the wages of their members, although there is some disagreement over the magnitude of the union wage gain. One recent review of the evidence estimated that the union relative wage advantage probably averaged 15 percent between the mid-1950s and the late 1970s and that, in general, this advantage is about as large for women as for men.[75] The union wage gain has fluctuated over time and appears to have been above this level in the 1970s and 1980s. Although not all workers gain to the same

---

[73]By 1988, 20 states had made some sort of pay equity adjustments (i.e., salary increases appropriated to female-dominated or minority-dominated job categories), and 6 states had fully implemented a pay equity plan; see Sara E. Rix, ed., *The American Woman: 1990–91* (New York: W. W. Norton, 1990), p. 392. See also Alice H. Cook, "Comparable Worth in the United States," *Labor Law Journal* 41, no. 8 (August 1990): 525–31.

[74]Freeman and Leonard, "Union Maids."

[75]H. Gregg Lewis, *Union Relative Wage Effects: A Survey* (Chicago: University of Chicago Press, 1986), cited in Robert J. Flanagan, Lawrence M. Kahn, Robert S. Smith, and Ronald G. Ehrenberg, *The Economics of the Employment Relationship* (Glenview, IL: Scott, Foresman, and Co., 1989), pp. 552–53. There is some evidence that union wage gains in the public sector are higher for women than men; see Freeman and Leonard, "Union Maids."

TABLE 7.3   The Representation of Women in Labor Organizations, Selected Years, 1956–1990

| Year | WOMEN AS A PERCENTAGE OF | | UNION MEMBERSHIP AS A PERCENTAGE OF ALL EMPLOYED WORKERS | | |
	All Employed Workers	Membership of Labor Organizations	Men	Women	Total
Unions only:					
1956	32.0	18.5	32.2	15.7	27.0
1966	35.6	19.3	30.7	13.1	24.4
Unions and associations:					
1970	37.7	23.9	32.9	16.9	26.8
1980					
All	42.4	30.1	25.1	14.7	20.7
Whites	41.7	28.3	24.4	13.4	19.8
Blacks[a]	48.1	40.7	31.5	23.2	27.5
1990					
All	47.2	36.9	19.3	12.6	16.1
Whites	46.7	35.4	18.8	11.7	15.5
Blacks	51.5	44.0	24.4	18.0	21.1
Hispanics	40.5	34.3	16.3	12.5	14.8

[a] Includes other nonwhites.

Source: U.S. Department of Labor, Bureau of Labor Statistics, "Earnings and Other Characteristics of Organized Workers," Bulletin 2105 (May 1980), Table 2, p. 2; Linda H. LeGrande, "Women in Labor Organizations: Their Ranks are Increasing," *Monthly Labor Review* 101, no. 8 (August 1978), Table 1, p. 9; *Employment and Training Report of the President* (1981), Table A-16, pp. 144–6; and *Employment and Earnings* 38, no. 1 (January 1991), p. 228.

extent by unionization—the union wage premium tends to vary by occupation and industry—there is little doubt that unions do increase the wages of their members. Hence the underrepresentation of women in unions lowers their wages relative to men's, all else being equal. At the same time, the higher participation of blacks than of whites in labor organizations raises the relative earnings of blacks somewhat, all else being equal.[76]

Unions have also been found to increase the fringe benefits of union workers relative to their nonunion counterparts. Indeed, the union fringe effect has been found to be greater (in percentage terms) than the union wage effect. Finally, unions impart nonpecuniary benefits to their members, chiefly by giving them a greater opportunity to shape their work environment by directly communicating

[76] Ashenfelter, "Discrimination and Trade Unions."

with employers in the collective bargaining process and by providing for grievance procedures. Richard Freeman has termed this the "voice effect" of unions.[77]

On the other hand, to the extent that the demand for labor is responsive to its cost, the advantages of higher wages and greater fringe benefits brought about by unionization would also be associated with lower employment. Hence, the gains of those who get greater rewards are in part at the expense of those who are not hired, or are displaced, due to unionization.

Reasons for the Underrepresentation of Women in Unions

In light of the advantages of union membership, how do we explain the underrepresentation of women in unions? It is commonly believed that women are less interested in unionism than men because of their lesser attachment to the labor force. This appears not to be the case, however. In 1977, among private sector workers who were not represented by labor organizations, women were considerably more likely than men to respond that they would vote in favor of union representation if an election were held—41 percent of women gave this response in comparison to 27 percent of men.[78] Interestingly, nonrepresented blacks also were more likely than nonrepresented whites to indicate that they would vote for union representation—69 percent of blacks in comparison to 29 percent of whites.

The primary reason for the underrepresentation of women in labor organizations is that they tend to be concentrated in industries and occupations where, for whatever reason, unionization is below average. Traditionally, unionization has been highest among blue-collar workers in manufacturing, whereas women have been concentrated in clerical and service occupations and in the service industries. Within the manufacturing sector, women are more likely than men to be employed in the more competitive industries, whereas unionization has been higher in monopolistic industries. One study found that over 80 percent of the male-female unionization differential was due to such workplace differences rather than any lesser desire for unionization among women.[79] Blacks, on the other hand, are more likely than whites to be in blue-collar jobs, and this helps to explain their higher rates of unionization.

---

[77]Richard B. Freeman, "Individual Mobility and Union Voice in the Labor Market," *American Economic Review* 66, no. 2 (May 1976): 361–68. The evidence on fringes is from Richard B. Freeman and James L. Medoff, *What Do Unions Do?* (New York: Basic Books, 1984).

[78]Freeman and Medoff, *What Do Unions Do?* Interpreting this result is complicated by the gender difference in the proportion of workers organized. Since more men are union members, one might expect on the margin a smaller proportion of nonunion men than nonunion women to desire unions. A study that takes this factor into account suggests there is no pure "taste" differential for unionism by gender; see Henry S. Farber, "The Determination of the Union Status of Workers," National Bureau of Economic Research Working Paper 1006, 1982, cited in Freeman and Leonard, "Union Maids."

[79]Freeman and Leonard, "Union Maids."

The policies of unions themselves have no doubt also contributed to the underrepresentation of women among their members. Male craft unions did not begin to admit women to their ranks until the late 1800s.[80] Even after unions began to officially open their doors to women, they have been criticized for their less than vigorous efforts to organize women workers and lack of support for women's own efforts to unionize. Moreover, it is claimed that unions have emphasized issues of concern to male workers at the bargaining table and neglected female concerns. This lowers the appeal of unions for women. For example, the emphasis of unions on fringe benefits like health insurance would be of less value to women than to men, because many women, as members of two-earner families, are already covered under their husbands' plans.[81] On the other hand, given the traditional division of labor in the family, provision of such benefits as parental leaves and day care is likely to be of greater interest to women than to men.

Part of the reason for the lesser attention of unions to women's issues has been the low participation of women in national union leadership positions. This is dramatically illustrated in Table 7.4, which gives this information for many large unions in 1985. As may be seen in the table, the representation of women among national officers and governing board members is consistently far below their share of membership. The reasons for this are complex, but most likely reflect the same types of barriers to women's participation encountered in other leadership positions. For instance, the situation is not unlike that in governmental elective offices. In 1991, only 31 women served in the United States Congress, comprising just 5 percent of members.[82] And it was not until 1984 that Geraldine Ferraro, the defeated Democratic candidate, became the first woman to be nominated for Vice President of the United States by a major political party. On the other hand, both within unions and in politics, women are making progress at the local level that should eventually be reflected in greater representation at the national level.[83]

Prospects for the Future

Unions have a strong interest in organizing female workers because unions must make inroads into traditionally female occupations and industries if they are to

---

[80] Barbara M. Wertheimer, "'Union is Power': Sketches from Women's Labor History," *Women: A Feminist Perspective,* 3rd ed., Jo Freeman, ed. (Palo Alto: Mayfield, 1984), pp. 337–52.

[81] Freeman and Medoff, *What Do Unions Do?* As discussed in Chapter 6, adoption of flexible benefit plans where workers can select benefit packages that meet their needs would be preferable for two-earner families.

[82] Robin Toner, "Women in Politics Gain, but Road is a Long One," *New York Times,* February 25, 1991. For an analysis of women's political attitudes and behavior, see Virginia Sapiro, *The Political Integration of Women* (Urbana, IL: University of Illinois Press, 1983).

[83] For example, in 1991, women comprised 18.1 percent of members of state legislatures, up from 4 percent in 1969. Similarly, three women were inaugurated as governors in 1991; this was 16 years after Ella Grasso of Connecticut became the first woman elected governor without being preceded by her husband. See Toner, "Women in Politics Gain."

TABLE 7.4   Representation of Women among Officers and Governing Board Members, Selected Labor Organizations, 1985

| | | OFFICERS/GOVERNING BOARDS | | |
| | | | WOMEN | |
Union	Women as a Percentage of Membership	Total Number	Number	Percent
Automobile workers (UAW)	13	25	1	4
Clothing and textile workers (ACTWU)	65	34	3	9
Communications workers (CWA)	52	18	1	6
Electrical workers (IBEW)	30	23	0	0
Electrical workers (IUE)	40	26	2	8
Government employees (AFGE)	31	19	2	10
Hotel and restaurant employees (HREU)	50	24	2	8
Ladies garment workers (ILGWU)	85	24	3	13
Machinists (IAM)	15	11	0	0
Service employees (SEIU)	50	50	9	18
State, county and municipal employees (AFSCME)	45	28	4	14
Steelworkers (USWA)	10	30	0	0
Teachers (AFT)	60	34	11	32
Teachers (NEA)	60	9[a] (121[b])	3[a] (61[b])	33[a] (50[b])
Teamsters (IBT)	26	21	0	0

[a] NEA executive committee.

[b] NEA board of directors

Source: Naomi Baden, "Developing an Agenda: Expanding the Role of Women in Unions," *Labor Studies Journal* 10, no. 3 (Winter 1986), p. 238.

reverse the decline in the share of the labor force that is organized and begin, once again, to expand. High-level union leadership has recognized this and is placing greater priority on efforts to organize women and giving more support to women's issues. The Coalition of Labor Union Women was founded in 1974 to increase the number of women in union leadership positions and to help organize women workers. Thus, the relative participation of women in unions, at all levels, may well increase in the future.

CONCLUSION

Economists define labor market discrimination as a situation where two equally qualified individuals are treated differently on the basis of gender (race, age, etc.). Such discrimination against a particular group is likely to be detrimental, both directly and indirectly, through feedback effects on their accumulation of human capital. Empirical studies have used available evidence on differences in the characteristics of male and female workers to explain the pay gap and the differences in occupational distributions between the two groups. Productivity-related factors have not been able to account for all of the gender differences in economic outcomes, suggesting that discrimination does play a part, accounting for perhaps half of the male-female earnings differential.

As much attention as has been focused on the issue of whether discrimination exists, there has been almost equal interest in the question who discriminates, why, and how. We reviewed theories suggesting that

- Employers, coworkers, or customers have tastes for discrimination against women
- Employers judge individual women in terms of the characteristics of the group (statistical discrimination)
- Women's wages are depressed because they are crowded into a few sectors
- Women are concentrated in dead-end jobs with few opportunities for on-the-job training and promotion

Last, we examined the government's equal employment opportunity policy and considered the role that unions have played in women's failure to achieve equal economic outcomes to men.

There is good reason to believe that each of these explanations contributes to our understanding of a complex reality, where factors keeping women in segregated and poorly paid jobs, rather than being mutually exclusive, are far more likely to have reinforced each other. By the same token, however, we pointed out that any reduction in one of the negative factors is likely to have feedback effects. By rewarding women more highly for their human capital, they are encouraged to accumulate more human capital on which they can gather rewards.

SUGGESTED READINGS

ARROW, KENNETH. "The Theory of Discrimination." In *Discrimination in Labor Markets,* Orley Ashenfelter and Albert Rees, eds. Princeton, NJ: Princeton University, 1973, pp. 3–33.

BECKER, GARY S. *The Economics of Discrimination,* 2nd ed. Chicago: University of Chicago Press, 1971.

BERGMANN, BARBARA R. *The Economic Emergence of Women.* New York: Basic Books, 1986.

BERGMANN, BARBARA R. "Occupational Segregation, Wages and Profits When Employers Discriminate by Race or Sex," *Eastern Economic Journal,* nos. 1–2 (April–July 1974): 103–10.

BLAU, FRANCINE D. "Discrimination Against Women: Theory and Evidence." In *Labor Economics: Modern Views,* William A. Darity, Jr., ed. Boston: Kluwer-Nijhoff, 1984, pp. 53–89.

CAIN, GLEN G. "The Economic Analysis of Labor Market Discrimination: A Survey." In *Handbook of Labor Economics,* Orley Ashenfelter and Richard Layard, eds. Amsterdam: North Holland Press, 1988, pp. 693–785.

DOERINGER, PETER B. and MICHAEL J. PIORE. *Internal Labor Markets and Manpower Analysis.* Lexington, MA: D. C. Heath, 1971.

FREEMAN, RICHARD B. and JAMES L. MEDOFF. *What Do Unions Do?* New York: Basic Books, 1984.

GORDON, DAVID M., RICHARD EDWARDS, and MICHAEL REICH. *Segmented Work, Divided Workers: The Historical Transformation of Labor in the United States.* Cambridge: Cambridge University Press, 1982.

MADDEN, JANICE F. *The Economics of Sex Discrimination,* Lexington, MA: Lexington Books, 1973.

RESKIN, BARBARA F. and HEIDI I. HARTMANN, eds. *Women's Work, Men's Work: Sex Segregation on the Job.* Washington, D.C.: National Academy Press, 1986.

RESKIN, BARBARA F. and PATRICIA A. ROOS. *Job Queues, Gender Queues: Explaining Women's Inroads into Male Occupations.* Philadelphia: Temple University Press, 1990.

STROBER, MYRA H. "Toward a General Theory of Occupational Sex Segregation: The Case of Public School Teaching." In *Sex Segregation in the Workplace: Trends, Explanations, Remedies,* Barbara F. Reskin, ed. Washington, D.C.: National Academy Press, 1984, pp. 144–56.

Chapter 8

DIFFERENCES IN JOBLESSNESS: DISCOURAGEMENT, FRICTIONAL AND STRUCTURAL UNEMPLOYMENT

In preceding chapters, we have dealt with decisions about the allocation of time as though individuals could choose freely according to their preferences. In reality, employment necessarily involves not only the willingness to a do a job but also the ability to find one. Thus, at any given time there are some people who are looking for work but who are not employed. Traditionally, such people have been categorized as being unable to find work; this would be a serious constraint on the individual's ability to maximize utility in the way that our models suggest.

We begin this chapter by defining unemployment and distinguishing between various types of unemployment. We then discuss the concept of full employment and the cost to the economy of not achieving it. Subsequent sections deal with the incidence of joblessness among various segments of the population, with emphasis on differences in the extent to which various factors influence women's and men's unemployment rates, and on the substantial narrowing that has occurred in the gender unemployment differential. Because the seriousness of the problem of unemployment for women has at times been questioned, we close by considering gender differences in the burden of unemployment.

DEFINITION OF UNEMPLOYMENT

The official definition of **unemployment** includes all individuals not currently working for pay but actively looking for work or persons temporarily laid off from a job to which they expect to return. This includes the **seasonally unemployed,** such as construction workers in the snow belt during the winter or ski instructors in the summer. Also, in a dynamic economy, there will always be new entrants and reentrants as well as job quitters and job losers looking for jobs.[1] Given imperfect information, it will take them some time to find jobs, even when enough appropriate job openings are available. This is referred to as **frictional unemployment.** Or there may be more serious **structural unemployment** when those looking for work do not have the right skills or are not in the right location to fill the vacancies that exist. Such unemployment is likely to be more persistent, because these difficulties are not easily or quickly remedied.

The type of unemployment that causes the most serious concern, however, is that associated with an overall deficiency in demand, when there is an excess of workers in relation to unfilled positions. This is most commonly referred to as **demand-deficient unemployment** or cyclical unemployment, because in advanced industrialized economies, such insufficient demand for labor tends to recur in cycles.

In addition to unemployment, there is also the problem of **underemployment,** when workers take jobs for which they are clearly overqualified, or when they work less than they would prefer to. Examples of the former would be a Ph.D. taking a house-cleaning job or a skilled automobile worker harvesting fruit. Examples of the latter are persons who work only part-time when they would prefer to work full-time. These situations tend to arise more often in a slack labor market, when the recorded unemployment rate is also high.

Last but not least, individuals who have searched for employment for some time without success may eventually stop looking. Others who would like a job may postpone their entry into the labor force until economic conditions improve. These individuals are generally referred to as **discouraged workers.** Relatively few men of prime working age fall into this category, because giving up on the labor market is not an acceptable option for them. It does, however, include many young people who often postpone entry into the labor market or return to school, older people who retire, and women who remain in or return to the household full-time. Such discouraged workers are considered to be out of the labor force

---

[1]This is so even though the majority of those who change jobs actually experience no unemployment because most workers search while holding on to the old job until they have found a new one. See J. Peter Mattila, "Job Quitting and Frictional Unemployment," *American Economic Review* 64, no.1 (March 1974): 235–39. Evidence also indicates that many labor market entrants never experience a period of unemployment. See Ethel B. Jones, *Determinants of Female Reentrant Unemployment* (the W. E. Upjohn Institute for Employment Research, 1983); Ronald G. Ehrenberg, "The Demographic Structure of Unemployment Rates and Labor Market Transition Probabilities," in *Research in Labor Economics* 3, Ronald G. Ehrenberg, ed. (Greenwich, CT: JAI Press, Inc., 1980): 253; and Ronald G. Ehrenberg and Robert S. Smith, *Modern Labor Economics: Theory and Public Policy,* 4th ed. (New York: Harper Collins, 1991, p. 605.)

rather than unemployed and, thus, are not included in the official estimates of the unemployment rate.[2] As we saw in Chapter 4, their numbers increase during recessions and decline during upswings.

COST OF UNEMPLOYMENT TO THE ECONOMY

Unemployment involves a loss for the economy because a larger output could be achieved with a better allocation of resources. One widely cited study found that for every additional 1 percentage point of unemployment, GNP declined by about 3 percentage points,[3] though more recently it has been suggested that the figure may now be closer to 2 percentage points.[4] This loss may, in part, be caused by the underemployment of some of the workers who do have jobs, as well as the idleness of those entirely without work. Excess capacity in plant and equipment is also likely to be a contributing factor.

Table 8.1 shows unemployment rates of men and women in the United States for years of relatively high and low unemployment between 1948 and 1990. During these years, the unemployment rate never approached the 1 in 4 rate reached during the depths of the Great Depression of the 1930s, but it was considerably higher than the 2 percent rate achieved in the wartime period of the early 1940s. Further, there appears to have been an upward trend. Unemployment rates in 1982 and 1983 were higher than in any of the previous 40 years, and have not been below 5 percent since 1973. The shortfall of GNP below its potential during many of these years was obviously substantial.

THE BURDEN OF UNEMPLOYMENT
FOR INDIVIDUALS

More controversial than the loss to the economy is the extent of the burden that falls upon the unemployed themselves. This is because the measured unemployment rate is not a perfect indicator of the degree of economic hardship for individuals.[5] How this is viewed depends in part on the reason why the person is out of work.

---

[2]However, Christopher J. Flinn and James J. Heckman, "Are Unemployment and 'Out of the Labor Force' Behaviorally Distinct Labor Force States?" *Journal of Economics* 1, no. 1 (January 1983): 28–42, report that, although the unemployed receive more job offers than those who are not in the labor force, some individuals go directly from being out of the labor force to a job. They conclude that the difference between the unemployed and "discouraged workers" is one of degree only.

[3]Arthur M. Okun, *The Political Economy of Prosperity,* Washington, D.C.: Brookings Institution (1970), Appendix, pp. 132–46.

[4]Robert J. Gordon and Robert E. Hall, "Arthur M. Okun, 1928–1980," *Brookings Papers on Economic Activity,* no.1 (1980): 1–5.

[5]For a more extensive treatment of this issue, see National Commission on Employment and Unemployment Statistics, *Counting the Labor Force* (Washington, D.C.: U.S. Government Printing Office, 1979).

TABLE 8.1 Unemployment Rates of Men and Women 16 Years and Older, Selected High and Low Years 1948–1990

Year	Total	Men	Women	Gender Differences[a]
1948	3.8	3.6	4.1	0.5
1949	5.9	5.9	6.0	0.1
1953	2.9	2.8	3.3	0.5
1954	5.5	5.3	6.0	0.7
1956	4.1	3.8	4.8	1.0
1958	6.8	6.8	6.8	0.0
1959	5.5	5.2	5.9	0.7
1961	6.7	6.4	7.2	0.8
1969	3.5	2.8	4.7	1.9
1971	5.9	5.3	6.9	1.6
1973	4.9	4.2	6.0	1.8
1975	8.5	7.9	9.3	1.4
1979	5.8	5.1	6.8	1.7
1982	9.7	9.9	9.4	−0.5
1983	9.6	9.9	9.2	−0.7
1989	5.3	5.2	5.4	0.2
1990	5.5	5.6	5.4	−0.2

[a]The female unemployment rate minus the male unemployment rate.

Source: *Employment and Training Report of the President* (Washington, D.C.: U.S. Government Printing Office, 1982); and *Employment and Earnings* 38 no. 1 (January 1991).

Though the very definition of unemployment appears to imply that it is involuntary, this is not necessarily the case. An individual who turns down a job and continues to search for a more attractive offer is making a voluntary decision and yet will be counted as unemployed. Indeed, the very notion of voluntariness is difficult to define and still harder to measure empirically. Is a Ph.D. who turns down a job doing house cleaning voluntarily unemployed? One commonsense definition of involuntary unemployment to which many economists would subscribe is the inability to find a position at the prevailing market wage for one's skills.[6] This would exclude persons who have received a reasonable offer but are holding out for higher rewards.

Unfortunately, no data are available to determine exactly what proportion of the unemployed would be classified as involuntary on the basis of this definition. It would, in any case, be a mistake to assume that a large proportion of the unemployment rate, particularly during times when it is high, can be ascribed

[6]See Orley Ashenfelter, "What is Involuntary Unemployment?" *Proceedings of the American Philosophy Society* 122, no.3 (June 1978): 135–38.

to individuals simply holding out for better offers. There is evidence that many of the unemployed never reject any offer at all.[7]

There are other reasons as well why the official unemployment rate does not perfectly measure the economic hardship of unemployment. For one, to the extent that the unemployed person uses some of the now available time to increase household production or to invest in human capital by getting education or training, the decline in money earnings would overestimate the decrease in economic welfare caused by the spell of unemployment.[8] On the other hand, no on-the-job training is acquired during a period of unemployment, and if the spell is prolonged, skills may depreciate. Hence, there may be a negative effect on future as well as on present earnings.[9] It has also been pointed out that the current loss of earnings will be cushioned for some individuals by unemployment insurance[10] or the earnings of other family members. Moreover, workers in seasonal or cyclically sensitive jobs probably receive higher wages to compensate for the irregularity of their work.[11]

Nonetheless, the figures in Table 8.2 make clear that unemployment causes considerable economic hardship. In 1989, a year of relatively low unemployment (5.3 percent), 32 percent of families with an unemployed householder had incomes below the poverty line, in comparison to only 6 percent of families with an employed householder. The economic hardship to families maintained by women was particularly serious, with the percentage of such families in poverty increasing from 17 to 65 precent when the householder was unemployed. It should also be noted that poverty rates tend to be considerably higher among minority families than among whites.

[7]See, for example, U.S. Bureau of Labor Statistics, Bulletin 1886, *Job Seeking Methods Used by American Workers* (Washington, D.C.: U.S. Government Printing Office, 1975), cited in Ronald G. Ehrenberg and Robert S. Smith, *Modern Labor Economics* (Glenview, IL: Scott Foresman and Co., 1982), p. 447; and Stanley P. Stephenson, Jr., "The Economics of Youth Job Search Behavior," *The Review of Economics and Statistics* 58, no. 1 (February 1976): 104–11. It must be noted, however, that an individual who is not interested in a job may not pursue it to the point of obtaining an offer.

[8]This implies that the welfare loss due to unemployment is smaller for groups whose members have a high value of nonmarket time relative to market earnings. This would include youth, who may return to school or devote full-time (rather than part-time) to their studies, older workers who are on the verge of retirement, and married women who, given the traditional division of labor in many families, are most likely to devote their time to household chores. The latter point has been used as an argument for considering female unemployment a less serious problem than male unemployment. We examine this viewpoint later in this chapter.

[9]See, for instance, Mary Corcoran, "The Employment and Wage Consequences of Teenage Women's Non-Employment," in *The Youth Labor Market Problem: Its Nature, Causes and Consequences,* Richard B. Freeman and David A. Wise, eds. (Chicago: University of Chicago Press, 1982), pp. 391–425; and David T. Ellwood, "Teenage Unemployment: Permanent Scars or Temporary Blemishes," in *The Youth Labor Market Problem,* Freeman and Wise, eds. pp. 349–90.

[10]Unemployment insurance, even for those who are eligible, is always less than the regular wage. Further, in the late 1980s, less than one-third of the unemployed were covered by unemployment insurance (*Statistical Abstract,* 1990).

[11]For evidence of such a compensating differential, see John M. Abowd and Orley Ashenfelter, "Anticipated Unemployment, Temporary Layoffs and Compensating Wage Differentials," in *Studies in Labor Markets,* Sherwin Rosen, ed. (Chicago: University of Chicago Press, 1981), pp. 141–70; and Daniel S. Hamermesh and John R. Wolfe, "Compensating Wage Differentials and the Duration of Wage Loss," *Journal of Labor Economics,* 8, no.1, pt.2 (January 1990): S175–97.

TABLE 8.2   Incidence of Poverty by Unemployment Status, Family Type, Race, and Hispanic Origin, 1989

	PERCENT IN POVERTY	
	Employed Householder	*Unemployed Householder*
Total		
All families	5.6	31.7
Married-couple families	3.6	17.7
Families maintained by women	17.1	64.8
Unrelated individuals	9.7	36.0
Whites		
All families	4.6	23.7
Married-couple families	3.3	15.7
Families maintained by women	14.4	53.5
Unrelated individuals	9.4	30.0
Blacks		
All families	13.7	59.3
Married-couple families	6.9	28.6
Families maintained by women	23.8	77.8
Unrelated individuals	12.8	60.5
Hispanics		
All families	14.6	45.2
Married-couple families	12.5	32.5
Families maintained by women	26.3	n.a.
Unrelated individuals	19.3	43.5

Source: Bureau of the Census, Current Population Reports, Consumer Income Series P-60, No. 168, "Money Income and Poverty Status in the United States, 1989."

These data suggest that the impact of unemployment on family income and poverty status is likely to be serious. Because searching for a job is likely to involve many expenses usually related to working, such as travel and clothing as well as a good deal of time away from home, this income loss may not be mitigated very much by declining job expenses and additional home production.

Individuals who are out of work not only fail to gain valuable labor market experience but may also lose tenure on the job, as well as insurance and pension benefits. Further, the unemployed suffer psychologically as well as economically by losing the feeling of dignity associated with being a productive member of society.[12]

[12] A study by Jeanne Prial Gordus and Sean P. McAlinden of the University of Michigan found that job loss was associated with depression, anxiety, aggression, insomnia, loss of self-esteem, and marital problems. The spouse of the unemployed worker also suffered psychological problems. In work settings where many have been laid off, even those who remain employed are negatively affected due to their need to cope with a highly stressful situation. Another study by Harvey Brenner of Johns Hopkins University found that the 14.3 percent increase in the unemployment rate during the 1973–74 recession was associated with a 7.3 percent increase in total mortality from all causes and a 2.8 percent increase in deaths by heart attacks. These studies are reported in the Bureau of National Affairs' *Daily Labor Report*, no. 128 (July 3, 1984): A–13 to A–15. See also a special issue of the *Journal of Social Issues* (vol. 44, no. 4, 1988), which presents reports on research from the United States and Europe concerning the psychological effects of unemployment.

Beyond that, a high unemployment rate slows the progress of disadvantaged groups. In occupations that have traditionally been restricted to white males, layoffs fall disproportionately on women and minorities, who tend to be more recently hired. The failure of new jobs to open up also reduces opportunities for hiring women and minorities to only those jobs that open up through attrition.

Finally, it should be pointed out that the official unemployment rate provides only incomplete information on joblessness in other respects as well. First, it tells us only the percentage of people who are unemployed at any one point in time. In order to learn how many people have been unemployed at some point during the year, and how long they were unemployed, we need to look at Table 8.3. In 1983, a year of recovery from the 1981–82 recession, but of continued high unemployment, 21 percent of men and 18 percent of women in the labor force were out of work at some time; and 54 percent of the unemployed men and 43 percent of the unemployed women were out of work for 15 weeks or more. Even in 1990, a relatively better year, a substantially higher proportion of individuals were out of work at some time in the year than were unemployed at any point in time.

In both years, the median duration of spells of unemployment was lower for women than for men, as was the incidence of long-term unemployment (15 weeks or more), quite possibly because women were more inclined to drop out of the labor force if unsuccessful in locating a job. The median duration of unemployment and the incidence of long-term unemployment declined for both men and women as economic conditions improved.

Second, as was pointed out earlier, the official definition of unemployment does not include a number of categories that could reasonably be viewed as representing joblessness. The data in Table 8.4 indicate the consequences of including two of these—discouraged workers and involuntary part-time workers. (Only one-half of the latter are included in the index of joblessness, to reflect

TABLE 8.3 Extent of Unemployment by Sex, 1983 and 1990

	1983		1990	
	Men	*Women*	*Men*	*Women*
Unemployment rate	9.9	9.2	5.6	5.4
Percent of labor force with unemployment at some time during the year	21.0	17.8	15.7	13.6
Percent of unemployment with				
1 to14 weeks	46.5	56.7	56.5	64.7
15 weeks or more	53.5	43.3	43.5	35.3
Median weeks of unemployment	15.2	12.3	12.7	10.9

Sources: Ellen Seghal, "Work Experience in 1983 Reflects the Effects of the Recovery," *Monthly Labor Review* 107, no. 12 (December 1984): 18–24; U.S. Dept. of Labor, Bureau of Labor Statistics, "Work Experience of the Population in 1990," *News,* September 11, 1991.

TABLE 8.4   Jobless Rates of Men and Women in 1979, 1983, and 1990[a]

	Official Unemployment Rate (%) (1)	EXPANDED LABOR FORCE DEFINITION[b]			
Year and Group		Unemployment (%) (2)	Discouraged Workers (%) (3)	(½) Involuntary Part-time (%) (4)	Jobless[c] (%) (5)
1979					
Total	5.8	5.8	0.7	1.6	8.1
Men	5.1	5.1	0.5	1.2	6.8
Women	6.8	6.7	1.1	2.1	9.9
1983					
Total	9.6	9.5	1.4	2.6	13.6
Men	9.9	9.8	1.0	2.2	13.0
Women	9.2	9.0	2.0	3.3	14.3
1990					
Total	5.5	5.5	0.7	2.0	8.2
Men	5.6	5.5	0.5	1.8	7.9
Women	5.4	5.4	0.9	2.3	8.6

[a]Data refer to civilians 16 years of age and over.

[b]The expanded labor force definition includes discouraged workers. It is the denominator in columns (2) through (5).

[c]The jobless include the unemployed, discouraged workers, and one-half of the involuntary part-time. Column (5) may not exactly equal the sum of columns (2) through (4) due to rounding.

Sources: Computed from data published in the *Employment and Training Report of the President* (1982), *Employment and Earnings* 31, no. 1 (January 1984), and *Employment and Earnings* 38, no. 1 (January 1991).

that they are only partially unemployed.) In 1979 and 1990, years of relatively low unemployment, inclusion of these categories would raise the estimate of joblessness by more than two percentage points to over 8.0 percent. In 1983, a year marked by the beginnings of recovery from a serious recession, the estimate of joblessness would be raised by 4 percentage points using the expanded definition.

Table 8.4 also illustrates that women are more likely to be discouraged workers or involuntarily employed part-time than are men. There is, thus, a larger disparity between the official unemployment rate and the jobless rate for women than for men. Indeed, although the measured unemployment rate was higher for men than women in both 1983 and 1990, in both cases, the jobless index was about one percentage point higher for women than for men.[13]

[13]The jobless rate was 0.7 percentage points higher for women than men in 1990 and 1.3 percentage points higher in 1983. Lest anyone be tempted to think it is not worth quibbling over such small differences, it should be noted that in 1990 each percentage point of female (or male) unemployment represented well over half a million people.

FULL EMPLOYMENT

It is clear from the above that the official unemployment data are not necessarily a fully accurate measure either of the waste of resources for the economy or the degree of hardship for individuals brought about by unemployment. Nonetheless, the unemployment rate undoubtedly reflects, to a considerable extent, both the degree of misallocation of resources and the economic and psychological difficulties for many of the jobless workers and their families.

At the same time, there is agreement that even an economy that has achieved full employment in the sense that demand for labor is not deficient must expect to have an unemployment rate higher than zero. There is, however, considerable disagreement about how much higher it needs to be.

Traditionally, the approach was to attempt to estimate the amount of unemployment that was seasonal and frictional and add the portion of structural unemployment that was considered inevitable. This would presumably result in the **full employment unemployment rate.** However, as the preceding discussion shows, it is both conceptually and practically difficult to draw a precise line between frictional and structural unemployment or to establish exactly how much of the latter is inevitable. Furthermore, all other types of unemployment tend to go up as demand-deficient unemployment increases. Hence, it is not surprising that not everyone agreed on a single figure, but for some time, there appeared to be a substantial consensus on 4 percent. When unemployment grew higher, many viewed it as the responsibility of government to implement measures that would increase the overall demand for labor.

As inflation became an increasingly serious problem in the late 1960s, the emphasis shifted increasingly toward controlling it, if need be, by permitting a higher rate of unemployment. In addition, opposition to government intervention also came from economists who subscribed to the new theory that traditional fiscal and monetary policy cannot be successful in the long run in reducing unemployment below its **natural rate** or can only do so at the expense of ever-accelerating inflation.[14] Accordingly, there was increasing opposition to government efforts to bring down unemployment rates.

Not all economists subscribe to these views. Some suggest that opponents of all government intervention hark back to the beliefs of theorists who, in the early part of the century, had complete confidence in markets. These early theorists argued that full employment is whatever volume of employment the economy is moving toward and that its achievement "requires of the government nothing more than neutrality, and nothing less."[15] Nonetheless, in light of increasing concerns

---

[14]This theory was proposed by Milton Friedman, "The Role of Monetary Policy," *American Economic Review* 58, no. 1 (March 1968): 1–17. For a very interesting alternative view, see Robert M. Solow, *The Labor Market as a Social Institution* (Cambridge, MA: Basil Blackwell, 1990).

[15]James Tobin, "Inflation and Unemployment," *American Economic Review* 62, no. 1 (March 1972): 1–18.

over the problem of inflation and in the face of demographic shifts in the labor force that occurred over the 1960s and 1970s, there was an increasing consensus among economists, even among advocates of government action, that the full employment target had shifted into the 5 to 6 percent range. Further changes in the last decade suggest, however, that it may again be possible to revise the target downward in the 1990s.[16] The nature of these demographic changes in labor force composition will be discussed in greater detail below.

INCIDENCE OF UNEMPLOYMENT

Although the unemployment rates of all groups in the labor market tend to move up and down with the business cycle, at any point in time there are considerable differences among some demographic groups. In contrast to differences in the unemployment rates of teenagers and adults and of minorities and whites, differences in the unemployed rates of men and women have tended to be relatively small, and, in recent years, have virtually disappeared.

Gender patterns of unemployment are nonetheless of interest, and the data in Table 8.1 and Figure 8.1 allow us to examine them in some detail over the 1948 to 1990 period. Three interesting points emerge from an examination of these data.

First, women's unemployment rates have been higher than men's in the past, and, as we have seen, this gap would have been larger and more consistent if a more comprehensive measure had been used. Second, the gender differential normally follows a cyclical pattern. The gender difference in unemployment rates has been *smallest* during *recessions* and *largest* during *prosperous times*. Third, an examination of Figure 8.1 reveals that, abstracting from cyclical variations, the size of the gap between men's and women's unemployment rates rose between the early 1960s and the late 1970s, but has virtually disappeared since then. These issues will be considered further in the next section. Here, we briefly examine the overall pattern of demographic differences in unemployment rates to place the gender difference in a larger context.

Table 8.5 shows unemployment rates by race, Hispanic origin, and age, as well as by gender for 1979, 1983, and 1990. Unemployment rates were relatively low in 1979 and 1990 and were considerably higher in 1983. In all years, unemployment rates are substantially higher for teenagers than for adults. Members of minority groups are also seen to have a considerably higher incidence of unemployment than whites. Even in 1979 and 1990, Hispanic rates are more than 1.5 times as great as those of whites; black rates are over twice as high. Female rates also were higher than male rates for each category of workers in

---

[16]Richard Krashevski, "What is so Natural about High Unemployment?" *American Economic Review* 78, no. 2 (May 1988): 289–93, cited in Ehrenberg and Smith, *Modern Labor Economics*, p. 603. See also Paul O. Flaim, "Population Changes, the Baby Boom, and the Unemployment Rate," *Monthly Labor Review* 113, no. 8 (August 1990): 3–10.

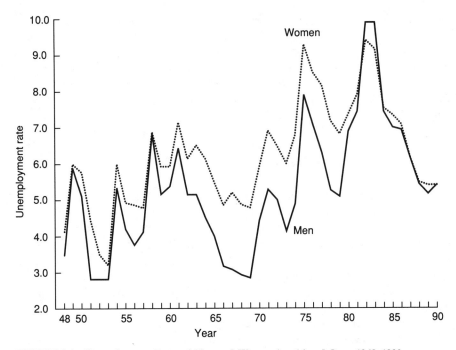

FIGURE 8.1   **Unemployment Rates of Men and Women Age 16 and Over, 1948–1990**

TABLE 8.5   **Unemployment Rates by Sex, Age, Race, and Hispanic Origin, 1979, 1983 and 1990[a]**

	1979	*1983*	*1990*
Age 16-19			
Men	15.9	23.3	16.3
Women	16.4	21.3	14.7
Age 20 and over			
Men	4.2	8.9	4.9
Women	5.7	8.1	4.9
Whites (age 16 and over)			
Men	4.5	8.8	4.8
Women	5.9	7.9	4.6
Blacks (age 16 and over)			
Men	11.4	20.3	11.8
Women	13.8	18.6	10.8
Hispanics (age 16 and over)			
Men	7.0	13.5	7.8
Women	10.3	13.8	8.3

[a] Civilian labor force.

Sources: *Employment and Training Report of the President (1982)*; *Employment and Earnings* 31, no. 1 (January 1984); and *Employment and Earnings 38, no. 1 (January 1991)*.

1979, although the differences were relatively small in comparison to the other demographic differentials. Moreover, in 1983, as the economy was moving out of a deep recession, the male rate was higher than the female rate and, in 1990, the unemployment rates for male and female adult workers were the same.

GENDER AND UNEMPLOYMENT[17]

As we have seen, there have been differences in the unemployment rates of men and women. These differences, however, have been relatively modest, given the substantial continued differences in many characteristics of male and female workers. Moreover, the extent of the gender unemployment difference has fluctuated over time and, in recent years, the differential has virtually disappeared. The discussion that follows suggests that this small "gender gap" is the net result of various factors working in opposite directions. The size of the gender difference has tended to change over time as the balance of these forces has shifted.

The first major factor affecting male and female unemployment is *labor force attachment*. On average, women are less firmly attached to the labor force than men, although the difference has been declining. (Gender differences in labor force attachment were discussed in Chapter 4). The higher labor force turnover of women in comparison to men has an ambiguous effect on their relative unemployment rates.

On the one hand, it contributes to the relatively larger proportion of entrants and reentrants among female labor force participants. The majority of women (72 percent of whites and 52 percent of nonwhites) enter the labor force without experiencing any unemployment, and the probability of such successful labor force entry is about the same for women and men.[18] Nonetheless, the higher proportion of women than men in the labor force who are entrants or reentrants is a factor that works to increase the female unemployment rate relative to the male rate. This is illustrated in Table 8.6, where we see that entrants and reentrants constitute a far larger proportion of the unemployed among women than among men.

On the other hand, as we have seen, unemployed women are considerably more likely to become discouraged workers, rather than to continue looking for work, as men tend to do. This is still true, despite women's growing labor force attachment and even though, with the growing proportion of two-earner couples,

---

[17]For interesting discussions of these issues, see Clair (Vickery) Brown, Barbara Bergmann, and Katherine Swartz, "Unemployment Rate Targets and Anti-Inflation Policy as More Women Enter the Workforce," *American Economic Review* 68, no. 2 (May 1978): 90–94; Ehrenberg, "The Demographic Structure of Unemployment Rates"; Janet L. Johnson, "Sex Differentials in Unemployment Rates: A Case for No Concern," *Journal of Political Economy* 91, no. 2 (April 1983); 283–303; and Ehrenberg and Smith, *Modern Labor Economics*, pp. 603–6.

[18]The rates for men are 68 percent for whites and 53 percent for nonwhites, as calculated from data on average monthly transition probabilities for January 1987 to December 1988 presented in Ehrenberg and Smith, *Modern Labor Economics*, p. 605.

TABLE 8.6 Percent of Unemployed Workers by Reasons for Unemployment: Men, Women, and Teenagers, 1979, 1983, 1990

	1979			1983			1990		
	AGE 20 YEARS AND OVER		AGE 16–19	AGE 20 YEARS AND OVER		AGE 16–19	AGE 20 YEARS AND OVER		AGE 16–19
	Men	Women	Both Sexes	Men	Women	Both Sexes	Men	Women	Both Sexes
Lost last job	63.6	37.4	20.5	77.7	49.5	20.2	65.0	40.8	19.0
Left last job	14.1	16.3	11.8	6.4	10.6	6.0	13.2	16.5	15.0
Reentered labor force	19.3	40.0	29.0	13.2	34.0	26.4	19.3	37.2	27.9
Never worked before	3.0	6.3	38.6	2.6	5.8	47.4	2.4	5.5	38.1
Total[a]	100.0	100.0	100.0	100.0	100.0	100.0	100.0	100.0	100.0

[a]May not add up precisely because of rounding.

Sources: *Employment and Training Report of the President*, 1982 (Washington D.C.; U.S. Government Printing Office); *Employment and Earnings* 31, no. 1 (January 1984); and *Employment and Earnings* 38, no. 1 (January 1991).

there are increasing numbers of men who could possibly drop out of the labor force. Because discouraged workers are not counted as unemployed, such behavior causes the measured unemployment of women to be lower than would otherwise be the case. For the 1987–88 period, the average proportion of unemployed workers who left the labor force was 26 percent for white women and 32 percent for black women. Among males, however, the comparable figures were only 15 percent for whites and 20 percent for blacks.[19] This greater propensity of unemployed women workers to exit the labor force probably also contributes to their lower average duration of unemployment (see Table 8.4).

The weaker labor force attachment of women helps to explain why the gap between female and male unemployment tends to narrow during economic downturns, as discouraged job seekers leave the labor force. Indeed, in the 1981–1982 recession the male unemployment rate actually exceeded the female rate. As conditions improve, previously discouraged workers enter the labor force and the gender differential in unemployment tends to widen.

Ironically, the growing labor force attachment of women may have contributed to the widening male-female unemployment differential during the 1960s and 1970s, because their probability of leaving unemployment to exit from the labor force declined during that time.[20] This appears to have counterbalanced the

[19]Ehrenberg and Smith, *Modern Labor Economics,* p. 605.

[20]Ehrenberg, "The Demographic Structure of Unemployment Rates," p. 262. See also Marianne A. Ferber and Helen M. Lowry, "Women—The New Reserve Army of the Unemployed," *Signs: The Journal of Women in Culture and Society* 1, no. 3, pt. 2 (Spring 1976): 213–32.

improvement in women's unemployment experience that would otherwise have been expected to result from their growing labor force attachment.[21]

The second major factor affecting male and female unemployment is that men and women tend to be employed in different occupations and industries. Like labor force attachment, gender differences in *occupational and industrial distribution* also have an ambiguous effect on the gender unemployment differential.

On the one hand, men are more heavily represented in blue-collar jobs and durable manufacturing, which have above average layoff and unemployment rates. Women are more likely to be employed in white-collar jobs which have lower layoff and unemployment rates, although they are also disproportionately represented in service occupations, which have unemployment rates that are above average. These gender differences in occupational and industrial distributions are one reason that a higher proportion of men than women are unemployed because they lost their last job (see Table 8.6).[22]

On the other hand, the characteristics of women's jobs (including the occupations and industries in which they tend to be employed) may indirectly raise women's unemployment rates relative to men's by increasing their propensity to quit their jobs. An indication that women's higher quit rates tend to raise their unemployment rates relative to male rates is that a higher proportion of female than of male unemployed workers have left (quit) their last job (see Table 8.6). Although some of the gender difference in quitting may be due to differences in family roles, some may be caused by the lack of substantial rewards for stable employment associated with the scarcity of career ladders in traditionally female jobs. It has, in fact, been found that holding everything else (including occupation) constant, there is no difference in male and female quit rates.[23]

Gender differences in occupational and industrial distributions help to explain why male unemployment rates increase relative to female rates during recessions. The blue-collar jobs and durable-goods manufacturing industries, which have a larger proportion of male workers, are subject to greater cyclical variations in employment. Thus, men's employment tends to decline more in downturns. As we have seen, during the 1981–82 recession, when the manufacturing sector was hit particularly hard, the male unemployment rate actually rose above the female rate.

---

[21] Specifically, over the same time period, women had a declining probability of leaving the labor force from employment. All else being equal, this aspect of their rising labor force attachment would *lower* their unemployment rates. See Ehrenberg, "The Demographic Structure of Unemployment Rates," p. 257–58.

[22] Among young workers, women were found to have lower layoff probabilities than men, on average. This remained the case even after controlling for a variety of personal and job-related characteristics. However, the occupational and industrial variables were quite aggregated and, thus, it is still possible that gender differences in detailed distributions are responsible for the observed layoff difference. See Francine D. Blau and Lawrence M. Kahn, "Causes and Consequences of Layoffs," *Economic Inquiry* 19, no. 2 (April 1981): 270–96.

[23] Francine D. Blau and Lawrence M. Kahn, "Race and Sex Differences in Quits by Young Workers," *Industrial and Labor Relations Review* 34, no. 4 (July 1981): 563–77; and W. Kip Viscusi, "Sex Differences in Worker Quitting," *The Review of Economics and Statistics* 62, no. 3 (August 1980): 388–98.

Returning to the issue of the overall gender unemployment differential, we see that male-female differences in labor force attachment and in occupational and industrial distributions have ambiguous effects. Each factor works in some respects to raise the unemployment rate of women relative to men, and in other respects to increase the unemployment rate of men relative to women. Thus, it is not surprising that the gender difference in unemployment rates has changed over time as the balance of these forces has shifted.

During the 1960s and 1970s, the net result of these opposing forces was that women's unemployment rates were higher than men's. A further contributing factor may have been that women faced increasing competition for some jobs from the growing number of young workers who were also seeking employment, as the large baby boom cohort entered the job market.[24]

Beginning in the 1980s, the gender difference in unemployment rates virtually disappeared. One factor producing this change may have been the relative decline during these years in the manufacturing industries, which disproportionately employ men, coupled with the growth of employment in the service industries, which have a high concentration of women.[25] In addition, as the baby bust cohort has entered the job market, there has been a declining number of young people competing for entry-level jobs, which are often also filled by women.

There are some indications that the balance of forces may change again in the 1990s. As the economy entered a recession in the summer of 1990, there were greater job losses in service industries than had been the case in previous downturns.[26] Some saw in this the beginnings of a retrenchment in the service sector, comparable to that which occurred in manufacturing in the 1980s. If, indeed, such a retrenchment comes to pass, it would put upward pressure on female unemployment rates. Whether the female unemployment rate actually rises above the male rate in response to this pressure will depend on a variety of other factors, including trends in female labor force attachment and whether the distribution of employment of men and women across occupations and industries continues to diverge or becomes more similar in the future.

WOMEN AND THE FULL EMPLOYMENT TARGET

As we noted above, demographic shifts in the composition of the labor force that occurred over the 1960s and 1970s led economists to revise their estimate of the

---

[24] For evidence that employers treat women and youths as substitutes in production, see James Grant and Daniel Hamermesh, "Labor-Market Competition among Youths, White Women and Others," *Review of Economics and Statistics* 63, no. 3 (August 1981): 354–60.

[25] For a discussion of these employment shifts, see Barry Bluestone and Bennett Harrison, *The Great U-Turn: Corporate Restructuring, Laissez-Faire and the Threat to America's High Wage Society* (New York: Basic Books, 1988), cited in Ehrenberg and Smith, *Modern Labor Economics*, p. 602.

[26] Sylvia Nasar, "Unexplored Territory: A Recession in Services," *New York Times*, February 3, 1991.

full employment target from 4 percent to the 5 to 6 percent range. The demographic shifts cited were the increase in the share of the labor force composed of women and youth. The share of women rose because of rising female labor force participation rates, and the proportion of youth increased as the baby boom cohort entered the job market. Because, as we have seen, both groups had relatively high unemployment rates, it was argued their rising shares of the labor force pushed the full employment unemployment rate upward.

When the two groups are aggregated, this does indeed appear to be the case, and demographic factors explain about half of the rise in the unemployment rate between 1957 and 1979.[27] However, what is frequently overlooked in such calculations is that the increased share of women explains very little of the unemployment increase; the major part is due to the rise in the proportion of youth. This is the case because, even in the 1960s and 1970s, when the female unemployment rate was higher than the male rate, the differential was relatively modest, whereas young people had considerably higher unemployment rates than adults (see Table 8.5). Thus, the increase in the women's share of the labor force, taken by itself, accounts for only 10 percent of the increase in the unemployment rate between 1957 and 1979.[28] This is only one-fifth of the total increase attributable to demographic factors.

With the aging of baby boom workers and the labor market entry of the smaller baby bust cohort, demographic factors are becoming more favorable to the attainment of lower unemployment rates. In addition, although the female share of the labor force is expected to continue to grow, this will not put upward pressure on the unemployment rate as long as women continue to have about the same unemployment rate as men.[29]

GENDER DIFFERENCES IN THE BURDEN OF UNEMPLOYMENT

Especially during the period in which the unemployment of women was higher than that of men, there was a tendency to downgrade the seriousness of women's

[27]Daniel S. Hamermesh and Albert Rees, *The Economics of Work and Pay,* 4th ed. (New York: Harper & Row, 1988), p. 414.

[28]In 1957, the unemployment rate was 4.3 percent; in 1979, the rate was 5.8 percent. If the female share of the labor force had remained at its 1957 level, the 1979 unemployment rate would have been 5.65 percent. That is, the increase in female labor force participation accounted for .15 percentage points of the 1.5 percentage point increase in the unemployment rate over the period. For further evidence that rising female labor force participation does not explain very much of the trend towards higher unemployment rates in the 1960s and 1979s, see Michael Podgursky, "Sources of Secular Increase in the Unemployment Rate, 1962–82," *Monthly Labor Review* 107, no. 7 (July 1984): 19–25. For international evidence, see Mary McCarthy and Lucrezia Reichlin, "Do Women Cause Unemployment? Evidence from Eight OECD Countries," *Review of Labour Economics and Industrial Relations* 2, no. 2 (Autumn 1985): 71–99.

[29]Flaim, "Population Changes, the Baby Boom, and the Unemployment Rate," found that demographic factors tended to drive up the unemployment rate during the 1960s and 1970s, but tended to lower it in the 1980s.

unemployment as a public policy concern.[30] A variety of reasons were offered for this position, and we consider some of the major ones here. We conclude that gender is too imprecise a measure of economic hardship to dismiss women's unemployment as less serious or less important than men's.

One argument for viewing women's unemployment as less cause for concern is that frictional factors, related to women's higher rates of labor force and job turnover, play a larger role in female than in male unemployment.[31] The fact that women's median weeks of unemployment are shorter than men's appears to suggest that they experience less difficulty in finding a job. Because frictional unemployment is viewed as being voluntary and of short duration, it is not generally perceived to be a serious problem.

But this characterization of female unemployment is not entirely accurate.[32] First, as we have previously observed, unemployed women are more likely to become discouraged and drop out of the labor force. Therefore, unemployment duration is not as reliable an indicator of their difficulty in obtaining employment as it is for men. Further, the "reason" given for a woman's unemployment may be misleading. For example, a woman may be fired from her job, become discouraged, and leave the labor force. If she returns to look for work, the reason for her unemployment is "reentry" rather than "lay off." Indeed, entrants or reentrants may be "job losers" in another sense; marital breakup has been found to be highly correlated with labor force entry for women who have become "displaced homemakers."[33]

Second, there is no direct evidence that women's higher unemployment is voluntary in the sense that we have defined—that is, that they decline offers at the prevailing market rate for their skills to a great extent than men do. On the contrary, they appear, if anything, to be too willing to curtail their search and accept a lower-paying job.[34] Finally, women's weaker labor force attachment may reflect not only their own voluntary choices but the indirect effects of labor market discrimination as well.

A second reason why women's unemployment problems are often viewed as less serious is because they supposedly do not need income as much as men do.[35]

---

[30] See, for example, the 1970 *Economic Report of the President;* Johnson, "Sex Differentials in Unemployment Rates"; and Ronald G. Ehrenberg and Robert S. Smith, *Modern Labor Economics: Theory and Public Policy,* 1st, 2nd, and 3rd eds. (Glenview, IL: Scott, Foresman, 1982, 1985, and 1988).

[31] Ehrenberg and Smith, *Modern Labor Economics,* 3rd ed., p. 614.

[32] See Nancy S. Barrett, "Women in the Job Market: Unemployment and Work Schedules," in *The Subtle Revolution: Women at Work,* ed. Ralph E. Smith (Washington, D.C.: The Urban Institute, 1979), pp. 63–98, for a good discussion of this issue.

[33] Francine D. Blau, "The Impact of the Unemployment Rate on Labor Force Entries and Exits," *Women's Changing Roles at Home and in the Job,* National Commission for Manpower Policy, Special Report No. 26 (September 1978), pp. 262–86.

[34] Steven H. Sandell, "Is the Unemployment Rate of Women Too Low? A Direct Test of the Economic Theory of Job Search," *The Review of Economics and Statistics* 62, no. 4 (November 1980): 634–38.

[35] See, for instance, Bettina Berch, *The Endless Day: The Political Economy of Women and Work* (New York: Harcourt, Brace, Jovanovich, Inc., 1982), ". . . during most economic downturns the myth that women do not 'need' to work is usually revived. . . ." p. 18.

This attitude is essentially based on the assumption that, even when a woman is employed, she is only an auxiliary wage earner.

It is true that in families where husband and wife are both employed, she tends to earn considerably less, only somewhat more than half as much as he does. This is not an insignificant contribution, though. In a good many cases, it is the wife's earnings that bring the family over the poverty line; in many more cases, they make the difference between mere adequacy and comfort. Accordingly, the loss of the woman's income results in a substantial reduction in the family's standard of living. In cases where the family has made substantial long-run commitments by buying on credit, the unanticipated loss of earnings can result in especially great hardship.

Even when the wife is a new entrant or reentrant, the family has made the decision that her labor market earnings would be more valuable than her full-time household production. Her inability to find work, thus, entails a decline in her family's welfare below what it would have been if she were employed. This is particularly serious when her labor force entry was prompted by a change in family circumstances that increased the need for her market income.

There is also a large number of women whose contribution to family income in absolutely pivotal, because they are the sole family head. Approximately 12 percent of all women in the labor market in 1990 fell into this category. They are likely to be more dependent on continuous employment than either spouse in a two-earner family.

The reasons for women's lesser need for income readily spring to mind; however, it is less often recognized that in some respects, men's unemployment is less likely to cause economic hardship than women's. Because men are job losers and full-time workers to a greater extent than women, they are more likely to be covered by unemployment insurance, which replaces at least part of their lost income. Moreover, since they are more highly unionized, they are more likely to receive supplemental unemployment benefits from their employer. (These are provided under many collective bargaining agreements.) Further, the wages of many male workers may already reflect a compensating differential due to their employment in seasonal or cyclically sensitive industries. Finally, today many men are members of two-earner families and can, thus, like many women, rely on the incomes of other family members during spells of unemployment.

On balance, it is not clear that women need income less than men. Although we have left behind the now thoroughly outdated view that women always have men to support them, and men's families are entirely composed of dependents, it will take longer to dispel the notion that women are only secondary workers. Meanwhile, the perception that women's inability to find market work is not so much of a problem is also likely to persist.

One reason for this is the assumption that a woman can always fall back on household work. Further, it has been pointed out that women's unemployment is exaggerated because those who search while working as homemakers are counted as unemployed, whereas men who search for a better job while employed are not counted.[36] Here again, however, this depiction is not likely to be entirely correct. As we pointed out earlier, the majority of women (and men) who enter the labor force experience no unemployment, just as the majority of individuals who change jobs move directly from one to the other without experiencing unemployment. Although the line between "employed" and "unemployed" search may be difficult to draw for married women who do some housework, the proportions suggest that women generally do not report themselves as unemployed until job search becomes a primary activity. Unemployed married women (like their employed counterparts) may do most of the housework in their families, but this does not seem adequate reason to consider their unemployment any less of a problem than their husband's.

In conclusion, a larger question needs to be raised about the fundamental assumption that the unemployment of men and women may be viewed differently because women are not dependent on their own income and because they can be productive in the household when they cannot find employment in the market. Not only was this view based on the premise that every woman was a member of a family that also included an adult male, but also that the division of responsibilities was necessarily a traditional one. The man needed to be employed because he had dependents; the woman did not need to be employed because she had a man to support her. The woman who was unemployed had the opportunity to take care of her household responsibilities, but a man had no such alternative. Gradual recognition that these views are no longer appropriate, and are likely to become increasingly less so, is a welcome development.

CONCLUSION

We began this chapter by defining unemployment and explaining the difference between seasonal, frictional, structural, and demand-deficient unemployment, as well as the related concepts of underemployment and discouraged workers. This was followed by a brief indication of the costs of unemployment for the economy and for the persons who are unemployed, and a discussion of the lowest level of unemployment an economy could expect to achieve and sustain. The next sections dealt with the varying incidence of unemployment in different population groups, examined differences in the extent to which various factors influence women's and men's unemployment rates, and sought to explain the substantial narrowing that has recently occurred in the gender unemployment differential. Finally, we considered the question of the extent to which unemployment is a burden for women.

We have seen that the issue of unemployment is one about which it is far easier to raise questions than to find definitive answers. There is not even

---

[36] Johnson, "Sex Differentials in Unemployment Rates."

complete agreement on a correct definition, let alone the causes of and solutions for unemployment. It is to be hoped that economists will make progress in all these respects in the future. Even with improved knowledge, however, disagreements over the relative importance of the problem of unemployment versus inflation will make solutions difficult.

SUGGESTED READINGS

EHRENBERG, RONALD G. "The Demographic Structure of Unemployment Rates and Labor Market Transition Probabilities." In *Research in Labor Economics* 3, Ronald G. Ehrenberg, ed. (Greenwich, CT: JAI Press, Inc., 1980), 241–91.

JOHNSON, JANET L. "Sex Differentials in Unemployment Rates: A Case for No Concern," *Journal of Political Economy* 91, no. 2 (April 1983): 293–303.

NATIONAL COMMISSION ON EMPLOYMENT AND UNEMPLOYMENT STATISTICS. *Counting the Labor Force,* Washington, D.C., Government Printing Office, 1979.

SANDELL, STEVEN H. "Is the Unemployment Rate of Women Too Low? A Direct Test of the Economic Theory of Job Search," *The Review of Economics and Statistics* 62, no. 4 (November 1980): 634–38.

SOLOW, ROBERT M. *The Labor Market as a Social Institution.* Cambridge, MA: Basil Blackwell, 1990.

BROWN, (VICKERY) CLAIR, BARBARA BERGMANN, and KATHERINE SWARTZ. "Unemployment Rate Targets and Anti-Inflation Policy as More Women Enter the Workforce," *American Economic Review* 68, no. 2 (May 1978): 90–94.

Chapter 9

CHANGING
WORK ROLES
AND THE FAMILY

In earlier chapters, we discussed the family as an economic institution and the allocation of time of husband and wife between the household and the labor market. We now turn our attention to the impact a woman's employment has on her family. The typical family today is one where both spouses participate in the labor force, at least for part of their married life; this topic, therefore, is of considerable importance. There is also a growing proportion of families where the woman is the single head of the household and the sole wage-earner. Such units have particular problems, because there is only one adult in the family and because that adult is a woman. Therefore, we devote special attention to them.

There is one basic difference between our approach here and in Chapter 4. There we accepted marital status and fertility as given, exogenous to our models, and focused on the effects of these factors on women's labor force participation. In this chapter, we turn the tables and examine the impact that women's labor force participation has on marriage, number of children, and the well-being of family members.

The first sections of this chapter deal with family formation, fertility, divorce, and the relationship of these to women's labor force participation.[1] After that, we first examine how much the wife contributes to family earnings. Secondly, we review what is known about the impact of women's work on the well-being and satisfaction of various members of the family. Finally, we conclude by considering the serious problems faced by the growing number of female-headed families.

MARRIAGE

What would be the expected effect of women's increased labor force participation on family formation? From the viewpoint of neoclassical economics, the determining factor in the marriage decision would be whether the benefits exceed the costs. Thus, the question is what effect rising female labor force participation has had on this cost/benefit calculus—do more or fewer couples find it in their economic self-interest to marry?

The answer to this question is not obvious from a theoretical point of view. That is, there are forces operating both to reduce and to increase the benefits of marriage, and their net effect is uncertain. The issue of costs is a bit more difficult to speculate about intelligently, but there may have been changes here as well. We first consider these theoretical issues and then review the empirical evidence.

On the one hand, women's increased opportunities for earning their own livelihood may have a negative effect on their incentives to marry. Market work presents a woman with a viable alternative to marriage, making it economically feasible to postpone or altogether forgo such a commitment. One may speculate that it has become more socially acceptable to do so as well.

Women's increased tendency to work outside the home may have reduced some of the economic benefits to marriage accruing to the couple as well. It may be recalled from Chapter 3 that one of the gains to marriage is that it makes possible the specialization and exchange that may potentially increase the couple's productivity and economic well-being. In general, the more the comparative advantage in producing home and market goods *differs* between the two partners, the larger the potential gain, for each may then specialize in his or her area of higher relative productivity. As women have been acquiring more market-oriented education and training, their market productivity has been rising relative to their home productivity. The traditional specialization of the husband in wage-earning and of the wife in

---

[1] Seminal work by neoclassical economists on the economics of the family was first done by Gary S. Becker and has been summarized by him in *A Treatise on the Family* (Cambridge, MA: Harvard University Press, 1991). A great deal of interesting work by some of the best-known researchers in this area is contained in *Economics of the Family,* a conference report of the National Bureau of Economic Research, ed. Theodore W. Schultz (Chicago: University of Chicago Press, 1974). Glenna Spitze, "Women's Employment and Family Relations: A Review," *Journal of Marriage and Family,* 50, no. 3 (Aug. 1988) provides a comprehensive survey of the literature on marriage, fertility, and divorce.

homemaking has become increasingly less advantageous, and, in general, the gains to marriage from specialization are reduced.[2]

On the other hand, as we also pointed out earlier, specialization and exchange is not the only economic benefit to marriage. Some of the other benefits need not be affected one way or the other by women's increased labor force participation. Such is the case for economies of scale and the consumption of public goods. Other benefits may be increased. For example, the externalities of joint consumption may be enhanced if an employed wife and her husband have more similar tastes. And, to the extent that the tastes of two-earner couples are more similar than those of traditional couples, potential disagreements over the combination of commodities to consume would be reduced.

Moreover, a working woman's income can have a positive effect on her propensity to marry because she can supplement her husband's earnings. When a traditional marriage is planned, it cannot occur unless or until the potential husband earns enough income to "support" his wife. A working woman's income may also make her a more attractive partner, at least to a man who values that income more than the services of a full-time homemaker.

With respect to the costs of marriage, the greater acceptability of market work for married women may have reduced these costs for women. Women today no longer choose between employment on the one hand or marriage on the other. Although many women continue to accommodate their paid work to what are still perceived to be their household responsibilities, they are far less likely than in the past to cut short their education or leave the labor market at the time they get married.

Only empirical evidence can show what the balance of these forces appears to be. The large increase in the proportion of single women between 1970 and 1989, from 35.8 percent to 62.5 percent for those between ages 20 and 24 and from 10.5 percent to 29.4 percent for those between ages 25 to 29, suggests that for relatively young people, the propensity to marry has declined. At the same time, the proportion of those 40 years of age or older who had never married actually fell slightly from 6.2 percent in 1970 to 5.2 percent in 1989.[3]

It appears that young women with increasingly acceptable alternatives are less likely to rush into marriage early on but that most of them do opt for it eventually. Even so, it is projected that the proportion of people who never marry in their lifetime, in recent years about 5 percent, may increase to perhaps 10 percent, as this large proportion of young singles moves through the life cycle.

Economic considerations are not the only ones that play a role in these demographic changes. One factor that undoubtedly has contributed to the growing

---

[2]The gains from specialization and exchange are not entirely eliminated unless there is no difference at all in comparative advantage between the two members of the couple.

[3]Bureau of the Census, *Marital Status and Living Arrangements: March 1989,* Current Population Report Series P-20, no. 445 (May 1989). The future projection given below was developed by Steve W. Rawlings of the Census Bureau and cited in Margot Slade, "Siblings: Now You Can't Live With Them or Without Them," *New York Times,* July 25, 1991, p. B1.

number of young people who are not married is the change in attitude toward sex outside of marriage and the corresponding increase in cohabitation. The really dramatic rise occurred after 1970. At that time, 523,000 unmarried couples were living together. This figure increased to 1,137,000 by 1978 and 2,764,000 in 1989.[4]

By sharing housekeeping, informal living arrangements provide the same possibility for economies of scale as marriage does, though they certainly do not provide the same legal guarantees for a partner who specializes in homemaking and forgoes the opportunity to maintain and increase labor market skills. But this is less important, as fewer partnerships are based on the husband's specializing in market work and the wife's specializing completely in housework, and the proportion of two-earner couples continues to grow. Furthermore, the status of a woman no longer seems to be solely determined by her marriage but rather is enhanced by her own educational and occupational accomplishments. Even so, cohabitation does not, for the most part, appear to be a substitute for marriage but, rather, a prelude to marriage or remarriage.[5]

The high rate of remarriage is another indication that, despite all the changes, marriage is still the cornerstone of American life. Most people who get divorced eventually remarry, although remarriage rates declined in the 1970s and 1980s. This recent downward trend may be due to an increase in cohabitation after marital dissolution.[6]

FERTILITY

We have seen that neoclassical economic theory contributes to our understanding of marriage. Similarly, it helps to shed light on the decision of whether to have children, how many to have, and to what extent scarce resources should be allocated to them. To make such decisions rationally, one must weigh costs against benefits.

The costs of raising children include more than the expenses incurred in feeding, clothing, housing, and educating them, substantial though these have become. A very large part of total costs consists of the time parents devote to childrearing, for children require a great deal of personal attention. Even when some child care is purchased, the final responsibility for finding suitable caretakers, taking care of emergencies, and providing affection and stability rests with the parents, most often the mother. The time and energy she devotes to these purposes could

---

[4]Data for the earlier years are from Paul C. Glick and Graham B. Spanier, "Married and Unmarried Cohabitation in the United States," *Journal of Marriage and Family* 4, no. 1 (February 1980): 19–30; the figure for 1989 is from *Marital Status and Living Arrangements: March 1989*, Bureau of the Census, Current Population Reports Series P-20, no. 445 (May 1989).

[5]In some instances, cohabitation also follows the termination of marriage among the elderly. Most likely this is spurred on by social security rules that would often severly reduce the incomes of such couples if they married.

[6]Andrew Cherlin, "Recent Changes in American Fertility, Marriage and Divorce." *Annals, AAPSS,* 510 (July 1990): 145–54.

otherwise be used to get more education or training for herself, to earn money, or to enjoy leisure. Giving up some or all of these constitutes the opportunity cost of rearing children.

In view of these considerations, women's growing potential for market earnings increases the opportunity cost of children and would, accordingly, be expected to have a negative substitution effect. This may well be one of the main determinants of fertility. At the same time, however, greater earnings would also be expected to have a positive income effect, since the family can now afford more children in terms of the money-costs associated with them. So long as fathers are not expected to give up much of their time for child care, their higher earnings would be expected to have such a positive effect.[7] For women, on the other hand, the either/or choice between labor force participation and children is still common enough that the substitution effect is likely to predominate.

As we have seen in Chapter 4, far more mothers of young children are employed now, but the proportion of full-time homemakers is nonetheless higher among these mothers than for other women. This has been found to be especially true for the first two years of a child's life. Also, mothers of preschoolers who are in the labor force are more likely to work part-time. Further, those who work full-time nonetheless spend less time on the job and tend to make less progress on the job.[8] This is as would be expected in terms of the economic theory of the family, for the value of the woman's contribution in the home is high relative to her (potential) market earnings during this period. Thus, young children continue to be an impediment to a woman working outside the home.

At the same time, there is also reason to believe that women's work plans influence their intended childbearing.[9] Women in the labor force, and particularly those who are highly educated and tend to have a stronger career orientation, have fewer children.[10] Accordingly, families have become smaller as women's

---

[7] The importance of both the substitution and income effect has been confirmed by research, such as William P. Butz and Michael P. Ward, "The Emergence of Countercyclical U.S. Fertility," *American Economic Review* 69, no. 3 (June 1979): 318–28. Another study, Michael Hout, "The Determinants of Marital Fertility in the United States, 1968–70, Inferences from a Dynamic Model," *Demography* 15, no. 2 (May 1978): 139–60, suggests that women's employment responds to the presence of children in the short run but that the total number of children a family has is determined by the women's employment status.

[8] Gus W. Haggstrom, Linda J. Waite, David E. Kanouse, and Thomas J. Blaschke, *Changes in the Lifestyles of New Parents* (Santa Monica, CA: Rand, 1984).

[9] Two studies that establish this relationship are Linda J. Waite and Ross M. Stolzenberg, "Intended Childbearing and Labor Force Participation of Young Women: Insights from Nonrecursive Models," *American Sociological Review* 41, no. 2 (April 1976): 235–52; and Michael Hout, "The Determinants of Marital Fertility in the United States, 1968–70."

[10] Kristin A Moore and Sandra L. Hofferth, "Women and Their Children," in *The Subtle Revolution*, Ralph Smith, ed. (Washington, D.C.: The Urban Institute, 1979), pp. 128–32. Evidence on very highly educated women is found in Marianne A. Ferber and Betty Kordick, "Sex Differentials in Earnings of Ph.D.'s," *Industrial and Labor Relations Review* 31, no. 2 (January 1978): 227–38. McKinley

education and labor force participation has been increasing. The growing demand for "higher-quality" children, with better health and more education, is related to rising incomes and would reinforce this effect.[11]

Table 9.1 shows the fertility rate since the 1940s. It declined sharply between the baby boom years of the 1950s, when fertility averaged more than three children per woman, and the late 1970s, when fertility averaged 1.8 children per woman.[12] It has risen somewhat since then. The sharp drop in the number of children in the early 1960s coincides with the rapid increase in the labor force participation rate of young women, already discussed in Chapter 4. It is unlikely that the modest rise in fertility during the 1980s portends further large increases. It was probably largely caused by the fact that some women who apparently chose not to have children earlier had them at a later age,[13] whereas younger couples may have decided not to wait so long to start a family when there had been a great deal of publicity about the fertility problems of older couples. Even with this increase, the fertility rate of 1.9 children per woman in 1988 remained well below the replacement level of 2.1.

As mentioned earlier, the long downward trend can be explained in part by the higher cost of dropping out of the labor force among women with stronger labor force attachment. One may also speculate that such women are inclined to hold less traditional jobs and are more likely to find their work absorbing and fulfilling. It should be noted, however, that the recent rise in the birthrate, albeit slight, helps to confirm that there is scant reason to expect a substantial increase in childlessness. So does the fact that the percent of married women who report that they do not intend to have any children continues to be quite modest, not exceeding 10 percent, except among the highly educated.

Nonetheless, since it is highly educated and career-oriented women who tend to have the fewest children, or even none, and both level of education and career orientation are continuing to increase, it may be that the long downward trend in family size will once again resume. There are those who predict that as young women continue to find the costs of childbearing increasingly unattractive, and alternative uses of their time and energy increasingly inviting, there will be a further decline in birthrates.[14]

L. Blackburn, David E. Bloom, and David Neumark ("Fertility Timing, Wages and Human Capital," National Bureau of Economic Research, Inc., Working Paper no. 3422, 1990) also found that higher potential earnings cause women to have their first child later.

[11]Becker, *A Treatise on the Family.*

[12]Even so, the proportion of ever married women who are childless has not risen very much: from 15.0 percent in 1960 to 18.8 percent in 1980 and 19.6 percent in 1988 (Bureau of the Census, Statistical Abstract, 1990).

[13]Blackburn et al., "Fertility Timing, Wages and Human Capital," suggest that this was associated with women's greater investment in human capital.

[14]See, for instance, Joan A. Huber and Glenna Spitze, *Sex Stratification, Children, Housework and Jobs* (New York: Academic Press, 1983).

TABLE 9.1   Total Fertility Rates, 1940–1988

Year	Total Fertility Rate[a]
1940–44	2523
1945–49	2985
1950–54	3337
1955–59	3690
1960–64	3449
1965–69	2622
1970–74	2094
1975–79	1774
1980	1840
1985	1843
1988	1932

[a] The number of births that a cohort of 1,000 women would have if they experienced the age-specific birth rates occurring in the current year, throughout their childbearing years.

Source: Department of Commerce, Bureau of the Census, *Statistical Abstract*, 1984, 1990; U.S. Department of Health and Human Services, *Monthly Vital Statistics*, 39, no. 4 Supplement (August 1990).

Such a trend would also be reinforced by increasing recognition that children cannot be viewed as "investment goods" in modern societies. Not only are the costs of raising and educating them very high, but children have increasingly been replaced by such institutional arrangements as insurance, pensions, and social security as providers of financial support for the elderly. On the other hand, the attraction of children as "consumer goods" may surely be expected to continue, possibly even to increase as fathers become better acquainted with them. Further, to the extent that fathers undertake a larger share of child care and organized child care becomes more readily available, the burden on young women would be reduced. In this case, fertility may not decline further and could even increase somewhat. Large increases in fertility are unlikely, however, in light of women's increasing commitment to market work.

DIVORCE

Two people who marry in anticipation of improving their well-being may nonetheless find that one or both of them later feel they would be better off if they terminated their relationship. This can occur because things do not always work out as anticipated at the time the initial decision is made. It is all the more likely to happen during a period when long-accepted standards and norms are rapidly changing. If, however, only one partner wants a divorce, it may be necessary to find a way to get the other partner to agree.

When considering the effect of women's labor force participation on marital dissolution, we are confronted once again by a complex situation. On the one hand, the great interdependence of the breadwinner husband and the homemaker wife clearly deters divorce. The wife earns no money and needs her husband's income to buy whatever she requires of market goods and services. The husband has little time and no training for household tasks and needs the wife to look after home and children. As this traditional division of labor breaks down, the economic incentives for remaining married are reduced. Also, the stress of overcommitment and possible role conflict in the two-earner family may place additional strains on a marriage.

On the other hand, when the wife works, couples enjoy to an equal, or even greater, extent the other benefits of marriage that we have discussed—economies of scale, public goods, joint consumption, and so on. Moreover, though such couples have less time, they have more money than those with only one paycheck. Not only does their higher income permit them to consume more of the market goods and services that they desire, it also presumably reduces at least one area of potential stress and disagreement—conflicts over allocating scarce dollars. Their higher income also gives them the opportunity to accumulate more wealth. This tends to inhibit marital dissolution because of the problems that are often encountered in dividing illiquid assets. Furthermore, sharing both market work and housework might be expected to create greater understanding and empathy between husband and wife.

In fact, as shown in Table 9.2, the divorce rate in the United States rose from 0.9 per 1,000 population in 1910 to 2.2 in 1960 and then increased very sharply to 5.2 in 1980. Since then, it has declined somewhat to 4.8 in 1988. Nonetheless, at current rates, it is estimated that about one-half of all marriages may end in divorce.[15] Accordingly, the chances of a child living in the same family until he or she establishes an independent household, and the chances of marrying only once in a lifetime, have been rapidly decreasing.[16]

Because of the conflicting considerations discussed above, it is not clear how the existing evidence of a rising divorce rate should be interpreted or what future developments are likely to be. Although, as we pointed out earlier, most people continue to live in families most of the time, there has been a radical change in family stability. This growing trend is usually regarded both as a symptom and a cause of society's malaise, for it is widely believed that two people who live together "forever after" are most likely to be happy and that children raised by

---

[15]Cherlin, "Recent Changes in American Fertility, Marriage and Divorce." Projections are, however, necessarily hazardous, because they are based on assumptions about future rather than merely past and present behavior. For each cohort, we only know their actual divorce rate up to their present age. Quite different conclusions may be reached about the proportion of their marriages that will eventually break up depending on projections for the future. See Robert Schoen, William L. Urton, Karen Woodrow, and John Bay, "Marriage and Divorce in 20th Century American Cohorts," *Demography*, 22, no. 1 (February 1985): 101–14.

[16]Suzanne M. Bianchi, "America's Children: Mixed Prospects," *Population Bulletin*, 45, no. 1 (1990).

TABLE 9.2 Divorce Rate per 1000 Population, 1910–1988

Year	Divorce Rate
1910	0.9
1920	1.6
1930	1.6
1940	2.0
1950	2.6
1960	2.2
1970	3.5
1980	5.2
1988	4.8

Source: U.S. Department of Commerce, Bureau of the Census, *Statistical Abtract*, 1984, 1990.

such a couple are most likely to grow up well-adjusted and successful.[17] There can, indeed, be no doubt that the breakup of a marriage, which generally begins with high hopes and excellent intentions, is at best sad and regrettable and often entails recrimination and bitterness. To the extent that women's work outside the home is associated with the high divorce rate, it may, therefore, have some undesirable effects.

This is, however, only one side of the story. First, empirical evidence on whether wives' employment tends to raise the divorce rate is rather mixed.[18] Thus, although rising labor force participation rates of married women over time have been associated with rising divorce rates, it has not been conclusively established that the former has caused the latter. However, even if this is to some extent the case, one might argue that similar life-styles of husbands and wives enhance the quality of some marriages, even if, by reducing interdependence, they facilitate the breakup of unsatisfactory ones. In such instances, divorce may be preferable to an unhappy marriage.

In terms of the future, it seems probable that any positive impact of married women's labor force participation on the divorce rate should diminish. First, strains are likely to be greatest when tradition still has a strong grip and is in conflict with existing reality. Once women and men have had the opportunity to adjust to new standards and norms, there should be fewer surprises and thus

[17]Interestingly, the increase in the proportion of children living in one-parent homes because of the rapid rise in the divorce rate has been at least partially offset by the decline in early deaths. The extent to which this is true can be gauged from the fact that among ever-married women less than 45 years old, the group most likely to have children still at home, 6.1 percent were widowed and 0.8 percent were divorced in 1890, whereas in 1989, only 1.9 percent were widowed, but 18.6 percent were divorced.

[18]A good summary of studies on both sides of this issue can be found in Sandra L. Hofferth and Kristin A. Moore. "Women's Employment and Marriage," in *The Subtle Revolution,* Ralph E. Smith, ed., Chapter 4. For an interesting paper that gives strong support to the hypothesis that an increase in women's wages causes a higher divorce rate, see Robert T. Michael, "Why did the U.S. Divorce Rate Double Within a Decade?" *Research in Population Economics,* 6 (1988): 367–99.

fewer problems. Second, the decreasing economic and social pressures to marry associated with women's rising labor force participation have led young people to postpone marriage. This should promote marital stability in that couples who get married at older ages are less likely to break up.[19] The evidence that the divorce rate began to level off in the early 1980s and has declined a bit since would tend to support such speculations. It may even decline somewhat more in the future, although it is not likely to fall to the levels that prevailed when husbands and wives were highly economically dependent on each other and when social attitudes towards divorce were extremely negative.

Whatever the pros and cons of divorce, it is clear that when it does occur, it is the full-time homemaker, along with her children, who is particularly vulnerable. She has been dependent on her husband not only for money income but also for her social status and even, at times, for much of her circle of friends. Because of their growing numbers, and the considerable attention they have been receiving in policy discussions, the plight of such female-headed families will be discussed at some length later in this chapter.[20] At the same time, it should not be forgotten that the proportion of families that do rather well, because they have two earners has also been increasing.

WIFE'S CONTRIBUTIONS TO EARNINGS

As we have seen in Chapter 4, by the late 1980s, 57 percent of all married women with husbands present were working for pay. The labor force participation rate for black women in this category was as high as 66 percent.

The earnings of these married women make a substantial contribution to the money income of their families. Between 1969 and 1985, average real income rose by 17 percent for white households with employed wives, and 38 percent for similar black households. During the same period, income for married couple households where the wife did not work for pay increased only 7 percent and 6 percent, respectively.[21] Having an employed wife increased family income by an average of 42 percent among whites and by more than two-thirds (67 percent) among blacks.[22]

---

[19] Alan Booth and Lynn White, "Thinking About Divorce," *Journal of Marriage and Family* 42, no. 3 (August 1980): 605–16.

[20] It is widely thought that no fault divorce legislation, increasingly widespread in recent times, has further contributed to financial settlements that favor the husband over the wife. See, for example, Lenore Weitzman, *The Divorce Revolution: The Unexpected Social and Economic Consequences for Women and Children in America* (New York: Free Press, 1985).

[21] These statistics and those that follow in this section are from Rebecca M. Blank, "Women's Paid Work, Household Income, and Household Well-Being," in *The American Woman 1988–89: A Status Report,* Sara E. Rix, ed. (New York: W. W. Norton, 1988), pp. 123–61.

[22] The figures are for nonelderly married couples in 1985. The average contribution of the wife to family income was 30 percent among whites and 40 percent among blacks.

The earnings of married women serve to bring a considerable number of families out of poverty status.[23] In many other instances, they make the difference between a barely adequate and a comfortable living. At the other end of the scale, married couples with employed wives were almost twice as likely as households overall to be in the top fifth of the income distribution. Even if we take into account the increased expenses of two-earner households, the loss of the services of the full-time homemaker, and the fact that such families may well be "time-poor,"[24] their standard of living is likely to be much improved.

As discussed earlier, a woman is expected to enter the labor market when the value of her earnings exceeds the value of her time at home. Therefore, it would appear that the well-being of her family must be increased when she decides to work for pay, presumably in response either to increased wages or to a decline in the value of her time at home. This approach, however, ignores the possibility that any change may improve the situation for some members of the family but could cause others to be worse off. We therefore turn to a more detailed examination of the impact of women's growing labor force participation on various family members.

SATISFACTION WITHIN THE FAMILY

Considerable work has been done to learn about the impact of women's labor force participation on their own and their husband's satisfaction with various aspects of life and on the development of their children. It is not easy to summarize the results of these studies concisely; the issues involved are very complex and findings are not always consistent.[25] One of the unresolved issues is the extent to which reporting on this sensitive subject is reliable.[26]

How the woman herself feels about taking a job outside the home depends on such considerations as the nature of the work; her health and energy level;

[23]It has been estimated that the presence of working wives decreases the poverty rate by 35 percent among white married couples, 39 percent among blacks, and 26 percent among Hispanics.

[24]This term was first introduced into the literature by Clair (Vickery) Brown, "The Time-Poor: A New Look at Poverty," *Journal of Human Resources* 12, no. 1 (Winter 1977): 27–48. The issue is also discussed in Clair (Vickery) Brown, "Women's Economic Contribution to the Family," in *The Subtle Revolution,* Smith, ed., pp. 159–200.

[25]Most of the research on these subjects has been done by psychologists and sociologists. Some of the best-known among these studies are Ronald J. Burke and Tamara Weir, "Relationship of Wives' Employment Status to Husband, Wife and Pair Satisfaction and Performance," *Journal of Marriage and Family* 38, no. 2 (May 1976): 278–87; Myra M. Ferree, "Working Class Jobs: Housework and Paid Work as Sources of Satisfaction," *Social Problems* 23, no. 4 (Spring 1976): 431–41; Francis I. Nye and Lois W. Hoffman, *The Employed Mother in America* (Chicago: Rand McNally, 1963); Glenna Spitze, "Women's Employment and Family Relations: A Review."

[26]Frank M. Andrews and Stephen B. Withey, *Social Indicators of Well-Being: Americans' Perceptions of Life Quality* (New York: Plenum Press, 1976) report that fully 60 percent of respondents in their survey claimed they were "delighted" with their children, 58 percent with their spouse, and 50 percent with their marriage, but only 22 percent were equally positive to all three combined. The authors suggest as one possible explanation that people are likely to be reluctant to express reservations about any individuals in their family but more willing to do so in response to more general questions.

supportiveness of her coworkers, friends, and family; the number and ages of her children; and the availability of services to replace those of the homemaker. The husband's attitude is likely to be influenced by many of the same factors but will be particularly affected by the extent to which his job requires his wife's involvement, his own taste for housework and leisure, and perhaps most of all, whether he wants a partner whose independence and accomplishments he can respect or a helpmate who devotes herself to creating a warm and relaxed home for him. The children's well-being is likely to depend on the extent to which the mother's work interferes with their demands on her time and energy, number of siblings, to what extent the father and perhaps other close relatives spend time with them, whether their friends' mothers are also employed, and last, but by no means least, the quality of the alternative arrangements that are made for their care.

Given the involvement of a number of individuals and a multitude of variables, it would be expected that the impact of the woman's labor force participation on the family will be quite different, depending on the context of various personalities, family situations, and social environments. In determining the nature of this impact, there are also such methodological problems as possible selection bias. For instance, women who are particularly family-centered are probably more inclined to become full-time homemakers, whereas those who have less patience with children and less tolerance for housework and are more interested in a career are likely to enter the labor market. Given all these complications, the results of different studies can be inconclusive and even contradictory. Hence, there is good reason to avoid hasty conclusions.

Wife

It has generally been found that employed women enjoy better physical and mental health, though the effect differs, depending on other circumstances. They also have higher self-esteem, and on the average live longer, than those who do not work for pay. This may show that the additional stimulation and rewards associated with market work have a positive effect but could in part also be the result of stronger, more confident women entering the labor force to begin with.

The findings on the relationship between women's employment and marital satisfaction have been mixed, some indicating it is positive, others suggesting it is negative, but most recent studies based on large national samples conclude that it is neutral.[27] In part, the outcome depends on such important factors as whether the woman works by choice or necessity, whether she is employed full-time or part-time, how well educated she is, what type of job she has, and how much housework the husband does. Also, the issue of selection bias arises once again. In this instance, it

---

[27]Sociologists, rather than economists, have done research on these questions. Much of the best-known work is summarized in Hofferth and Moore, "Women's Employment and Marriage," and Spitze, "Women's Employment and Family Relations: A Review."

may be negative, because those who have higher ambitions and more demanding standards as well as those who are specifically dissatisfied with their marriage are most likely to work for pay, all else being equal.

To the extent that any conclusion may be drawn, it appears that when husband and wife are both employed, they tend to have more common concerns and more understanding of each other's problems, but also that mothers, especially those working full-time, frequently complain of being overcommitted and experience more anxiety and guilt. Regrettably, we have no evidence how much of this is caused by societal pressures. At the same time, employed women also enjoy their children more. It is not farfetched to ascribe the latter to diminishing utility of additional time spent with children. As was suggested in Chapter 3, even the most pleasurable activity palls when a great deal of time is devoted to it, and what may at first be a minor nuisance is likely to become a major annoyance over a long period. Hence, the quality of time may well be quite different for a parent who looks forward to spending time with his or her children on evenings and weekends than one who spends more or less seven days a week with them. Last, it is also interesting to note that education is positively related to satisfaction with paid work but negatively related to satisfaction with homemaking. Thus, the picture for working women is not all rosy, but the pluses appear to outweigh the minuses for most of them.

This optimistic view has not, however, gone unchallenged. There are those who point out that women have increased their labor force participation without correspondingly reducing the amount of housework they do, and that men continue to do little housework. They further argue that this increase in workload, coupled with the substantial rise in the proportion of women who support themselves and often their children as well, has resulted in a decline in the ratio of the estimated income per hour worked for women as compared to men.[28] In fact, however, as we saw in Chapter 3, the data in the United Nations report suggest that the total amount of market work plus housework done by men and women remained virtually unchanged from the mid-1960s to the mid-1980s.

Other questions also need to be raised about the conclusion that women's overall well-being has declined as their labor force participation has risen. It tacitly assumes that the benefits of family income are shared equally among spouses, regardless of who is the wage earner. As discussed previously, this is hardly realistic. Also, the possibility that many women may enjoy doing more market work and less housework is not considered. Most important, however, the fact that women who have to support themselves and their family would be even worse off

---

[28]Most notably this is true of Victor R. Fuchs, "His and Hers: Gender Differences in Work and Income, 1959–1979," *Journal of Labor Economics,* 4, no. 3 (July 1986): S245–S272; and Victor R. Fuchs, *Women's Quest for Economic Equality* (Cambridge, MA: Harvard University Press, 1988). Rena L. Repetti, Karen A. Matthews, and Ingrid Waldron, "Employment and Women's Health," *American Psychologist,* 44, no. 11 (November 1989): 1394–1401, conclude that on average, employment has positive effects on women's health, but they also point out that heavy family demands and low control appear to increase health risks.

COPING WITH HOME AND JOB RESPONSIBILITIES:
A MANAGERIAL APPROACH

Although combining career and family is not easy, growing numbers of women are finding that the benefits outweigh the costs. In this column from the *Wall Street Journal,** a "managerial approach" to coping with family responsibilities is advocated—and one need not be a professional manager to benefit from the advice offered. Although it is assumed in this piece that the working mother will hire a nanny, other, more affordable arrangements, such as organized day-care centers, can provide the quality and reliability advocated.

A September article in this paper described a working mother—a major account executive for an advertising firm—who almost missed an important meeting because she had to dash out into the snow to buy diapers for her child. Her housekeeper called and said they had run out. The mother left the office, spent $20 on cab fare for a $10 box of diapers and arrived back at the office feeling as if she'd "been to California and back."

The tone of the article was summed up by an "expert" who was quoted as saying that most women find combining career and family an impossible situation. "I'm not sure," said the expert, "how any woman can avoid being overwhelmed. Simply dropping out may be the only alternative."

Maybe. But there are many women with children doing very well out there in law firms, accounting offices, government and other professional capacities. Of course it is difficult for a professional woman to manage a successful career and be a mother. But women in management have an edge they might not be using to the full advantage: They can put their management skills to use in managing their lives as working mothers.

Taking a managerial approach to home life doesn't mean you have to haul in McKinsey & Co. to do a work-flow study on your kids. And it certainly isn't recommending a tough-cookie approach to home and hearth. Far from being callous, an effective management approach to childrearing is the most loving, caring and respectful course a professional woman can take. When arrangements are slapdash, when no one knows what to do next, when Mommy is too torn and crazed to be effective as an investment banker or as a mother, then everyone suffers.

If the woman who almost missed her meeting had paid more attention to managing her inventory (diapers) and to hiring an employee who could take expected initiative (going out and buying the diapers), she probably would not have ended up in such a frazzled state.

A three-step management approach is required for the effective manager-mother:

1. *A feasibility study.* Some jobs in some companies may not be compatible with family life. Sixty-hour weeks, a two-hour commute and a heavy travel schedule don't leave much time for kids. (Of course, this is true for men as well as women.)

*Claudia P. Feurey, "Manager's Journal: Kids Plus Careers Needn't Keep Mom in Arrears," *Wall Street Journal,* June 4, 1984, p. 20. Reprinted by permission of the *Wall Street Journal,* ©Dow Jones & Company, Inc. (1984). All rights reserved.

Does the culture of your organization support families? Management attitudes can make or break a company as a place where women can have both families and careers. While management should not be expected to go out of its way to accommodate unreasonable demands, it is generally in a company's interest to ease the transition when its employees become parents.

2. *Making your decision and setting your priorities*. If you decide you can work, do you still want to? They may not get into this at Wharton, but if you have other sources of income, you do not have to work at a particular job. There is no disgrace in not working or in working part time and devoting the rest of your time to family and home.

If you decide to go to work, however, get your priorities straight. As a managerial mother, you may not be able to keep up your previous social life, be den mother to the Cub Scouts or see every play that comes to town. If family and career come first, carefully evaluate the costs and benefits of other claims on your time.

3. *Implementation*. The next step is organizing your life so that you can combine home, children and career with the minimum strain.

- Decide what your child-care needs are. If your job involves late nights, early meetings or extensive travel, then be sure your husband or your help can cover for you during these times. Or make standing arrangements with reliable sources.
- Bite the bullet and pay for the best child care you can afford. It is astonishing how many high-income families try to make do with ad hoc arrangements or bottom-of-the-barrel help. Would you trust the person you hire to deal with an emergency or get a sick child to the doctor? If not, you have made a mistake. Hire the best person you can afford, treat her well and let her do the job.
- Have a reliable temporary agency or nurses' registry on call for those days the nanny is ill. These agencies exist in virtually every community and may be a lot less hassle than getting your mother to come over on a snowy Tuesday.
- Ferret out every neighborhood store that delivers and set up local charge accounts at these stores.
- Learn to appreciate the virtues of take out food.

Even with the most sophisticated management approach, there will be times when your husband is out of town, when your three-year-old has thrown up on your best suit and you are late for work. It is easy to succumb to playing the part of the working heroine, a martyr for the movement. When this happens, it is wise to think of the many, many women who are working — and often raising their kids alone — without the privileges and the psychic and financial rewards of management positions. At these times, look at your family, look at your accomplishments and count your blessings . . . .

---

if they had not been in the labor market before is ignored. In light of all these considerations, we conclude that, on balance, women are likely to be better off as a result of their higher labor force participation, even though not as much as one might wish.

This does not mean that there are no problems. The evidence suggests that the number of hours full-time homemakers work has declined considerably. At the same time, the persistently unequal distribution of homemaking responsibilities when both spouses are employed results in a heavy burden for employed women, particularly for those who are employed full-time and must also care for children or infirm family members. Further, as we shall see later in this chapter, women who are heads of families have a disproportionate share of difficulties.

Husband

The effects of the wife's employment on the husband have been found to be, overall, less favorable.[29] A number of studies report less marital satisfaction, less physical and mental well-being, and even greater job pressures. These negative effects are especially strong for men in the lower class, though less so when the wife works by choice or works less than full-time. Such results seem rather puzzling, because we know the husband shares in the benefits of additional income, has more opportunity to change jobs (at least within the same geographic region), and may find that an employed spouse is a more interesting companion, whereas the wife normally carries the main burden of the additional work. But there are a number of plausible explanations.

Once again, the likelihood of a negative selection bias exists, because wives may be especially likely to enter the labor market when the marriage is not satisfactory. Furthermore, wives of unsuccessful husbands are more likely to seek to supplement family income. Beyond that, it is widely accepted that there are still husbands who perceive the shift to the two-earner family as a loss of status and power for themselves and view any increase in household responsibilities as demeaning and as interfering with their work. They see recent changes as eroding their secure position and even as threatening their masculinity. The wife, on the other hand, believes she is expanding her sphere, as well as increasing her influence and her security.

Several studies confirm that the status and power of the wife within the family increases vis-à-vis that of the husband when she too is a wage earner.[30] Men have a more dominant role in important family decisions when their wives do not work for pay. The fact that women who are employed are more likely to have their

[29] Again summarized in Hofferth and Moore, "Women's Employment and Marriage," and Spitze, "Women's Employment and Family Relations: A Review."

[30] See Marianne A. Ferber, "Labor Market Participation of Young Married Women: Causes and Effects," *Journal of Marriage and Family* 44, no. 2 (May 1982): 457–68; Gerald W. McDonald, "Family Power: The Assessment of a Decade of Theory and Research, 1970–1979," *Journal of Marriage and Family,* 42, no. 3 (Aug. 1980): 841–54. An alternative view is that the sex ratio in the population plays an important role in determining the relative status of husband and wife. Marcia Guttentag and Paul F. Secord, *Too Many Women? The Sex Ratio Question* (Beverly Hills, CA: Sage, 1983) proposed what came to be known as the "marriage squeeze" hypothesis. They suggested that women are less likely to be in the labor force and will also be more highly prized in societies where there is a surplus of men, and vice versa. This view remains controversial, and is not supported by most of the available evidence; see Marianne A. Ferber and Helen M. Berg, "Labor Force Participation of Women and the Sex Ratio: A Cross-Country Analysis," *Review of Social Economy,* 48, no. 1 (Spring 1991): 2–19.

CHANGING GENDER ROLES: A MALE PERSPECTIVE

A small but increasing number of men are actively sharing responsibility for home as well as market work. This excerpt from an article in the *New York Times** summarizes some of the costs and benefits of these changes from a male perspective.

Change is not easy, and many men have come to feel a good deal of anger and resentment in their lives. There is a sense that somehow we have been deprived of the chance to become the sort of men we expected to be as we grew up—men who, like those of earlier generations, possess a surefooted sense of what is expected and of how to meet those expectations.

Contradictions increasingly rule our lives. On the one hand, a majority of people now believe that both sexes should enjoy equal employment opportunities. On the other, most believe that children may be harmed psychologically if their mothers work outside the home. Says Dr. Joseph Pleck, a prominent researcher in this field: "One fundamental American value is that family and parenthood are important, and this belief is now being extended to include men to a much greater degree. This contradicts the traditional belief, however, that a man should be mainly the breadwinner."

The result can be considerable strain and tension. . . . I, too, am often beset by such anxieties. My wife now works more than 40 hours a week, mostly in the afternoon and evening. As a result, I frequently must cut short my own workday in order to pick up our 18-month-old son from day care or to spend time with my older child. Often, I am also the one who is on call in case of illness, who prepares many of the meals and who keeps the house clean.

I have many fewer hours available for work than I wish, and sometimes I am too exhausted at the end of a day to resume my work when the children have gone to bed. I cannot pretend to feel comfortable about this, and at times I explode with rage or I withdraw into sarcasm and moodiness. There is no question that the rewards of sharing career achievement and child rearing with one's spouse are great, but the price paid can be high. It is a price, finally, that many of us never imagined we would have to pay, and therein lies much of the trouble.

Maybe some of us might be able to do this. Maybe we might learn—in the words of my departmental colleague—to give up the amenities of life in order to concentrate on the essentials, adhering not only to precise daily schedules but working late into the night (a major ingredient in the success of many men who seem to be able to combine the demands of work and family). We might, in addition, learn to exult in the career attainment of our wives, even if we must sacrifice some of our own professional ambitions. We might find the time, as well, to be with our children and to be involved as a matter of course in the necessary household chores. We might even learn to give up the anger and resentment that is often engendered by the need to do all of these things, and to do them well.

We might. But most of us, as yet, cannot hope to follow such a program, nor should we berate ourselves if we do not live up to the "superman" image. Despite the things we did learn from our own fathers, we usually did not find out how to balance full participation in work and in family. Now we are exploring uncharted territory, with all of the missteps and false starts that such exploration requires.

Still, if we think about it, we might ultimately come to gain from the new requirements in our lives. On the morning I was to begin writing this column, my 18-month-old son woke up with a low-grade fever. My wife had a full schedule at the office, and this sick child clearly could not go to his baby sitter. The only solution was for me to alter my plans and to stay home, where I diapered, played with, worried over and comforted a still-energetic but cranky baby. I could feel my bitterness and resentment boiling—for lost hours at work, for missed deadlines, for unprepared classes. "Men today," I found myself thinking, "really have a raw deal."

Then I discovered that my son had learned something new. For the first time, he was able to give a proper kiss, puckering up his lips and enfolding my face in his arms. "Kees Dada," he said as he bussed me on the nose and cheeks. No amount of gratification at work could have compensated for that moment. I found out another thing that morning, a discovery that came as a bit of poetic justice. I suddenly realized that in sacrificing my workday, I had learned a lot about how fathers might care for their sons. And I found that I had learned something further about what it means to be a man, something that goes beyond simply bringing home the paycheck.

---

own credit cards and bank accounts points in the same direction. One may also conjecture that the sole breadwinner has more bargaining power because an angry "if I do not like it, I do not have to put up with this," or an impatient "if you do not like it, you can go," has far more credibility coming from him than from his "dependent" wife.

Past research necessarily included many men who did not anticipate at the time they married that their wife would be in the labor market. There is much evidence that unanticipated changes tend to cause problems, and thus that these results are likely to be more negative than will be the case for young cohorts.[31] It is

[31] Alan Booth, "Wife's Employment and Husband's Stress: A Replication and Refutation," *Journal of Marriage and Family* 39, no. 4 (Nov. 1977): 645–50, reports that stress is caused by a change in the wife's labor force status in either direction, not by the wife being in or out of the labor force. Further evidence on this point is provided by Catherine E. Ross, John Mirowsky, and Joan Huber, "Dividing Work, Sharing Work, and In-Between: Marriage Patterns and Depression," *American Sociological Review* 48, no. 6 (December 1983): 809–23. They found that those husbands of employed wives who preferred her to be a full-time homemaker tended to be depressed, but that this was definitely not the case for those husbands who preferred that their wife work for pay. They conclude that it is the transition, when the wife's employment status has changed but the husband's traditional attitudes have not, that causes the problem.

entirely possible that, in time, men may come to enjoy a partnership marriage more than they ever did the traditional one. They will no longer need to shoulder the total responsibility of financial support of the family. Many surely will enjoy getting to know their children better. They will be better prepared to fend for themselves in emergencies. Last, but not least, they will often have a happier wife.

Children

The most emotionally charged issue is the question of the effect of maternal employment on children.[32] In principle, the question should be asked about parental employment in general; however, it is still commonly accepted that the father will be working in any case and, as of now, that is a realistic assumption. It is more difficult to understand why most research on this subject goes so far as to ignore the role of the father entirely, considering that he can do much to compensate for the reduced home-time of the mother.

This is only one of the many variables that need to be taken into account when the effect of the mother's labor force participation on her children is to be investigated. Some of the others are the age and sex of the children, the number of children in the family, the affection they receive from relatives and other friends, the quality of care they receive from hired sitters and teachers, and the quality of time the family spends together. As noted in previous chapters, it is not obvious that the mere fact that a mother works has any clear predictable effects on her children.[33]

Recent extensive research on this subject clearly shows the complexities of the situation. First, children's development is determined by a variety of factors in addition to mother's employment status, including the innate characteristics of the child itself, the level of resources of the child's family, the role of the father, and the quality of out-of-home care, as well as conditions in the society at large. Second, children's development involves not only progress in cognition, the measure most frequently employed by economists, but also biological and socio-emotional development. Third, children's needs in all these respects differ

[32] Interestingly, virtually none of the research addresses a question that was of much concern in earlier times: possible disadvantages of a mother with few outside interests who tries to live vicariously through her children. How quickly we have forgotten "Portnoy's Complaint," a phrase that became popular because of the 1969 novel of the same name by Philip Roth about a man who blamed his numerous neuroses on his overprotective mother.

[33] See Urie Bronfenbrenner and Ann C. Crouter, in one of the most thorough reviews in recent years, "Work and Family Through Time and Space," in *Families That Work: Children in a Changing World,* S. B. Kamerman and C. D. Hayes, eds. (Washington, DC: National Academy Press, 1982).

markedly by age.[34] Last but not least, all these factors merely influence the probability of different outcomes.[35]

Some of the findings of studies that have been taking such complexities into account are particularly instructive. No evidence has been found of any adverse effects of quality day care (with an adequate number of qualified personnel), even for preschoolers, and a number of studies discovered favorable results, especially with respect to social adjustments. The only exception to this is some evidence indicating that unfavorable effects of out-of-home care may predominate for infants up to about six months or one year of age.[36]

The impact on school-aged and older children when mothers are successful in their paid work appears to be overwhelmingly favorable, perhaps because she herself is more satisfied, is likely to have more structured and consistent rules in her relationship with her children, is less passive, and fosters greater independence in her family. Daughters, particularly, hold their mothers in higher esteem and adopt them as role models, but their sons also are more likely to favor equality for women. There are some indications of a negative influence on the academic achievement of sons[37] but not on daughters, where some evidence of a favorable effect has been found.

These findings should prove useful in helping individuals make better-informed decisions about childrearing. They should also reduce controversy about the usefulness of parental leaves and of quality day-care centers. They cannot, however, be regarded as definitive. For one, little research has been done so far on the long-term consequences of maternal employment apart from educational attainment. Such questions as the impact on career, marital problems, and success in raising their own children remain to be investigated.

[34]Francine D. Blau and Adam J. Grossberg, "Maternal Labor Supply and Children's Cognitive Development," *Review of Economics and Statistics* (forthcoming) found in their research on 3- and 4-year-olds that mother's employment during the child's first year appears to have a somewhat negative effect, but that the opposite is true for the second and later years.

[35]Cheryl D. Hayes, John L. Palmer, and Martha Zaslow, eds. *Who Cares for America's Children? Child Care Policy for the 1990s,* National Research Council (Washington, DC: National Academy Press, 1990).

[36]Two comprehensive reviews of the issues involved may be found in M. Rutter, *Maternal Deprivation Reassessed* (Middlesex, England: Penguin Books, 1981); and Edward F. Zigler and Meryl Frank, eds., *The Parental Leave Crisis: Toward a National Policy* (New Haven, CT: Yale University Press, 1988).

[37]See, for instance, O. D. Duncan, D. L. Featherman, and B. Duncan, *Socioeconomic Background and Achievement* (New York: Seminar Press, 1972); Lois W. Hoffman, "Effects of Maternal Employment on the Child," in *Working Mothers,* Lois W. Hoffman and Francis I. Nye, eds. (San Francisco: Jossey-Bass Publishers, 1974); Belton M. Fleisher, "Mothers' Home Time and the Production of Child Quality," *Demography* 14, no. 2 (May 1977): 197–212; and Sheila F. Krein and Andrea H. Beller, "Educational Attainment of Children From Single-Parent Families: Differences by Exposure, Gender, and Race," *Demography* 25, no. 2 (May 1988): 221–34.

Policy Issue:
Parental Leave and Child Care Subsidies

Public subsidies for child care, common in many other countries, have been to some extent instituted in the United States as well. As of 1990, the Federal Government permitted employed parents to credit up to 30 percent of actual expenses up to $2,400 for the care of one child, and $4,800 for the care of two or more children, against their income tax liabilities for returns with an adjusted income up to $10,000, falling to 20 percent for returns with an adjusted income above $28,000. Further, in 1990, Congress approved a measure appropriating $2.5 billion over the next three years to help states improve and expand available child care. As discussed in Chapter 4, such policies are likely to raise women's labor force participation, all else being equal. There is also interest in the impact of such policies on the welfare of children.

Increasingly, many of those who believe that parental care is best for very young children advocate legislation that would require employers to provide some leave for one or both parents when a child is born or adopted, with provision of health insurance, or at least the opportunity to buy coverage, and with a guarantee of being able to return to the same or to a comparable job. Even parents who are strongly committed to the labor market may benefit from greater flexibility in the time available to them to make alternative arrangements before they return to work, and the children may well receive better care as a result. Virtually all other advanced industrialized countries, and a good many developing countries, have mandatory maternal or parental leaves. Such policies are frequently justified not only because they help families, but also because both the community and employers have a stake in the quality of future generations of citizens and workers.

There is less agreement whether this option should be available only to mothers or to fathers as well, but a strong case can be made that offering it to women only is, on the one hand, discriminatory and, on the other hand, gives employers an incentive to favor male employees. Equally controversial is the question of whether the mandate should be for paid leave. Advocates point out that it is the poor, and hence the most needy, who could not afford to take leave without pay. At the same time, opponents argue that paid leave would be far more costly to employers. Therefore it would be expected to create hardships for some businesses, especially small ones, and to generate strenuous opposition from employers generally.[38]

Those who believe parental care is better for older children as well often oppose day-care subsidies because they tend to encourage maternal employment. The evidence we have reviewed, however, suggests that adequate substitute care need not be harmful to children. Further, a substantial portion of mothers already

---

[38]Opposition to such policies should not be underestimated. In 1990, President Bush vetoed a bill mandating 12 weeks of *unpaid* leave on the grounds that it would constitute too much of a burden for many businesses.

work outside the home, and their numbers are likely to increase to some extent, regardless of government policy. Those concerned with child welfare might thus more fruitfully focus their attention on how best to provide good alternative child care rather than on whether or not it should be provided.[39] However, given strongly held and often emotional beliefs, negative attitudes on this subject are likely to remain a factor.

In spite of the sharp decline in birth rates, opposition to subsidies also continues because it is commonly believed that reducing the costs of raising children will encourage people to have more of them and that, in any case, parents should be responsible for all of the expenses. Both these points deserve careful examination.[40]

Economic analysis tells us that reducing the price of any good will generally result in an increase in the quantity demanded, and there is no reason to assume this effect would not exist in the case of children. From this perspective, subsidized child care could increase the number of children women have. But this is not likely to be the only effect. As we have seen, providing subsidized care will also encourage mothers to enter the labor market. To the extent that women acquire more—and more market-oriented—education in anticipation of this, and accumulate more work experience, they will have higher earnings. Hence, the opportunity cost of additional children will also increase. Further, it may be that women who work develop stronger preferences for market goods, or perhaps for having their own income, and a greater feeling of independence.

It is not possible to determine, a priori, which set of forces is likely to be stronger. However, in the various advanced industrialized countries that have introduced child care subsidies, none have experienced a large increase in the birthrate. In particular, Sweden, which among Western countries provides the most financial support, has a relatively lower birthrate and a substantially higher labor force participation rate of women than in the United States. On the other hand,

---

[39]How good some of this care can be is obvious when one reads about schools for "nannies" where the students, many of them college graduates, are trained in nutrition, child development, cardiopulmonary resuscitation, and even party planning. Trainees from such schools, however, were reported to receive about $600–$800 a month in 1984, putting them out of reach of most parents (*Newsweek*, May 21, 1984, pp. 63–64). There are also child care centers where children get excellent care. But these are also very expensive, even though their employees are generally poorly paid, often only half as much as elementary school teachers. At the other extreme there are families, mostly those in dire poverty, who permit even quite young children to be home alone for extended periods of time. Although there have been alarming estimates of the numbers of such "latchkey" children, ranging from 4 to 10 million, a 1984 Census Bureau Survey (cited in Bianchi, "America's Children: Mixed Prospects") found that only about 2.1 million children between the ages of 5 to 13 cared for themselves after school. An additional 0.3 million cared for themselves or were under the care of a sibling under age 14 at other times, such as before school or at night. Most of these children were alone for less than one hour before school and less than two hours after school, and since the incidence of self-care increased with the age of the child, many were not necessarily too young to care for themselves. A course for parents and children on coping strategies for self-care is described in an inset on pages 283–84.

[40]A thorough discussion of these issues is found in Myra H. Strober, "Formal Extrafamily Child Care—Some Economic Observations," in *Sex, Discrimination and the Division of Labor*, Cynthia B. Lloyd, ed. (New York): Columbia University Press, 1975), and in Hayes, Palmer, and Zaslow, *Who Cares for America's Children? Child Care Policy for the 1990s*.

it is widely believed in Sweden that these arrangements, together with generous provisions for parental leave, have helped to arrest the decline in fertility that might otherwise have occurred.

The question of how costs of raising children should be allocated is also quite complex. Children's parents, undoubtedly, have a special responsibility for their care. Unfortunately, some of them, especially single parents, are unable to discharge their responsibilities at an acceptable level, often through no fault of their own. Further, it is generally recognized that the nation benefits, even in narrowly economic terms, when children grow up to be healthier, better-educated, and better-trained adults, for they will be more productive, will contribute more both as workers and as taxpayers, and are less likely to be a burden on the public. In other words, there are significant positive externalities when children are better cared for that benefit not only their parents, but the whole community. Additionally, subsidies for child care help compensate for the advantage that families with full-time homemakers have, because earnings are taxed, but the value of goods and services produced at home is not.

These considerations may have influenced legislators when, as noted earlier, in 1990, they passed the first federal bill since World War II that supports child care for employed parents outside of welfare and employment programs by providing not only higher tax credits than previously, but also grants. In addition, the bill requires states to establish registration, health, and safety requirements for child-care establishments.

Another long-run economic advantage resulting from subsidized child care is that more mothers will be able to take jobs that offer valuable experience and on-the-job training opportunities, even if the initial wages paid are low. Thus, instead of permitting their human capital to deteriorate, they would be adding to it, enabling them to become taxpayers rather than, in some cases, welfare dependents. Such women will also provide better role models for their children. Greatly expanded day-care facilities would even help to provide jobs for many women, not only for trained teachers, but also for relatively unskilled women, who would often make excellent teacher's aides.

Those who believe that all individuals deserve as nearly an equal chance in life as can be provided would find this another argument for public subsidies for child care. Nor is such a view unprecedented, even in the United States, which lags considerably behind other advanced industrialized countries in this respect; this country does have a long, and apparently well-nigh universally accepted, policy of paying out public funds for primary and secondary education.[41] In recent years,

---

[41] Vocal opponents of public schools, among whom Milton Friedman is perhaps one of the earliest and best known, do not advocate that the government should stop paying for education but rather that it should do so by giving parents vouchers. They could then send their children to any school of their choice. See Milton Friedman, *Capitalism and Freedom* (Chicago: University of Chicago Press, 1962), pp. 85–107.

the government has also contributed substantially to public institutions of higher education. One might argue that it makes little sense to do all that for youngsters from age 5 or 6 on, but to permit many younger children to live under conditions that do not enable them to benefit to any great extent from these advantages when they reach school age.

In addition to parents and the public, employers have a potential interest in child care. In the long run, they also benefit collectively from any arrangements that help today's children become more productive workers. But more immediately, parental leave and subsidized child care are likely to attract more workers to the particular firm and to increase women's labor force attachment (making them more stable workers). Child care also helps to reduce absenteeism brought about by undependable arrangements for children, and, to the extent that other employers do not provide similar services, job changing is reduced. This is why, in 1988, slightly more than one-third of full-time employees of medium and large firms were in firms that offered some child care leave to new mothers and 17 percent worked at firms that offered such leaves to new fathers.[42] (Provision of leave was, however, less common among small firms.) In addition, there were 1,000 on-or near-site child-care centers by 1989, though some of them require employees to pay part or all of the costs.[43] Among the advantages of on-site care are that parents do not have to make a separate trip to take children elsewhere, and that they are nearby in case of emergencies. There are disadvantages, however: children may have to be taken out of their own neighborhood, perhaps travel large distances, and must change caretakers when parents change jobs. In addition, smaller firms may not have enough employees with small children to warrant establishing their own center.

In recent years, it appears that employers are increasingly likely to contract with independent operators, whether commercial or not-for-profit, or pay subsidies to employees directly. Some also provide information about existing child care. Such arrangements enable parents to make their own choices, and perhaps to find a place in their neighborhood. Although firms offering child-care benefits or services of any kind are still a minority (11.1 percent of establishments with 10 or more

[42]This is apart from whatever leave workers are able to piece together from short-term disability, paid vacation and sick leave, and so on. See Joseph R. Meisenheimer, "Employer Provisions for Parental Leave," *Monthly Labor Review* 112, no. 10 (Oct. 1989): 20–24. It is also interesting to note that by 1990, as many as 15 states had passed some form of family leave laws, albeit generally with exemptions for small employers (Institute for American Values, *Family Affairs* 2, nos. 2–3, Summer–Fall 1989 and 3, no.1, Spring 1990).

[43]Most of these are at hospitals, where large numbers of women of childbearing age who have to work nonstandard hours are employed. There are also a very few innovative employers who are combining care for children and for the elderly, such as the Stride Rite Intergenerational Center (Marianne A. Ferber and Brigid O'Farrell, with Larue Allen, *Work and Family: Policies for a Changing Workforce*, National Research Council (Washington, DC: National Academy Press, 1991).

employees in 1987), they are a growing group that includes such trend-setting firms as IBM, AT&T, and Polaroid.[44]

Because, as we have seen, parents, employers, and the public all potentially stand to gain from good child care, such changes toward sharing the costs of providing it may be seen as a step toward finding an equitable way of allocating the burden. Parents might pay a fee on a sliding scale, according to ability to pay. Large employers might provide facilities; others might subsidize employee use of centers located elsewhere. The government could make up the remainder of the expenses. There would, no doubt, be a good deal of disagreement about any precise formula, but if arrangements could be worked out where each of the three parties received benefits that equaled or exceeded their contributions, it should be possible to reach a consensus. One of the effects of making progress in this direction would be to enable more mothers of young children to remain in, or to enter, the labor market.

Given the extremely low levels of support for child care from either government or employers, parents have resorted to whatever means of providing for their children they have been able to afford. It is not uncommon for parents to have multiple arrangements. Table 9.3 displays data on the various kinds of child

TABLE 9.3   Child Care Arrangements Used by Employed Mothers in the United States for Children Five Years and Younger (Percent Distribution)

	1965	*1982*	*1988*
Care in child's home	47.2	25.7	29.1
By father	10.3	10.3	12.9
By others	36.9	15.4	16.2
Care in another home	37.3	43.8	32.6
Group care[a]	8.2	18.8	31.2
Under 2 years	n.a.	n.a.	11.8
2–3 years	n.a.	n.a.	32.6
4–5 years, not in school	n.a.	n.a.	52.4
4–5 years, in school	n.a.	n.a.	25.7
All other arrangements	7.3	11.7	7.3

[a]Includes day-care center, nursery or preschool, kindergarten, extended day care and day camp.

Sources: For 1965 and 1982, U.S. Department of Commerce, Bureau of the Census, Current Population Reports, Special Studies Series P-23, no. 117; for 1988, U.S. Department of Health and Human Services, National Center for Health Statistics, Advance Data, no. 187, October 1, 1990.

[44]This includes nearly one-third of firms with 250 employees or more. See Howard V. Hayghe, "Employers and Child Care: What Roles Do They Play?" *Monthly Labor Review* 111, no. 9 (September 1988): 38–44; and *New York Times* (August 4, 1985): p. F1. A study of employer-sponsored child care conducted by Renne Y. Magid for the American Management Association found that employers who did provide such facilities claimed that benefits far outweighed costs. The gains reported included less employee absenteeism, improved morale, and greater ability to attract and keep superior employees. Reported in Bureau of National Affairs, *Daily Labor Report*, no. 39 (February 28, 1984), pp. A-5, A-6.

AN INNOVATIVE EMPLOYER PROGRAM:
SELF-CARE INSTRUCTION FOR CHILDREN

No one advocates that young children should be left without an adult to take care of them, but all children need to learn to take care of themselves sooner or later, whether or not both parents are employed. Employer programs that are supportive of families make it easier for workers, particularly women, to combine job and household responsibilities. This, in turn, is likely to make them more productive employees. One such program is described below.*

The question is every parent's nightmare, but it was raised matter-of-factly enough in the room full of children:

"Problem: You are walking home alone from school and you think that a man in a car is following you," Evie Herrmann-Keeling read from her work sheet, as 11 children followed the question on their own printed sheets. "What would you do? (A) Stand still and see what he does. (B) Walk quickly home and lock yourself in the house. (C) Walk to a neighbor's home and stay there. (D) Stop and ask the person what he wants. (E) Other.

"Well," Mrs. Herrmann-Keeling asked, "what do you think?"

A hand shot up, and Mrs. Herrmann-Keeling called on Kristin, an 11-year-old. "I think that if you go to a neighbor's house, well, an adult you know will be there–and they can help if you need it." She paused for a moment "But if you go home and lock yourself in the house, you could be followed, and there might not be anyone there to help you."

A murmur of voices signalled agreement from the children, all of whom were between 9 and 13 years old. They began talking animatedly, and soon agreed that to "Stop and ask the person what he or she wants" is a very, very bad idea indeed.

It was a typical exchange in the weekly courses for "latchkey" children run by Mrs. Herrmann-Keeling, executive director of Parents Anonymous of Connecticut. What made the session unusual was that it took place in the offices of a large corporation—the Phoenix Mutual Life Insurance Company—and was offered free to the company's 1,900 employees in the Hartford area. . . . The course of five 90-minute sessions at Phoenix Mutual is intended to make both children and parents aware of the problems—and the opportunities for growth—that confront millions of American families who have "latchkey" children, those who spend time not directly supervised by a parent or adult.

Studies have estimated that there are between 4 and 10 million such children, but there are no reliable statistics on the phenomenon. Since the term "latchkey child" has become something of a pejorative, Parents Anonymous and other groups prefer the term "self-care" to describe children who are on their own, usually after school.

These children are the shock troops of a family revolution that has seen a dramatic increase in two-career marriages and single-parent families. Although

*Glen Collins, "Course for 'Latchkey' Children and Parents," *New York Times*, March 19, 1984, p. C-10. Copyright ©1984 by The New York Times Company. Reprinted by permission.

only 19 percent of mothers were working in 1947, 58 percent of all mothers with children under 18 were in the work force by 1980.

"It's very logical to approach the problem of latchkey children through the work place," said Mrs. Herrmann-Keeling. "Corporations are the very places where parents most need this service. It's very important for companies to be supportive of families."

A small but rapidly increasing number of corporations accept that premise, including companies as varied as Bankers Trust, Exxon, Philip Morris and Phoenix Mutual. They have been hosts to a variety of parent-education programs, have offered referrals to local social-service agencies and have established child-care networks among employees.

"At most companies, from 3 PM on," said Mrs. Herrmann-Keeling, "there is much covert telephoning going on. Parents feel they have to call to see if their children are safe. Yet it's so silly for this kind of thing to have to be underground. The more supportive the company can be of family life, the more productive workers will be.". . .

The positive aspects of "self-care," she said, can make it a growth experience for families that develops children's sense of responsibility and involves parents in monitoring the progress of their independence. "We want parents and children to understand that they are working together to achieve a common goal," said Mrs. Herrmann-Keeling.

---

care used in the United States in recent decades. They show a substantial decline in the percentage of young children of employed mothers who were cared for in their own home from 47.2 in 1965 to 25.7 in 1982, but a slight rise since then to 29.1. The percentage cared for by their fathers actually increased marginally from 10.3 in 1965 and 1982 to 12.9 in 1988. Care in another home, on the other hand, rose somewhat over the first years, then declined a good bit.

Some individuals who take youngsters into their homes do, of course, provide excellent care. But informal arrangements are generally unregulated and of very uneven quality. Parents who can afford to do so tend to prefer to have infants cared for in their own home, partly because they get more individual attention, partly because they are less exposed to infectious diseases. For somewhat older children, group care has the advantage of contact with other children, and of being regulated, at least to some extent. On the other hand, the ratio of children to care providers is about twice as high in nursery school, preschool, and day-care centers as in the homes of nonrelatives or in the child's own home. Some of this reflects differences in the average age of children in each type of arrangement, with older children being more likely to be cared for in group settings.

Whatever the relative merits of different types of care may. be, it is the share of children in group centers that rose most sharply, from 8.2 percent in 1965 to 18.8 percent in 1982 and 31.2 percent in 1988. The increase has been even greater in a number of other advanced industrialized countries. The experience in other countries will be discussed further in Chapter 10.

FEMALE-HEADED FAMILIES[45]

Although there has been considerable interest in families with working mothers, special concern has focused on those where the mother is the main breadwinner and often the only adult. Such attention is appropriate in part because the proportion of families in this category has been rising rapidly and because they experience a disproportionate share of economic problems.

Female-headed families are generally composed of women and dependent children. Historically, there were always children without a father in some homes, but the main cause used to be death. Today, the causes are primarily divorce and separation, with the greater number of births to unmarried women being an additional contributing factor. Mothers and their young children also are more likely to form separate families today, rather than to live with other relatives. Overall, the proportion of families headed by women has increased substantially, from 9 percent in 1950 to 17 percent in 1989.

Table 9.4 shows the relatively low income and high incidence of poverty among female-headed families. Their median income was less than half that of married couples. Nearly one-third of them were poor, compared to only 5.6 percent of married couples, and one-quarter were on welfare. This gives some indication why there is much discussion about the "feminization" of poverty.[46] These data also show that the incidence of female headship is higher and the poverty problem is particularly serious in the black and Hispanic communities.

Among blacks, 43.8 percent of families had female heads by 1989, and almost half of these lived in poverty. The incidence of female-headed families among Hispanics was 23.1 percent, but the poverty rate among them was just as high. By comparison, the 12.9 percent of female-headed families among whites and the poverty rate of somewhat above one-fourth seem relatively modest, although it is worth noting that since 1950, the proportion of female-headed families has been increasing at about the same rate in all three groups. By 1988, only 73 percent of children under age 18 lived in two-parent families, compared to 88 percent in 1960. Demographers estimate that, of children born today, at least one-half— perhaps as many as 60 percent—will spend some time in a female-headed family.[47]

---

[45] We use the term "female-headed" because it represents general usage. Technically, it should be "single-parent family headed by a woman." For an interesting discussion of these issues, see Irwin Garfinkel and Sara McLanahan, *Single Mothers and Their Children: A New American Dilemma* (Washington, DC: Urban Institute Press, 1986).

[46] The poverty line in 1988 dollars was $9,435 for a family of three, adjusted according to family size. Critics charge that this is too low, because it is based on the estimate of family needs calculated in 1963, using data from 1955.

[47] Suzanne M. Bianchi, "America's Children: Mixed Prospects."

TABLE 9.4   Incidence of Poverty by Type of Family, 1989

	Number (thousands)	*Percent of families[b]*	*Median income*	*Percent in poverty*
All families	66,090	100.0	$34,213	10.3
White	56,590	85.6	35,975	7.8
Black	7,470	11.3	20,209	27.8
Hispanic origin[a]	4,840	7.3	23,446	23.4
Type of family				
Married couple families	52,317	79.2	38,547	5.6
Male householder, no wife present	2,884	4.4	27,847	12.1
Female householder, no husband present	10,890	16.5	16,442	32.2
White	7,306	11.1	18,946	25.4
Black	3,275	5.0	11,630	46.5
Hispanic origin[a]	1,116	1.7	11,745	47.5

[a]May be of any race.

[b]Calculated.

Source: U.S. Department of Commerce, Bureau of the Census, Current Population Reports, Consumer Income Series P-60, no. 168. *Money Income and Poverty Status in the United States: 1989*, Tables 7, 18.

The prevalence of female-headed families and the economic problems they face is a major reason why the proportion of children living in poverty is larger than that of any other age group. In 1989, fully 19.6 percent of all children, 14.6 of white, 36.2 percent of Hispanic, and 43.7 percent of black children lived in poverty.[48]

It has been noted that the income figures used to determine poverty status do not include such items as food stamps, Medicaid, housing subsidies, and other in-kind transfers so that they understate real income. Less attention has been drawn to the fact that families with a single adult are at a great disadvantage compared to mother-father families because all household responsibilities fall upon that person, in addition to whatever work she does for pay. This double burden can be a serious constraint on the woman's labor force participation, not to mention reducing her leisure time.

It is not surprising that female-headed families generally have economic problems. As we have seen, women tend to earn considerably less than men with comparable qualifications. Married women also tend to accumulate less labor market experience than their husbands, and this is especially so when they have children. As of 1988, one out of three women, but only one out of one hundred

[48]U.S. Department of Commerce, Bureau of the Census, CPR Special Studies Series P-23, no. 154, *Child Support and Alimony.*

men, had quit paid work at some time to care for children.[49] Hence, women are often ill-equipped to cope with the double role of single parent and breadwinner.

In addition to blacks and Hispanics, never married mothers of all racial and ethnic groups, many of them teenagers, are among the most disadvantaged. In 1988, about one-fourth of all births, and almost two-thirds of births to women under age 20, were to unmarried mothers. This represents an increase from 18 percent of all women and 48 percent of younger women in 1980.[50] It is widely believed that when the need to raise children by themselves is combined with the lack of education, work experience, and self-esteem so prevalent among these young mothers, they and their children are very likely to face a life of poverty and deprivation. Often they qualify only for the types of jobs that offer low pay and no family benefits such as child care, so that many can not afford to continue working.[51]

Recent research has raised some questions about the conclusion that teenage childbearing is the cause of the persistent poverty of this group.[52] Other new work finds that for both blacks and whites, but particularly for whites, the negative effects of early childbearing on earnings are greater for those who are married than for unmarried mothers.[53] In any case, however, there can be no doubt that it is primarily poor, uneducated women with very low potential earnings who are most likely to become unmarried mothers. Nor can there be any question that children from such families will be seriously disadvantaged, especially without concerted efforts to provide public assistance.

In recognition of the difficulties they face, women heading families may receive alimony to compensate for their reduced earning power and child support as payment of the father's share of the expense of childrearing. Everyone has at one time or another heard stories of very large divorce settlements. These tend to convey the erroneous impression that generous payments are common. In fact, of the almost 20 million ever divorced or currently separated women in this country in 1985, only 14.6 percent had been awarded any alimony payments, only 4.4

---

[49]U.S. Department of Labor, *Child Care: A Workforce Issue,* Report of the Secretary's Task Force, April 1988. According to *Mothers-Only Families,* General Accounting Office Report to Congressional Committees, April 1991, 35 percent of single mothers would not earn enough to escape from poverty even if they worked 40 hours per week. Further, they are likely to face not only low earnings, but are vulnerable to layoffs and other interruptions, lack important fringe benefits, and have relatively high child-care expenses.

[50]U.S. Department of Health and Human Services, *Monthly Vital Statistics Report* 39, no. 4, Supplement (August 1990) and Children's Defense Fund, *CDF Reports* (May 1991).

[51]Sar A. Levitan and Elizabeth A. Conway, *Families in Flux* (Washington, DC: The Bureau of National Affairs, Inc., 1990). See also Irwin Garfinkel and Sara McLanahan, *Single Mothers and their Children.*

[52]Arline T. Geronimus and Sanders Koreman, "The Socio-economic Consequence of Teen Childbearing Reconsidered," Paper presented at the National Bureau of Economic Research Labor Studies Summer Institute, Cambridge, MA, July 1990.

[53]Shelly Lundberg and Robert D. Plotnick. "Teenage Childbearing and Adult Wages," Department of Economics, University of Washington, Seattle, Working Papaer # 90-24, August 1990.

percent were due payments that year, and only 3.2 percent actually received any money, on average $3,730. Problems also arise in dividing family assets at the time of the divorce. This is particularly true in the case of human capital, which husbands are considerably more likely than wives to have accumulated, whether it be advanced education or on-the-job-training.

A substantially larger proportion of eligible mothers had obtained a child support award. Among those who had been married, 74.5 percent received awards, but only 18.4 percent of those who were single; among nonblacks 70.4 received awards, compared to only 36.4 percent of blacks, and 42.8 percent of Hispanics. The amounts awarded to all mothers were, however, only $2,494 on average, $1,419 for those who had not been married, $1,278 for blacks, and $1,334 for Hispanics. The mean amount per child was a mere $1,638. Furthermore, in spite of federal legislation to enforce payments, only about 74 percent of mothers with awards received any payments, and only half received the full amount.[54]

Many factors contribute to this dismal situation. In some instances, the father has died; more frequently, he is himself poor and genuinely unable to pay more. Collection and redistribution of all child support payments by the state, so that the amount each mother gets is not directly dependent on the payments by the particular father, or public assistance would be the only possible solutions in such cases. But there are other causes for inadequate support by the father that might be amenable to appropriate changes in legal arrangements and, particularly, to more conscientious enforcement of existing laws. This issue is an important one, because it is generally the women who are least able to stand on their own, with little education, little or no labor market experience, and few other resources, that are also least likely to receive any support from their ex-husbands.

One study found that during the first year after the marriage was terminated, the income of the female-headed family was only 66 percent of that of the family before the divorce, leaving the woman and her children substantially worse off financially, even when the smaller number of individuals left in the family is taken into account. On average, three-fifths of the income of those families consisted of the earnings of the mothers whose labor force participation rose substantially from the previous year, only one-tenth was contributed by the fathers, and one-twentieth came from welfare.[55] This reality differs substantially from the popular image of the lady of leisure supported generously by her ex-husband or the lazy welfare mother taking advantage of the taxpayer.

---

[54] Andrea H. Beller and John W. Graham, "Trends in Child Support Payments," unpublished manuscript, 1992. According to "The Child Support Enforcement Program: Policy and Practice" (report by the Subcommittee on Human Resources of the Committee on Ways and Means of the U.S. House of Representatives, Dec. 5, 1989), the situation has improved somewhat since the mid-1980s and may be expected to improve further as states implement changes authorized by a 1988 law.

[55] Greg J. Duncan and Saul D. Hoffman, "Economic Consequences of Marital Instability," in *Horizontal Equity, Uncertainty and Well-being,* Martin David, ed. (NBER Conference Volume, Chicago: University of Chicago Press, 1985).

Policy Issue: Raising the Incomes of Female-Headed Families[56]

The preceding discussion suggests a variety of measures that would improve the economic status of female-headed families. Their primary sources of income are threefold:

1. Private transfers
2. Public transfers
3. Their own labor market earnings.[57]

We consider the prospects for increasing income from each of these sources in turn.

Private transfers are court-awarded alimony and child support payments. Federal legislation to enforce child support obligations more stringently was passed in 1981 and 1988 and appears to be having some effect. State enforcement services are now available to mothers, regardless of whether or not they are on welfare. In cases of overdue child care payments, withholding of wages, as well as of state and federal income tax refunds, may be obtained.[58] However, as we have seen, the amounts involved are small, so that improved collection of currently owed child support by itself would bring about only very modest improvements in the economic status of female-headed families. Nor is there likely to be much public support for a policy to substantially raise the level of such awards, because this would probably be considered too great a burden on the father.

Public transfers stem from a variety of sources, particularly the federal welfare program, Aid to Families with Dependent Children (AFDC). Although such programs do provide a minimum level of support, they generally leave the family with an income below the poverty level. Given the attitudes of taxpayers toward such arrangements, more generous welfare provisions are unlikely. Further, in contrast to private transfers, there are work disincentives associated with these public transfers, because payments are reduced as labor market earnings increase.

These work disincentives are illustrated in Table 9.5. Assume that a female-headed family receives $3,500 when the mother is not employed, and

---

[56]For an excellent summary of the problems of such families, as well as possible solutions, see Chapter 10, "Poverty and Single Parents," in Barbara R. Bergmann, *The Economic Emergence of Women* (New York: Basic Books, 1986).

[57]Evidence of the potential effectiveness of these various approaches is reported and discussed in Barbara R. Bergmann and Mark D. Roberts, "Work and the Single Parent: Work, Child Support and Welfare," in *Gender in the Workplace,* Clair Brown and Joseph A. Pecman, eds. (Washington, DC: Brookings Institution, 1987).

[58]The new legislation enabled Wisconsin to adopt the innovative Child Support Assurance System, which obliges all absent parents to pay 17 percent of their income for one child, and 25, 29, 31, and 34 percent for two, three, four, and five or more children. If the noncustodial parent pays less than a stipulated minimum benefit, the state makes up the difference. In addition, low-income custodial parents are paid for work expenses, such as child care, in order to encourage them to seek employment. Since August 1987, the appropriate share of the wages of the absent parent are directly withheld by the state. Subcommittee on Human Resources, Committee on Ways and Means, U.S. House of Representatives, *The Child Support Enforcement Program: Policy and Practice* (Dec. 5, 1989).

TABLE 9.5   An Illustration of Alternative Welfare Programs

LABOR MARKET EARNINGS (1)	GOVERNMENT WELFARE PAYMENT (2)	TOTAL FAMILY INCOME (1+2)
PROGRAM A (100% tax rate)		
$ 0	$3,500	$3,500
2,000	1,500	3,500
3,500	0	3,500
PROGRAM B (50% tax rate)		
$ 0	$3,500	$3,500
2,000	2,500	4,500
3,500	1,750	5,250
7,000	0	7,000

these payments are reduced by an amount equal to what she is paid when she takes a job. This amounts to a 100 percent implicit tax rate on her wages up to $3,500. Such an arrangement ensures saving a full dollar of public funds for every dollar a welfare recipient earns but, as illustrated by Program A in Table 9.5, will also greatly reduce the incentive to work for pay, especially for women who can earn little more than $3,500. This is all the more so because working outside the home generally involves job-related expenses such as commuting, better or special clothing, and child care.

The disincentives will be smaller if the reduction in payments is only a fraction of earnings, particularly if such provisions for retaining a share of earnings are generous. This is illustrated by Program B in the table. In this case, a woman's welfare payment is reduced by only one-half the amount of labor market earnings (an implicit tax rate of 50 percent). Such an arrangement substantially increases the incentive to work, as indicated by the increases in the total income of the family that occur in this case. The government's outlay to the welfare family is also reduced as market earnings increase. Although this reduction is not as large as under Program A, as noted earlier, an individual receiving welfare is unlikely to work under that program. On the other hand, under Program B, families with considerably higher incomes, up to $7,000, are eligible for welfare. This would be expected to reduce their incentives to work to some extent.

Thus, a reduction of the implicit tax rate potentially decreases program costs by encouraging welfare recipients to supplement their transfer payments with market earnings and, perhaps, shorten the period of time until they can find jobs that pay enough to enable them to leave the welfare rolls entirely. But a reduction of the implicit tax rate potentially increases program costs in the short run by making a larger number of families (at higher income levels) eligible for some welfare payment.

The AFDC program was developed during a time when it was assumed that the only proper role for a mother was to stay at home and look after her family. When no other resources were available, it was accepted that such a family without a breadwinner was to receive welfare payments, although these payments were never very generous. Welfare payments were reduced dollar-for-dollar with market earnings. However, as this view of women's roles gradually changed, there came to be growing concern that the recipient would have little incentive to look for a job or to make adequate efforts to collect child support payments from the absent parent. As we have seen, this concern was not unfounded.

It is therefore not surprising that by 1967, the law was changed. Welfare payments were no longer reduced by the full amount earned, and recipients were allowed to keep $30 per month, plus one-third of their earnings. This change did not prove to be very effective in achieving its intended goal, perhaps in part because the family would lose in-kind benefits such as health coverage and food stamps if their income exceeded a relatively modest specified amount. In view of mounting distress with welfare expenditures, in 1981, the policy was rescinded in order to save money, and the new, more liberal provisions were restricted to the first four months of employment, after which the dollar-for-dollar deduction once again applied.[59]

The realization that the attendant savings were very short-run led to another shift in policy in 1988. Rather than seeking to induce change with incentives, the new law simply requires the recipients of AFDC to find employment, go to school, or sign up for a training program. To enable them to do this, the government in turn is obliged to make child care available, either directly or by giving the parents vouchers or cash that will enable them to purchase it. Beyond that, some community services, including counseling, are made available in order to help the family to function better in the long run, and recipients also receive some help with establishing paternity, locating the absent parent, and collecting the child support they are owed.

It remains to be seen whether this new approach will succeed not only in reducing the number of people on welfare,[60] which was clearly the main intent of many backers of these reforms, but also in enabling single parents to earn enough to achieve an acceptable standard of living, and to give their children a decent start in life. In any case, the reforms of the late 1980s are likely to be at least a step in the right direction, by recognizing that parents should continue to share responsibility for their children after separation or divorce, and that single custodial parents often need help if they are to successfully raise their children.

---

[59]Ronald G. Ehrenberg and Robert S. Smith, *Modern Labor Economics: Theory and Public Policy,* 2nd ed. (Glenview, IL: Scott Foresman, 1985), pp. 181–190.

[60]Welfare rolls increased sharply in the early 1990s, in part due to the recession. The number of families on welfare rose by 24 percent (900,000) between July 1989 and October 1991. (See Jason DeParle, "Fueled by Social Trends, Welfare Cases are Rising," *New York Times,* January 10, 1992, pp. A1, A9).

Perhaps equally important, the 1988 law appears to accept the fact that, although private and public transfers have a role to play, they have not been, nor are they likely to be, sufficient to substantially improve the economic status of female-headed families. To accomplish that more ambitious goal, policies are needed that will improve the earnings potential of women who head families.

Because all women (and their children) are at risk of living in a female-headed household, policies to benefit female heads are, in the last analysis, the same as those needed to raise the earnings of women in general. Such measures, discussed at various points in this book, range from ending preferential tax and social security treatment of traditional families (in order to increase incentives for women to acquire more labor market experience) to encouraging women to invest in market-oriented education and training and to combatting labor market discrimination. They also include more flexible terms of employment, such as part-time jobs that do not involve undue penalties in terms of pay, promotions, and fringe benefits, as well as flexitime and the availability of family leaves when the occasion warrants.

CONCLUSION

This chapter has considered the effect of a woman's labor force participation on the formation, operation, and possible breakup of families, as well as the special problems of households in which the woman is a single family head. These subjects continue to be highly controversial; however, we interpret the preponderance of the evidence to show that the dominant effects of the wife working outside the home are likely to be benign for the whole family and particularly so for her and the children. Perhaps the chief negative effect of women's employment is its apparent association with the rising divorce rate. Here we would point out that though a divorce inevitably is fraught with disappointment and problems, in some instances ending an unhappy marriage may be the lesser of two evils. In any case, it is clear that, should a marriage terminate, whether because of death or divorce, it is the woman who has maintained her labor market skills and contacts who will be able to best fend for herself and for her children.

SUGGESTED READINGS

BECKER, GARY S. *A Treatise on the Family.* Cambridge, MA: Harvard University Press, 1991.

BIANCHI, SUZANNE M. "America's Children: Mixed Prospects," *Population Bulletin* 45, no. 1 (1990).

BLANK, REBECCA M. "Women's Paid Work, Household Income, and Household Well-being." In *American Woman 1988–89: A Status Report,* Sarah E. Rix, ed. New York: W. W. Norton, 1988, pp. 123–61.

FERBER, MARIANNE A. and BRIGID O'FARRELL, with LARUE ALLEN, eds. *Work and Family.* Washington, DC: National Academy Press, 1991.

FUCHS, VICTOR R. *Women's Quest for Economic Equality.* Cambridge, MA: Harvard University Press, 1988.

GARFINKEL, IRWIN AND SARA MCLANAHAN, *Single Mothers and Their Children: A New American Dilemma.* Washington, DC: Urban Institute Press, 1986.

HAYES, CHERYL D., JOHN L. PALMER, AND MARTHA ZASLOW, eds. *Who Cares for America's Children? Child Care Policy for the 1990's.* National Research Council, Washington, DC: National Academy Press, 1990.

HUBER, JOAN A. AND GLENNA SPITZE. *Children, Housework and Jobs.* New York: Academic Press, 1983.

KAMERMAN, SHEILA B. AND CHERYL D. HAYES, eds. *Families that Work: Children in a Changing World.* Washington, DC: National Academy Press, 1982.

SCHULTZ, THEODORE W., ed. *Economics of the Family.* A conference report of the National Bureau of Economic Research. Chicago: University of Chicago Press, 1974.

SPITZE, GLENNA. "Women's Employment and Family Relations," *Journal of Marriage and Family* 50, no. 3 (August 1988): 595–618.

Chapter 10

GENDER DIFFERENCES IN OTHER COUNTRIES: WHAT CAN WE LEARN FROM INTERNATIONAL COMPARISONS?

Up to this point in the book we have focused almost entirely on the situation in the United States. Throughout, we emphasized the influence of economic factors in determining the status of women. This is not to suggest that nothing else matters, but rather that, everything being the same, economic considerations play an important role. Of course, in the real world, everything else is generally not the same. Societies differ in their political systems, in their cultures, and in their religions. In this chapter, we turn to a consideration of women in other countries, on the one hand, to shed light on the causes of the substantial diversity in their status, and, on the other hand, to see what we can learn about institutions and policies elsewhere that have retarded or enhanced improvements in the position of women.

We begin by presenting information on various indicators of the economic status of women as compared to men and discussing regularities as well as differences among various countries and regions. Because of serious limitations in terms of availability, accuracy, and comparability of data, particularly for developing countries, evidence is often limited to only selected countries and must be interpreted with great caution. It should also be noted that data on the former Union of Soviet Socialist Republics (which in 1992 became the Commonwealth of Independent States) and other Eastern European countries refer to the period before the dramatic changes in their economies in 1989 and the subsequent political reunification of East and West Germany. We believe that it is nonetheless worthwhile to examine the situation in these countries during the earlier period to learn about the effects on the status of women of the ideology that prevailed at that time. Throughout, we use the country names that applied during the period to which our data refer, even if they were subsequently changed. We go on to present a brief interpretation of the findings, acknowledging that we have much to learn about the determinants of existing differences. Last, we briefly examine some of the issues of special concern in developing countries, with their serious problem of low per capita income, and in two advanced industrialized countries, the former Union of Soviet Socialist Republics (USSR) and Sweden, each of which, in its own way, has had an explicit commitment to equality for women.

INDICATORS OF WOMEN'S ECONOMIC STATUS

There are a number of measures that, by general agreement, are regarded as useful indicators of women's economic status. We consider labor force participation first. Unless women can participate in production beyond homemaking, few can expect to have their own income or to achieve status in their own right. In other words, they will be restricted to the role of economic dependent, even if they are fortunate enough to obtain a relatively high standard of living. Many will not be that fortunate. For this reason, the labor force participation rate is an important indicator of women's progress toward equality.

The second criterion to be discussed is the degree of occupational segregation, which is often viewed as representing the exclusion of women from rewarding and challenging jobs. The third item to be addressed is the male-female earnings gap, obviously an issue of great relevance to women's economic status. Next, we consider the extent to which government and employer programs are provided in different countries. Last, we present the evidence that is available on the amount of housework done by women and men, which is likely to affect women's relative status in and out of the work force.

Labor Force Participation

We begin by discussing women's labor force participation because, as noted above, it is an important determinant of their well-being as well as of the standard of living of their family. Although women who do not work for pay share, to a greater or lesser extent, in the income earned by other members of their household, they have little opportunity to achieve independence or status in their own right. Money income is perceived as making a more important contribution than provision of services to the family, and it confers greater power and influence in decision making within the family. Comparisons of the status of women in different countries tend to confirm the importance of labor force participation.[1]

Labor force participation is determined by demand and supply factors that vary from place to place, as well as over time, depending in part on the level of economic development and the industry mix of each economy. The nature of the jobs available in the labor market influences the demand for women workers. Both the availability of goods and services for purchase, and the relative value of market earnings as compared to time spent in household production, influence the supply of female labor.

A number of models have been developed concerning the relationship between economic development and women's labor force participation. One hypothesis that receives some degree of support from the evidence presented in this chapter, as well as from the historic evidence briefly noted in Chapter 2, is that female labor force participation declines during the early stages of economic development as the locus of production moves out of the household, but then rises as opportunities for employment increase during industrialization and in postindustrial economies while the need for domestic labor declines.[2]

Demographic factors also play an important role. An unusually large proportion of women in the population necessarily means a large number of them will be unmarried (at least in countries where monogamy is the rule) and will have little incentive or opportunity to become full-time homemakers. An unusually high birthrate necessarily means families with large numbers of children, giving women, especially those in advanced industrialized societies, more incentive to become full-time homemakers. At the same time, as discussed in Chapter 9, fertility is itself influenced by the extent to which women expect to seek employment. Recent research suggests that women's labor force participation also influences the allocation of resources, hence their survival chances and the sex ratio in the population, particularly in poor developing countries.[3]

It would also be a mistake to overlook the importance of such other factors as the preferences of employers for male workers rather than female workers, perceptions of what type of work is appropriate for each sex, general attitudes toward the appropriate roles for women and men, and tastes for market goods as compared to commodities mainly produced at home. A comparison of varying labor force participation rates sheds some light on these issues.

Most countries provide data on the number of economically active males and females in the adult population; these data enable us to calculate the labor force participation rates for men and women. The information provided must, however,

---

[1] Susan P. Joekes, *Women in the World Economy,* An INSTRAW Study (New York: Oxford University Press, 1987).

[2] John D. Durand, *The Labor Force in Economic Development* (Princeton, NJ: Princeton University Press, 1975).

[3] Marianne A. Ferber and Helen M. Berg, "Labor Force Participation of Women and the Sex Ratio: A Cross-Country Analysis," *Review of Social Economy* 48, no. 1 (Spring 1991): 2–19.

be interpreted with great caution, for there are a number of factors that can produce misleading results.

First, when two otherwise similar countries include populations from a different minimum age, the one that uses a higher cutoff will appear to have a higher labor force participation rate. This is so because younger individuals are more likely to be in school. Second, when there is a larger proportion of the population in age groups that still tend to be in school, or that are already retired, there will be a lower labor force participation rate. Third, the number of years young people generally spend in school and the typical retirement age obviously influence the proportion of those who are economically active.

Insofar as these variables influence the proportion of men and women who are economically active in the same way, their effect can be neutralized by computing the ratio of female to male labor force participation rates in each country. For this reason, and because we are in any case primarily concerned with the relative status of women, we rely on this ratio in our discussion. Because male labor force participation has declined somewhat in the advanced industrialized countries during this century, this ratio has risen slightly more rapidly than women's labor force participation.

Even these data, however, have substantial limitations. Serious issues arise because of problems that do not affect men and women to the same extent. As was explained in Chapter 4, in the United States, all individuals 16 years of age and over who are employed or self-employed for at least one hour per week are included in the labor force; among unpaid family workers, only those working at least 15 hours a week are counted. Similar definitions are used by many, though not all, other countries. Predominantly, women are considered to be unpaid family workers, whereas men in the same family enterprise are most often considered to be self-employed; this distinction causes women's labor force participation to be relatively low, both as compared to men in the same country and as compared to women in those countries where all family workers are treated as self-employed or family enterprises are less prevalent.

Distortions are greatest in the Third World, where a substantial part of the population continues to be occupied in family establishments, most often subsistence agriculture, and are aggravated by the inevitable inaccuracy of estimates of hours worked in such an informal setting. In addition, those countries where women's labor force participation is genuinely low also appear to be most likely to undercount marginal female workers, thus exaggerating gender differences in labor force participation across countries.[4] Hence, there are serious questions about comparability.

---

[4]"In cultures where women's role in productive activity is not readily acknowledged and valued, there is likely to be a tendency to undercount the number of women who are working." United Nations, *The Economic Role of Women in the ECE Region* (New York, 1980), p. 3. This is, however, increasingly less likely to be the case with the universal shift from family and self-employment to formal employment. Also, Ester Boserup, *Women's Role in Economic Development* (New York: St. Martin's Press, 1970) suggests that an analysis of women's status should, in any case, focus on their participation in paid employment, because work in the family does not put them in as good a position to advance economically in modernizing economies.

Last, one additional problem deserves mention. As in the United States, those who work only in the household are not counted as members of the labor force. This omission is far more serious in developing countries, where water and fuel are often carried by women for long distances, clothes are washed in the river for lack of running water, and food must be procured and prepared on a daily basis for lack of refrigeration. Many goods and services generally purchased in economically advanced countries are produced at home.

For all these reasons, cross-country comparisons of labor force participation are, at best, only rough indications of actual differences in the extent to which men and women participate in productive work. In spite of these shortcomings, the data are instructive.

Table 10.1 shows the average ratio of female to male labor force participation for individual countries, as well as the mean (giving each country equal weight) for seven relatively homogeneous regions,[5] ordered from the highest to the lowest ratio according to the most recent data. There were substantial variations in the ratio between regions; the even larger variations between individual countries ranged, in the late 1980s, from 11.3 percent in Pakistan and 11.9 percent in Iran to 94.5 percent in Sweden and 88.9 percent in the former East Germany. These differences can only partly be explained in terms of differences in economic development.[6]

The least economically developed countries, those with the lowest per capita income,[7] mainly the Sub-Saharan African countries (group II), have only recently moved from the horticultural to the agricultural stage. As would be expected, they have a rather high ratio of economically active women relative to men. Many of the women continue to grow, sometimes process, and also sell food. But this is also the only group in which the ratio of economically active women to men decreased between 1950 and 1980, although even there the decline was, overall, quite modest, and the sparse data from more recent years suggest that this phase appears to be over.

---

[5]Data are not shown for the period 1985 to 1988 for the African countries, although they were available in a number of cases, because their erratic variations raised doubts about their reliability. It must also be noted that the basic grouping in this table is, inevitably, to some extent judgmental, as for instance in drawing the line between North Africa and the remainder of the continent, and between South Central and East Asia. Data are available for virtually all countries for 1950 and 1980 from *Economically Active Population: Estimates and Projections* (Geneva: International Labour Office, 1986), but for a far smaller number for the late 1980s.

[6]We would not, however, go as far as some other authors, in arguing that economic development has little or no uniform effect on female labor force participation. For that point of view, see, for instance, Nadja Youssef, *Women and Work in Developing Societies* (Berkeley: University of California Press, 1974); and Guy Standing, *Labour Force Participation and Development,* 2nd ed. (Geneva: International Labour Office, 1981). At the same time, substantial variations among regions and among individual countries within regions suggest that differences in the form that economic development takes, as well as many other factors, influence female labor force participation.

[7]Income data for various countries expressed in a single currency inevitably depend for their comparability on the exchange rate values used, which are at best approximations of their respective purchasing power. However, the differences in per capita income between countries and regions are so great in many instances that they tend to dwarf possible inaccuracies caused by such deficiencies.

The ratio of women's to men's labor force participation in the Latin American countries (group VI), most of them solidly in the agricultural phase, is considerably lower, but it has been increasing substantially in recent decades. Similarly, this ratio has been rising in most of the rest of the world, particularly in the 1980s. Growth was slowest in East Asia (group V) and Eastern Europe (group I), both areas where women's labor force participation was already quite high in 1950. Except for those regions, the upward trend may not yet have run its course.[8]

Overall, the data seen in Table 10.1 are consistent with the hypothesis that urbanization in its early stages tends to confine women to the household more than they had been in rural areas,[9] and that women's labor force participation tends to decline during the earliest stages of development, only to increase again as modernization progresses. There have, however, been many variations idiosyncratic to individual countries and regions that do not conform to the general pattern. For example, the Caribbean (Group IV) is not much more economically advanced (in terms of per capita income) than Latin America (Group VI), but it has a far higher ratio of women's to men's labor force participation. Or again, the region of North Africa, the Middle East, and South Central Asia (Group VII) includes countries that are at very different stages of economic development (per capita income in 1988 ranged from $172 in Bangladesh to $13,540 in Kuwait), but labor force participation of women tends to be very low in all of them. No doubt, such incongruities occur because economic development does not follow the same path everywhere, and that other factors than economic development often play an important part in determining female labor force participation.

As was briefly noted in Chapter 2, women's roles varied during the earliest economic stage of hunting and gathering, depending on the resources of the area, and the same was true of later stages. Thus different traditions were established, and their influence tends to linger long beyond the era during which they were shaped. For instance, the fact that the people of North Africa and the Middle East generally were pastoral, rather than horticultural, may help to explain why women's role there is so heavily centered in the household.

The importance of the nature of economic development in different countries is also illustrated by the high labor force participation of women in the Caribbean, where tourism is a major industry, and the low participation in such countries as Iran and Iraq, whose economies are dominated by oil production. There is reason to believe that guest workers (foreigners temporarily working in a country but not

---

[8]One thorough study, which analyzes labor force participation by age in various regions, reaches the different conclusion that "intensified efforts are needed if progress, rather than stagnation or declines of economic opportunities for women is to characterize the last years of the twentieth century"; see Shirley Nuss, in collaboration with Ettore Denti and David Viry, *Women in the World of Work* (Geneva: ILO, 1989), p. 119. The admittedly incomplete evidence for the 1980s, however, suggests that their projections may have been too low, as for many years used to be true of the projections in the United States.

[9]Lourdes Beneria, ed., *Women and Development: The Sexual Division of Labor in Rural Societies* (New York: Praeger, 1982).

TABLE 10.1 Ratio of Women's to Men's Labor Force Participation by World Region, 1950–1988[1]

	1950[a] (%)	1980[a] (%)	1985-88[b] (%)	Per Capita GNP 1988 ($)
I. Eastern Europe	65.3	77.1	–	6125
(Subset)	(56.7)	(75.1)	(79.4)	7096
Albania	73.0	70.1	–	981
Bulgaria	75.1	85.4	85.9[d]	6004
Czechoslavakia	57.1	82.0	81.0[c]	8862
Germany, Dem. Rep.	64.9	75.4	88.9[c]	11240
Hungary	38.4	73.4	78.9[j]	6780
Poland	68.6	78.7	–	4734
Romania	78.8	83.3	–	5107
Union of Soviet Socialist Republics	83.9	85.8	–	8819
Yugoslavia	47.8	59.5	62.1[c]	2596
II. Sub-Sahara Africa	65.8	62.5	–	522
Angola	69.9	66.0	–	1364
Benin	85.6	92.2	–	363
Botswana	62.0	55.4	–	1011
Burkina Faso	94.6	89.8	–	240
Burundi	96.9	91.5	–	209
Cameron	62.8	53.1	–	1167
Cape Verde	25.4	32.5	–	742
Central African Rep.	93.5	86.0	–	401
Chad	29.5	28.0	–	189
Comoros	73.6	71.9	–	–
Congo	65.9	64.1	–	928
Equatorial Guinea	70.2	67.5	–	407
Ethiopia	67.8	64.4	–	114
Gabon	68.9	62.7	–	3083
Gambia	72.6	71.1	–	256
Ghana	79.1	69.2	–	349
Guinea	73.0	69.8	–	327
Guinea-Bissau	73.6	69.7	–	149
Ivory Coast	84.7	57.0	–	780
Kenya	74.7	71.3	–	354
Lesotho	83.1	78.2	–	444
Liberia	47.5	46.0	–	488
Madagascar	72.7	68.8	–	156
Malawi	79.2	73.8	–	181
Mali	19.6	19.6	–	221
Mauritania	28.3	24.5	–	484
Mauritius	23.3	28.8	–	1737

(continued)

TABLE 10.1 Ratio of Women's to Men's Labor Force Participation by World Region, 1950–1988 (*continued*)

	1950[a] (%)	1980[a] (%)	1985-88[b] (%)	Per Capita GNP 1988 ($)
II. Sub-Sahara Africa (*continued*)				
Mozambique	97.3	96.7	–	68
Namibia	27.0	31.1	–	–
Niger	91.5	90.7	–	324
Nigeria	59.4	56.7	–	256
Réunion	21.0	47.6	–	–
Rwanda	99.5	94.8	–	316
Senegal	70.3	68.9	–	649
Sierra Leone	57.7	51.0	–	219
Somalia	71.2	66.8	–	203
Sudan	27.7	24.6	–	306
Swaziland	74.7	67.5	–	829
Tanzania	101.3	96.2	–	118
Togo	62.7	60.7	–	390
Uganda	75.0	73.3	–	271
Zaire	80.3	58.0	–	178
Zambia	39.4	37.0	–	484
Zimbabwe	61.4	56.9	–	628
III. Advanced Industrialized				
Nations	36.9	56.3	–	15835
(Subset)	(36.8)	(55.6)	(64.3)	(15531)
Australia	28.8	59.9	64.5[f]	14120
Austria	55.1	60.8	58.9[f]	16330
Belgium	30.3	49.0	61.1[f]	15110
Canada	29.2	65.2	73.3[f]	18090
Denmark	49.5	76.3	81.2[f]	20300
Finland	64.2	81.2	81.5[f]	19980
France	43.3	62.2	70.0[f]	16490
Germany, Fed. Rep	50.3	56.4	58.6[f]	19900
Greece	27.7	34.0	52.3	5225
Iceland	38.8	73.0	–	23140
Ireland	36.5	39.5	43.6[f]	8108
Israel	28.3	49.9	62.3[f]	10140
Italy	31.1	43.8	53.1[f]	13860
Japan	59.9	58.7	63.4[f]	23290
Luxembourg	40.1	46.0	50.5[f]	24380
Netherlands	30.6	44.3	57.5[f]	15320
New Zealand	30.4	50.8	69.2	12290
Norway	30.5	65.7	80.9[e]	21620
Portugal	25.3	50.0	66.0	3906
South Africa	24.7	50.9	53.2[d]	2397

(*continued*)

TABLE 10.1   Ratio of Women's to Men's Labor Forces Participation by World Region 1950–1988 (*continued*)

	1950[a] (%)	1980[a] (%)	1985-88[b] (%)	Per Capita GNP 1988 ($)
III. Advanced Industrialized Nations (*continued*)				
Spain	17.2	29.8	49.4	8418
Sweden	35.9	76.5	94.5[e]	20880
Switzerland	38.6	55.1	57.0[j]	28660
United Kingdom	37.1	60.4	67.0[f]	14080
United States	39.1	67.7	73.3[f]	19840
IV. Caribbean	53.6	64.4	–	2249
(Subset)	(53.6)	(63.7)	(63.0)	(2249)
Barbados	63.2	80.7	76.8[f]	6088
Guadeloupe	57.6	69.7	75.9[f]	–
Guyana	21.3	32.2	40.5[f]	412
Haiti	90.2	76.1	64.8	349
Jamaica	54.2	82.8	69.6	1136
Martinique	53.6	69.1	–	–
Trinidad & Tobago	34.8	40.5	50.4[f]	3262
V. East Asia	59.8	64.4	–	1585
(Subset)	(45.8)	(56.6)	(60.9)	(2541)
Bhutan	58.5	53.8	–	–
Burma	65.2	64.3	–	278
Cambodia	73.1	71.3	–	–
China	71.0	80.8	–	501
Hong Kong	38.8	59.9	60.8	–
India	49.7	40.1	–	329
Indonesia	34.0	45.2	63.0	414
Korea, Dem. Rep	81.3	82.9	–	1328
Korea, Rep	48.6	62.2	61.7[f]	3950
Laos	91.6	87.2	–	–
Malaysia	35.8	53.7	55.0[f]	1972
Mongolia	80.9	83.5	–	–
Nepal	54.8	56.1	–	173
Philippines	53.8	49.3	58.0[f]	639
Singapore	24.1	54.8	59.8[f]	9367
Sri Lanka	35.9	38.2	47.4	415
Thailand	95.0	89.5	81.2[c]	1031
Vietnam	83.9	85.6	–	202
VI. Latin America	20.7	31.1	–	1652
(Subset)	(21.5)	(33.1)	(44.7)	(1840)
Argentina	26.1	36.4	35.9	3087

(*continued*)

TABLE 10.1 Ratio of Women's to Men's Labor Forces Participation by World Region 1950–1988 (*continued*)

	1950[a] (%)	1980[a] (%)	1985-88[b] (%)	Per Capita GNP 1988 ($)
VI. Latin America (*continued*)				
Bolivia	24.0	28.2	29.4	624
Brazil	18.0	36.8	48.6	2473
Chile	24.6	36.7	40.2[f]	1609
Colombia	22.4	29.1	58.8[h]	1168
Costa Rica	17.7	27.6	37.3[h]	1569
Cuba	15.4	44.3	56.1[f]	3353
Dominican Republic	10.9	14.4	–	568
Ecuador	19.9	24.2	43.2	937
El Salvador	19.6	33.5	–	1042
Guatemala	15.0	16.4	31.0	867
Honduras	13.3	18.7	–	841
Mexico	14.9	37.0	42.7	2076
Nicaragua	15.6	27.5	44.4	311
Panama	25.0	37.0	45.2[f]	1920
Paraguay	26.2	26.1	–	1328
Peru	26.8	32.4	66.3	1846
Puerto Rico	27.0	39.1	52.1[e]	–
Uruguay	29.9	41.0	46.1	2567
Venezuela	22.3	35.6	38.6	3198
VII. North Africa, Middle East, South Central Asia	9.6	16.4	–	3927
(Subset)	(15.0)	(19.2)	(20.7)	(3874)
Afghanistan	6.7	8.2	–	214
Algeria	2.9	8.8	12.6	2160
Bahrain	3.8	17.3	24.2[f]	6062
Bangladesh	5.0	7.1	12.2	172
Egypt	7.3	9.7	19.1[i]	1455
Iran	11.6	18.7	11.9[i]	6132
Iraq	3.6	23.2	14.0	3742
Jordan	5.6	9.2	–	1476
Kuwait	5.8	20.1	37.4[f]	13540
Lebanon	12.3	29.0	–	–
Lybia	5.1	8.8	–	6022
Morocco	7.4	22.6	–	753
Oman	3.1	8.5	–	5673
Pakistan	9.8	12.5	11.3	338
Qatar	2.9	12.0	–	12560
Saudia Arabia	3.2	7.9	–	5308
Syria	9.1	17.9	–	1275
Tunisia	5.0	27.0	–	1236

(*continued*)

**TABLE 10.1   Ratio of Women's to Men's Labor Forces Participation
by World Region, 1950–1988 (continued)**

	1950[a] (%)	1980[a] (%)	1985-88[b] (%)	Per Capita GNP 1988 ($)
VII. North Africa, Middle East, South Central Asia (continued)				
Turkey	84.9	55.7	43.5[h]	1263
United Arab Emirates	2.9	12.1	–	11820
Yemem, Arab Rep.	6.3	12.5	–	407
Yemen, Dem. Rep.	7.6	11.7	–	849

[a]Data are for the economically active population aged 10 years and over relative to the total population (no age restriction).

[b]Data are for the most recently available year between 1985 and 1988 and are for population 10 years of age and over, unless otherwise indicated. Data are not shown for the Sub-Saharan African countries because information was available for only 7 countries and tended to vary erratically relative to previous values.

[c]Employees only.

[d]20 years of age and over.

[e]16 years of age and over.

[f]15 years of age and over.

[g]14 years of age and over.

[h]12 years of age and over.

[i]6 years of age and over.

[j]total population (no age restriction).

Sources: Years 1950 and 1980 from *Economically Active Population: Estitmates and Projections 1950–2025*, Geneva: International Labour Organization Office, 1986; years 1985–1988 from International Labour Organization, *Yearbook of Labour Statistics*, 1988, 1945–1989, and 1989–1990; for Czechoslavakia, Germany, Dem. Rep., Thailand, and Yugoslavia, from United Nations, *Demographic Yearbook*, 1988.

expected to remain there) in such Western European countries as the former West Germany and Switzerland may to some extent be substitutes for female workers and therefore have a depressing effect on women's employment.[10] Last, the negative effect of large numbers of children, even though it is not as great in agricultural economies as in industrialized ones,[11] helps to explain the situation in Latin America, as well as in North Africa, the Middle East, and South Central Asia (groups VI and VII).

[10]Patricia Roos, *Gender and Work: A Comparative Analysis of Industrial Societies* (Albany, NY: SUNY Press, 1985) suggests that the sharp increase in women's labor force participation in Sweden coincided with a substantial cutback in use of workers from abroad.

[11]This was found by a number of studies of developing countries, such as Jere R. Behrman and Barbara L. Wolfe, "Labor Force Participation and Earnings Determinants for Women in the Special Conditions of Developing Countries," *Journal of Development Economics* 15 (1984): 259–88, and Allen C. Kelley and Lea M. deSilva, "The Choice of Family Size and the Compatibility of Female Workforce Participation in the Low Income Setting," *Revue Economique* 31, no. 6 (November 1980): 1081–1101.

It is clear, however, that such factors as ideology and religion also play an important part. For one, fertility is, to a greater or lesser degree, influenced by governmental policies and religious doctrines. In numerous countries, there have at one time or another been laws prohibiting various types of family planning. Divine sanctions have frequently been invoked against those who chose not to follow the command to "be fruitful and multiply." On the other hand, in China and Singapore, for instance, there have been severe penalties for having more than a specified number of children. Second, beliefs in what are appropriate roles for men and women, whether shaped by the dogma of philosophers, church, or state, appear to have considerable influence on the extent to which women's activities are confined to the home.

In general, universalistic, egalitarian standards tend to be positively related to the role women play in the economy. It has been found, for instance, that a more equal distribution of income is associated with higher female labor force participation,[12] as is a larger share of resources allocated to social welfare.[13] Marxist ideology, which strongly advocates women's entry into the work force, surely helps to explain the situation in Eastern Europe up to 1989. It remains to be seen what the long-term impact of the dramatic changes that took place during that year will be.

Religion, as well as other ideologies, appears to play a part. For instance, in predominantly Catholic countries, women's labor force participation tends to be relatively low, as is clearly the case in Latin American countries (group VI). Similarly, within the industrialized nations (group III), the ratio of women's to men's labor force participation rate tends to be lower in the predominantly Catholic countries (for example, Austria, the former West Germany, Ireland, Luxembourg, and Spain). Further, the highest ratios are found in the Scandinavian countries, which are not Catholic, and where there is also a notable dedication to an egalitarian ideology. Group VII, on the other hand, consists entirely of Moslem countries, which have emphasized women's roles as wives and mothers to the virtual exclusion of activities outside the home.[14] Even here, however, women carry on income-earning activities in the home, which are not taken into account as labor force participation.

An inspection of labor force data in Table 10.1 also reveals that the changes in women's work roles, which we have seen in the United States in recent decades, are reasonably representative of other advanced industrialized countries in general. This

---

[12]Moshe Semyanov, "The Social Context of Women's Labor Force Participation: A Comparative Analysis," *American Journal of Sociology* 86, no. 3 (November, 1980): 534–50, using a regression with industrialization, fertility, and the divorce rate as additional variables, finds that a higher degree of inequality leads to a lower labor force participation rate. The measure of inequality used is the percentage of income going to the top 5 percent of the population.

[13]Jane Weiss, Francisco Ramirez, and Terry Tracy, "Female Participation in the Occupation System: A Comparative Institutional Analysis," *Social Problems* 23, no. 5 (June, 1976): 593–608.

[14]A substantial proportion of the small minority of women who do work outside the home have jobs that involve working with girls and women, most notably as teachers, nurses, and servants.

may also be seen in Figure 10.1, where we look in greater detail at patterns in six countries. There have, however, been some exceptions. Labor force participation of women in Italy and Japan declined somewhat in the 1960s as the agricultural sectors, where women were heavily represented, were shrinking. More recently, women's influx into the modern sector has halted the downward trend there.[15]

As can also be seen in Figure 10.1, labor force participation has risen more for women between ages 20 and 60 than for those younger and older. As more of the former remained in school longer, and more of the latter retired earlier, participation rates for these groups actually declined in some instances, reducing the increase for women as a whole. This has been all the more true because the proportion of elderly in the population has been increasing.[16]

Finally, Figure 10.1 shows that lifetime participation patterns vary across countries.[17] In Italy, and especially in Ireland, female labor force participation still declines with age after an early peak. As we have seen, this was also characteristic of the United States before World War II. In Japan and the United Kingdom, there is an M-shaped pattern; labor force participation decreases during the childbearing years but increases to a second peak later. This pattern prevailed in the United States between World War II and the early 1970s. Of the countries seen here, only the United States and Sweden show an inverted U pattern, similar to that for men, where labor force participation rises during the early years, reaches a plateau, and eventually declines as retirement age approaches.

Occupational Segregation

Just as there are substantial differences in women's labor force participation, so there are in the degree of occupational segregation.[18] There are a number of reasons why occupational segregation is a matter of concern. Jobs vary in terms of the skills, effort, and preparation they require, as well as the challenges, rewards, and opportunities for power and influence they offer. There may be differences between men and women in the assortment of characteristics they typically prefer. Because, however, not everyone is "typical," but on the contrary, there is considerable variation within each group, gender typing to the point that

[15]Constance Sorrentino, "International Comparisons of Labor Force Participation, 1960–81," *Monthly Labor Review* 106, no. 2 (February 1983): 23–36.

[16]A good example is the former West Germany of the 1970s, which experienced substantial growth in the participation rates of most age groups, but approximate stability for the total population of women.

[17]At the same time, it must be noted, as was pointed out in Chapter 4, that cross-sectional participation rates tend to be misleading when the experiences of cohorts is changing.

[18]Both are, in part, artifacts of biases in data collection. There is evidence that some countries particularly understate women's participation in agriculture, as, for instance, discussed in Lourdes Beneria, "Conceptualizing the Labor Force: The Underestimation of Women's Economic Activities," *Journal of Development Studies* 17, no. 3 (April 1981): 10–28.

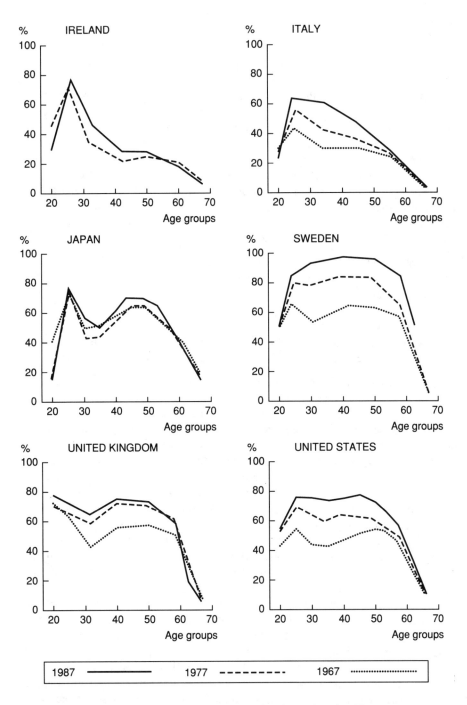

Note: When the last age bracket is 65 and over, this has been plotted at 67½ years.

Source: Organization for Economic Co-operation and Development, *OECD Employment Outlook* (September 1988), Ch. 5, pp. 132–33. Reprinted by permission.

FIGURE 10.1   Female Labor Force Participation Rates by Age, 1967–1987

particular occupations are virtually monopolized by one sex would appear to unnecessarily reduce options for many individuals.

As we have seen, in the United States, there has been and continues to be a considerable amount of occupational segregation by gender. There also continues to be a great deal of disagreement as to why this is the case. Though available data are far from ideal for this purpose and, as we shall see, have serious limitations, comparing the situation in different countries can shed some light on this question.

The main problems are that many countries provide no detailed data on the occupational distribution of men and women at all, and those that do tend to use various classification schemes. The only standardized grouping available for a large number of countries is that of the seven very broad occupational categories in the International Labour Organization Yearbook. They are as follows:

- Professional, technical, and related workers
- Administrative and managerial workers
- Clerical and related workers
- Sales workers
- Service workers
- Agricultural, animal husbandry and forestry workers, fishermen and hunters
- Production-related workers, transport equipment operators, and laborers

As discussed in Chapter 5, the most common measure of occupational segregation is the index of segregation, which is equal to the percentage of one group that would have to change jobs in order for the occupational distribution of the two groups to be the same. It will also be recalled that this measure gives substantially different results depending on how detailed the occupational categories are. Only a few large groupings are used here; we would therefore expect relatively low levels of segregation as compared to those found when more detailed occupational categories are used. The results are shown in Table 10.2.

It is obvious at first glance that there is considerable variation in the degree of occupational segregation among the countries, from a low of 9.7 in China and 9.9 in Thailand to a high of 62.3 in Qatar and 60.2 percent in the United Arab Emirates. The causes of these extreme differences are not obvious. If the requirement for physical strength were the primary reason for keeping women out of some jobs, segregation would be expected to decline as technology becomes more sophisticated. If women chose different occupations mainly because they did not expect to spend much time in the labor market, segregation would be expected to be lower where women's labor force attachment is greater. If the dominant cause were that men and women are better suited to or prefer different types of work, the degree of segregation would be expected to be fairly similar across countries. Further, women would tend to be over- or underrepresented in the same occupational categories. The existing situation does not, for the most part, conform to any of these hypotheses.

Clearly, the occupational structure of an economy can have a considerable effect on the degree of occupational segregation. Take the extreme case where

TABLE 10.2 Occupational Segregation by World Region[a]

	Occupational Segregation Index		*Occupational Segregation Index*
I. Eastern Europe	**31.3**	**IV. Caribbean**	**41.7**
Bulgaria	26.2	Bahamas	41.0
Czechoslavakia	32.7[b]	Barbados	31.6
Hungary	34.8	Belize	55.9
Poland	30.7[b]	Bermuda	41.7
Yugoslavia	32.1	French Guyana	39.8
		Grenada	32.8
II. Sub-Saharan Africa	**20.5**	Guyana	47.1
Botswana	27.0	Haiti	35.3
Burundi	10.1[b]	Montserrat	49.2
Cameroon	22.2[b]	Netherlands Antilles	50.6
Central African Rep.	18.6[b]	St. Christopher and Nevis	33.1
Comoros	14.8	St. Lucia	34.2
Gambia	22.3	St. Pierre and Miquellon	45.6
Ghana	20.8	St. Vincent and the Grenadines	39.0
Liberia	25.1	Trinidad & Tobago	46.7
Togo	11.9	Turks and Caicos	34.2
Zambia	29.7	Virgin Islands (British)	57.1
Zimbabwe	23.2	Virgin Islands (U.S.)	36.3
III. Advanced Industrialized Nations	**39.5**	**V. East Asia**	**17.9**
		China	9.7
Australia	31.9	Hong Kong	15.0
Austria	44.5	India	19.8
Belgium	38.5	Indonesia	13.7
Canada	39.8	Korea, Rep.	17.8
Denmark	48.0	Malaysia	16.0
Finland	42.7	Philippines	35.8
France	38.4	Singapore	26.6[c]
Germany, Fed., Rep.	36.9	Sri Lanka	14.7
Gibralter	42.4	Thailand	9.9
Greece	25.4		
Ireland	49.3	**VI. Latin America**	**43.5**
Israel	42.1	Chile	49.4[c]
Japan	23.2	Colombia	32.4
Luxembourg	48.9	Costa Rica	42.5
Netherlands	38.5	Cuba	45.7
New Zealand	41.5	Dominica	46.5
Norway	46.3	Dominican Rep	48.6
Portugal	26.0	Ecuador	46.5
South Africa	45.6	Guatemala	57.2
Spain	36.4	Mexico	39.0
Sweden	41.7	Panama	53.2
Switzerland	39.3	Paraguay	46.4
United Kingdom	44.5	Peru	30.2
United States	36.6		

(continued)

TABLE 10.2   Occupational Segregation by World Region (*continued*)

	Occupational Segregation Index		Occupational Segregation Index
Puerto Rico	36.1	Egypt	24.6
Uruguay	30.8	Iraq	47.8[b]
Venezuela	48.6	Kuwait	51.1
		Pakistan	18.6
VII. North Africa, Middle East,	**43.0**	Qatar	62.3
South Central Asia		Syria	45.9
		Tunisia	19.3[b]
Bahrain	57.9	Turkey	43.2
Brunei	41.7	United Arab Emirates	60.2

[a]Data are for the 1980s, unless otherwizse indicated. Bangladesh was omitted because the data for 1981 show occupational segregation of 0.1 percent, entirely out of line with data for earlier years.
[b]Data are from the 1970s.
[c]Employees only.
Source: Calculated from data in ILO *Yearbook of Labour Statistics*, 1988, 1989–1990, and 1945–1989.

agriculture, possibly subsistence farming, is the only way of making a living. There may well be a substantial division of labor within that sector, but obviously, all men and women will be in the same "occupation," using the broad definitions employed in Table 10.2. Although this is not entirely true for any country, agriculture tends to be the dominant sector in the countries in Sub-Saharan Africa, where the index of occupational segregation ranges from 10 to 30 percent. The proportion of the economically active population in the agricultural sector ranges from 50 percent in Botswana to 93 percent in Burundi. At the same time, women in these countries are represented in agriculture to about the same extent as, or even to a greater extent than, in the labor force.[19]

On the other hand, in some Latin American countries, there is also a large proportion of the economically active population in agriculture. In these countries, however, according to official statistics, women are very underrepresented in this occupation, and the index of occupational segregation is high.

It is this type of incongruity that raises serious questions about explaining occupational segregation primarily in rational, economic terms. When women do much of the agricultural work in developing African countries, and very little in North America and Western Europe, it is easy to point to the differences in what such workers do. But when we find that the representation of women differs substantially among countries where agricultural practices differ far less, it becomes

---

[19]Interestingly, occupational segregation is also low in Hong Kong, where manufacturing dominates, but which is one of only two countries where the proportion of women among production workers is at least as great as their proportion in the labor force.

obvious that similar work is considered appropriate only for men in some societies, but viewed as equally or even more appropriate for women elsewhere.

There are other puzzling differences in the occupational distribution among countries as well, which suggest that the determination of what jobs came to be designated male or female is likely to be influenced by discrimination and tradition, rather than solely by objective ability to do the work. In the vast majority of cases, women are less heavily represented among administrative and managerial workers (interestingly, the United States is one of only three countries where women make up one-third or more of persons in this occupation) and among production workers than in the labor force. But in other occupations, there is considerable diversity.[20] The great range of differences in the proportion of women in each occupational category in individual countries may be seen in Table 10.3.

The data we have used for these calculations have serious limitations. As previously mentioned, they represent broad categories and provide no information about the extent of segregation by more detailed occupations, which may be substantial. Second, they do not tell us to what extent women are distributed throughout the hierarchy within each occupational group. Third, the nature of particular occupations may vary radically from one economy to another, particularly when they are at very different levels of economic development. Secretaries may copy letters longhand or operate sophisticated word processing machinery. Agricultural workers may till the land with a hoe or use complex farm equipment. Transport workers may lift heavy boxes or push buttons.

Even with all these shortcomings, the picture that emerges is instructive. An examination of Table 10.3 dispels the view that most clerical and service work is always done by women or that only an extremely small proportion of women is capable of doing managerial or blue-collar work. We, therefore, conclude that the substantial degree of occupational segregation found in many countries cannot be explained simply by inherent differences between women and men alone. On the contrary, not only economic factors but such considerations as social norms, traditions, religious beliefs, and other noneconomic considerations appear to play an important part in the varied pattern of the distribution of men and women by occupation.

Similar hard-to-explain differences are also found in the representation of women in elected public positions in various countries. For instance, as of 1987, women made up more than one-fourth of parliamentary representatives in Denmark, Finland, Norway, and Sweden. The same was true in most East European countries, Cuba, and Mongolia, but representatives in those countries arguably had little real power. On the other hand, in large numbers of countries in Africa, Latin Amer-

---

[20]There tends to be less diversity within regions. For instance, women are underrepresented among professional workers in virtually all Sub-Saharan African countries, and overrepresented in the great majority of countries in the other regions. Similarly, women tend to be overrepresented in agriculture in most Sub-Saharan African, East Asian, and East European countries, but underrepesented in almost all countries in other regions.

TABLE 10.3   Percent of Workers Who are Women by Major Occupational Categories

	3 Highest Percent	3 Lowest Percent	United States
Professional, technical, and related workers	64.0 Philippines 60.3 Denmark 58.2 Uruguay	15.2 Pakistan 16.3 Central African Republic 17.8 Cameroon	49.8
Administrative and managerial workers	39.2 Virgin Islands, U.S. 37.9 U.S. 33.4 Haiti	0.0 Comoros 0.9 Qatar 1.2 United Arab Emirates	37.9
Clerical and related workers	84.5 Bulgaria 83.1 Czechoslovakia 82.0 Bermuda	3.1 Pakistan 6.4 India 7.3 Iraq	80.1
Sales workers	89.7 Haiti 89.0 Ghana 85.4 Togo	1.1 Qatar 1.2 United Arab Emirates 1.8 Syria	48.0
Service workers	79.0 Finland 77.5 Norway 77.1 French Guyane	5.5 Comoros 6.0 Syria 6.3 Central African Republic	60.6
Agriculture, animal husbandry and forestry workers, fishermen and hunters	55.7 Burundi 54.1 Gambia 53.9 Bulgaria	0.0 Gibralter 0.0 Qatar 0.0 St. Pierre and Miquelon	15.8
Production-related workers, transportation and equipment operators and laborers	44.8 Ghana 38.0 Togo 35.4 China	0.1 Qatar 0.1 United Arab Emirates 0.2 Kuwait	18.2

Source: Calculated from data in ILO *Yearbook of Labour Statistics*, 1988, 1945–1989, and 1989–1990.

ica, and Asia, women comprised less than 4 percent of these bodies. Women also held 37 percent of ministerial positions in Norway, 25 percent in Bhutan, 22 percent in Dominica, 17 percent in Sweden, 16 percent in Tanzania, 14 percent in Norway, and 13 percent in Canada, Senegal, and Uruguay, as well as 10 percent or more in ten other countries; however, women are entirely unrepresented in numerous other nations. Finally, as of the end of 1990, 17 women had been elected heads of state during this century, only five of them from Europe, and none from North America.[21]

The Male-Female Earnings Gap

As we have seen, the patterns of labor force participation and occupational segregation in various countries are anything but simple. This is no less true of the earnings gap and its relation to labor force participation and occupational distribution. As we shall see, though the difference between men's and women's earnings has declined in most countries for which data are available, this is not universally true, and the rate of change varies substantially. Nor is there a discernable relationship between the size of the earnings gap and the degree of occupational segregation.

Table 10.4 provides data on the ratio of women's to men's hourly earnings in manufacturing in advanced industrialized countries, except for the United States, for which only weekly earnings are available.[22] Because weekly earnings are influenced by the number of hours and days worked, the earnings differential in the United States is likely to be larger than if hourly wages were compared. There are also differences in the precise definition of wages among various countries, concerning such issues as whether the data are restricted to adults, and whether they include income in kind, family allowances, and so on. Further, the question may be raised to what extent wages in manufacturing are representative for the whole economy. However, the evidence for countries that provide data both for manufacturing and for all nonagricultural workers shows that the differences in the size of the earnings gap are relatively small and can be in either direction. Most importantly, the trend for the two series has been very similar in all instances.

Contrary to what might be expected, the earnings gap is small in a number of countries where occupational segregation is relatively high, such as Sweden and Denmark, whereas in Japan, for instance, it is quite large, though occupational segregation is relatively low. This evidence suggests that the size of pay differentials within and among different occupations as well as gender differences in occupational distribution are important.[23] Until we learn more about this intriguing issue we shall not be able to answer the various questions raised by

---

[21] United Nations, *The World's Women in 1970–1990: Trends and Statistics,* 1991.

[22] A few other countries also provided earnings data for men and women; however the data tend to fluctuate erratically over quite short periods of time, raising serious questions about their reliability.

[23] Similar conclusions were reached by Donald J. Treiman and Patricia A. Roos, "Sex and Earnings in Industrial Society: A Nine-Nation Comparison," *American Journal of Sociology* 89, no. 3 (April 1984): 612–46. They found that there was almost no effect of occupational distribution on earnings but quite substantial and complicated effects of rates of return for men and women within major occupational groups. The suggested explanation is that the observed differences reflect the legacy of traditional patterns of disadvantages and discrimination (p. 643).

TABLE 10.4   Ratio of Women's to Men's Hourly Earnings in Manufacturing: Selected Years, 1955–1988

	1955	*1973*	*1982*	*1988*
Australia[a]	69.0	69.4	78.2	79.6
Belgium	56.8	68.7	73.5	74.5
Denmark[b]	65.3	82.3	85.1	84.4
Finland[c]	67.6	71.7	77.1	77.2
France	n.a.	76.8	77.7	79.2[j]
Germany, Fed. Rep[d]	62.8	70.9	73.0	73.0
Greece	64.7[g]	65.5	73.1	78.0
Ireland	56.3	59.9	68.5	68.9
Japan	44.7	53.9	48.8	48.5[i]
Luxembourg	–	55.3	60.1	58.4
Netherlands	58.8	75.5	74.1	74.8
New Zealand	62.8	65.8[h]	70.8	74.6
Norway[a]	67.4	76.2	83.2	84.3
Sweden[e]	69.2	84.1	90.3	90.0
Switzerland[d]	63.7	65.4	67.0	67.5
United Kingdom	58.6	60.7	68.8	68.0
United States[f]	–	61.7	65.4	70.2

[a] Earnings of employees only.
[b] Excludes vacation pay.
[c] Includes mining and quarrying, electricity.
[d] Includes family allowances paid by employers.
[e] Includes holiday and sick pay, and value of payments in kind.
[f] Usual weekly earnings of full-time workers.
[g] 1961.
[h] 1974.
[i] 1986.
[j] 1987.
Sources: Calculated from data in International Labour Organization, *Yearbook of Labour Statistics*, various years, except U.S. data are from the U.S. Department of Labor, *Employment and Earnings*, various issues; and Japanese data are from Organizational for Economic Cooperation and Development, *Employment Outlook* (September 1988), p. 212.

the existing relationships between occupations and earnings in various countries. The overcrowding model presented in Chapter 7 suggests that relative supply and demand conditions in female and male jobs would be an important factor. Further, government policies, which may set a floor on wages or limit pay differentials among occupations, could also play a role.

Thus, no uniform patterns emerge from an examination of the data in Table 10.4, except that women are always paid less than men. Scholars who have examined this situation have tended to put far more emphasis on this fact than on the very substantial extent to which the size of the earnings gap differs, even among

COMPARABLE WORTH IN AUSTRALIA

In the 1960s, among full-time, year-round workers, women earned 60 percent as much as men in both Australia and the United States. By 1976, the wage ratio in Australia had increased to 77 percent; while it had remained roughly constant in the United States. The implementation of equal pay and, particularly, of comparable worth in Australia appears to account for the sharp increase in women's earnings there. The following is a description of these changes.*

Australia has an unusual wage determination system that differs markedly from that in the United States. In Australia, minimum wage rates for occupations are determined by government wage tribunals. Up to 1969, the Australian pay structure explicitly discriminated against women. Until World War II, female award rates were set at 54 percent of male rates; in 1950, this was raised to 75 percent. In 1969, the concept of equal pay for equal work was implemented, and the award rate was raised to 100 percent. Predominantly female occupations were, however, excluded from the equal pay provisions. In 1972, the federal tribunal moved towards comparable worth by deciding that the "equal pay for equal work" concept should be expanded to "equal pay for work of equal value" in order to cover female employees in predominantly female jobs. As noted above, the result of these policies, particularly the implementation of comparable worth, was a 17 percentage point reduction in the gender pay gap.

During these years, the unemployment rate of women continued to fall relative to that of men, and employment continued to grow faster for women than for men. However, implementation of comparable worth appears to have been associated with a decline in the *relative* employment of women; that is, their employment increased less rapidly than would have been expected if their wages had not risen.** The explanation for the fairly small negative impact of comparable worth on women's employment is thought to be that the persistent high degree of occupational segregation constituted a substantial barrier to the replacement of women by men as the wage gap declined.

Clearly, the Australian institutional structure, with its reliance on wage tribunals to determine occupational pay rates, facilitated the transition to pay equity. The Australian

---

*This account is based on Robert G. Gregory and Vivian Ho, "Equal Pay and Comparable Worth: What Can The U.S. Learn from the Australian Experience?" (The Australian National University, Centre for Economic Policy Research, Discussion Paper no. 123, July 1985); R. G. Gregory and A. E. Daily, "Can Economic Theory Explain Why Australian Women are So Well Paid Relative to Their U.S. Counterparts?" paper presented at the 8th conference on Women's Wages: Stability and Changes in Six Industrialized Countries, Chicago, March 1990; Mark Killingsworth, *The Economics of Comparable Worth* (Kalamazoo, MI: W.E. Upjohn Institute for Employment Research, 1990); and Francine D. Blau and Lawrence M. Kahn, "The Gender Earnings Gap: Some International Evidence," paper presented at the NBER Comparative Labor Markets Project Conference on Differences and Changes in Wage Structures, London, September 1991.

**See Killingsworth, *The Economics of Comparable Worth.* June O'Neill, Michael Brien, and James Cunningham ("Effects of Comparable Worth Policy: Evidence from Washington State," *American Economic Review* 79 [May 1989]: 305–309) also found negative effects on women's relative employment when comparable worth was introduced in Minnesota, Washington State, and San Jose.

experience also suggests that there were costs to the adoption of this policy. Nonetheless, the finding that a large and rapid increase in the relative wages of women did not have large adverse effects on their employment is certainly of considerable interest and may have implications for other countries as well.

---

advanced industrialized countries.[24] Similarly, there has been more emphasis on the fact that the earnings gap has, for the most part, been declining in the countries in our sample than that the rate of change has varied considerably.[25]

As can be seen in Table 10.4, the earnings gap was greater in the United States than in 12 of the 16 other advanced industrialized countries in 1973, than in 14 in 1982, and than in 11 in 1988. In addition, between 1973 and 1982, when most of the change in the other countries took place, the earnings gap declined more slowly here than in 10 of the other countries. It should be noted, however, that only one other country experienced a decline in the earnings gap equal to the decline in this country between 1982 and 1988. If this trend continues, the picture may be expected to be significantly different by the end of the century.

---

[24]Examples include Marjorie Galenson, *Women and Work: An International Comparison* (New York State School of Industrial and Labor Relations, 1973) and Treiman and Roos, "Sex and Earnings in Industrial Society." This is somewhat less true of Jacob Mincer, "Inter-Country Comparisons of Labor Force Trends and of Related Developments: An Overview," in *Trends in Women's Work, Education, and Family Building,* Richard Layard and Jacob Mincer, eds., *Journal of Labor Economics* 3, no. 1, Part 2 (January 1985). A recent paper suggests that these intercountry differences are related to the extent of wage inequality in each country. The authors find that although U.S. women compare favorably with women in other industrialized countries on several measures of skill relative to men, their earnings relative to men are reduced by the much larger wage penalty that the U.S. labor market places on those with below-average levels of market skills. The higher level of wage inequality in the United States fully accounts for the lower gender ratio in the United States in comparison to the Scandinavian countries and Australia, the countries with the smallest gaps. See Francine D. Blau and Lawrence M. Kahn, "The Gender Earnings Gap: Learning from International Comparisons," *American Economic Review* 82, no. 2 (May 1992).

[25]Two interesting, but conflicting, interpretations of why the earnings differential decreased in Great Britain are to be found in B. Chiplin, M. M. Curran, and C. J. Parsley, "Relative Female Earnings in Great Britain and the Impact of Legislation," in *Women and Low Pay,* P. J. Sloan, ed. (London: Macmillan, 1980) and A. Zabalza and Z. Tzannatos, "The Effect of Britain's Anti-Discriminatory Legislation on Relative Pay and Employment," *Economic Journal* 95, no. 379 (September 1985): 679–99. Similarly, conflicting views are found about the situation in Australia, for instance in R. G. Gregory, R. Austie, A. Daly, and V. Ho, "Women's Pay in Australia, Great Britain and the U.S.: The Role of Laws, Regulations, and Human Capital," in *Pay Equity,* Robert T. Michael, Heidi Hartmann, and Brigid O'Farrell, eds. (Washington, DC: National Academy Press, 1989 and Mark R. Killingsworth, *The Economics of Comparable Worth* (Kalamazoo, MI: Upjohn Inst., 1990), Chapter 6.

Government and Employer Programs for Working Families in Advanced Industrialized Countries

Employers in some of the advanced industrialized countries have been providing fringe benefits to their employees for a very long time. Such benefits proliferated considerably after World War II and in recent years have increasingly included programs particularly helpful to two-earner and single parent families. There has also been progress in offering more flexible terms of employment, which are intended to make it easier for workers to meet their responsibilities both to job and family. These policies have at times been voluntary or the result of collective bargaining, but they have frequently been the consequence of government mandates. In addition, governments are providing a variety of programs themselves.

Most other countries have gone much further much faster than the United States, not only in providing government services, but also in imposing government mandates. As a result, social welfare expenditures for mandated programs, substantial even in this country, tend to be considerably larger in the other nations; these are, however, in part offset by greater voluntary expenditures in the United States (see Table 10.5).

Among the benefits other governments require employers to provide are relatively generous provisions for public holidays, ranging from 6 in the United States to 11–13 in Germany,[26] and annual paid leave, not yet introduced in this country, but as long as 30 days in Denmark.[27] Except for the United States, all advanced industrialized countries (as well as many others) have mandated paid maternity leave, from 12 weeks in the Netherlands to 11 months in Finland. Further, the Scandinavian countries and Germany provide for paternity leave at the time of childbirth, and Italy and Sweden require some parental leave for child care.

As previously noted, employers often go beyond compliance with government mandates in accommodating workers with dual responsibilities. Opportunities for part-time work have been growing in most countries, occasionally including job sharing, and flexible schedules are becoming increasingly common. Such flextime arrangements may take many forms, from modest adjustments in starting and leaving time to employees virtually setting their own schedules, as long as they get their job done.

One of the benefits that has received considerable attention is child care, whether paid for by employers or government. Progress in making it available has been uneven, but the proportion of preschoolers aged 3 to 5 who are cared for in

[26]Organization for Economic Cooperation and Development, *Living Conditions in OECD Countries,* 1986.

[27]Organization for Economic Cooperation and Development, *Employment Outlook,* 1986.

TABLE 10.5   Social Welfare Expenditures of Selected Countries in the European Community as Percent of Gross Domestic Product

| Country | EXPENDITURES | | |
	Mandated	Non-Mandated	Total
Belgium	27.9	1.5	29.4
Denmark	27.6	1.1	28.7
France	23.1	5.4	28.5
Germany	26.9	2.2	29.1
Italy	22.3	1.0	23.3
Netherlands	29.6	4.1	33.7
U.K.	19.5	4.6	24.1
U.S.	14.1	7.5	21.6
Average, excluding U.S.	25.3	2.8	28.1

Notes: Social Welfare Costs include customary spending and other expenditures of a social nature.

Source: Adapted from Martin Rein, "The Social Policy of the Firm and the State," paper prepared for the Panel of Employer Policies and Working Families, Committee on Women's Employment and Related Social Issues, Commission on Behavioral and Social Science and Education, National Research Council, Washington, DC, 1989. Adapted by permission.

publicly funded or employer-subsidized centers in the European countries has been growing and is as high as 95 percent in Belgium and France.[28]

Taken in their entirety, these and other programs in advanced industrialized countries add up to a substantial package of benefits for "working families," which help to facilitate women's entry into the labor market, as well as their advancement on the job after entry. Although further progress is likely to be slow during periods of recession and high government deficits, and may even be temporarily reversed, the outlook in the long run is toward further expansion, because the growing proportion of families without full-time homemakers may be expected to continue to exert their influence.

Household Work[29]

As was discussed at some length in earlier chapters, the roles of women and men in the labor market are closely interrelated with their roles in the household. We found that in the United States, although women's participation in the labor market

[28] Peter Moss, *Consolidated Report to the European Commission on Child Care and Equality of Opportunity,* London, England, February 1988.

[29] This discussion draws freely on Francine D. Blau and Marianne A. Ferber, "Women's Work, Women's Lives: A Comparative Economic Perspective," in *Work in Modernizing and Industrial Countries,* Hilda Kahne and Janet Z. Giele, eds., forthcoming.

TABLE 10.6   Time Spent on Housework and Market Work (hours per week)

		TOTAL WORK		HOUSEWORK		MARKET WORK	
		Men	*Women*	*Men*	*Women*	*Men*	*Women*
Denmark	1964	45.4	43.4	3.7	30.1	41.7	13.3
	1987	46.2	43.9	12.8	23.1	33.4	20.8
Finland	1979	57.8	61.1	13.8	28.6	44.0	32.5
Hungary	1977	63.7	68.9	12.9	33.8	50.8	35.1
Japan	1965	60.5	64.7	2.8	31.5	57.7	33.2
	1985	55.5	55.6	3.5	31.0	52.0	24.6
Norway	1971	53.2	54.6	15.4	41.3	37.8	13.3
	1980	51.0	50.6	16.8	33.0	34.2	17.6
Sweden	1984	57.9	55.5	18.1	31.8	39.8	23.7
U.S.	1965	63.1	60.9	11.5	41.8	51.6	18.9
	1981	57.8	54.4	13.8	30.5	44.0	23.9
USSR*	1965	64.4	75.3	9.8	31.5	54.6	43.8
	1985	65.7	66.3	11.9	27.0	53.8	39.3

*The sample is from the city of Pskov.

Adapted from F. Thomas Juster and Frank P. Stafford. "The Allocation of Time: Empirical Findings, Behavioral Models, and Problems of Measurement," *Journal of Economic Literature* 29, no. 2 (June 1991), p. 477. Adapted by permission.

has been increasing rapidly for some time, participation of men in housework began to increase only more recently. The continued unequal division of responsibilities influences both the amount of leisure men and women have and their achievements on the job. Hence, inevitably, it also influences the quality of their lives.

Table 10.6 shows broadly similar patterns for time spent on housework and market work by men and women in the eight advanced industrialized countries for which data are available. Men spend far more time on market work and women spend far more time on housework, although the total amount of work done by women and men is considerably more similar. Data collected by various organizations in 16 industrialized countries, and hence less likely to be strictly comparable, point to the same conclusion.[30] Unfortunately, data are not available separately by women's employment status. Evidence from the United States, however, suggests that women who are in the labor force, and especially those who are employed full-time, tend to work longer hours than men, whereas full-time homemakers work fewer hours than men. This may be partly explained by the fact that men spend about the same amount of time on housework whether or not their wife is

[30]United Nations, *The World's Women 1970–1990*.

employed. This situation is a matter for concern, in part because many women accommodate household demands by working part-time, and because the additional energy spent at home may in some cases inhibit the progress of full-time workers.

On the other hand, it should be noted that in all the countries where information is available for more than one year, (Denmark, Japan, Norway, the United States, and the former USSR), the number of hours men spent on housework increased over time to a greater or lesser extent, while the number of hours they spent on market work declined. The opposite was true for women, except in Japan, where the amount of time women spent in the labor market declined.

In spite of the similarities noted above, there are considerable differences between countries in the ratio of men's to women's hours of housework. For the most recent year, it ranges from 11.3 percent in Japan to 56.9 in Sweden. These patterns and trends suggest that the allocation of housework between men and women is at least to some extent responsive to government policies, as well as to changes in women's labor force roles. For example, it is widely believed that the introduction of parental leave in Sweden—rather than merely maternal leave, as is the case in most other countries—has encouraged fathers to participate in child care. In general, there appears to be some movement toward greater equality in the household as women's opportunities in the workplace continue to improve. Assuming that this trend continues, women should in turn be able to take more advantage of labor market opportunities.

Among the few developing countries for which data are available, mainly based on small individual surveys,[31] the number of hours per week women spent on domestic work ranged from 18.9 in Cameroon to 49.0 in Mexico. The figures for men were, once again, considerably lower, varying from 1.4 hours in Cameroon to 18.9 in Mexico. Overall, there is reason to conclude that, throughout the world, women do the bulk of housework and men tend to do more market work. Although, as previously noted, the amount of time spent on both together is roughly comparable for women and men in the wealthier countries, fragmentary evidence, as well as reports from observers, suggest that in poor countries women often work longer hours than men, and that the total number of hours they work is very large.

PATTERNS AND INTERPRETATIONS

One fact that clearly emerges from the evidence presented in the previous sections is that there is substantial variation in the status of women between different countries

---

[31] Such data are provided for five countries (Bangladesh, Cameroon, Mexico, Nepal, and Venezuela) in various essays in Luisella Godschmidt-Clermont, *Economic Evaluations of Unpaid Household Work: Africa, Asia, Latin America and Oceania*. (Geneva: International Labour Office, 1987). Data for Botswana and Nepal are also found in F. Thomas Juster and Frank P. Stafford, "The Allocation of Time: Empirical Findings, Behavioral Models, and Problems of Measurement," *Journal of Economic Literature* 29, no. 2 (June 1991): 471–522.

for which data are available, as measured by any of the indicators used. Labor force participation of women, as presented in official statistics, varies from negligible to a level almost equal to that of men. Segregation, with respect to major occupational categories, is so low in some countries that scarcely more than one in ten women workers would have to change jobs to duplicate the male pattern of distribution, whereas in at least one country it would involve over six out of ten women making such a change. Women in manufacturing earn between 49 and 90 percent as much per hour as men. Furthermore, the rate of change in the male-female earnings ratio has varied considerably. Even concerning housework, we found differences both in its allocation between women and men, and in the total amount done in various countries.

We began with the hypothesis that economic factors influence the status of women as compared to men, and our data provide some clues as to what a few of these might be. They also show, however, that for the most part, the situation is very complex, and that noneconomic factors also play an important role. Further, we saw that women may be doing well in a country in terms of some criteria but not in terms of others.[32] It appears that we shall have to wait for more and better data before we can learn more from international comparisons. Meanwhile, we may be able to gain some insights from comparing developing countries, where there are especially serious problems, and two countries, the former USSR and Sweden, where women appear to have made considerable progress. Also, an inset in this chapter tells us something about the situation of women in one country, Saudi Arabia, where women continue to be rigidly confined to their traditional role.

WOMEN IN DEVELOPING COUNTRIES

In our examination of the status of women, we have been emphasizing how they are doing as compared to men, whether it be in terms of labor force participation, occupational distribution, or earnings. The justification for this is obvious. For instance, women in one country may have high earnings compared to the inhabitants of a much poorer nation, but this tells us nothing about the degree of equality they have achieved with men. It is, nonetheless, clear that the absolute level of well-being is hardly a matter of indifference. Even a cursory examination of the lives of women in developing countries will dispel any doubts one might have on that score.

---

[32] A similar conclusion, that the relation of economic development and women's status is at least to a degree erratic and not readily explainable, was reached by Shirley Nuss and Larraine Majka, "The Economic Integration of Women: A Cross National Investigation," *Work and Occupations* 10, no. 1 (February 1983): 29–48.

SAUDI WOMEN

As a result of the 1991 Persian Gulf War, more attention was focused on the Middle East in general, and on Saudi Arabia in particular. Information is provided here about this most traditional of countries, and the obstacles that confront would-be reformers there. The specific occasion for the newspaper column we have excerpted* was that, encouraged by the upheavals of the pre-war period, and the presence of large numbers of foreign troops, a small group of Saudi professional women staged a protest against the ban on women operating cars, and drove through the capital city. They were stopped, arrested, and jailed. Further, they lost their jobs and their passports.

Saudi women may have been officially banned from driving, but in many other ways at least some of them appear intent on stretching the narrow limits of this male-dominated Islamic society.

Safe in the privacy of their homes, Saudi women often reveal a taste for the most stylish clothes and a willingness to ridicule social precepts drawn from a narrow interpretation of Islam, neither of which is in evidence in public.

Not surprisingly, some of the more outspoken and enterprising women here are not finding the going easy.

Their collision with the largely male-ordained traditionalism may reflect the experience of a minority of women here. But their complaints may also indicate the kinds of conflicts lying ahead in a society that despite its rules and regulations is very much in flux.

"I'm at the point of seriously thinking about leaving the country or getting myself in a lot of trouble," said a professional woman here who asked not to be named so she would not suffer punishment from the Government, or from her father and brothers.

Although almost 30 years old, she is still forced to live with her family, since in Saudi Arabia it is against the law for her to live alone as an unmarried woman. If she chooses to leave the country, she said, the only way she can get a passport or board a plane is with her father's written permission.

Legally, neither she nor any other single Saudi woman can go out alone, drive, work with men, travel alone, stay in a hotel, go out to eat, or do anything else alone that might allow them to somehow encounter a man on their own.

The woman who said she was frustrated sipped a whiskey at a private party, danced and, after a long conversation, confided that she was divorced and recently had a lover.

But, she said, Government officials had found out about the relationship and investigated her. Her father threatened to lock her in the house and one of her brothers threatened to kill her.

"It makes me want to go crazy," the woman said.

Judging from several anecdotes from women, another growing source of tension is the unwillingness of some Saudi men to marry highly educated women.

A doctor, who asked to be identified only as Miriam, said her boyfriend of five years had recently told her he was going to marry a much younger woman who did not have a university education.

*James LeMoyne, "Some Saudi Women Push Change," *New York Times* (December 8, 1990), p. 6. Copyright © 1990 by The New York Times Company. Reprinted by permission.

"He told me that I am too independent, too strong for him." she said. . . .

The trend is a problem in a society where more women are educated. The challenge they face is even tougher because they are prohibited from holding most jobs, assertedly on the grounds they cannot have contact with men.

As a consequence, a number of educated women who are not able to find work spend their time in quiet frustration in their homes or in the company of other unemployed and often affluent women. Judging by conversations, they appear to share in a strongly bonded society of women, removed from public view.

Drinking alcohol, dancing, mixing of the sexes and a great deal else is officially prohibited here as non-Islamic. In spite of such formal strictures, drinking, dancing and a great deal else that is non-Islamic regularly goes on behind closed doors. . . .

In public, Saudi women are required to wear a black robe covering almost all of their body and usually a veil to cover their hair and face as well.

But in the privacy of their homes, these nun-like figures have a talent for dropping their robes to reveal short skirts, spike heels, blinding colors and plunging necklines. It reflects the near-absolute division here between private freedom and public stricture that women appear to exploit to the fullest. . . .

Although the Saudi Government has officially decreed that women cannot drive and has instituted a crackdown, debate on the issue continues to surge here.

Yet many and perhaps most of the women here remain quite traditional. Unlike some would-be reformers and frustrated professional women, the more traditional women wear a veil out of choice, think almost any premarital contact with a man is bad and criticize the women who drove cars in protest.

When asked why driving by women was such a threatening issue, a Muslim religious teacher of literature and history who said he would speak more frankly if his name was not used explained, "Driving could lead to temptations that would hurt the sanctity of women."

To provide anything like an adequate coverage of the situation of women in the Third World would require a book larger than this one.[33] One reason for this is the tremendous variation in many respects among individual countries. Included are some that can only euphemistically be called "developing," and others that are soon likely to join the ranks of the "advanced industrialized" nations. Some are rich in resources only waiting to be exploited, others have almost none. Among many additional issues that might be mentioned, there are also substantial differences in the extent and the way that women participate in productive labor, and, as previously mentioned, differences in statistical reporting. We cannot even begin to give proper attention to all such complex topics, but these diverse countries do share one characteristic—low per capita income. Consequently, they also share

---

[33] A number of very useful books on women in developing countries have been written since 1970. The pioneering work among these was Boserup, *Women's Role in Economic Development,* followed by Nadja Youssef, *Women and Work in Developing Societies* (Berkeley, University of California Press, 1974), and more recently, Ester Boserup, *Economic and Demographic Relationships in Development* (Baltimore: Johns Hopkins University Press, 1990).

problems that are somewhat different from those in more affluent nations. One of these is particularly ominous and deserves to be at least mentioned here.

Not only do women and men share in scant education, hard labor, general deprivation and, as a result, a short life, but there is reason to believe that women carry a disproportionate part of this burden. Further, this appears to be particularly true where women's productive contribution outside the household is small. Among the 13 countries where per capita income in the late 1970s was less than $500 per year, and where the labor force participation of women was less than one-fourth that of men, the average number of women was only 98 for 100 men, while it was 105 in the other 39 countries at the same low level of income.[34] One need not go so far as to suspect female infanticide, though that has not been unknown historically.[35] An unequal allocation of food and medicine, under conditions when both are scarce, would be quite sufficient to explain this situation.

Similarly, there is evidence that improved techniques of production have generally been initially monopolized by men, in part because so many of the technical assistance programs have targeted this group. Thus the gap between skill levels of women and men has tended to widen in the early stages of economic development, reinforcing the inclination of large enterprises to recruit male craftsmen and apprentices for skilled and supervisory jobs, while hiring women to do jobs requiring only routine skills. Hence, the near-term outlook for women in these countries is not bright.[36]

WOMEN IN THE FORMER
UNION OF SOVIET SOCIALIST REPUBLICS:
MARXIST IDEOLOGY AND SOVIET PRACTICE[37]

From the days of World War I through the 1980s, the government of the former Union of Soviet Socialist Republics (which in 1992 became the Commonwealth of Independent States) subscribed to Marxist ideology, including the

[34] Marianne A. Ferber and Helen M. Berg, "Labor Force Participation of Women and the Sex Ratio: A Cross-Country Analysis."

[35] The existence of such practices in the past appears to be well-established. See, for instance, Elisabeth Croll, *Feminism and Socialism in China* (London: Routledge and Kegan Paul, 1978), with reference to China before the revolution: "Girls were the main, if not exclusive, victims of infanticide and tended to have a higher infant mortality rate in times of poverty and famine. In a nineteenth century survey the 160 women over 50 years of age who were interviewed, and who between them had borne a total of 631 sons and 538 daughters, admitted to destroying 158 of their daughters; none had destroyed a boy. As only four of the women had reared more than three girls, the field workers felt that the number of infanticides confessed to was considerably below the truth" (p. 24).

[36] Boserup, *Economic and Demographic Relationships,* pp. 37–38.

[37] The source of data on the USSR is Gail Warshafsky Lapidus, *Women in Soviet Society* (Berkeley, CA: University of California Press, 1978). An interesting discussion of the issues considered here is also found in Hilda Scott, *Does Socialism Liberate Women? Experiences from Eastern Europe* (Boston: Beacon Press, 1974).

relevant views about the role of women. The same was presumably true after World War II in other Eastern European countries. We focus, however, on the former USSR, not only because it was the largest of these countries, and had the longest time to implement its ideas, but also because it was, to a considerable extent, the model for the others.

The leaders who successfully carried out the revolution and shaped the ideas that dominated the country during the early years saw the relationship between men and women as inextricably entwined with the revolutionary reconstruction of society. They essentially espoused the view that the abolition of private property and class structure is both necessary and sufficient for achieving equality between women and men. They struck down all legal discrimination against women. Equal treatment in the educational system and in the labor market was mandated. Liberal family laws were introduced, making the marriage contract egalitarian and legalized abortion readily available, though some of this legislation was later modified.[38]

Because there was, generally, not only full employment but often a labor shortage, doctrinal belief in labor force participation of women was reinforced by the need for them to help with the rapid industrialization that was the main goal of the regime. But for the very same reason, little progress was made in "socializing housework," the Soviet solution for women's double burden. Such work was to be made unnecessary by the provision of public services, from communal dining rooms to day-care centers. Women were told that these would be made available as soon as the higher priority goals had been achieved.

In practice, this meant that, almost 70 years after the revolution, much house-work still needed to be done in the former Soviet Union, most of it by women. To the extent that official notice was taken of this at all, the proposed solution was still that, with growing affluence, the state was offering somewhat more of the promised facilities and would continue to do so. Sharing of household responsibilities between men and women has never been part of the Marxist ideology espoused by the regime.

The results of this mixed situation were, inevitably, also mixed. Not only was the status of women clearly better than in prerevolutionary Russia, but in some respects it compared favorably with that in other advanced, industrialized countries. Labor force participation in the USSR for women of prime working ages, between 20 and 49, has for some time been close to 90 percent. The proportion of those with secondary education changed from 8.5 percent for women and 11.6 percent for men (a ratio of .73) in 1939 to 49.4 percent for women and 56.6 for men (a ratio of .87) in 1977. The comparable figures for higher education changed from 0.5 percent for women and 1.1 percent for men (a ratio of .45) to 5.3 percent for women and 6.5 percent for men (a ratio of .82).

During the same years, the proportion of women in the most heavily male sectors of the economy was 24 percent in transportation, 29 percent in construction, and 44 percent in socialized agriculture. Not only were 7 out of 10 physicians

---

[38]This was particularly true during the Stalinist period when, for instance, abortions were made illegal.

women, but also 4 out of 10 engineers. The former occupation was not very well paid, but the latter was.

This is, however, only one side of the story. In the former Union of Soviet Socialist Republics, as in the United States, there was a noticeable tendency for women to be heavily represented in the low-paying occupations. There is ample evidence that they also tended to be concentrated at the lower levels of occupational hierarchies. They did the least sophisticated and least mechanized work in agriculture, which also brings the lowest rewards. In the health professions, virtually all nurses were women, as were 90 percent of pediatricians. On the other hand, only 6 percent of surgeons and 50 percent of all chief physicians and executives of medical institutions were women. Last, but not least, there have been virtually no women in the top echelons of the powerful government hierarchy.

No official data have been available from the USSR on men's and women's earnings. The only Soviet-bloc country that provided such information was Czechoslovakia, where the ratio of women's to men's earnings had been about 68 percent since the early 1970s, well within the range of figures for the Western advanced industrialized countries. One estimate of the earnings ratio for the USSR is that it was about 70 percent between 1960 and 1980.[39] A survey conducted in Soviet Armenia in 1963, for the purpose of carrying out a methodological study on estimating family income distributions, provided, as a by-product, data on earnings of all family members. A careful analysis of these data suggests that, at that time, women brought home about 65 percent as much as men.[40] This is interpreted to be largely the result of the greater amounts of time and energy women, as compared to men, spent on housework—a situation which, as we have seen, continued into a later period.

Life would, no doubt, have improved for women in the USSR if they had been relieved of more family work. This would not, however, have resolved all of what was generally referred to as "the woman question" there. Such tasks as food preparation, laundry, and child care tended to be low status and poorly paid when they were done outside the home, and they were almost exclusively performed by women. Also, not all housework can be "socialized." Thus, the Marxist solution, even in principle, leaves something to be desired.[41] For an approach that endeavors to get to the heart of the problem of stereotypical gender roles, we must look not to the Soviet model but to Sweden.

[39] Mincer, "Inter-Country Comparisons of Labor Force Trends."

[40] Michael Swafford, "Sex Differences in Soviet Earnings," *American Sociological Review* 43, no. 5 (October 1978): 657–73.

[41] Though a good deal has been written about the development of women in China since the revolution, the information offered tends to be based on necessarily selective personal observations, since virtually no data are available. See, for instance, Elisabeth Croll, *Feminism and Socialism in China* (London: Routledge and Kegan Paul, 1978) and Phyllis Andors, *The Unfinished Liberation of Chinese Women, 1949–1982* (Bloomington, IN: Indiana University Press, 1983). It is nonetheless clear that here, as in the USSR, women have made considerable progress since the days when their feet were bound and Confucian ideology consigned them to an entirely subservient position, but they have failed to achieve anything like full equality either in the household or in the public sphere.

SWEDEN: IDEOLOGY VS. TRADITION[42]

In the late 1960s, the Swedish government officially accepted the view that a policy attempting to give women an equal place with men in economic life while at the same time confirming women's traditional responsibility for care of the home and children has no prospect of fulfilling the first of these aims. It was the first country to put such emphasis on the achievement of equality of men and women in the household, as well as in the labor market. The stage was set for a struggle between a profound commitment to this egalitarian ideology and a deeply rooted traditional paternalism.[43]

The government has pursued a consistent campaign to change the institution of the family ever since. Considerable efforts have been made to discourage gender-based stereotypes at all levels of the education system. Legislation was introduced to make marriage an equal partnership, including abolishing the right of the wife to be supported. All gender differences in public aid were removed. The joint income tax for spouses was eliminated (except for nonwage income) and replaced with a system of individual taxation.[44] Generous arrangements for parental leave, which may be taken by fathers or mothers, were provided. Such benefits are allotted in proportion to forgone earnings, so that there are strong incentives for women to have a job before the birth of the first child and again before the second child is born. Heavily subsidized day-care is available for more than half of preschool children. This compares favorably with most other countries.[45]

Women's education has been increasing more rapidly than men's, gradually narrowing the difference between the two, even though segregation by field continues in higher education. Hence, women were in a good position to take advantage of the removal of barriers to entry into the labor market in general, and into better paid jobs in particular. At the same time, all low wage earners benefitted from the concerted efforts of the powerful, centralized union movement in Sweden to reduce inequalities between classes of workers.

All this adds up to an impressive set of favorable circumstances for women to make progress toward the professed goals of an egalitarian family and equality in the

---

[42]Much of the information in this section is derived from Siv Gustafsson and Roger Jacobson, "Trends in Female Labor Force Participation in Sweden," in *Trends in Women's Work, Education, and Family Building*, Layard and Mincer, eds.; Siv Gustafsson, "Equal Opportunity Policies in Sweden," in *Sex Discrimination and Equal Opportunity*, Gunther Schmid and Renate Weitzel, eds. (Aldershot, England: Gower Publishing Company Limited, 1984), pp. 132–54.

[43]Interestingly, the labor force participation rate of women in the nineteenth century was only about half as great in Sweden as in the United States.

[44]The importance of this must not be underestimated. When the income tax is highly progressive, as it is in Sweden, the applicable rate for the wife is much lower when she is taxed as an individual rather than a second earner. Further, any amount she earns by entering the labor market leaves them more disposable income than the same amount of *additional* earnings he may be able to make by working harder, longer hours, or whatever. The effect of the tax structure on labor force participation in the United States was discussed in Chapter 4.

[45]It is worth noting, however, that this figure is in excess of 90 percent for children aged 3 to 5 in Belgium and France; see OECD, *Employment Outlook*, July 1990.

labor market. Up to 1980, however, the stress was almost entirely on social policy rather than on any antidiscrimination legislation. The Act on Equality between men and women was passed in 1980; however, it must be expected to take some time before its effects can be fully felt. Thus, it is not surprising that the record, as of the 1980s, was somewhat mixed. By 1987, 81 percent of all women aged 16 to 65 were in the labor force, and for women aged 35 to 49 the figure was as high as 92 percent.

Nonetheless, it would be a mistake to conclude that homemaking no longer interferes with women's paid work. In 1982, fully 53 percent of women who were in the labor market were employed part-time (compared to 28 percent in the United States). Thus women constituted only 31 percent of the full-time labor force, even though they comprised 45 percent of the total labor force. Further, about one-fifth of female workers were absent for the whole week during which the data were collected, most of them on parental leave. This is easier to understand when we learn that the demand for child care still exceeds supply at existing prices and that women continue to do about two-thirds of the housework. It appears that here, as elsewhere, changes in women's labor force participation tend to be far more rapid than changes in men's share of household responsibilities.

As was mentioned previously, occupational segregation in Sweden continues to be high, with women disproportionately represented in clerical and other white-collar jobs. The quadrupling of women in the government sector in recent decades while the number remained almost constant in the private sector has no doubt been one of the factors inhibiting any significant decrease in segregation. Thus, it would appear that, in spite of all the efforts, men have not been fully integrated in the household nor women in the labor market.

Some Americans who have analyzed the position of women in Sweden tend to end on this negative note. This does not do justice to the very real achievements. It must not be dismissed as a technicality that women in the United States often quit their job when they have a child, whereas women in Sweden tend to take paid leave. Not only are the latter receiving payments while they are at home, but they are guaranteed the right to return to their job and without loss of seniority. Similarly, working part-time is likely to be less disruptive to maintaining and accumulating market skills than dropping out entirely. Nor should one dismiss the importance of providing, in principle, parental leaves to both men and women, even when fewer men than women take them, or providing government supported day-care, even when its supply is less than fully adequate. Both do provide an official stamp of approval for new and different arrangements, and appear to have reduced the qualms of young people who might wish to use them. For instance, fathers are increasingly likely to take leave when the baby is born, and later to care for their children.[46]

---

[46] Although few fathers availed themselves of parental leaves when they were first instituted, by the late 1980s, about 85 percent took an average of 8.5 days of the 10-day postconfinement benefit, 25 percent took an additional month during the child's first year, and 30 percent of fathers with children

Last, but certainly not least, Sweden is foremost among the countries that have succeeded in rapidly reducing the earnings gap between men and women. It is true, as has been pointed out, that it is only hourly wages of women in industry that are as high as 90 percent of those of men and that this must, in part, be credited to the impact of unions in narrowing earnings differentials. But the ratio of the annual earnings of all full-time, year-round female to male workers increased from 72 percent in 1973, the year these data first became available, to 81 percent in 1980. This compares very favorably with the situation in the United States, where the comparable figure was 71 percent as recently as 1990.

Clearly, no amount of effort and goodwill can fundamentally change a society overnight, especially one that, in many ways, had been more traditional in its gender roles than the United States ever was. But reason dictates that we recognize that moving toward a goal, albeit slowly and at times uncertainly, is better than standing still, because utopia cannot be achieved quickly.

CONCLUSION

Our survey of several indicators of the economic status of women showed that there are great differences with respect to all except the division of housework. It is likely that if we could get data on other factors that influence the extent to which men and women are unequal, such as polygamy, seclusion, legal rights, and so on, we would find even greater variations between different economies and cultures. These cannot readily be explained without taking into account factors other than merely varying economic conditions. We conclude, therefore, that there is a possibility for discretionary changes, though it may be neither easy nor painless to make them.

Although cross-country comparisons also show that progress toward equality in one respect is no guarantee of progress in all other respects, they provide no evidence of negative relationships. On the contrary, we find, for instance, that in the advanced industrialized countries, for which extensive data are available, recent decades saw both a substantial growth in women's labor force participation and a decline in the male-female earnings gap. Increasing women's labor force participation does not appear to increase occupational segregation or depress their wages as compared to those of men. Thus, there appears to be no cause to worry about negative feedback. There is also evidence, both in the former Union of Soviet Socialist Republics and in Sweden, that the government has played a significant role. In previous chapters of this book, we have considered existing and possible future

---

under age 12 took an average of 5 days' leave for child care per year. Joseph Pleck, "Family Supportive Employer Policies and Men's Participation," paper prepared for the Panel on Employer Policies and Working Families, Committee on Women's Employment and Related Social Issues, Commission on Behavioral and Social Sciences and Education, National Research Council, Washington, DC, 1990.

policies that might be used in the United States to reduce inequality between men and women in opportunities and economic outcomes. Our review of the experience of other countries leads us to be reasonably optimistic about the potential role of government intervention in this area.

SUGGESTED READINGS

BENERIA, LOURDES, ed.   *Women and Development: The Sexual Division of Labor in Rural Societies*. New York: Praeger, 1980.

BOSERUP, ESTER.   *Women's Role in Economic Development*. New York: St. Martin's Press, 1970.

BOSERUP, ESTER.   *Economic and Demographic Relationships in Development*. Baltimore, MD: Johns Hopkins University Press, 1990.

JUSTER, F. THOMAS AND FRANK P. STAFFORD.   "The Allocation of Time: Empirical Findings, Behavioral Models, and Problems of Measuremenrement," *Journal of Economic Literature* 29, no. 2 (June 1991): 471–522.

LAPIDUS, GAIL WARSHAFSKY.   *Women in Soviet Society*. Berkeley, CA: University of California Press, 1978.

LAYARD, RICHARD AND JACOB MINCER, eds.   *Trends in Women's Work, Education, and Family Building*, special issue of *Journal of Labor Economics* 3, no. 1, part 2 (January 1985).

Organization for Economic Cooperation and Development. *Employment Outlook*, Sept. 1988, Chapter 5.

ROOS, PATRICIA.   *Gender and Work: A Comparative Analysis of Industrial Societies*. Albany, NY: SUNY Press, 1985.

SCOTT, HILDA.   *Does Socialism Liberate Women? Experiences from Eastern Europe*. Boston: Beacon Press, 1974.

UNITED NATIONS.   *The Economic Role of Women in the ECE Region*. New York: Author, 1980.

YOUSSEF, NADJA.   *Women and Work in Developing Societies*. Berkeley: University of California Press, 1974.

EPILOGUE

We have seen throughout this book that women's roles in the economy have been changing rapidly in recent decades. We also learned that many policies affecting women have been changing, albeit often slowly, in ways that have tended to enhance the status of women as compared to men. At the same time, however, we showed that we are far from having achieved equality between the sexes. What does all this portend for the future?

On the basis of the low birthrate, the continuing tendency of young women to get more, and more job-oriented, education, the growing recognition that husbands and wives do not always live together happily forever after, and the increasing acceptance of the two-earner family, we would expect the labor force participation of women to continue to increase, though not necessarily as rapidly as in the 1980s. If new technology should greatly reduce the demand for clerical workers—still by far the largest single source of employment for women—or if the general unemployment level should remain high for extended periods, women's labor force participation rate may rise relatively slowly for some time. But virtually no reasonably foreseeable conditions are expected to cause an actual downturn.

As the labor force participation of women remains high and is likely to continue to increase, young women will be even more likely to invest in their human capital in preparation for market work and to continue moving into less traditional occupations. Both these trends should continue to reduce the male-female earnings gap, perhaps even at a faster pace than in the past. To the extent that existing laws and regulations are enforced, labor market discrimination should be reduced. This, too, would be expected to directly contribute to a narrowing of the pay gap and also to encourage women to further broaden their horizons.

At the same time, increased experience with women workers should reduce statistical discrimination and prejudice to the extent that these are based on stereo-typical ideas of women as unsuited for nontraditional jobs, while women's growing attachment to the labor force should help to counter the view that they are unstable workers. Finally, as women stay in the labor market more consistently and for longer periods of time, and as those who have been successful help to open the doors and smooth the path for others, women may be expected not only to move into a greater variety of occupations but also to rise to higher levels within them. All of this does not mean that occupational segregation or the earnings gap are likely to disappear overnight. It is possible that they will never disappear entirely. However, this does not detract from the importance of any substantial move in that direction. The experience of other countries, such as Sweden, suggested that substantial increases in economic equality between men and women are certainly feasible, given appropriate government policies.

Next to occupational segregation and the earnings gap, the disparity between men and women that has for a long time proved most resistant to change has been in the amount of time devoted to housework. The amount of market work done by women has been increasing rapidly, but, until recently, there has been little evidence of men doing more work in the household. To the extent that the "housework gap" diminished in the seventies, this was because of a decline in time devoted to housekeeping by women, both full-time homemakers and participants in the labor force. Smaller families, the availability of attractive market substitutes for home-produced goods and services, and possibly tolerance of less exacting standards of housekeeping most likely contributed to this trend. In the 1980s, there was also some evidence of growing participation of husbands in housework, and there is good reason to expect this trend to continue. Thus, men and women in the "liberated" family of the future may more equally share household tasks and also find additional ways of reducing the work that needs to be done.

Lest this concluding section sound too much like a prediction of utopia, it should be noted that not all market work is fun, challenging, and highly paid. There are dangerous jobs in mines, boring jobs on assembly lines, jobs with low pay and low prestige in laundries. Similarly, it would be unrealistic to assume that housework can be reduced to a well-scheduled and minimal routine that will never interfere with a career. Appliances break down, family members become ill, children expect parents to be present at school events at unpredictable times. As long as work is often a chore, and as long as job and household responsibilities tend to come into conflict, there will be problems in allocating responsibilities in the two spheres among spouses. There will also be people who will look back with nostalgia to the days when such problems did not exist, because men and women knew their place.

Nonetheless, more and more couples continue to opt for two jobs and two paychecks. Although men have clearly not been as eager to participate in housework as women have been to take on market work, they appear to be increasingly willing to make some compromises to accommodate the two-earner lifestyle. Virtually all signs point toward a continuation of these trends. The only real question is at what rate further changes are likely to take place.

AUTHOR INDEX

A

Abbott, Edith, 23n
Abowd, John M., 177n, 242n
Abraham, Katherine G., 167n, 168n
Adelson, Andrea, 155n
Aigner, Dennis J., 208n
Allen, LaRue, 281
Alpert, William, 183n
Andors, P., 336n
Andrews, Emily, 150n, 225n
Andrews, Frank M., 268n
Ardrey, Robert, 15n
Arrow, Kenneth, 200n, 205n, 208n, 210n, 217n
Ashenfelter, Orley, 99n, 191n, 200n, 204n, 232n, 241n, 242n
Austie, R., 316n

B

Baden, Naomi, 235n
Baran, Barbara, 129n
Barcher, Ann, 219n, 229n
Baron, James N., 124n
Barrett, Nancy S., 254n
Bartlett, Robin L., 211n
Bay, John, 265n
Becker, Brian E., 199n
Becker, Gary S., 34, 34n, 49n, 81n, 141n, 161n, 173n, 189n, 200n, 202n, 205n, 207n, 259n, 263n
Behrman, Jere R., 304n
Belkin, Lisa, 195n
Bell, Duran H., 111n, 274n
Beller, Andrea H., 123n, 134n, 225n, 277n, 288n
Beneria, Lourdes, 299n, 306n
Berch, Bettina, 254n
Berg, Helen M., 155n, 161n, 273n, 296n, 324n
Berger, Joseph, 144n
Bergmann, Barbara R., 54n, 207n, 212n, 217n, 227n, 249n, 289n

Berryman, Sue E., 179n
Bianchi, Suzanne M., 123n, 127n, 265n, 285n
Bielby, Denise D., 173n
Bielby, William T., 124n, 173n
Birnbaum, Bonnie G., 35n, 43n
Blackburn, McKinley L., 263n
Blank, Rebecca M., 184n, 267n
Blaschke, Thomas J., 262n
Blau, Francine D., 7n, 58n, 92n, 109n, 121n, 123n, 124n, 127n, 134n, 136n, 175n, 177n, 191n, 197n, 205n, 206n, 212n, 215n, 217n, 251n, 254n, 277n, 315n, 316n, 318n
Blaug, Mark, 148n, 149n
Blinder, Alan, 194n
Bloom, David E., 263n
Bluestone, Barry, 252n
Blumrosen, Ruth G., 227n
Blumstein, Philip, 45n
Booth, Alan, 267n, 275n
Boserup, Ester, 297n, 323n, 324n
Boskin, Michael J., 99
Bowen, William, 81n
Brenner, Harvey, 243n
Brien, Michael, 315n
Brinton, Mary C., 154n
Bronfenbrenner, Urie, 47n, 276n
Brown, Charles, 224
Brown Claire (Vickery), 32n, 35n, 86n, 87n, 105n, 249n, 268n
Brown, James N., 168n
Brown, Murray, 49n
Burke, Ronald J., 268n
Burkhauser, Richard V., 60n
Butz, William P., 262n
Byrnes, Eleanor, 183n, 186n

C

Cabral, Robert, 199n
Cain, Glen G., 54n, 81n, 91n, 99n, 111n, 112n, 191n, 208n, 215n
Cantor, Milton, 24n, 28n, 74n

SUBJECT INDEX

A

Ability, gender differences, employer discrimination and, 209
Absolute advantage, 38, 39t, 40
Act on Equality, 328
Added worker effect, 96
Administrative positions, distribution
by gender, 121, 121t, 122t
by race and ethnic group, 121, 122t
Administrative support positions, distribution
by gender, 120, 121, 121t, 122t
by race and ethnic group, 121, 122t
Administrators
male, compared to female, 209
women, 127
AFDC, *see* Aid to Families with Dependent Children
Affirmative action, 221, 225–27
Africa
north
labor force participation in, gender differences, 299, 303t, 304t
occupational segregation in, 310t
Sub-Saharan
labor force participation in, gender differences, 298, 300t, 301t
occupational segregation in, 309t, 310
AFSCME. *see* American Federation of State, County and Municipal Employees
Age
-earnings profile, gender differences in education and, 175–76, 176f
labor force participation and, 76, 78
of women, 76–77, 78
unemployment rates and, 247, 248t, 250t
Agriculture, agricultural societies, 29
occupational segregation in, 310–11
women's roles in, 20–21
Aid to Families with Dependent Children (AFDC), 112, 118, 289, 291
Alimony, 287–88, 289

American Federation of State, County and Municipal Employees (AFSCME), 229n
Antidiscrimination, government efforts in, 224–25
Artisans, women and, 21
Asia
labor force participation in, gender differences, 299, 302t, 303t, 304t
occupational segregation in, 309t, 310t
Assignment, occupational, gender differences in, 217
Assumptions
simplifying, 4
in traditional economics, 3
Australia, women's labor force participation in, 22, 315–16

B

Baby boom, 107, 253, 263
Bachelor's degree, attainment, gender differences in, 143t, 144, 145t
Bargaining approaches, 49–50
Barriers, removal of, 126
Behavior
gender differences, employer discrimination and, 209
human, genetic components, 17–18
optimizing, in women, 177
teaching, 148
Benefit plans, flexible, 185
Birthrate, 341. *See also* Fertility rate
Blacks
child support for, 288
educational attainment of, 143, 143t
female
earnings of, 136, 137, 137t
employment of, during industrialization period, 24
unemployed, 250